ISBN 978-0-259-94455-3
PIBN 10254930

This book is a reproduction of an important historical work. Forgotten Books uses
state-of-the-art technology to digitally reconstruct the work, preserving the original format
whilst repairing imperfections present in the aged copy. In rare cases, an imperfection in
the original, such as a blemish or missing page, may be replicated in our edition. We do,
however, repair the vast majority of imperfections successfully; any imperfections that
remain are intentionally left to preserve the state of such historical works.

1 MONTH OF
FREE
READING

at

www.ForgottenBooks.com

By purchasing this book you are eligible for one month membership to ForgottenBooks.com, giving you unlimited access to our entire collection of over 700,000 titles via our web site and mobile apps.

To claim your free month visit:

www.forgottenbooks.com/free254930

English
Français
Deutsche
Italiano
Español
Português

www.forgottenbooks.com

Mythology Photography **Fiction**
Fishing Christianity **Art** Cooking
Essays Buddhism Freemasonry
Medicine **Biology** Music **Ancient
Egypt** Evolution Carpentry Physics
Dance Geology **Mathematics** Fitness
Shakespeare **Folklore** Yoga Marketing
Confidence Immortality Biographies
Poetry **Psychology** Witchcraft
Electronics Chemistry History **Law**
Accounting **Philosophy** Anthropology
Alchemy Drama Quantum Mechanics
Atheism Sexual Health **Ancient History**
Entrepreneurship Languages Sport
Paleontology Needlework Islam
Metaphysics Investment Archaeology
Parenting Statistics Criminology
Motivational

A DIARY

OF THE

HOME RULE PARLIAMENT

1892 1895

HENRY W. LUCY

AUTHOR OF "PEEP'S TWO PARLIAMENTS"
"A DIARY OF THE SALISBURY PARLIAMENT"

WITH A FRONTISPIECE

CASSELL AND COMPANY LIMITED
LONDON, PARIS & MELBOURNE
1896

A DIARY

OF THE

HOME RULE PARLIAMENT

1892—1895

BY

HENRY W. LUCY

AUTHOR OF "A DIARY OF TWO PARLIAMENTS"
"A DIARY OF THE SALISBURY PARLIAMENT"

WITH A FRONTISPIECE

CASSELL AND COMPANY, LIMITED

LONDON, PARIS & MELBOURNE

1896

To the Memory of

LORD RANDOLPH CHURCHILL,

BORN 1849; MEMBER FOR WOODSTOCK, 1874;

CHANCELLOR OF THE EXCHEQUER AND LEADER OF THE

HOUSE OF COMMONS, MIDSUMMER TO MIDWINTER, 1886;

DIED 24TH JANUARY, 1895.

A DIARY OF THE HOME RULE PARLIAMENT, 1892—1895.

THE result of the General Election which took place in July, 1892, is inadequately indicated by bare record of the fact that it placed Mr. Gladstone in power with a majority of forty. In order to realise the stupendous variation in public opinion marked at this epoch it is necessary to consider the leeway to be made up before Lord Salisbury was overtaken and the race for power started afresh on level terms. As in 1886, the issue at the polls was distinctly, if not with equal exclusiveness, fought on one question—to wit, Home Rule. At the earlier trial the Home Rulers were routed all along the line. When on the 5th of August, 1886, the new Parliament met, Mr. Gladstone found himself in a minority of 116.

On the eve of the General Election of 1892 things from a Liberal point of view were not quite so bad as that, but the wall to be scaled looked hopelessly high. By a process of bye-elections, aided, to some slight extent, by stirring of conscience among seceded Liberals, the anti-Home Rule majority had at the time of the Dissolution been reduced to sixty-six. This was swept away at the polls, with the net result that the new Parliament met with 355 members pledged to Home Rule and 315 banded against it. The 302 Conservatives holding seats at the time of the Dissolution were reduced to 269 ; the 66 Liberal Unionists had been brought down to 46. Of Liberals, including what were known as Labour Candidates, the total had run up from 216 to 274, whilst of the Irish Home Rulers, now formally, even fiercely, divided into two camps, there were 81 against 86 who had seats in the Salisbury Parliament. Of these, nine followed the banner of Mr. John Redmond, 72 being ranged under the leadership of Mr. Justin McCarthy.

Further dissecting the component parts of the new Parliament, it will be found that Ireland sent a Home Rule majority of fifty-seven, Scotland of twenty-eight, and Wales of twenty-six. This total of 111 was met by a majority of seventy-one against Home Rule contributed by the electors of English counties and boroughs.

Thus the new Government pledged to carry a Home Rule Bill started with a majority of 40.

Mr. Gladstone was staying at Dalmeny when there arrived a telegram announcing the issue of the last doubtful contest in the General Election. The little group gathered in the library was not ungovernably enthusiastic at the aggregate results. One, gallantly putting the best face on it, said, " Well, we shall have a majority of forty."

" Too small, too small," said Mr. Gladstone, slowly shaking his head and speaking in those deep, tragic tones he reserves for occasions of greatest storm and stress.

Whether, and how, this early prognostication, made upon swift review of the momentous task taken in hand, was verified will appear in the following pages. It should be said that they are transcribed from notes made under the dates affixed. The freshness of impression thus preserved may, perhaps, to some extent atone for the inevitable accompaniment of hasty judgment and only partial knowledge.

CONTENTS.

Note.—Lord Randolph Churchill commissioned Mr. Ward to paint a replica of the portrait which serves as a frontispiece to this volume. On the eve of his departure for South Africa he presented it to his mother, the Duchess of Marlborough. In the original painting, here reproduced, the artist has introduced the clever fancy of throwing on the glass of the bookcase a reflection of his own face as he sat at the easel and of Lady Randolph Churchill's looking over his shoulder as he worked.

THE

HOME RULE PARLIAMENT.

—•◆•—

CHAPTER I.

SESSION OF 1892.

END OF THE SALISBURY MINISTRY.

4th Aug.
Opening Day.

A QUARTER OF AN HOUR before the business of the Thirteenth Parliament of Queen Victoria commenced, the House of Commons presented a curious appearance. A throng of members stood in the centre of the floor, in continuation of the gathering that stretched forth under the main entrance and peopled the lobby. The benches were tenantless, save for a collection of hats planted out, as it were, brim uppermost. To every hat was attached a ticket, bearing the name of the member who had secured this particular seat and would presently come to claim it.

As two o'clock approached the throng on the floor of the House thinned and the hats on the benches gave place to their wearers. Mr. Arthur Peel was discovered at the corner of the second bench, behind that on which Ministers sit, to the right of the empty chair. He was in plain morning dress, and evidently enjoyed the opportunity, long intermitted, of wearing his hat in the House. When he was discovered, members from both sides flocked up with effusive greeting. To him presently entered Mr. Addison, who disposed himself on the step of the gangway at the feet of the Speaker-designate. In

B

this humble position, partly obscured by the crowd and partly by the back of the benches, only his smiling, beardless face visible, the learned Q.C., in conjunction with the tall, grave figure of Mr. Peel, irresistibly suggested the idea of a cherub poised below a portrait, as is sometimes seen in Florentine galleries.

Two o'clock was sounding from the Clock Tower when Mr. Balfour briskly stepped in, hailed by a cheer from the Conservative side. He wore a pale pink carnation in his coat, and as he beamed upon his applauding friends and shook hands with those who pressed around him, he looked much more certain of approaching victory than conscious of pending defeat. Sir John Gorst, accidentally anticipating coming events, entered from behind the Speaker's chair on the Opposition side, and had proceeded some way by the table when he turned about and entered into conversation with the clerk. At this time Mr. Mundella came in, and shook hands with everyone within reach. Mr. Chamberlain and Sir Henry James, bereft of the companionship of Mr. Heneage, took their old places at the end of the Front Opposition Bench, shaking hands with former colleagues nearest them as if nothing had happened since they sat there before.

At seven minutes past two the doorkeeper, breaking through the throng at the Bar, loudly announced "Black Rod!" That functionary, certain that at least on this occasion he was not in danger of interrupting ordered speech, advanced with the customary genuflexions, albeit the Speaker's chair was empty and the Mace was under the table. In response to the invitation to "this Honourable House" to repair to another place to hear the Royal Commission read, Mr. Palgrave, the Chief Clerk, rose from his seat at the table and prepared to follow. This promptitude led to some temporary embarrassment. Black Rod, having advanced bowing thrice, must needs retire with an equal number of obeisances. The present incumbent of this ancient and honourable office is not to be hurried on State occasions. So Mr. Palgrave had to halt in the middle of the floor whilst Black Rod, not hastening a step nor abating an obeisance, safely backed himself out over the Bar. Mr. Balfour, most of the Ministers, and nearly all the new members, went off to the House of Lords to attend on the Royal Commission and receive Her Majesty's commands to proceed to the choice of some proper person as Speaker.

The Victor at the Polls. They had not gone many minutes when a cheer from below the gangway announced some new episode. Mr. Gladstone was discovered entering from behind the Speaker's chair. At sight of him the still crowded ranks of the Opposition rose to their feet enthusiastically cheering, Mr. Gladstone bowing acknowledgment of the spontaneous reception. Mr Peel had remained behind when the procession fared forth to the House of Lords. Catching sight of him, Mr. Gladstone nimbly rose and crossed the floor. The Speaker-designate, emulating the courtesy of kings, made haste to meet his distinguished visitor, intercepting his progress at the foot of the gangway. The Treasury Bench was in convenient contiguity for purposes of conversation, and Mr. Peel made a motion for Mr. Gladstone to seat himself thereon.

"Not yet," he replied, laughingly shaking his head.

So Mr. Peel led the way to the bench behind, where the two right hon. gentlemen sat for a few moments in conversation. When it was over and Mr. Gladstone prepared to return to his own place, Sir John Mowbray, one of the oldest members left to the House of Commons, ran after him with friendly greeting, heartily responded to. On regaining the Front Opposition Bench the Leader for the first time noticed seated thereon Sir Henry James and Mr. Chamberlain, and to each in succession held out the right hand of fellowship.

Re-election of the Speaker. By this time Mr. Palgrave was back in his chair at the table, and the crowd which had gone forth to see Lord Halsbury and his brother Commissioners, arrayed in crimson garments, seated on the Woolsack, were returning. When all were seated the Clerk rose and pointed three fingers at Sir Matthew White Ridley, who sat in close companionship with Mr. Peel on the bench behind Ministers. At this signal the burly baronet, who at one time seemed himself on the way to the Chair, rose, and in brief speech proposed the election of the Right Hon. Arthur Wellesley Peel as Speaker. Mr. Gladstone, following, received renewed ovation from a crowd that now filled every part of the House, including the side galleries. It was doubtless owing to the fact that the gallery immediately facing him was thronged with Liberals that the welcoming cheers with which the Liberal host greeted their chief seemed to be echoed and prolonged from the Ministerial side. Mr. Gladstone was evidently in blooming health, and though his voice betrayed some huskiness, that was the sole sign of his recent indisposition.

It was noticed, as being in accordance with the general condition of change in the new House, that whilst Mr. Balfour, contrary to his habit, had decked himself with a flower, Mr. Gladstone, rarely without a flower in his buttonhole when he takes a prominent part in Parliamentary proceedings, to-day wore none. His speech in seconding the motion was brief and to the point, his graceful recognition of long friendship with Mr. Peel—"dating from the middle of my life and from a very early portion of his "—eliciting a general burst of cheering.

Mr. Gladstone having made an end of speaking, the three fingers of the Clerk at the Table again went forth, this time pointing to Mr. Peel. When the hearty cheer his rising evoked had subsided, Mr. Peel, addressing "Mr. Palgrave," made a passing reference to the unusual but not unprecedented fact that this was the fourth time the same member had been invited to take the Chair of the House of Commons. If the invitation were confirmed, he trusted he might have the support of every member. "Without that the Speaker could do nothing. Having it, there is little he cannot do."

There was a pause when Mr. Peel resumed his seat. Sir Matthew Ridley half rose and looked across at Mr. Gladstone, who stepped briskly across the floor and assisted in conducting Mr. Peel to the Chair. As the Speaker-elect stood and faced the House under the canopy of the Chair, members on both sides with one accord rose to their feet. The Sergeant-at-Arms, advancing, withdrew the Mace from its place of retirement and set it on the table. At a signal from Mr. Peel, members reseated themselves; and Mr. Balfour, rising in his capacity of Leader of the House, offered his congratulations to the new Speaker. In response, Mr. Peel unreservedly placed himself in the hands of the House, a remark with which the interesting ceremonial, eagerly watched by the crowded House, was completed.

Whilst people were wondering what would happen next, the Speaker-elect, rising again, said, in his official voice (a distinctly different organ from that employed during the earlier proceedings): "The question is that this House do now adjourn." To this, the very first question formally submitted to the new House of Commons—Sir Matthew Ridley's motion was not put—no objection was taken, and the Speaker leaving the Chair, the assembly rapidly melted away, the proceedings having occupied rather less than an hour.

At noon the Speaker-elect took the Chair
5th Aug.
The Speaker's in the House of Commons, his chrysalis
Progress to state being marked by the circumstance
the Chair. that, instead of the full-bottomed wig and flowing robe in which he is accustomed to preside, he presented himself in Court dress, topped with what is irreverently known as a "bob" wig. There was a full attendance of members, who filled the House with a buzz of conversation. After a lapse of a quarter of an hour Yeoman Usher of the Black Rod entered and, with carefully regulated approach to the table, summoned the Commons to the other House.

On arrival, the Speaker-Elect and his following of Commoners found the Lord Chancellor dressed in the red gown of a peer of Parliament, seated on a bench between the Throne and the Woolsack, in company with the Duke of Rutland, Lord Balfour of Burleigh, Lord Knutsford, and Lord Cross. These were the Lords commissioned by the Queen to receive the Speaker, who "presented himself with all humility for Her Majesty's gracious approbation." The Lord Chancellor announced that "Her Majesty does most readily approve and confirm you as their Speaker."

The Speaker, now duly installed, made the time-honoured claim for access to Her Majesty, liberty of speech in debate, and freedom from arrest. Still following the ancient formula, he begged that the most favourable construction might be put upon all the proceedings of the House of Commons, chivalrously adding the request that if any error were committed, it might be imputed to him, not to Her Majesty's faithful Commons. All this the Lord Chancellor—now addressing Mr. Peel as "Mr. Speaker"—graciously conceded. Whereupon the Commoners retired, and the Lords went forward with their business of swearing-in.

Hard Swearing. On returning to the Commons, the Speaker, instead of taking the Chair, passed out behind it, returning fully arrayed in wig and gown. He reported to the House his visit to the Lords, and the approval signified by the Queen of the Commons' selection of their Speaker. Mr. Palgrave, the Chief Clerk, administered the oath to the Speaker, whose name was written first on the roll of the New Parliament. Immediately afterwards Sir M. Hicks-Beach, Lord George Hamilton, Mr. Matthews, and other Ministers were sworn in, a couple of tables having been placed lengthwise by the Clerk's table. On these were laid copies of the New Testament and the Oath, and for the next four hours the process of swearing-in went on without intermission. Members of the Ministry, members who had been Ministers, and Privy Councillors had precedence. Thus it came to pass that Sir Charles Dilke happened to be sworn in with the same batch as that in which the Attorney-General took the oath.

Sir Charles was watched with peculiar interest when he entered, there being some curiosity as to where he might select his seat. He chose it on the Front Bench below the gangway, with Mr. Labouchere as his immediate companion in the corner seat. It was in this seat, or rather the corresponding one on the opposite side of the House, that more than twenty years ago he made his mark, and here he begins again. He must have been much encouraged at the start by the reception he met with, few members who had known him in former days passing without stopping to shake him by the hand and express their pleasure at seeing him back again.

Mr. Davitt arrived early on the scene and was sworn in without controversy. Mr. Keir Hardie, sauntering down the House, wearing a cap of

nondescript appearance, was sternly called to order by
the Speaker, not because his headgear happened
to be unconventional, but because no member may
move about the House with his head covered. Mr.
Naoroji elected to affirm, as did a considerable
number of other members. Lord Randolph Churchill,
coming in towards four o'clock, when the crush had
abated, took the oath. By a quarter-past four all
the members on the premises had been sworn, and
the sometimes turbulent tide ebbing, the House
adjourned.

Business commenced in earnest when the
7th Aug.
The Glove
Thrown Down. Speaker took the chair after an interval
following on the ceremony of proceeding
to the Lords to hear the Queen's Speech
read. Mr. Gladstone seized the opportunity to take the
oath and sign the Roll of Parliament, the process being
watched with interest by an already crowded House.

The Address having been duly moved and
seconded, Mr. Asquith rose to move an amendment.
He was loudly cheered, the applause being redoubled
when he resumed his seat after a brilliant and
effective speech kept well within the limits of forty
minutes. The amendment humbly proposed to add
at the end of the Address words pointing out that
it is essential the Government should possess the
confidence of the House and the country, and
affirming that that confidence is not possessed by
Her Majesty's present advisers.

Mr. Asquith declined to go into the question of
the bearings of the coming Home Rule Bill to
which he had been invited by Mr. Barton, who
moved the Address. The sole question before them
was, Did the Government or did it not possess the
confidence of the House and the country? The field
of inquiry was strictly narrowed. The Government
had selected the tribunal, they had fixed the issue,
they had even named the day for their trial, and

the result had been that the mandate of 1886 had been revoked by the constituencies. There now remained for the House of Commons the task of rendering effective the deliberate judgment expressed at the poll. The speech was full of polished and barbed sentences. Perhaps no passage created more effect than the slowly-spoken words in which Mr. Asquith described the Tory party as having been engaged through six years in abandoning a historic position, pursuing a peddling and huckstering system of progressive legislation at the bidding of an ephemeral and accidental combination, born the day before yesterday, doomed to forgetfulness the day after to-morrow. To angle in other people's waters and catch nothing, to poach in other people's preserves and take nothing, but be taken themselves —that, Mr. Asquith said, amid enthusiastic cheers from the Opposition, is a blunder which in politics is worse than crime.

Mr. Burt, in seconding the amendment, reviewed various Bills passed by the Government avowedly in the interest of the working classes, and showed how what was good in them had been introduced from the Opposition side of the House, and had met with strong resistance from Ministers. Mr. Goschen rising to reply from the Treasury Bench, there was a movement towards the door by members who had been in close attendance for upwards of two hours. Those who went missed Mr. Goschen in his most sprightly mood, apparently already invigorated by the prospect of relief from Ministerial responsibilities. He deprecated Mr. Asquith's view that the question before the House was strictly that of confidence or no confidence in the Government, and insisted on the necessity and the desirability of learning from gentlemen on the Front Opposition Bench something of their proposed measures, supposing they came into office, more particularly that touching Home Rule.

B *

Mr. John Redmond, whose rising excited much interest on the Conservative side, early succeeded in chilling it by announcing his intention to vote for the amendment. That, he said, was the duty of every Irish Nationalist. After six years of misgovernment the day of judgment had come, and he was not disposed to stand in the way of its decrees. He also thought it desirable that the Liberal party should have an opportunity of fulfilling their pledges to Ireland, which were that the Irish Home Rule Question should be taken first, and that the scheme should be final. Other demands he peremptorily made on the coming Government were that they should extend an amnesty to the Fenian prisoners, and should summon Parliament to a winter session in order to deal with the case of the evicted tenants.

9th Aug.
Mr. Gladstone comes to the Front.

There was another splendid audience to-night for the resumption of the debate on the Address. Some uncertainty existed as to the hour at which the House would meet, and at which Mr. Gladstone would find his opening. Many members were under the impression that he would not speak till after four, and did not put in an appearance till that time. But the attendance just now is so large and the interest so overpowering that a few scores are not missed. When late comers arrived they had considerable difficulty in finding even standing room.

The Leader of the Opposition spoke for an hour with remarkable force and vigour. He had evidently bestowed great pains upon the composition of his speech, more especially on those parts devoted to reply to the categorical inquiries of the Irish members. For greater accuracy he had written out the carefully-weighed phrases, and read them from his manuscript.

He began by commenting on the circumstance that the House should now be engaged upon this particular debate. That the Government, having been defeated at the poll, should persist in hanging on to office was, he affirmed, contrary to the manly precedent set by Mr. Disraeli in 1868, and followed at succeeding General Elections up to 1886. The debate was ostensibly arranged with the object of supplying opportunity for defending the conduct of the Government whilst in office. But the Chancellor of the Exchequer, who had appeared as the mouthpiece of the Government, entirely skipped over the grounds of the vote of "No confidence," devoting the greater portion of his speech to denunciation of the coming Government, "a nebulous hypothesis" whose certainty to go wrong was alleged by him as the sole reason for keeping the present Government in office.

As for the order of legislation, "the Irish Question," Mr. Gladstone said, "is everything to me. It is my sole link with public life, my primary and absorbing interest, and so it will remain. When the Home Rule Bill comes before the House of Lords it will be a great question for the Empire at large, a greater question, possibly, for themselves." This remark, spoken in low, solemn voice, led to the fiercest outburst of enthusiasm that marked the delivery of the speech. Its significance was quickly seized on the Opposition side, and cheers rose again and again. If the Lords rejected the Bill, Mr. Gladstone continued, it would not be either politic or just to observe the course adopted by Lord Melbourne's Government between 1835 and 1841. The duty of the Liberal party would remain unweakened and unchanged. It would be impossible for them to regard rejection of the Bill as terminating their duties towards the Irish people

An Omen: For whom? The scene during Mr. Gladstone's significant reference to the House of Lords was made more notable by a curious atmospheric effect. A black thunderstorm gathered over the House, suddenly steeping it in deepest gloom.

Fortunately the gas in the roof had been turned on, and no inconvenience arose during the six or seven minutes that the heavens were overcast, and what should have been a bright summer afternoon became dark as night.

One other incident was the tendency below the gangway, shown in a very limited circle, to renew an attitude towards Mr. Gladstone familiar enough in a former Parliament, but from which the late House of Commons, more particularly in its closing session, was conspicuously free. It was, as Mr. Gladstone suggested, probably only a single member who broke in upon his speech with noisy laughter. Once the Speaker interposed with a grave cry of "Order! order!" and after Mr. Gladstone had observed, amid general cheering, that before the House of Commons emerged from a possible conflict with the House of Lords it would be no laughing matter, better manners prevailed, and there were no further interruptions.

Mr. Balfour. Mr. Balfour has been in the merriest humour since the fall of his Government was decreed at the poll. He came up smiling to-night, and delighted his own side with the vigour with which he hit out very early in his speech. Ministers, he admitted, were beaten, but they looked forward with hope and confidence, knowing that the future was with them.

"For you, the victorious party," Mr. Balfour said, stretching his hand out towards the smiling face of Sir William Harcourt, "the future holds nothing but perplexity and dismay."

11th Aug. Still on the Address. At fi minutes past four Mr. Balfour was on his feet, replying to a question, possibly the last in the present Parliament he will have addressed to him on a departmental point. Suddenly his remarks were broken in upon by a loud, sharp cheer, which grew in volume when Mr. Gladstone was seen advancing to his place from behind the Speaker's chair. Mr. Balfour waited till the enthusiastic outburst had subsided, and then went on reading his answer, as Charlotte, when she first saw Werther, "went on cutting bread-and-butter."

Mr. Chamberlain. Mr. Chamberlain rose to resume the debate on the Address, and was hailed with a cheer from the Tory benches such as is usually reserved for a recognised Leader of the Party.

At this moment the House was crowded, even more densely than it has been at any period since the new Parliament met, a circumstance accounted for by the imminence of the division and the full response made from all sections of parties to the various whips. So overwhelming was the crush, so inadequate the seating accommodation, that the Speaker authorised the introduction of chairs, which were placed in a row by the front benches below the gangway. But among so many these dozen chairs were nothing. Members crowded both side galleries, sat in pairs on the steps of the gangway, swarmed around the Speaker's chair, and stood in a dense throng at the bar. It was a magnificent audience, and through the hour he spoke Mr. Chamberlain played upon it with the skill of a master of Parliamentary debate. He concluded an adroit and able speech by a peroration delivered with much more appearance of passion than he usually permits himself in his Parliamentary efforts. It contained a direful prophecy of what would befall a majority which, he gravely feared, might not, even at this last moment, be induced to take the better course and refrain from turning out the Government.

14th Aug. Mr. Chaplin holds the Bridge. It was just midnight when Mr. Chaplin resumed his seat, flushed with the achievement of having contributed the last speech to a historic debate that led up to the overthrow of a powerful Ministry. The

division might have taken place three-quarters of
an hour earlier but for the fact that three members
of the Conservative majority still tarried on their
way back to Westminster. There was a time, not
far distant, when Mr. Balfour would not have
thought of keeping 660 gentlemen waiting because
three of his supporters unduly lingered over their
coffee and cigars. With a majority exceeding sixty
and a long series of easy triumphs behind him, an
Isaacson more or less in the division lobby did not
matter. To-night things are changed. A majority
of sixty has become a minority of forty. This is
the first trial of strength between the newly-
marshalled hosts, and it would not do for the forty
to be increased beyond their time-honoured number.

Accordingly, Mr. Chaplin volunteered to step
forward and hold the bridge till the reinforcements
came up. When the crowded House, eager for the
division, discovered the right hon. gentleman at the
table, a quick, sharp roar of execration went up,
threatening to crack the glass roof. Mr. Chaplin,
affecting to misunderstand the reception, resumed
his seat and looked across inquiringly at Sir Wm.
Harcourt. That particular shout, he seemed to say,
could be meant only for Mr. Gladstone's chief lieutenant,
an invitation to contribute to the debate the reply
to Mr. Chamberlain naturally expected from him.
But Sir Wm. Harcourt sat unresponsive, and Mr.
Chaplin rising again, and being greeted with an
even more angry howl from members opposite, who
thought he had abandoned his intention of speaking,
smilingly bowed his acknowledgment.

A stormy three-quarters of an hour followed.
Taking it altogether, comparing the time occupied by Mr. Chaplin's ordered speech with the
interruption that came from what should have
been the audience, it is probable the latter had
the lion's share. Whenever there was an opening,

Mr. Chaplin inserted the fragment of a sentence.
When there was none, he meditatively sipped from
a glass of apparently unfiltered water with which he
had thoughtfully provided himself. Once he effectively filled up a pause of fully two minutes by
staring with Jovelike frown at the smiling visage
of Sir William Harcourt, of whose recent conduct
in some not clearly defined situation fragmentary
denunciation had earlier floated above the uproar.

At the end of twenty minutes news
The Strayed reached the Treasury Bench that one of
Revellers.
the strayed revellers had returned. Mr.
Chaplin, turning to his notes with renewed energy,
continued his interesting but necessarily disjointed
remarks. Twenty minutes later Mr. Akers Douglas,
standing at the Bar, signalled another sail in sight.
At ten minutes to twelve, in a sudden lull in the roar
of multitudinous voices, Mr. Balfour, who had been
enjoying the scene with as complete *abandon* as if no
black shadow hung over Downing-street, was heard to
say, " That'll do, Chaplin. All in." But by this time
the blood of the President of the Board of Agriculture
was up, and it was not cooled by the hilarious cheer
with which this accidentally overheard remark was
greeted from below the gangway opposite. One sheet
of Mr. Chaplin's somewhat mixed notes had the
corner carefully turned down so as to secure identi-
fication. On this his peroration, worthy of the last
moments of a great Ministry, was fairly written out,
and it should be recited if he stood there all night.

More boisterous grew the uproar on the Opposition
benches. " Never before," said Mr. Chaplin sternly,
gazing through his eyeglass on the face of Sir William
Harcourt, which seemed to have a curious fascination
for him, " has a responsible Minister of the Crown
been treated thus in the British House of Commons."

This dignified reproof only made matters worse.
Mr. Chaplin, firmly holding the sheet of manuscript

with its turned-down corner in his right hand, faced
the tumult and worked hard at the peroration. He
cleared the obstacle at last—not as in Leicestershire a
horse goes clean over fence and stream, but as in
Ireland the hunter surely, but by degrees, scrambles
over wall and spreading mound, and comes down
lightly on the other side.

Now the miscellaneous murmurs and
shouts merged in a mighty cry of "Divide! divide!" The Speaker slowly rose
and put the question.

The Division
on the Address.

"Those that are of that opinion say 'Aye,'" he
said, having read the terms of the amendment which
spoke the doom of the Government.

Never was so brief a monosyllable made so much of
since shouting began.

"The contrary, 'No,'" said the Speaker, continuing
the catechism.

Another roar, the more sonorous negative giving
the advantage to the minority.

Then it seemed as if an earthquake had disturbed
the chamber, men rising on either side and hastening
down the floor of the House, making their way to the
lobbies. The division bell clamoured through all the
rooms and corridors. But there were few to call,
since members had long been packed as closely as
they could stand or sit in the House. As the hand
of the clock touched ten minutes past twelve a strange
contrast was presented. The House was deserted,
even the Speaker's chair empty, and the Sergeant-at-
Arms on guard by the lobby door. In another
minute the returning stream poured in, the murmur
of voices growing higher as the flood broadened
over the floor of the House, and benches were again
filled up. Mr. Balfour, getting back early, took up a
blotting pad and sheet of paper, and began his letter
to the Queen, just as on a memorable June night
in 1885 Mr. Gladstone had done. But, whilst Mr.

Gladstone on that famous occasion steadily wrote on, so that when the division was announced he had nothing to do but to fill in the figures that proclaimed his dismissal, Mr. Balfour toyed with pen and paper, and with smiling face watched the excited throng.

Mr. Akers Douglas was back first. He Expectation. had been counting the Ministerialists, and since they were in a minority his earlier return from the division lobby was a matter of course. All eyes were bent upon the doorway under the clock, whence would issue the Whips bringing the tally of the Opposition muster. They seemed to be an unconscionably long time coming. The Opposition grew increasingly buoyant, hoping for unexpected mercies. Whilst they looked the crowd massed at the bar slowly parted. A white head was seen making its way through the narrow lane, and Mr. Gladstone struggled into full view. With one accord the Opposition sprang to their feet, some leaping on the benches, all waving hats and madly cheering. Mr. Gladstone started at the sudden outburst, quickly recovered his self-possession, and, with head erect, marched down the cheering line to take his seat for the last time in the present Parliament—possibly for the last time in a long life—on the Front Opposition Bench.

There was more waiting for the Opposition tellers. It was probably only a moment. It seemed an hour. At length there was another movement in the mass at the door, and Mr. Marjoribanks, with arms aloft as a strong swimmer struggles among the breakers, was seen making his way through. On the very edge of the seething throng, delivered from its impact with sudden impetus, he fell over Sir George Trevelyan, nearly bringing to a tragic end a blameless life.

The cheering now grew incessant. There Defeat of the was no uncertainty as to the result, but Government. the late arrival of the tellers from the Opposition lobby had, with increasing force, spread the conviction that the majority against the Government had somehow exceeded the normal point. "A majority of fifty!" a voice below the gangway shouted. It proved to be only forty. That was enough to bring the Opposition once more to their feet, cheering and waving hats.

Hardly could the Speaker find opportunity to declare the figures—310 for the Government, 350 against. Whilst he made the effort, Mr. Balfour leaned forward with one hand on the box, the other holding the virgin sheet on which his letter to the Queen had yet to be written. At a signal from the Speaker he rose, and with him the Ministerial Party, whose ringing cheer was the last tribute to the young Leader whose dauntless courage and brilliant capacity had frequently illumined the otherwise dull progress of the dead Parliament. Mr. Balfour's heart must have swelled with pride at this spontaneous recognition. But there was no inflexion in his tone nor sign of emotion in his face as he quietly moved, in view of the division just taken (which he casually admitted was important), the adjournment of the House till Thursday next.

Here ended the story of the Salisbury Ministry, and the crowd outside Palace Yard, patiently waiting for hours, took up the thunderous cheers that welcomed Mr. Gladstone back to office.

CHAPTER II.

PROROGATION.

LORD HALSBURY, preparing for his holiday, pleased with the retrospect of an honourable and honoured life, must have his thoughts slightly ruffled by reflection on the incomprehensible favouritism of fortune. For six years he has lent grace and dignity to the Woolsack. To see him enter, preceded by the Purse-bearer and accompanied by Black Rod, has been for the few peers present a lesson in deportment. The way he has gathered up his flowing robes with intent to step aside from the Woolsack and merge the President in the debater has at times been more effective than a syllogism. Long practice, combined with natural gifts, has enabled him to put the question and declare "The Contents have it" in briefer space of time than has sufficed for any modern Lord Chancellor.

On the very last day the House of Lords met under his Presidency he performed a feat which extorted admiration from an audience with whom frequent repetition had worn off the gloss of surprise. When Lord Salisbury, his heart light and his spirits high with the sense of coming deliverance from official thraldom, had gravely poked fun at Lord Kimberley, and Lord Kimberley had made response in his gossamer style, motion was made that the House adjourn to Thursday. Agreement thereto was taken as a matter of course. Nevertheless, the motion was one which the forms of the

House permitted to be debated at whatever length it might please noble lords to speak. In the almost imperceptible pause that followed on the proposal being made there rose from the table a tall, gaunt figure, over whose grey face and eyes, looking wearily out on a world prone to misunderstanding, was set a red skull-cap.

" My Lords—" said this picturesque figure suddenly projected on a commonplace scene.

In an instant the Lord Chancellor was on his feet. " Question-is-that-this-House-adjourn-till-Thursday. The-House-will-now-adjourn." Thus he, breathless, spoke, and, almost skipping away from the Woolsack, left Lord Denman standing forlornly at the table, his face grown visibly sadder with the reflection that once more the right of free speech had been violated, and the conspiracy to prevent his being heard amongst his peers had again triumphed.

That was on Monday. To-day the scene Prorogation. was the same, but the actors were changed.

Lord Halsbury had retired from the Woolsack, his place to be for some indefinite time occupied by Lord Herschell. From among the new Lord Chancellor's companions on the bench before the Woolsack the red beard of Earl Spencer was spied beneath the muffler of the quaint red cloak he, in common with other Commissioners, wore. The Ministerial bench was empty. Not a single bishop lingered in the fold above the gangway. The benches opposite were a tenantless waste. In all the broad space allotted to the Peerage of the United Kingdom there sat only Lord Stratheden and Campbell, that Siamese twin of Diplomacy and Oratory.

At the Bar stood the Speaker, as dignified and imposing as if he were playing a part in the pageant of the opening of a new Session, with his

Sovereign seated on the Throne at the other end
of the House. He had just come from another
curious scene, presented in three shifts. First, there
was the meeting of the Commons at three o'clock
for the business of moving the writs for vacancies
created by acceptance of Ministerial office. Then
came the suspension of the sitting and its resumption
at half-past four. Once more the sitting was suspended, a few members furtively reassembling at
nine o'clock to be present at the ceremony of the
Prorogation.

"Don't, Keir-
Hardie." At the first meeting Mr. Keir-Hardie,
his withers unwrung by the labours of
a Parliamentary Session already accomplished, was eager, in the interests of the Working
Man, that there should be an autumn Session by
way of getting into training for an ordinary Session
which promises to be amongst the most lively and
laborious of recent years. He was all in the wrong
on points of procedure, and the Speaker explained
the matter to him in tone and manner of winning
courtesy. The Member for Ham, as he put on
again his *fin de siècle* Cap of Liberty, moved uneasily in his seat, and presently rose with intent
to argue the matter out. He was "being done,"
somehow. Mr. Burt was probably at the bottom
of this. The British Working Man was once
more, at the instance of the aristocracy and with
the assistance of traitors, betrayed. If he had
them out at Ham, or under the Reformers' Tree
in Hyde Park, he would let them know that the
British workman is not to be trampled on with
impunity. But here, with this stately personage
in the Chair, with his ordered speech, sonorous
voice, and air of being accustomed to command,
it was different. Mr. Keir-Hardie hurriedly looking
round and finding no help coming, from the hills
or anywhere else, subsided, and what had long

promised to be a stirring scene lapsed into a commonplace incident.

In the Commons. At this first hour of meeting the House was remarkably full, bubbling with excitement. There were yet some offices in the new Ministry unallotted, and hope still flickered in as many breasts, telling the flattering tale that the message of invitation to Carlton-gardens was only delayed. On both sides it was an army without generals, only here and there a subaltern to represent absent authority. The Conservatives had crossed over to the left of the Speaker, the Liberals jubilantly ranging themselves along the frontier of the Promised Land on which through six years they had longingly looked. The Government were represented by the Financial Secretary to the Treasury and the Secretary to the Admiralty, with Mr. Marjoribanks, acclaimed the new Liberal Whip, bulging out at every pocket with new writs which he was commissioned to move.

There was odd contrast between the Whip's flurried recital of the formula of the motion and its stately repetition of the Speaker as he put the question. The tiresome rotund sentence seemed to gather fresh grace of literary composition and fuller depth of meaning as time after time, exceeding a score in all, it rolled forth from beneath the sounding board over the Chair. So perfect is Mr. Peel's elocution that if in some dull dinner hour he were to get up and repeat the multiplication table up to twelve times twelve, the House would quietly fill with members who would sit entranced at the rhythmic sound, strangely moved by the familiar truths.

In the absence of Mr. Arthur Balfour, already gladly making holiday, Mr. Ashmead-Bartlett, faithful to the last to duty's call, entered the House, and naturally fell into the place of the Leader of the Opposition. As he sat there, nursing the secret the morning papers should disclose,* he from time to time looked sharply round to the seat corresponding with that in which Mr. Blundell Maple was accustomed to sit on the other side. But his brother knight, less used to facing a curious throng, was blushing unseen in some place of retirement, and will not reappear in the parliamentary arena until, by domestic practice, he has grown accustomed to be hailed Sir John. Gradually the statesman soon to be Sir Ellis submitted to the soothing influence of the Speaker's monotone, sitting enraptured whilst the syllables rose and fell in stately cadence.

"The question is that Mr. Speaker do issue his warrant to the Clerk of the Crown to make out a new writ for the election of a member to serve in this present Parliament for the county of Edinburgh, in the room of the Right Hon. William Ewart Gladstone, who since his election for the said county has accepted the office of First Commissioner for executing the office of Treasurer of the Exchequer of Great Britain and Lord High Treasurer of Ireland."

More Meteorological Omens. It was in the last scene of all, which preluded and accomplished the prorogation of the first Session of the thirteenth Parliament of the Queen, there befel the incident upon which Lord Halsbury may have reflected with pardonable envy. More than half a dozen times he has been called upon to perform the function over which the new Lord Chancellor presided to-night, but never in such circumstances of superhuman splendour. Never before, as far as memory goes, did Nature so lavishly contribute to the efforts Art makes to invest the Prorogation of Parliament by Royal Commission with suitable environment. As the Speaker stood at the Bar, with the Sergeant-at-Arms by his side, a

* Among the honours conferred by Lord Salisbury on retiring from office were knighthoods for Mr. Ashmead-Bartlett and Mr. Blundel Maple.

little group of members in the rear, there suddenly
broke forth a regal peal of thunder that rumbled
round the Clock Tower and threatened to crumble
Westminster Abbey into the ancient dust on which it
stands.   There was no Queen's Speech to read, only
Her Majesty's commands to "prorogue this Parliament till Friday, the 4th day of November next."
These were contained in a single sentence.   But it
was punctuated as Queen's Speech never was, peals of
thunder coming in where Lord Halsbury in his time
had been supplied only with commas, the final word
being marked by a full stop that made all the
windows rattle, and seemed to presage the Crack of
Doom.

In the candelabras by the Throne and in the
brackets under the galleries multitudinous candles
burned.   But their ineffectual flame paled beneath
the constant flashes of lightning that lit up the
Chamber, gleaming along the Mace on the Sergeant-
at-Arms' shoulder, playing with lambent, lurid flame
around the heads of the five cloaked figures on the
bench before the Woolsack.

CHAPTER III.

SESSION OF 1893.

BRISK BEGINNING.

THE wholesome impetus given to political life by the result of the General Election was testified in striking manner by the multitude gathered outside Palace Yard. At all new Sessions a similar crowd assembles in hope of catching a glimpse of the faces of prominent members. Never did it reach such proportions as to-day, a considerable body of police being requisite to keep the roadway open. The people assembled as early as ten o'clock, formed in dense numbers at noon, and showed with additional force between three and four, at which hour members rapidly passed in.

31st Jan. The First Muster.

At four o'clock the Speaker took the chair. At this moment Mr. Gladstone was discovered standing in front of the crowd at the Bar, with Mr. Marjoribanks on one side and Mr. Herbert Gladstone at the other. These were his escort, bringing him up to the table to take the oath. As he advanced, wearing a white flower in his coat and a smile on his face, members had the opportunity of satisfying themselves that he seemed in excellent health and spirits. He led in single file his colleagues in the Ministry re-elected during the recess. The various Ministers were cheered with divers degrees of unanimity. But there was nothing like a scene, the event taking place more promptly than had been expected, befalling at a time when the House was not full, and when the larger portion of those present were struggling for places in the line that led up to the table where the book lay on which members desiring to give notices of motion enter their names for the ballot.

By an odd accident there came between Mr. Gladstone and Sir Wm. Harcourt, who followed next in the line of Ministers, Mr. Chamberlain, entering by the doorway under the clock, followed closely by Sir Henry James. The leader of the Dissentient Liberals was sharply cheered by his friends—a thin black line on the third bench below the gangway on the Ministerial side, the prevailing tone of colour varied by the bold buff of Mr. Courtney's waistcoat—the welcome being taken up from the Conservative benches.

The process of swearing-in new members occupied just half-an-hour.

Whilst it was going forward Mr. Goschen arrived, and was probably surprised at the heartiness of the cheer on the Conservative side with which he was greeted, contrasting as it did with their habitually cold manner towards him in the last Parliament. Just before half-past four Mr. Balfour came in from behind the Speaker's chair, and, the House being now crowded, he received the loudest cheer of all.

New members having taken their places,
Jabez Balfour. there followed the moving of writs for seats vacated during the recess. The motion for a new writ for Burnley, in the place of " Spencer Balfour, Esq., who since his election has accepted the office of Steward of the Chiltern Hundreds," was received with ironical laughter from the Conservatives, forgetful of analogous cases on their own side not many sessions ago. Mr. Coddington asked why " in view of the great frauds Mr. Balfour had committed " he was permitted to take an office of honour. Sir Wm. Harcourt

explained that some time ago all reference to the office of the Chiltern Hundreds being a place of honour had been struck out of the formula. By Sir Stafford Northcote, the Chancellor of the Exchequer said, but was quickly corrected by Mr. Gladstone, who laughingly observed, " I struck out the words."

The Struggle for Seats. At this time the House was densely crowded. Not a seat was vacant on the floor of the House, whilst the side benches in the gallery were eagerly appropriated. There was time, whilst the Speaker proceeded with the monotonous reading, to observe that the Irish Nationalist members had secured their old places below the gangway on the Opposition side, including all the corner seats. Mr. James Lowther, who had made gallant efforts to secure a seat corresponding with that he occupied on the other side during the last Parliament, retired baffled to the Front Opposition Bench, where sanctuary was provided for him. Lord Randolph Churchill held unchallenged his corner seat immediately behind the Front Opposition Bench. On the other side Sir John Pender, one of the early birds, had caught a worm in the shape of the top corner seat below the gangway. Below him sat Mr. Chamberlain, with the opportunity of contemplating the figure of Mr. Picton in the corner seat below him, and that of Mr. Labouchere in the corner seat corresponding with his old camping ground when in Opposition. Then, as now, beside the member for Northampton sat Sir Charles Dilke.

The Address. It was half-past nine when Mr. Balfour rose to take part in the debate on the Address. The House, at the time depressingly empty, began to fill up. As the benches behind him were peopled, the cheering rose with a volume that encouraged the right honourable gentleman to those flights of invective Mr. Gladstone later

deplored. A ringing shout of applause, echoed from
the third bench below the gangway on the Ministerial
side, approved Mr. Balfour's declaration that the dealing
with the manumitted prisoners was not an exercise of
the prerogative of mercy as it should be used, but
rather as the wielding of a political weapon. He was inclined to reserve his criticism of the Bills promised in
the Queen's Speech till the measures were before the
House. But he adventured the remark, again cheered
by his friends, that the proposal to shorten the duration of Parliament was not of immediate interest, since
no one supposed the life of the present one would be prolonged. As to the Home Rule Bill, he declared, amidst
strident cheers from the Opposition, it was regarded
with passionate, ineradicable aversion by one-third of
the Irish people ; by another third with sentimental
approval, not unmixed with impulse towards spoliation ;
whilst the other third regarded it as an opportunity
of extracting more strength from the Empire.

Mr. Balfour spoke for an hour, and was followed
by the Premier, whose appearance at the table was
the signal for a prolonged burst of cheering. He had
evidently been moved by the hot speech of the Leader
of the Opposition, and commenced in tones of deepest
indignation, with animated gestures that belied the
fables about his waning strength. After the first
out-burst he subsided into more placid mood, and
reviewed in order the various points of the Queen's
Speech raised by Mr. Balfour. With respect to the
Home Rule Bill, he expressed the hope that gentlemen opposite would await its appearance, and thereafter bestow upon the problem a calm, a patient, even
a benevolent consideration.

Whilst the ceremony of opening Parliament by Royal Commission is a melancholy, almost grotesque affair that might
well be dispensed with, there is an earlier
performance much more dramatic. This is the search

1st Feb.
In Search of
Guy Fawkes.

through the vaults of the Houses of Parliament, done as punctiliously in these closing days of the nineteenth century as it was 300 years ago, when it was first ordered. The business was yesterday morning carried out with a gravity perfectly delightful. The first essential is secrecy. If you are going to drop upon a conspirator, you do not approach his hiding-place with blare of trumpets and the beat of drums.

It is the Lord Chamberlain, one of the highest Ministers of State in the kingdom, to whom is personally entrusted the duty of seeing the thing through. Possibly, when fresh to the office, he may go the round. This year Lord Lathom had nothing new to learn, and his place was taken by the Vice-Chamberlain. The House of Commons was represented by the Deputy-Sergeant-at-Arms. The civil force was present in the person of an inspector of police. The Clerk of the Works acted as guide; and, for fear ruffians traced to their lair should turn at bay, the little procession was escorted by four of Her Majesty's Guard of Yeomen, armed to the teeth. All the passages and chambers under the House of Commons are lighted either by gas or electricity. Three hundred years ago these elements in domestic life were non-existent, and search was made with the assistance of lanterns. So to this day lanterns are carried, albeit they flare dimly in the brilliantly illuminated recesses that underlie the Houses of Parliament.

The search was thorough and effective. The safety of Imperial Parliament was committed to the charge of this little body of devoted men, and they did not shirk it. Silent and resolute they tramped along the corridors, peering in at innumerable vaults, unresting till they had made the full tour of the place and were able with clear consciences to testify that all was well. The fact that the search has been made, and that no trace of iniquitous design has been revealed by the light of the lantern, is gravely reported in .the Lord Chamberlain's office.   In former times a horseman was despatched to the residence of the Sovereign, with a missive from the Lord Chamberlain attesting the fact, and announcing that the attendance of Majesty on the opening of Parliament might be safely undertaken.   Now the work is done by telegraph; and though the Queen had not the slightest intention of risking life or limb, a despatch was gravely committed to the telegraph wires informing Her Majesty at Osborne that the Houses of Parliament had been searched, and that she might safely repair thither for the opening.

Bringing in Bills.   The debate on the Address, resumed at noon, was adjourned at four o'clock in order to provide opportunity for members to bring in Bills.

This led to a scene which must have conveyed a curious notion of the business qualities of the House of Commons to the few strangers in the Gallery. Yesterday two clear hours of the most precious time of the sitting were wasted by the process of publicly balloting for precedence for private Bills and motions. This is a mechanical performance that might well be added to the useful labours of the clerks, leaving the Speaker and the House of Commons opportunity for devoting their energies to more delicate duties.* What happened to-day were the second and third acts of a farce that has not even a flash of humour to recommend it.

The ballot having been settled, and something like 400 notices of motion given, there remained the process of bringing in Bills.   There were 142 on the list, and the process goes on in this way: The Speaker, taking the list in hand, calls by name on a

---

* This suggestion was adopted by the Speaker at the opening of the Session of 1894.

member. The member responds by lifting his hat.
Thereupon the Speaker recites the title of the Bill,
and puts the question: "The question is that leave be
given to bring in a Bill to assimilate the Laws of
Heritable Succession to those of Movable Succession
in Scotland. Those of that opinion say 'Aye'; the
contrary, 'No.' Who is prepared to bring in this
Bill?"

The gentleman in charge rises and reads the list of
members, modestly concluding with himself. Then
the Speaker proceeds to the next in order, and so the
thing goes on by the yard and the hour.

*2nd Feb.
"A Murder-
ous Ruffian;
or, the Excited
Politician."* Just before half-past four Colonel Saunderson found opportunity to resume the
debate on the Address. He had, whether
strategically or by treaty, succeeded in
obtaining the corner seat on the Front
Bench below the gangway, on the opening day of the
Session appropriated by Dr. Tanner. He proceeded
with moderate success for the space of half-an-hour,
devoted chiefly to an attack upon the Evicted Tenants
Commission. This led him on to the release of the
dynamite prisoners, and of those connected with the
Gweedore murder. Having occasion to allude to the
parish priest, he styled him "that ruffian McFadden."
This drew forth a roar of protest from the Irish
members sitting immediately behind the Colonel,
who was supported by a sympathetic cheer from
above the gangway, where the party of Law and
Order are massed. When there came a lull in the
storm, the Colonel obligingly offered to vary the
phrase, and in a loud, emphatic voice denounced
"This murderous ruffian McFadden."

There was another shout of indignation from the
Irish members, one jumping up, excitedly shouting,
"The expression itself is ruffianly." The Speaker,
interposing, quietly observed that the member who
had risen was himself out of order. Mr. Dillon

shouted at the Speaker the inquiry whether Colonel
Saunderson was in order in bringing an accusation of
murder against a man who had never been put on his
trial for such offence.

"Withdraw! withdraw!" the Irish members
roared.

"I withdraw nothing," said Colonel Saunderson,
who was standing in close contiguity to his excited
countrymen.

Attempting to proceed with his speech, he was met
with continuous cry of "Divide! divide!" to which
the Conservatives above the gangway contributed a
shout of "Order! order!" The Speaker, again
rising, explained that it was not competent for him
in the circumstances to call Colonel Saunderson to
order. The hon. and gallant gentleman was within
his right in using the phrase with respect to a person
—"outside the House," the Speaker significantly
added. It was for him to consider whether it was
a proper one.

Colonel Saunderson attempted to proceed amid
renewed cries for the division. Mr. Dillon once
more dashed in and, amid prolonged cheering from
the Irish members, moved that Colonel Saunderson
be no longer heard. Above the gangway, Mr.
Bartley rose with intent to say something. His
voice was lost in the roar. The Speaker, amid loud
cheers from the Conservatives, declared his inability
to put the motion, and suggested that Colonel
Saunderson should modify the expression.

"I cannot help taking my own view," the
Colonel said doggedly.

Whereat the uproar broke forth afresh. Whenever the Colonel opened his mouth, he was gagged by
cries for the division.

It seemed as if the struggle might go on for
another hour. Suddenly and unexpectedly a new
turn was given to it. From above the gangway

came the advice, audibly addressed to Colonel Saunderson, " Move the adjournment." The Colonel, who throughout the excited scene had lost nothing of his customary coolness, quickly took the tip.

" I beg to move," said he, " that the debate be now adjourned "; at which there was a roar of triumph from the Conservatives.

Before the Speaker could put the question, Mr. Gladstone was on his feet with prefatory appeal to the Irish members to exercise patience. Turning to Colonel Saunderson, he submitted to his judgment whether such an expression as he had used " with regard to a gentleman——." Mr. Gladstone was rudely interrupted by laughter and ironical cheers from above the gangway at this mode of reference to the parish priest, a fresh insult responded to with angry cheers by the Irish members. Taking no notice of either demonstration, Mr. Gladstone quietly repeated the word—" A gentleman," he said, " who was known to be held in respect and esteem by his parishioners." He appealed to Colonel Saunderson, in the name of the dignity and honour of the House, to close the scene.

Colonel Saunderson was about to rise when Mr. Balfour interposed. Stillness suddenly fell upon the House, curious to know what line the Leader of the Opposition would take. A moment's reflection suggested that in such circumstances he would, as a matter of course, support the Leader of the House in his effort to quell the riot that had burst forth at the instance of one of his own followers. Mr. Balfour had no such intention. On the contrary, at the very moment peace seemed about to follow upon the joint exertions of the Speaker and Mr. Gladstone, he threw oil on the embers of the fire. He, indeed, joined in the appeal that the scene should terminate; but, what was much more effective in another direction, he tacked on the

c

reminder that language not less strong had been heard in the House levelled against innocent police-men, and had gone unrebuked.

It seemed after this that Colonel Saunderson would persist in the attitude he had stubbornly maintained up to the moment Mr. Gladstone had interposed. But he proved wiser than his leader.

"I will," he said, "for the words complained of substitute——." Here was a pause, members on both sides eagerly bending forward to catch the first indication of what might mean peace or renewed, even more bitter war. "I will substitute the words," continued Colonel Saunderson, "excited politician."

This anti-climax was welcomed with a roar of laughter, in which Mr. Gladstone heartily joined, and thereafter the Colonel ambled peacefully along to the end of his speech.

4th Feb.
"Honest
John."

Second only to the welcome accorded to Mr. Gladstone when on Tuesday he ap-proached the table to take the oath on re-election after acceptance of office was that which greeted Mr. John Morley.

Nothing succeeds like success, and upon top of his great triumph at Newcastle there comes to Mr. Morley a flood of personal popularity. He has always been esteemed by the people, but has never before this hard-won fight succeeded in touching their affection. He was known as "Honest John" during the general election. A man of letters, a statesman and a scholar, he was opposed by a local gentleman, in personal appearance and general characteristics not without reminiscences of Mr. Micawber in his prosperous days. This personage is locally known as "Old Charlie," and as he strutted about, his more than seventy years taking on springtime again, with summer suit, light covert coat of latest fashion, and high white hat jauntily set on one side of his head, men and boys followed him, jubilantly cheering when he lightly kissed his hand to girls, pretty or otherwise, who had brothers or husbands with votes. Between Mr. Charles Hammond and Mr. John Morley there is fixed as great a gulf as may possibly yawn between two works of the same Creator. People laughed at Old Charlie and listened attentively to the weighty speeches of Honest John. But when the poll was declared it was found that on an unprecedentedly large poll Old Charlie was 3,000 ahead, whilst Honest John retained his seat only by grace of 219 voters, who at the last moment plumped for him.

That was a severe blow for a man of Mr. Morley's position, seeing it was dealt in a constituency which in point of numbers and standard of intelligence ranks high among Liberal boroughs. It would have paralysed some men. It has been the final making of John Morley. It stirred him to his deepest depths, and they have proved to be richly profound. When, on his acceptance of office, the ring was cleared at Newcastle for another tussle, Mr. Morley flung himself into the fray with a courage that might have been expected from him, but with a vigour, a verve, and a light, sure touch with the people, capability for which was hitherto unsuspected.

It was almost fatally late in life that he entered the arena of active politics. He was in his forty-sixth year when he entered the House of Commons as Member for Newcastle, a splendid age, the very prime of manhood, but, except in rare cases, too far advanced for happy entrance upon a term of apprenticeship in the House of Commons. Mr. Morley ranks to-day as one of the ablest debaters in the House of Commons. But the position was slowly acquired. He always had it in him, but could not for some time get it out —or, to be more accurate, could not be induced to let himself go. To his almost ascetic literary taste the looser style of expression more fitting for a public audience was shocking.

His Maiden
Speech.

Those present will not forget his maiden speech, looked forward to with interest in the House of Commons, listened to with a feeling of disappointment his warmest friends could not disguise. It happened that he followed at brief interval the late Mr. Joseph Gillis Biggar. That personage was in his primest mood. Lord Randolph Churchill had sparkled earlier in the sitting, and Joey B., who shared with the monkey its mimetic faculty, had, as was his custom, unconsciously adopted a travesty of the noble Lord's incisive style and emphatic manner. The House roared with delighted laughter. Mr. Biggar, fluent, self-possessed, never at a loss for a word, not too particular as to its *nuance* of meaning, talked on for a full half hour, as complete a master of this critical assembly as was Mr. Gladstone or Mr. Bright. Then came John Morley with his carefully-thought-out treatise, glistening with polished sentences gleaming through profound depths of thought. The House generously cheered him when he rose, and sat in silent sympathy as he painfully struggled through the opening sentences of his speech.

It was a curious contrast, not without its note of sadness, to think of Mr. Biggar saying nothing with easy fluency, and to look on this embodiment of culture, this man teeming with thoughts, this master of a perfect literary style, standing with parched lips and strained eyes, endeavouring to recite his sedulously prepared essay.

A great deal has happened since then, among other events an accident that was the turning-point in Mr. Morley's Parliamentary career. It chanced a year or two ago that he was called upon to address a great conference of Liberals, held at Leeds. It was a time at which the tide of Liberalism in the constituencies had begun to flow with unmistakable strength and persistency. The delegates gathered in thousands at Leeds were in high spirits, which in the

course of the meeting were communicated to the
austere statesman on the platform.

Delivering himself from the trammels of
On the
Platform.his notes, Mr. Morley talked to his enthusiastic audience in a frank, hearty
manner which delighted them, and probably astonished
himself. That speech was a great success, not only
with the audience within the building, but with
the larger and wider circle that read the verbatim
report in the newspapers. Mr. Morley has never
turned aside from the new departure made that night.
It was as if a man floating on the water had by
accident been deprived of his life-belt and discovered
that he could swim very well without it. Mr. Morley
will never plunge into the stream of debate, whether
in the House of Commons or on the platform, with the
burly joyousness that distinguishes Sir William Harcourt. But he improves every year, and made a long
stride forward during the recent contest at Newcastle.

Even if he had lost the election instead of winning
it by an unexpectedly large majority he would have
been indebted for the opportunity of bringing himself
much nearer the heart of the English people than he
ever stood before. Accustomed to an attitude of
mobility common to politicians on both sides at times
of electoral contests, people found a time of refreshment in this spectacle of Mr. Morley standing with
his back to the wall, immovable in an attitude taken
up on the labour question at a time when the contest
was far off and seemed in any case free from danger.
Wound up to a high pitch by the excitement of the
contest, Mr. Morley, finding himself on the platform or
talking to enthusiastic crowds in the streets, finally " let
himself go," with happiest results. Never before has
he spoken with such force or effect, and probably never
again will he be borne down by the mystical burden
of a House of Commons audience whose influence he
early admitted his inability to dissect or define.

3rd Feb.
New Phases
of the Irish
Question. The House of Commons since it met, for what prophets are agreed in forecasting as a momentous Session, has been busied with many things. Egypt, Uganda, and Ireland have severally passed in review. But Ireland has, in its familiar manner, been the lean kine that swallowed up the rest. All Parliamentary roads lead to Ireland. With whatever object or prospect a sitting may commence, some Irish question is safe to interpose. Publicists are used to speak of "the" Irish Question as if it existed in the singular number. There is, truly, only one Irish Question, as the earth has only one atmosphere. But it is everywhere, varying as the atmosphere varies, yet ever present.

"Who Stole the Deer?" It came before the House in delightful fashion when incorporated in the person of Mr. John Roche. Mr. Roche entered the House three years ago in succession to Mr. Mat Harris. He has modestly kept in the background, and only to-night leaped into parliamentary fame. It was Colonel Saunderson who acted as his introducer, incorporating in his speech last night an interesting biographical sketch of the hon. member. This was given as pertaining to a witness before the Evicted Tenants Commission, and probably not one in ten of the members who followed its details knew that the John Roche alluded to was the member for East Galway. Indeed, when the hon. member appeared on the scene and called in question some particulars of the narrative, Colonel Saunderson blandly asked, How was he to know that the John Roche who stole a deer at Woodford was their esteemed fellow member?

Mr. Roche had, in the interval between the delivery of Colonel Saunderson's speech and the meeting of the House to-day, made his identity known, and challenged the Colonel's perfect accuracy. It had been said he made a personal attack on an obnoxious bailiff, who a few days later was brutally murdered. The date of the murder was five months later. To that extent the Colonel retracted and apologised. But that John Roche had stolen a deer he still insisted, and read to the House a certified copy of the magisterial order in the case. This showed that John Roche did, on the 4th of October, 1876, carry away from the Derry Crag a deer ; that, being indicted, he pleaded guilty,. expressed his poignant regret, and consented to pay all costs.

Mr. John Roche.

It was at this stage that from a bench near the Serjeant-at-Arm's chair there uprose a quiet-looking gentleman who stood for the moment silently regarding the House. His action was so gentle and his manner so unobtrusive that the Speaker might have been forgiven if he had not observed him, and, concluding the incident was closed, proceeded to call on the next business. But the Irish members, who of course knew their compatriot, loudly cheered, and all eyes were turned in the direction where the unfamiliar figure stood. He still made no attempt to speak, and the silence was growing embarrassing when with deliberate action he folded his arms across his chest. That seemed to break the spell. As when one drops a penny in the slot something (occasionally) happens, this folding of the arms seemed to loosen the chords of Mr. Roche's voice. He spoke at first slowly and in low tone. As he proceeded he grew excited, and there was a ring of triumph in his voice when, turning towards Colonel Saunderson, he shouted, " If I was fined, where is the fine ? "

That he had shot a deer was true ; but what was the deer doing on his farm ? If he found one there to-morrow he would shoot it : whereat the Irish members, probably anticipating a friendly distribution of haunches of venison, loudly cheered.

Here the incident ended, and the House had time to forget Mr. John Roche, when, once more, he appeared on the scene, in the same deliberate

manner, with the same prelude of silence, broken
again by the tragic folding of his arms.   This time
it was Mr. Carson who dropped the penny in the
slot.   Referring to the proceedings before the Evicted
Tenants Commission, he expressed his regret that
he had not been allowed to cross-examine Mr. John
Roche as to the circumstances under which he had
advised the Clanricarde tenantry to throttle an obnoxious neighbour "till his glass eye fell out of his
head."

"Mr. Speaker," said Mr. Roche, when he found
his voice, "I did not tell the tenantry to throttle him."

That was satisfactory, and if Mr. Roche had forthwith sat down, the House, in accordance with its
polite usage, would have felt bound to accept the
disclaimer.   But his arms being folded, Mr. Roche
went on to explain.   "I told them that by adopting
the Plan of Campaign they would adopt means by
which they would throttle him."   That was a *nuance*
the delicate shade of which the House recognised with
uproarious merriment.   Thus encouraged, and resolved that his explanation should be honestly full,
Mr. Roche, still confidentially addressing the Speaker,
continued :—"In the heat and excitement of the occasion I did go so far as to say that by adhering loyally
to the Plan of Campaign they would throttle him."
Here another burst of laughter broke in, for the
moment uncontrollable.

But there still remained the glass eye, and as Mr.
Roche, with no responsive smile flickering over his
solemn countenance, remained on his feet with folded
arms, there was reasonable expectation that if quietness were restored the House might even hear the
glass eye drop out.   Nor were they disappointed.

"Also, Mr. Speaker," said Mr. Roche, going on
with a jerk when silence was restored, "I did say that
I hoped they would not loose their grasp until the
glass eye fell out of his head."

CHAPTER IV.

THE HOME RULE BILL BROUGHT IN.

THERE were some curious changes notable
this afternoon in the locality of eminent
persons seated in the House. Lord
Randolph Churchill, who the other night,
finding his usual corner seat occupied, accepted the
proffered sanctuary of the Front Opposition Bench,
sat there through questions this evening, in friendly
conversation with Mr. Goschen, Sir M. Hicks-Beach,
and other of his former colleagues. On the opposite
side of the House, when Mr. Chamberlain rose to put
a question to the Premier, he had, so to speak, to
round the promontory presented by the person of
Mr. T. B. Potter anchored in what the member for
West Birmingham had regarded as his own particular
seat. It happens that the seat selected by Mr.
Chamberlain on the opening of the session corresponds
with that Mr. Potter occupied on the other side of the
House during the last Parliament. Being no party to
the appropriation Mr. Potter was down bright and
early to-day, and, while benefitting by the advantage
of taking part in the devotional exercises that precede
the business of the day, was able to reflect that he had
got in before Mr. Chamberlain. When the right hon.
gentleman arrived he found Mr. Potter in his place,
and, there being no appeal, he dropped down on the
other side of him.

The Ministerialists have through the week
been growing in aggressive spirit. There
was talk at the beginning of the Session
of their actually dwindling majority of

*6th Feb.
Faces and
Places.*

*9th Feb.
The
Ministerial
Back put up.*

c *

forty further disappearing. Successive divisions have brought out the surprising and unexpected fact that Ministers may, upon occasion, command majorities of twice forty. Of course this can easily be explained away. It is due to accidental circumstances, and does not disturb the stubborn fact that when forces are mustered for pitched battle, as they will be on stages of the Home Rule Bill, the Government majority will be reduced to its actual proportions. Still, there are the majorities of eighty and more, and no one familiar with Parliamentary warfare will be inclined to under-rate their significance.

Those so disposed should endeavour to realise what would have been the effect supposing things had gone the other way, and, instead of being doubled, the Ministerial majority had, in identical circumstances and from corresponding causes, been reduced by one-half. The figures at least show that at the outset of the campaign, without special incentive in the way of danger to the Ministry, the admirably whipped Ministerial host are standing shoulder to shoulder, filling up their ranks to a man, and voting in platoons. Other direful things prophesied in advance have not only not been realised, but matters have turned out greatly to the advantage of the Government. Two clouds which loomed darkly over their fortunes at the opening of the Session have proved full of mercy, and have broken in blessings on their head. It turned out upon inquiry that it was all a mistake about leaving Sir Gerald Portal without adequate instructions and letting Uganda shift for itself. The attack in force on this position was at a critical moment abandoned, a similar fate attending the equally threatening action directed against the Home Secretary in the matter of the release of Egan and Callan. Then to-night comes in swift succession the news that Halifax is safe and Walsall recaptured.

In the existent topsy-turvy condition of 10th Feb. The Irish Members Shocked. affairs in the House of Commons there is nothing more striking than the manner in which the Irish members have become the stern and sensitive custodians of orderly conduct and language. The other night Mr. Tim Healy brought tears to the long-unused eyes of hardened door-keepers by his rebuke of Mr. Balfour, who had blocked a number of Government measures, including Mr. Henry Fowler's Registration Bill. Mr. Healy's voice trembled with ·emotion as he declared that never in his parliamentary experience had he known obstruction so wanton and so reckless.

Mr. Johnston, of Ballykilbeg, when he recovered his breath, asked the Speaker if it was not the fact that two nights earlier Mr. Healy had himself blocked this very Bill, persisting in the action in spite of the pleading of Mr. Fowler and the stern remonstrance of Sir William Harcourt ? But Ballykilbeg is situated in the north of Ireland, and Mr. Johnston is bereft of the priceless faculty of humour.

All the indignation that had flooded Mr. Healy's breast when he discovered Mr. Balfour frustrating the aims of a beneficent Government welled up again to-night when he heard the right hon. gentleman dropping remarks that might be construed as disrespectful to Mr. Gladstone. The Irish members sitting in the very same seats, tossing about with the same turbulence, vividly recalled scenes of nightly occurrence in the Parliament of 1880-5. Then their fierce visages were turned a little further to the left, their glowering eyes bent on the Treasury Bench, their strident voices uplifted in bitter, passionate denunciation of Mr. Gladstone, his colleagues, and all their works. One remembers a remark of the late Mr. Biggar, spoken at a time of strongest tension between the Irish members and the Government in which Mr. Forster was Chief Secretary. " A vain old

gentleman" was the phrase in which Joseph Gillis
dismissed Mr. Gladstone from further consideration.
The phrase, taken by itself, is not complimentary,
scarcely respectful. At the time, by comparison with
others in current use by his compatriots, it somehow
had a genial, almost a friendly sound.

Those days have fled, and much has happened
since. Other times, other manners, or, rather,
much the same manners, only their force directed
in a different quarter. To-day the Irish members
are Mr. Gladstone's bodyguard, and the Irish
Secretary finds his most zealous protector in the
person of Mr. Tim Healy.

Mr. Balfour was probably meditating on these
things as he bowed his head to the storm, and
waited till it had so far spent itself that he might
say what he had at heart. Some moments passed
whilst the outraged advocates of Parliamentary de-
corum seated below the gangway incessantly clamoured
for apology. To make apology for what was described
as offence unwittingly given was, it turned out, the
purpose with which Mr. Balfour rose, and when
silence was partially restored he accomplished it.

" Mr. Gladstone," he said, with an inclination of
the head to which the Premier, ready to for-
give anyone but Mr. Jesse Collings, graciously responded, " is the last person in this House whose
feelings I should desire to hurt."

The House, in the aggregate the most generous-
minded assembly in the world, ever shows itself most
eager to accept apology. Mr. Balfour's was received
with general cheering, and there, as when earlier he
had stood up, the incident seemed to close. But next
to the Premier sat Sir Wm. Harcourt, smiling at
the happy turn events had taken. Mr. Balfour
was in contrite mood, really sorry that he should
have wounded one who long ago won his youthful
admiration and still retains it. But the sight of

Sir Wm. Harcourt's beaming visage was irresistible. Hardening his voice and straightening his back, Mr. Balfour, as he resumed his seat, snapped forth the words, " I was not attacking him, but the right hon. gentleman the Chancellor of the Exchequer."

The House had seethed with indignation at certain words used by Mr. Balfour and assumed to be addressed to Mr. Gladstone. When Mr. Balfour, in a lull in the storm, managed to explain that the words objected to were meant, not for Mr. Gladstone, but for his esteemed lieutenant, all anger vanished, animosity was extinguished in a burst of hilarious cheering and uncontrollable laughter. The best of it was that no one more than Sir William Harcourt enjoyed the turn given to events.

13th Feb.
The Home
Rule Bill.
It was half-past three o'clock when Mr. Gladstone, making his way through the cheering multitude outside, entered the House of Commons. The Chamber with one or two notable exceptions was filled to its uttermost limits. As on the last occasion a Home Rule Bill was expounded, chairs were brought in and placed on the floor to accommodate a small portion of the overplus of members. But what were thirty-two chairs amid so many? Nevertheless, massed by the Bar they disproportionately added to the crowded appearance of the House. Both side galleries were full, members on the back benches standing up through the speech. The privileged strangers were early in their places. More unusual was the rush of the Peers, who, as soon as their gallery opened, filled every seat (save three) over the clock. Lord Rosebery and Lord Spencer had special places in the Diplomatic gallery, whence they regarded with complaisance the struggle of their peers to find accommodation in another quarter.

Mr. Chamberlain secured his corner seat, having for companions Sir Henry James and Mr. Courtney.

Mr. Jesse Collings, less fortunate, found a seat on one of the chairs. A group of members stood at the Bar; for them there were no seats in any part of the House. Another congregation of outcasts found standing room behind the Speaker's chair. More fortunate members perched on the steps of the Chair itself, whilst all the gangway steps were occupied. Lord Randolph Churchill, now a regular occupant of the Front Opposition bench, was seated side by side with his old companion, Sir John Gorst. Mr. Labouchere and Sir Charles Dilke had the good fortune to retain accustomed seats on the front bench below the gangway.

The Rush for Places. Long before noon, all the approaches to Palace Yard were blocked by a crowd anxious at least to see some of the people who would presently hear Mr. Gladstone expounding his Bill. They were not the rose, but they would live near it. The multitude were rewarded by the spectacle of over two hundred M.P.'s flocking down in cabs and hansoms. But for the wise provision of the Speaker, this rush would have taken place before daybreak. It was felt to be quite enough once in a Session to have members turning up in the House of Commons at five o'clock in the morning. Accordingly the Speaker issued a mandate forbidding the unlocking of the doors till noon. ·

When twelve o'clock began to chime from Big Ben the door was unbolted and the stream of members, young and old, waiting in the lobby, dashed inward like a cataract. In far-off days, before Lord Randolph Churchill began to grow bald and a statesman, he made a bet that between the first note of the chimes for midnight and the last stroke of twelve he, starting from the Surrey side, would run across Westminster Bridge, bringing up by the steps under the Clock Tower. A not less remarkable feat was performed when, in precisely that space of time, the

empty and astonished House of Commons was suddenly
filled. The proceedings partook rather of the character of a stampede than of the gathering of one of
the Chambers of the High Court of Parliament.

Among the personal encounters that took
place in various parts of the battle-field
the fight between Colonel Saunderson and
Mr. Wallace, member for Limehouse, attracted exceptional attention. The Colonel had, Mr.
Wallace said, dropped into his seat. Certainly he
had dropped on to his hat, which chanced to be
on the seat. Mr. Wallace, though representing a
London constituency, is, like the Colonel, an Ulster
man. When under provocative circumstances Ulster
meets Ulster there is naturally a fight, and this
incident supplied no exception to the rule. Mr.
Wallace tried to pull the Colonel out of the seat.
The Colonel stands six feet high, is all bone and
muscle, and was born fighting. He gently but firmly
laid Mr. Wallace on his back and resumed his seat.

There was talk of the incident coming before
the House, a consummation devoutly desired by
Colonel Saunderson, who would have liked nothing
better than to tell the tale of the fight to an appreciative audience. But Mr. Wallace was better advised,
and the Colonel promising him a new hat, the story
has been reserved for private circulation.

The first intimation of Mr. Gladstone's
approach was given by a cheer from
members near the door behind the
Speaker's chair. It was taken up all along the ranks
—save in respect of the two benches appropriated by
the Liberal Unionists—to the right of the Speaker,
taken up by the Irish members, who sat massed
below the gangway. As the cheers resounded
members rose to their feet, the Irish members waving
their hats as they shouted. Mr. Gladstone looked
better than ever, possibly the slight flush called to his

Colonel Saunderson Takes a Seat.

Mr. Gladstone.

cheek by this royal welcome having something to do with the effect. The applause continued for several moments, members still standing.

As the enthusiastic uproar subsided, the Prince of Wales, accompanied by the Duke of York, entered the Peers' Gallery. The Heir Apparent took his seat over the clock, the third to the left of the Duke of York being occupied by the Duke of Teck. At this moment there was only one vacant seat visible, and that was the prominent one pertaining to the leader of the Opposition. Mr. Balfour was able philosophically to subdue his curiosity till the very last moment, sauntering into the House just after Mr. Gladstone had risen.

It was understood that all the usual preliminary business would be passed over in order that the Premier might, at the earliest moment, deliver the message for which all the world waited. Some surprise was manifested when Mr. Milman opened the box on the table containing an appalling number of ballot papers, and the doomed system of publicly balloting interposed nearly a quarter of an hour between the impatient House and the waiting orator.

When the last immaterial number was reached, the Speaker called upon members desiring to take their seats to approach the table. This was easier said than done, the gangway being almost blocked by the chairs. A narrow lane was left through which the new members approached, with accidental but dramatic effect. They had to pass in single file. First Sir Arthur Hayter, who recaptured Walsall, and next Mr. Shaw, who retained Halifax, each accompanied by an escort of introducers. This procession of Liberal victors was greeted with prolonged cheering from the Ministerial benches.

It was a quarter to four when the Speaker called upon "The First Lord of the Treasury." A moment of curious embarrassment followed. Mr. Gladstone

either did not hear the signal or misunderstood it.
He did not rise till his attention was called to the
situation by Mr. Morley and Sir William Harcourt.
When he appeared at the table, ringing cheers once
more broke forth, the Ministerialists with one accord
leaping to their feet, the ranks below the gangway
obscuring the view of the double row of Liberal
Unionists, who stubbornly kept their seats.

The first sentences spoken by the Premier showed
he was in full possession of his splendid voice, and it
may be here mentioned that only twice in the duration of a speech that lasted two hours and a quarter
did he have recourse to the historical " pomatum
pot " with which he came prepared, and, as a preliminary to his speech, laid on the table by the side
of his notes. Recurring, at the outset, to the state
of the question as it had been approached in 1886,
he touched upon the various methods of dealing with
the Irish question, propounded, amongst others, "by
those politicians whom we term Dissentient Liberals."
These devices had all vanished, but the reality
remained. The only choice lay, he insisted, between
autonomy and coercion. Dropping easily into argumentative mood, he started with two contentions.
The first was that a permanent system of repressive
law inflicted upon a country from without, in
defiance of the views and the judgment of the vast
majority of the people, constitutes a state of things of
such a character that whilst it subsists you have not,
and cannot have, the first condition of harmony and
good government. A second contention was that
this system is a distinct and violent breach of the
promises upon the faith of which the Union was
obtained.

Incidentally he mentioned, among the broken
pledges of which Ireland complained, that while it
had been his honoured destiny to sit in Cabinet
Council with between sixty and seventy statesmen,

not one, with the exception of the Duke of Wellington, was an Irishman.

That Home Rule was demanded by the vast majority of the Irish people was shown by the present position of the representation. In 1832—"the first Parliament I sat in," added Mr. Gladstone, in one of those personal parentheses which illumined his speech, and drew forth sympathetic cheers—there existed the largest majority known in constitutional history. The party of Sir Robert Peel was supported by only 150 members. But the majority against him did not reach the proportions in which the Nationalist members for Ireland in the present Parliament overpowered those of their countrymen opposed to Home Rule. He admitted that the enemies of Home Rule were chiefly garrisoned in England. "But," he asked, "is the mind of England irrevocably fixed in the direction of refusing Home Rule to Ireland?" This he effectively answered by citation of two sets of figures. In 1886, of 465 English members of the House of Commons, only 127 were favourable to Home Rule, 338 being opposed to it. At the present time that minority of 127 had swollen to 197, whilst the majority of 338 had sunk to 268. A majority of 211 against Home Rule, which existed amongst English members in the House of Commons in 1886, has in the present year sunk to the more modest figure of seventy-one.

"I want to know," Mr. Gladstone asked, looking triumphantly round the House, "who will be the effective guarantor that this remainder will not also vanish?"

These introductory passages were listened to with frequent cheers from the Ministerial side, with respectful attention from the Conservatives. This last condition was varied only once by a little group of members behind the Front Opposition bench, who broke into a guffaw when the Premier alluded to "the protection of the secret vote" in Ireland, and

what it had wrought for the people. Mr. Gladstone
paused, and, looking across at his interrupters, asked
whether they approved the principle of secret voting.

" If not," he added with lowered voice but flashing
eyes, "I advise them to go to their constituents and
make their opinion known."

This was the only interruption of a kind, once
painfully familiar, that varied the triumphant flow
of the speech.

His undertaking, delivered at the end of
What the Bill Proposes. the first half-hour, to "endeavour to give
some intelligible account of the Bill,"
quickened the already absorbing interest. In 1886,
he said, there were five principles laid down as underlying the measure then introduced. To those principles
the new Bill would be found closely to adhere, though
there were certain important changes in details. The
first principle was the establishment of a legislative
body sitting in Dublin, charged both with legislation
and with the administration of Irish affairs, as distinct
from Imperial affairs. Perfect equality between the
kingdoms was to be established. There was to be equitable distribution of Imperial charges. Precautions were
taken for the protection of minorities; and, lastly, the
plan of Home Rule ought to be of such a character
as to bring about a real and continuous settlement of
the Irish Question. In the preamble of the Bill
would be found a phrase which established the
supremacy of the Imperial Parliament, running to
the effect that: "Whereas it is expedient, without
impairing or restricting the supreme authority of
Parliament," etc.

Amid breathless attention Mr. Gladstone went on
to explain that the Bill constitutes an Irish Legislature authorised to make laws for Ireland in matters
exclusively relating to Ireland. This was subject to
the reservation of certain matters for the consideration
of the Imperial Parliament. The heads reserved

related to the Crown, the Viceroyalty, peace and war, defence, foreign treaties, dignities and titles, coinage, and everything which belongs to external trade. In order to divest the Viceroyalty of party character, the Bill provides that the office of Viceroy shall run for six years, independent of the coming and going of Ministries. The Viceroy would be assisted by the appointment of an Executive Committee of the Privy Council in Ireland, which would serve him in the capacity of a Cabinet. This Executive Committee would advise the Viceroy as to whether he should give or withhold his assent to Bills passed by the Irish Parliament, subject, of course, to the control of the Sovereign.

There would also be a Legislative Council, to be elected by a new constituency composed of persons of £20 rating, whether as owner or occupier. Mr. Gladstone added that a clause appeared in the Bill which would enable these electors to vote only in one constituency—an adoption of the principle of one man one vote much cheered below the gangway.

This Legislative Council would consist of forty-eight members, who would sit for eight years. The Legislative Body would consist of 103 members, elected for five years. In order to provide against deadlocks, the Bill proposed that in cases where any measure had passed the Legislative Assembly more than once at intervals of two years, or after a dissolution, the two assemblies should meet and settle the matter. The prospect here conjured up of possible contingencies among combative legislators led to some laughter below the gangway.

The judges would be irremovable by the new Legislature, and for six years would continue to be appointed as they now are. The meeting of the new Parliament the Bill provides shall take place on the first Tuesday of September. The quiet matter-of-course manner in which Mr. Gladstone announced this

practical conclusion of promised legislation was recognised with cheers and laughter. The constabulary, as
it at present exists, would be gradually replaced by a
body appointed under the direction of the new Legislature. During the time of the transition the force
would remain under the direction of the Viceroy.

Mr. Gladstone next touched upon the question of
the retention of Irish members at Westminster, at
mention of which there was a rustling sound of
quickened attention. He slowly elaborated a scheme
whereby Irish members are to be retained at Westminster, but only to the number of eighty, that being
their fair representation according to numbers. " Are
the Irish to vote eighty strong in matters purely
British ? " Mr. Gladstone asked, with eloquent dubiety.
That was a question, he said, which would require
the exercise of all the reflective and reasoning powers
of the House. There were strong reasons on both
sides, and he was not able to forecast on which the
House would decide.

There was, however, no difficulty in classifying
topics coming before Parliament, whether as Irish or
Imperial. Certain provisions for the limitation of the
voting power of the Irish members would be found
inserted in the Bill. The Irish members are not to
vote on any Bill expressly stated to be confined to the
interests of Great Britain. They are not to vote any
money otherwise than for Imperial purposes. Nor
are they to vote upon any motion or resolution "exclusively affecting Great Britain or things or persons
therein." They are not to vote on any motion or
resolution incidental to the foregoing except to the
first—Mr. Gladstone explaining, in response to gestures
of inquiry, that the Irish members are not to vote on
such a Bill, but may take part in a division upon a
motion incidental to it.

As to finance, the Customs duties are to be appropriated as Ireland's contribution to Imperial finance,

leaving the new Legislature the excise, local taxes,
Post Office, and Crown lands. Ireland will have to
meet the whole of the Government charges, except
that of the constabulary, of which Great Britain will
bear one-third. There are also the charges for collection of Inland Revenue and Postal Services. From
these sources of revenue Ireland would receive
£5,660,000, whilst it would expend £5,160,000, leaving a clear surplus of half-a-million " to start on
her own account."

A Last Appeal. Folding up and laying aside the notes on
which his explanation of the details of the
Bill were based, Mr. Gladstone in a noble
peroration, the music of which was long sustained,
pointed to the future. If this controversy was to end
the sooner they stamped and sealed the deed that
was to efface all former animosities the better. For
his part, he never would, and never could, be a party
to bequeathing to his country a continuance of the
heritage of discord handed down through seven centuries, from generation to generation, with hardly a
momentary interruption.

"Sir," he continued, in a voice struggling with
emotion, " it would be a misery to me if I had omitted
in these closing years any measures possible for me to
make towards upholding and promoting the cause I
believe to be the cause, not of one party nor of another,
not of one nation or another, but of all parties and all
nations inhabiting these islands." " Let me entreat
you," he added, in last words spoken in clear though
low voice—" if it were with my latest breath I would
entreat you—to let the dead bury its dead. Cast behind you every recollection of bygone evils, and
cherish, love, sustain one another through all the
vicissitudes of human affairs in the times that are
to come."

It was just six o'clock when the Premier resumed
his seat, members behind him and the Irish members

on the benches below the gangway opposite once more
rising and enthusiastically cheering.

One accustomed to see Mr. Gladstone day
The Orator. by day through successive years is least
able to appreciate change in him. A
gentleman who sat next to me whilst the speech was
in progress, who had heard the earlier one on the same
subject, and who had not chanced to see the Premier
for fully two years, was much struck with his altered
appearance, finding him sadly aged. Save for the
failing voice, which grew hoarse and, in distant
galleries, inaudible at the end of the speech, there
was no outward and visible sign of the inevitable
change. Certainly there was no falling away in
mental power or in oratorical effect. The explanation
of the intricate measure was a model of lucidity;
the opening passages of the speech soared on lofty
heights of eloquence; the stately peroration that
closed it will take rank with its most famous
predecessors.

The House of Commons has to-day re-
14th Feb. sumed in various directions its normal
Mr. Balfour
on the Bill. appearance. The chairs which yesterday
blocked the passage across the floor are
removed, the ordinary seating accommodation being
more than equal to the calls upon it. The Strangers'
Galleries are filled to the utmost capacity, and there
is an unusual gathering of peers, with the Duke of
Teck over the clock, in the place yesterday occupied
by the Prince of Wales.

It was ten minutes past five when Mr. Balfour
rose, the House at the time being full, though falling
far short of the crowded and animated appearance presented when yesterday the Premier opened the debate.
The interposition of the Leader of the Opposition was
hailed by a loud cheer from his supporters. He
opened his criticism of the measure by asking whether
any Bill was required, and reached the conclusion

that no adequate reason for the present one was to be
found.   Since, however, it had been introduced, Mr.
Balfour felt bound to look thoroughly into it, and,
behold ! it was very bad.   It inflicted gross injustice
on the constabulary.   It placed the judges in an
intolerable position.   Every time one went in opposition to the popular will a vote to reduce his salary
would be brought forward in the new Irish Parliament—a Parliament elected upon an extraordinary
and complicated system of constituencies.   The
Imperial supremacy provided for in the preamble
of the Bill was a mere sham.   The Irish did not
object to its being mentioned there if it would never
be exercised.   Mr. Balfour announced, amid cheers,
that he and his friends were determined there should
at least be variations in the process.   What would
follow would be a spasmodic interference with the
affairs of Ireland, according to the balance of parties
in the Imperial Parliament.   The Irish members,
under the provisions of the Bill, might turn out a
Ministry, but might not vote on a road Bill.   The
consequence would be that whilst now three-quarters
of the time of the Imperial Parliament was taken
up with Irish affairs, in the new order of things its
whole time would be so appropriated.   As for the
landlords, they saw nothing before them but the
prospect of illimitable plunder—a remark the dubiety
of which escaped the attention of the Conservatives
who loudly cheered it.   In brief, "the Irish having
been engaged in a lawless contest, we (the Conservatives) have been beaten, and the war indemnity is now
demanded."

    This gloomy picture had its natural effect upon the
audience, gradually thinning it out.   Having finished
the dolorous sketch, Mr. Balfour plucked up heart and
raised the spirits of his friends by declaring that all
was not yet lost.   The party of Law and Order were
not beaten, and the Irish Nationalists would find that

the resources of civilisation were not yet exhausted.
Finally, he asked himself and the House how it came
about that after seven years' meditation and opportunity of g   information, a Ministry not without
talent had brought forth this strange abortion of a
measure, this belated combination of Federal and
Colonial Government and the British Constitution.
It was, he answered, because they had attempted an
impossible task.

Mr. Chamberlain found opportunity for
resuming the debate on the Home Rule
Bill as early as a quarter-past four.

15th Feb.
Mr. Chamber-
lain.

Possibly this was unexpected. Certainly
when the right hon. gentleman rose, with a starlike
orchid flaming from his buttonhole, the attendance
was unusually small. As he proceeded through a
speech that will rank high in his Parliamentary efforts,
the benches filled up and the interest deepened. His
interposition in debate was welcomed by a loud cheer
from the Tories, and it was from that side of the
House the applause which frequently punctuated his
speech came.

At the outset Mr. Chamberlain announced that he
had resolved to let Posterity judge between himself,
his friends, and what he called "the large majority of
the Liberal Party" now committed to the advocacy of
Home Rule. He would not consider the motives
that may have actuated them in taking that course,
but would proceed forthwith to consider the Bill.
Amid some laughter from the Ministerialists, he
explained that in voting against the measure he and
his friends would not be making a declaration hostile
to Home Rule, but against a Bill which did not fulfil
their just expectation.

The unusual moderation of tone imposed upon
himself by Mr. Chamberlain added something to the
interest and much to the power of his speech. For a
moment he was incited to personal conflict with a

person ordinarily so unobtrusive as is Mr. Bryce. But the temptation to wrangle was yielded to only for a moment, and he resumed the judicial air and attitude assumed at the outset. Remembering, and he had been abundantly reminded, of some things said by him in 1885, his position was one of great delicacy and peculiar difficulty. That only enhanced the admiration with which the House watched him gliding, sometimes over dangerously thin ice, always with graceful movement and irresistible force. Whilst the matter of the speech was consummately contrived and skilfully marshalled, the delivery was simply perfect. Some who have heard most of Mr. Chamberlain's speeches since he entered the House are agreed in regarding this as excelling all.

18th Feb. An Excited House. When on the stroke of one o'clock this morning Mr. Gladstone walked up the floor of the House with a piece of paper in his hand purporting to contain the text of the Home Rule Bill, the Ministerialists leaped to their feet and wildly waved their welcome. This sudden uprising with uproarious cheer is so effective a demonstration that it is a pity to have it made too cheap, a tendency prominent in the week now closing. It was well enough on Monday, when Mr. Gladstone entered a Chamber crowded in anticipation of his speech. It was his great opportunity, reached after arduous struggle, and none would grudge him the personal triumph. But when, an hour or two later, on the conclusion of his speech, enthusiastic members were discovered again on their legs, shouting and waving hats as before, it was felt that there might be too much of a good thing. A lower depth was reached last night, when, at the conclusion of Mr. Blake's harangue—a compendious effort with something subtly colonial in its character—half a dozen excited Irishmen went through the too familiar process.

The House was curiously empty, considering
that a milestone in the course of the Bill's
journey had been reached. Mr. Balfour
has always been a master of the effective
art of absenting himself. In the early days of his
leadership he had a provoking way of showing what
he thought of the aggregate value of questions on
the paper by staying away till more than half had
been put and answered. Since he is Leader of the
Opposition he must needs be in his place when the
Premier expounded the principal measure of the
Session. But, as recorded, he did not arrive to take
it till the last moment.

Last night, also, yielding to the imperative necessity of the situation, he remained in his place whilst
his colleague, Mr. Goschen, with unwonted fervour,
declaimed against the Home Rule Bill. But he was
not absolutely bound to sit out Mr. Morley's speech,
with its inevitable conclusion of the bringing in of the
Bill. So he went off, an example loyally followed by
his friends. The Home Rule Bill must needs be
brought in, but they need not be in their places to
witness the exultation of the enemy.

Mr. Gladstone was in a position of equal personal
freedom. At the commencement of the Session he
fell into the habit of being in his place up to eight
o'clock, not returning after the dinner hour. This
week he has departed from that custom, and on more
than one occasion has been in his place till the Speaker
left the chair. Any one of his colleagues whose names
were on the back of the Bill might have acted as his
substitute and gone through the ceremony of bringing
it in, whilst he rested after the labours of the week.
But Mr. Gladstone is apparently not tired yet. With
a brief absence for dinner he sat through the more
than eight hours' talk of the night, and though he did
not make ordered speech, he contributed a constant
series of conversational remarks. Whilst Mr. Goschen

was speaking, the Premier was filling up a spare moment by writing a letter, with blotting pad on his knee. That task engrossed only one ear and one eye. The others were sharply opened to what Mr. Goschen said, and to what was going on in the House.

"What do you say, for instance," asked Mr. Goschen, turning triumphantly to the Radicals below the gangway—"what do you say to the payment of a war indemnity of seventeen millions?"

"Seventeen millions!" echoed Mr. Gladstone, in a tone of dramatic contempt that greatly amused the House.

"Yes, seventeen millions!" Mr. Goschen reiterated.

"It is ridiculous," said Mr. Gladstone, in his deep chest notes, and went on writing his letter.

When the debate was over and the first reading of the Home Rule Bill had been agreed to, without spoken dissent from the half-empty Opposition benches, the Premier jumped up. With head erect and swift, springy step, he walked down to the Bar, wheeled sharply round, and brought in his new Home Rule Bill, with no visible diminution of vigour as compared with his appearance when seven years ago he made the same pilgrimage on an identical errand.

20th Feb.
Return of the
Prodigal.

Lord Randolph Churchill's return to the Parliamentary scene has been second in interest only to Mr. Gladstone's appearance at the table to explain his Home Rule Bill. The crowd gathered to hear his speech on Thursday was less only by a score or so than that which tumultuously gathered to hear the Premier. Lord Randolph grievously suffered from the preliminary scene of excitement sprung upon the House in the matter of a charge of breach of privilege. Such an accident is fatal to the full success of any endeavour. It was peculiarly trying to Lord Randolph, who, unsuspected as the fact may be, never, even in his most audacious days, got over that feeling of House of Commons fright which to the last possessed Mr. Bright. A scene like that of Thursday acts and reacts upon the intending orator and the waiting House. The latter, having come prepared for an ordered feast, is surfeited in advance. To the intellectual palate the boisterous scene of Thursday night acted much as the preliminary pudding administered before meat operates in the economy of some school dinners. As for the hapless orator sitting fuming on the bench for an hour and a half, not daring to leave the House lest he lose his opportunity, the experience is cruelly wearisome.

That Lord Randolph felt it was shown in the opening sentences of his speech, which were delivered in so low a tone, with such faltering accent, that they barely travelled across the House. Remembering his old aggressive style, his perfect command over himself, and his consequent control over the House, there was something sad in the spectacle of the former Parliamentary *sapeur* thus blenching on the threshold of the fight. But the influence was only temporary, and when Lord Randolph warmed to his work there flashed forth the keen fire of former days, and the House felt that the still young statesman whom it affectionately calls "Randolph" may, if he please, come back and resume his commanding position, whether above or below the gangway.

CHAPTER V.

THE POSITION OF PARTIES.

THE House of Commons is, even in dull times, the focus of London life. Just now it is, in fashionable parlance, " the thing," and the competition for the few private rooms available, or for seats in the room where strangers, including ladies, are permitted to dine, is severe. Tea on the terrace has, of course, not yet commenced, but there are signs abroad that when opportunity offers it will be even a more popular function than it has been during previous Sessions, when Sir Richard Temple and other *preux chevaliers* were nearly worked off their feet in discharge of the pleasing duty of escorting ladies over the place.

21st Feb. Tea on the Terrace.

The rush between five and seven o'clock grew, in the summer months of last year, to proportions seriously embarrassing. The terrace, corridor, and lobbies were as full of fashionably dressed ladies as is the Park at church parade on fine Sundays. After being everywhere else, the ladies generally finished up by peeping at the House through a glass window within the main entrance. The regulation hitherto has been that a member may conduct two ladies at a time to this coign of vantage. The consequence was that there was a shifting crowd of ladies blocking up the lobby, waiting their turn. The Speaker has stopped that by ordering that no ladies shall be so privileged before seven o'clock in the evening. As by seven o'clock it is time to go off to dress for dinner, this will prove practically prohibitive.

That listeners.hear no good of themsélves
is an ancient axiom, to the truth of
which the Bishop of St. Asaph is able to
testify. To-night being fixed for the discussion of the Welsh Church Suspensory Bill, his
lordship arranged his engagements so as to leave
him free to spend the night in the House of Commons.
For greater fulness of the anticipated enjoyment he
made tryst with his old co-worker and colleague, now
Principal of Lampeter College, better known in the
Principality as " the fighting Dean of St. Asaph." It
was necessary, or at least desirable, that captain and
lieutenant should sit together, so that, as the fight
below proceeded, they might exchange confidences.
The arbitrary scheme for the seating of strangers in the
House of Commons does not easily lend itself to such
an arrangement. The Dean might not sit in the Peers'
Gallery with the Bishop, and though, as Lord Spencer
and Lord Rosebery showed on the night when the Home
Rule Bill was introduced, Peers may sit in the front row
of the Gallery to the right of the clock where the
Dean was placed, the position had less exclusive
privilege in the matter of free movement.

A happy thought occurred to the Lord Bishop.
If he sat at the extreme end of the Peers' Gallery
and the Dean secured the place at the extreme end
of the Diplomatic Gallery, they might sit shoulder
to shoulder, with only the division of the Benches
(very properly) marking their several positions in
Church and State. Thus it came about with fortunate results, including the marked prominence of
the two representatives of a militant Church in an
assembly that presumed to discuss its existence as if it
were a School Board or a parish vestry. The Bishop
with his sheaf of sermon paper, on which he diligently
made notes, his reverend henchman on the right
in animated conversation, acted upon the placid
Welshmen massed beneath the part the intrinsically

(marginal note:) 23rd Feb. Bishop and Dean.

inoffensive red rag plays with the super-sensitive
bull.

Fortunately for the peace of the House, the
Welsh members were depressed by the consciousness
of a self-denying ordinance upon which they had
entered, all unknowing of this pending presence in
the Peers' Gallery. What they chiefly desired was
to get the Suspensory Bill read a first time. To that
end it was consonant with ordinary practice that they
should contribute argument. They shrewdly concluded that it would be more effective to contribute
silence. Accordingly they arranged that Mr. Stuart
Rendel should voice their concentrated eloquence,
they sitting dumbly by.

In ordinary circumstances this would have been
well enough. But, given the Bishop of St. Asaph
seated up aloft jubilantly whispering to the Dean,
Mr. Stuart Rendel was a little mild-mannered.
Goaded by the spectacle of the inarticulate anguish
that surrounded him in the person of his compatriots, Mr. Rendel did his best, and made some
personal references to the Bishop and his work in
Wales that provided opportunity to Welsh members
of utterance for their overcharged feelings.

Sir John
Gorst.
Up to this epoch the Bishop had an
almost uninterrupted bad time. Mr.
Asquith prefaced a vigorous uncompromising speech by the blunt declaration that the
Bill was the first step towards the disestablishment
of the Church of Wales. Sir John Gorst, coming
forward in his new character as a University member,
had undertaken the defence of the Church, and
when in succession to the Home Secretary he appeared at the table, Bishop and Dean exchanged a
congratulatory look across the wooden fence. But
Sir John was decidedly, even dangerously, disappointing. At the outset his manner, artistically
subdued to his new association, was depressing His

hands moved uneasily about as if feeling for the
surplice that would have formed an appropriate
sartorial adjunct to his address. When, as he proceeded, and, incited by cheers and counter-cheers,
lapsed into his older self, matters grew even worse.
It seemed at one time as if, feeling the necessity in the
circumstances of assuming a Biblical character, he was
about to adopt that of Balaam. Mr. Goschen, sitting
near him on the Front Opposition Bench, visibly shrank
with apprehension. What if Sir John were about
to revive memories of his famous Manipur speech,
and, rising with avowed purpose of defending the
Church in Wales, were to treat the institution as
he had dealt with the Government of India, poking
fun at the Bishop of St. Asaph, as he had then
scoffed at the equally revered figure of his esteemed
chief, the Viscount Cross ?

Through a painful succession of sentences, it
seemed as if the temptation would prove irresistible
to the member for Cambridge University. Perhaps
if the manner of the Ministerialists had been less
restrained their triumph would have been greater.
Sir John's position at the table prevented him from
observing the anxious looks of his colleagues on the
Front Bench, or the perturbed countenances of supporters of Church and State on the back benches
above the gangway. But he could not fail to note
the smiling faces of the expectant throng on the
Ministerial benches, and pulled up just in time.

At best it was a chilling effort, suggestive, as
the Premier's hilarious fancy pictured, of having
been composed in the refrigerating chamber of an
Atlantic steamer. It was fortunate that Mr. Vicary
Gibbs was in the House, and, later, caught the
Speaker's eye. Young Vicary (Antony Gibbs and
Son, 15, Bishopsgate Street Within, E.C.), rushing
in where Sir John Gorst had so gingerly trod,
under-wrote, as it were, the Welsh Church, a proof

D

of confidence in the institution that greatly cheered the Bishop of St. Asaph, of whom the hon. member spoke with almost paternal commendation.

Lord Randolph Himself again. This did something to raise the drooping spirits in the gallery over the clock. But a greater champion of the Church than Mr. Vicary Gibbs was at hand. A more dutiful son than Sir John Gorst put lance in rest. It was past ten o'clock when Lord Randolph Churchill interposed, the House at the moment not having recovered from the desertion through the dinner hour. It had been rumoured through the evening that he was to speak about ten o'clock, and for the pleasure of hearing him men would even dare to cut the dinner hour short. As he proceeded members trooped in, and before he was half-way through the House was crowded in every part, buzzing with that intense emotion which only three, or at most four, members can at will command.

It was Lord Randolph's second appearance since his return to Parliamentary life. The first had piqued the abiding interest in his fascinating personality. Would he be better or worse than he had been adjudged in his speech last week on the Home Rule Bill? The thronged audience were not long left in doubt. Lord Randolph had evidently got over the fright that on his earliest reappearance on the familiar stage clogged his tongue and hampered his movements. Possibly he was, all unconsciously, happier in the circumstances of the hour. Mr. Balfour's regrettable illness still kept him from the House. Lord Randolph had the Front Opposition Bench all to himself, with no beginning of the making of a rival in right hon. gentlemen who at the moment sat on it. He was not now, as happened on Thursday, worn out with waiting for opportunity whilst purists of Parliamentary order seated below the gangway clamoured for the vindication of the privileges of the House. His

withers were unwrung, and the audience were freshly
gathered in anticipation of his speech. Nor were
they disappointed. Lord Randolph was himself
again, and new members, to whom his earlier fame
is a tradition, learned with delight upon what substantial basis it rests.

Draws Mr.
Gladstone. There was one member on the benches
opposite who watched with entranced
attention the vigorous onslaught. Lord
Randolph Churchill has ever had a strong attraction
for Mr. Gladstone—an influence mutually felt with
at least equal force. The Premier, contrary to
his wholesome custom, had returned after dinner,
and sat through the speech with hand to ear and
flaming eyes fixed on the successor of Henry the
Eighth as Defender of the Faith. He did not
indicate by note-taking intention of following in
debate. But when Lord Randolph resumed his seat
he sprang to his feet with alacrity that mocked the
burden of his more than fourscore years. He was
evidently burning to fly at Lord Randolph, but before
commencing the onslaught he paused to notice in due
place the earlier speech of Sir John Gorst. These few
sentences he spoke in the slow, deliberate tones, with
the infectious smile and dramatic gestures, that mark
his lighter moods. Then he flung himself upon Lord
Randolph with an impetuosity and vigour that delighted and astonished the House, fresh though it was
from witness of his effort on introducing the Home
Rule Bill.

There was something almost pathetic in his
seething anger at the restriction of time laid upon
him. It was half-past eleven when he rose, and
within half an hour he must needs conclude or
defeat his cherished object of seeing the Bill
brought in at that sitting. So towering was his
rage that he magnified the enormity of Lord
Randolph's iniquity, declaring that he had been

speaking for two hours, whereas he had actually occupied little over an hour for his speech. As has happened before, this limitation of time proved of substantial service. The passage being narrow, its boundaries unalterable, Mr. Gladstone must perforce adapt himself to them. So it came to pass that his stormy eloquence rushed like a torrent through the narrow gulf where, in other circumstances, it might have spread to the dimensions of a stream, wider but less picturesque and effective.

28th Feb.
Position of
Parties.

Without going the length of insisting upon adversity lurking behind these bright days, it is quite true that the Government are just now in the hey-day of prosperity. By-and-by, when Bills get into Committee, difficulties on minor points will arise, not threatening the existence of the Government, but leading to worry and resentment. In the meanwhile, it is a great thing to have made a good start. The ball has been set rolling with remarkable impetus, and, considering the Session is only four weeks old, it has travelled far.

The exultation on the Liberal benches is accompanied by a corresponding fit of depression in Opposition circles. As usually happens when things are wrong, the Tories turn and display a disposition to rend their idol, Mr. Balfour. He has just come back to his post after a bout of illness, and shows evident signs of the lassitude of mind and body that follows on influenza. He arrived in time to share the fresh damage to the Opposition cause, arising out of the attitude towards bimetallism, into which it was forced by its leaders. As the division list showed, the Conservatives are not at one in belief in bimetallism, whilst the Liberal Unionists are pretty evenly divided, with Mr. Joseph Chamberlain and Sir John Lubbock on one side, Sir Henry James and Mr. Courtney on the other. The consequence was that Mr. Goschen, in supporting Sir H. Meysey-Thompson's motion, was obliged to wobble, protesting that he was not supposed to be declaring in favour of bimetallism, only feebly and vaguely demanding an inquiry.

A Transformation Scene. The most prejudiced Tory could not fail to contrast with this attitude the appearance at the table of Mr. Gladstone, who at least knew whither he was going, or, rather, whither he would not be led. Almost casually interposing in the debate, evidently having made no deliberate preparation beforehand, he talked for an hour, literally fascinating a House full to the doors. Rarely in a long career has his personal supremacy been vindicated in the triumphant fashion displayed to-night. The subject was one it seemed impossible for anyone, though he spoke with the tongue of men and angels, to make attractive, even bearable, to the House of Commons. Sir Henry Meysey-Thompson had tried it for a full hour, bringing the House down to the penultimate stage of depression. The final limit was reached when Mr. Montagu followed, seconding the motion. By this time Mr. Gladstone seemed to be almost the last man left in the audience. Even Mr. Goschen had succumbed, temporarily withdrawing from the post of observation.

When word went round "Gladstone is up," the House began to fill, as twice a day the Severn fills when the tide rushes in. Before he had been five minutes on his legs the aspect of affairs changed as if by magic. When he sat down, amid prolonged cheers, the scene resembled that witnessed in the same place on the eve of a political crisis.

This is the third great speech he has made since the Session opened, and it would seem that the nearer ninety he grows in point of years the more marvellous are his intellectual powers. The speech on introducing the Home Rule Bill was evidently the result of long preparation. His vigorous harangue on the

Welsh Church Suspensory Bill sprang out of a condition of political heat that naturally created fire and
flame in this sensitive organisation.   But here was an
empty House, perhaps the dreariest of all topics, and
an impromptu speech which infused life into the dry
bones and made the bleak wilderness blossom like a
rose garden.

CHAPTER VI.

THE NEW CHAIRMAN OF COMMITTEES.

THE most remarkable and significant Parliamentary portent of the week has been the recrudescence of Mr. James Lowther. For many years this eminent statesman, once a prominent figure in the House of Commons, has been in the background. Eskdale rejecting him just at the time when his party were emerging from the wilderness of Opposition, he missed a great opportunity. Except inasmuch as he has in his time figured as a Law-giver, Mr. Lowther does not recall the personality of Moses. But having loyally assisted in leading the Opposition in days of depression, it was a cruel fate that deprived him of a small holding or allotment when they crossed the borders of the Promised Land. It was during his enforced retirement that he found himself on the judicial bench, conducting the case submitted to him by the Jockey Club with a dignity, impartiality, and judiciousness that extorted encomiums from the envious Bar. The Louth division of Cumberland would not have him, nor Eskdale either, it being reserved for the Isle of Thanet to find for him sanctuary.

Returned to the House again in the last Parliament, he found a seat below the gangway, regarding without mean envy dignities to which other and lesser men had, by reason of his enforced absence, attained on the Treasury Bench. Whilst his political friends were yet in office Mr. Lowther was content to fill the place of a Parliamentary *amicus curiae*. He shrank from taking prominent position in party controversy. But

*3rd March.
An Old War-
Horse.*

upon occasion he would interpose, and, in style and
manner possessing an ancient flavour unfamiliar to
new members, gently distil counsel.   He seemed
to be evermore drifting nearer and nearer to the
Scaean Gate, to join the reverend throng who

> Lean'd on the walls and basked before the sun ;
> Chiefs who no more in bloody fights engage,
> But wise thro' time and narrative with age,
> In summer days like grasshoppers rejoice.

This week, with difficulties gathering in the neighbourhood of the Chair, he has blossomed into fuller
vigour.   It is curious to see how insensibly he has
gravitated towards the seat of the Leader of the
Opposition.   When, driven from his corner seat below
the gangway by an incursion of Picts and Scots, he
crossed the gangway and quartered himself on a bench
to which his rank as Privy Councillor gives him access
he modestly appropriated a seat at the uttermost end
of the bench.   Gradually, as the conflict heated, he
worked his way along the bench, and it was from Mr.
Balfour's temporarily unoccupied seat that he addressed the House on those "great many times this
afternoon" to which Sir William Harcourt to-night
alluded.

It has seemed through these years past that Mr
Lowther's pulse no longer beats responsive to the
battle cry.   Till this week he has never, since he represented the Isle of Thanet, approached his old manner
familiar when in years gone by he consorted with Mr
Cavendish Bentinck, hearing the chimes at midnight
and as long after as was necessary to thwart the
designs of a Minister returned to power with mission
to disestablish the Irish Church and harry the Irish
landlords.   This week, more particularly to-night, the
old war-horse, scenting the battle from afar, has
rushed in and capered round with even disconcert-
ing activity.

Occasion presented itself in Committee under the direction of a new Chairman.

Mr. Courtney has retired into private life, and Mr. Mellor rules (or rather sits in the Chair) in his stead. Mr. Gladstone has already had opportunity of pondering over the advantages secured by abstaining from re-electing the old Chairman of Committees. It is said the Premier was disposed to take the more generous course, but that his hand was forced by representations made to him on the part of supporters sitting below the gangway. If that be true, it will presently appear that a tremendous price has been paid for the unnatural privilege of the tail wagging the dog. Regarded purely as a matter of expediency, the Premier would have done well, if the boon were not obtainable on other terms, to go down on his knees and beseech Mr. Courtney to retain the Chair, at least till the Home Rule Bill was through Committee.

The supervision of a Committee to which such a Bill is referred is sufficient to tax the energy and probe the knowledge of the most experienced Chairman. There are special reasons, obvious to a most careless glance, why Mr. Courtney would have been invaluable to the Government in his position as Chairman of a Committee through which the Home Rule Bill passed. Whilst the most virulent and prejudiced Liberal (if such there be) would shrink from whispering a word in challenge of Mr. Courtney's impartiality in the Chair, Unionists would feel that in his hands they would obtain justice. With a consciousness of his own political tendencies, an honourable man like Mr. Courtney would be prone to tinge his decisions rather in favour of the Bill than against it. Thus the advantage in the case of Mr. Courtney would have been distinctly in favour of the Government, and would have been immeasurably added to by the disinclination of the Opposition to embarrass a personal and political friend in the Chair.

D *

These are considerations apart from the important one of the desirability or otherwise of placing in the Chair a new and inexperienced man at a time when the Committee is about to undertake the moulding of an intricate and important measure, round which party passion boils like geyser pools. It will probably turn out that the change of Chairmanship will prove a more active agency in defeating, or at least in postponing the passage of, the Home Rule Bill than all the speeches now in preparation, or all the amendments that will in due course crowd the paper. Mr. Gladstone might have done otherwise, and he has done this.

7th March. Lord Randolph and the Conservative Party. The remarkable reception given to Lord Randolph Churchill by the Conservative party meeting at the Carlton Club yesterday is much talked of in the lobby of the House of Commons. It exceeded in warmth that tendered either to Lord Salisbury or Mr. Balfour. It is regarded as an incident not calculated to strengthen the hands of the present conjoint leadership of the Opposition in the House of Commons. Lord Randolph Churchill had attended the meeting without intention of taking part in the proceedings, and yielded only to the persistent call with which he was greeted.

8th March. At the Top of the Tree. A good story is told about Colonel Saunderson. Discussing with him the Home Rule Bill, with special reference to the opening afforded by it to Irishmen to come to the front in national affairs, a friend said few would have a better chance than the popular colonel.

" You are sure to come to the top of the tree."

" Yes," said the colonel; " hauled up by a rope round my neck."

9th March. A Diner-Out. The Premier, like a wise man, absented himself from the House during the earlier part of the week, profiting by the sunlight and sea air of Brighton. He is back in his place to-night, looking as brisk and buoyant as if his holiday had extended over three months instead of being limited to three days. It might be thought that his official work, followed by his labours attendant on his commanding position in the House of Commons, would prove sufficient for the strength of a man half his age. When Mr. Gladstone leaves the House of Commons it is only to enter upon a fresh phase of active life. He dines out nearly every night, varying the course by giving an occasional dinner at his own house.

These last are probably designed as a species of resting time. When he is the guest of the evening it is usual to invite to meet him the most brilliant available talent of various developments. With these as his audience, the Premier naturally and quite easily strains to the full his conversational power. When he himself entertains he goes to the other extreme, his guests for the most part being amiable, good men, of steady Liberal principles, but not provocative of fatigue to the brain of the host by their intellectual activity.

10th March.
Manœuvring.

A great many things have been talked of in the course of the week, but all action has been undertaken with eye steadfastly fixed on a particular goal. No one speaks, at least not in Parliament, of the Home Rule Bill. Nevertheless, that is the sole object of consideration and meditation on both sides. Mr. Gladstone put down the second reading for Monday next. The Opposition at the time scoffed at the idea of the decks by that time being so completely cleared that action might commence. The way to realise their aspirations and intentions was plain enough. Certain votes in Committee of Supply must needs be agreed to before legislative business can be taken in hand. If only they discussed these votes at sufficient lengt h to spread the time out over Monday, the Home Rule Bill must be delayed, and its chances of passing the second reading before Easter diminished accordingly.

Organised Attacks on the Chairman of Ways and Means.

That is the key to the Parliamentary situation. It explains everything, including the attacks on the Chairman of Committees and the insistence on taking two nights for discussion of the first Navy vote, a thing which, as Sir William Harcourt pointed out, has happened only once in thirteen years. The exception, by a singular coincidence, is found in the year 1886, when Mr. Gladstone brought in his first Home Rule Bill.

The attack on the Chairman, successful as it seemed at the time in upsetting the equanimity of the new comer and weakening his authority, turned out to be one of the best things that could have befallen Mr. Mellor. It was proved upon inquiry that he was absolutely right in the ruling which Mr. Balfour described as introducing "an entirely novel principle," and which Mr. Chamberlain, from the other side of the House, sharply denounced as an unwarranted limitation of the privileges of debate.

The House, always generously inclined, conscious that it had been momentarily drawn into harsh and unjust treatment of the new Chairman, has since been eager to make amends. Thus encouraged, Mr. Mellor is coming to be firmly seated in the saddle, out of which when he first mounted it seemed he would be promptly thrown.

It was observed at the time that Lord Randolph Churchill studiously withdrew from even the appearance of participation in the baiting of the Chairman of Committees. He does not disguise his opinion that, however such proceedings may commend themselves as part of the more desperate tactics of Opposition, they should not be participated in from the Front Bench. One of the prime duties of the Front Opposition Bench, in his opinion not less imperative upon it than with the Treasury Bench, is to support the authority of the Chair.

11th March. A Saturday Sitting. To old members there is something uncanny in the spectacle presented at Westminster this afternoon. It is Saturday. Outside, a bright spring day, with the Parks in sunlight, the trees budding, the crocuses starring the lawns; beyond, the broader belt of country, sea and land, inviting the tired legislator to make holiday. Within the House there is the ordinary appearance of a Wednesday sitting; the Speaker in the Chair, the Mace on the table, the Sergeant-at-Arms alert in his chair by the Bar. A score or so of members are scattered over the benches, whilst one descants at length. Where the marvel comes in, the shivering apprehension of something out of tune, is on discovery that the Irish benches are empty. It is eminently respectable people, like Mr. James Lowther and Mr. Hanbury, who have made a Saturday sitting necessary, and it is the colonels of the British Army who are counted upon to see that within its limits as little as possible of Government business is transacted. If the wraith of Mr. Joseph Gillis Biggar revisits the glimpses of Westminster Clock it will contemplate the proceedings of yesterday and those following to-day with what, for a ghost, may be described as mixed feelings. There will be regret that what should have been a monopoly for his own countrymen has been appropriated by others—regret not unmixed with a soothed sense of the flattery conveyed by imitation. All can grow the flower now, for all have got the seed. But we cannot, even were we disposed, forget the hand that first scattered it.

A Deadlock. The fight being formally entered upon, it may be expected that next week will see a renewal of it with even bitterer intensity.

The Prime Minister has fixed the second reading of
the Home Rule Bill for Thursday, and quietly says he
means to proceed with it then, and day by day thereafter, with the object of having the second reading
taken before the Easter holidays. The Opposition is
determined this shall not be, and since it is in a
minority, predestined to defeat in the division lobby,
it resorts to the old Irish tactics of talking against
time.

The way the process works out will probably
strike the Man in the Street as a little quaint. Mr.
Gladstone says he must have two Army Votes and the
remaining Navy Vote this week, so as to leave the
ground clear on Monday for discussion of the proceedings and conclusions of the Evicted Tenants'
Commission. There remained Friday and Saturday
for the accomplishment of the work. No members
of either party want to sit on Saturday, whilst arrangement of a Saturday sitting at the end of a heavy week
is a positive injustice to the Speaker, the officials of
the House, and others who must needs be present. In
these circumstances, recognising the inevitable, it
would seem natural that the House should get to
work on the Friday and dispose of it so as to leave
Saturday free. But these things are managed differ-
ently at Westminster. Friday's morning sitting, set
apart specially for discussion of the votes in question,
is occupied up to its very last moment in discussing
whether there shall be a Saturday sitting or not, and
if so, in what circumstances of time it shall be
conducted. When the third division is taken,
approving by a small majority the arrangements
originally submitted by Ministers, it is found to
be seven o'clock, at which hour a morning sitting
automatically closes. It is, therefore, absolutely
necessary to sit on Saturday in order to do what
might easily and comfortably have been accomplished
on Friday.

The simple statement of these occurrences reads like a passage from "Through a Looking-Glass," though it lacks the humour of that phantasy. It is the baldest statement of two days' proceedings in the most perfect, most important, and best regulated assembly of business men the world contains.

To sit through yesterday's proceedings was an experience calculated to eclipse the gaiety of the most mercurial temperament. When the Irish members were responsible for the play it was at least amusing, occasionally exciting. Yesterday it was not more entertaining than watching the performance of a champion walker pledged to do only half his accustomed task, or sitting by the bedside of Mr. Succi when he had undertaken to fast merely for a week. The House was uncheered even by the element of uncertainty as to the result. It met at two o'clock, and the sitting must needs be suspended by seven. The interval at its full length was nothing for a minority mustering over 200 to fill up with talk. As the scornful prisoner in the dock sometimes retorts on the magistrate who has passed sentence, they " could do it on their 'ed."

Sir William Harcourt, replying to a question from Mr. Balfour, announced that, owing to the delay in the progress of Estimates, it will be necessary to abandon the intention of taking the second reading of the Home Rule Bill before Easter.

13th March.
Check to the
Premier.

There is no question that this is a check to Ministers and a triumph for the Opposition. Whether it was reasonable or worth while, especially in view of the early fixture of Easter, to arrange for taking the second reading before the holidays is a question which, it is understood, divided the Cabinet. The youngest, and therefore most impetuous, man in the Cabinet —the Premier to wit—insisted it could be done, and so it was ordered. The announcement having been

made, there is a pained feeling in Liberal circles that
the decision should have been stuck to, and at whatever cost carried. It is easy to say this, and quite a
different thing to work it out. The late Government
might have done it; but they lived and worked amid
widely different circumstances. They had a majority
beginning at ·116, dwindling down to sixty-five, but
never falling below that figure. They were not met
by obstruction, and they had the priceless advantage
of the Closure in regular use.

Abrogation of the Closure. In each one of these particulars the present Government is at a disadvantage.
Their maximum majority is forty-two, the
Closure is practically abrogated, and they are faced by
the most resolute and reckless party of obstruction
known since Mr. Parnell was in the height of his power
and the thick of the fight. The worst of all is the
withdrawal of the Closure. This follows upon the in
terpretation put by the Speaker upon the situation
and the duty it devolves upon him. It should be said,
in justification of conduct much discussed in Parliamentary circles, that from the very first the House of
Commons has been insistent upon having the Closure
applied only when supported by an excessively large
majority. It was some time before it was brought to
the point of consenting to the principle of a bare
majority, and then it insisted on the safeguard of
interposing the arbitrary discretion of Speaker or
Chairman. Mr. Peel, recollecting these things, and
imbued with the sentiment, holds the opinion that
with a Ministerial majority of forty the Closure may
only occasionally be invoked.

Whether he be right or wrong, this is an intelligible proposition, and its application is likely to have
far-reaching effect. It places the Government at a
serious and unforeseen disadvantage, and is for the
Opposition the most cheering discovery made since the
Home Rule Bill was introduced.

16th March.
A Devoted
Judge Advo-
cate General.
Mr. Campbell-Bannerman, in charge of the Army Estimates, enlivened a dull afternoon with an interesting story, charmingly told, about the late Judge Advocate General. Inquiry was made as to the circumstances under which the office of Judge Advocate General remained unappropriated. The Secretary for War undertook to make a clean breast of the business. It appears that the late Judge Advocate General, Sir William Marriott, had a somewhat variegated experience, occasionally being paid and anon receiving no salary. At length it was arranged to attach to the office a salary of £500 a year, money down, with fees for business transacted payable up to the amount of another £500.

Last year was, as Mr. Campbell-Bannerman observed, one of some risk to the Government of which Sir William Marriott was a distinguished ornament. But that apparently not entering into his calculations he, on the 1st of April—the first day of the new financial year—applied to the Treasury for his salary, and received a cheque for £500. Having pocketed this, Sir William proceeded with such amazing energy to attack the business of his office that before the Government went out in August last he had absorbed the remaining £500, payable as fees for specific purposes, with the exception of a small balance of about £150. The consequence was that when the new Government came in they found no money at their disposal for the office of Judge Advocate General.

"That is the reason why," said Mr. Campbell-Bannerman, amid prolonged laughter from a suddenly interested House. "It is all owing to the exceeding devotion to his public duties of the late Judge Advocate General."

CHAPTER VII.

RIFTS IN THE LUTE.

Mr. Gladstone looked in this afternoon,
17th March everyone glad to know that what might
have been serious indisposition has lightly
passed. It is a week since he was last in his place,
and in resuming it there probably recurred to him a
phrase spoken long ago from the same bench by Mr.
Disraeli. A great deal has happened since Friday
last. The Premier was then resolved that, come
what might, the Home Rule Bill should be read a
second time before Easter. To that end a Saturday
sitting was ordered, and Mr. James Lowther's devout
mind was stirred by apprehension lest once more the
sound of Sabbath bells should break in on the work-
a-day labours of a hardened Legislature. But as the
morning sitting on Friday had come to naught, so
Ministerial intentions had through the Saturday
been withstood and finally frustrated by the Opposition. On Monday, Mr. Gladstone being confined
to his room, Sir W. Harcourt came down, and with
a meekness of demeanour that deeply touched the
House announced capitulation.

This was not a cheerful theme for meditation
for a statesman impatiently bent on seeing the
Home Rule Bill added to the Statute Book.
There were other circumstances connected with
his reappearance that, to any but a man of indomitable hope, must have been fatally depressing.
Mr. Gladstone was called upon to answer two
questions indicating separate rifts in the lute of the
Ministerial majority. One voiced the dissatisfaction

of Scotch members with the state of affairs as
affecting the business of their constituencies. The
example of Ireland in forcing itself upon the attention of the House of Commons proves increasingly
infectious. Gallant little Wales has come to the
front, insisting upon time and opportunity being
found for at least opening the trenches against the
fortress of the Established Church. After long
resistance the Welshmen, proving otherwise irre-
concilable, had their way, and why should Scotland
wait ? If there were no other means at the disposal
of the Premier, why should he not set aside a
succession of Saturdays, through whose pleasant
hours Scotch members might revel in the quiet
pastures of the Sea Fisheries Regulation Bill, or in
those marked out by Parochial Boards ?

Threatened
Radical
Revolt.
This was a question put to the Premier
this afternoon by way of cheering him
on his convalescence with prospect
of a long vista of cheerful Saturday
afternoons. More embarrassing was the other question
pressed upon his attention. It was put on behalf of
the Radical section of the Ministerial forces, and
imperatively demanded a pledge that by some means
or other, " whether by legislation, Budget arrangements, or otherwise," provision should be made for
the payment of members of Parliament. The dissatisfaction in Scotland was awkward enough, but
not dangerous. It might be kept within bounds by
privily informing the Scotch members that if they
persisted in pestering the Premier their demand for
Saturday sittings should be conceded. That, it is
safe to predicate, would promptly bring them to
their knees. It is a very different thing with the
Radicals, reputed to be a hundred and forty strong,
with Mr. Storey as their leader and mouthpiece.
Through his long official life Mr. Gladstone has had
many opportunities of studying them and learning

of what they are capable.   One of his earliest
lessons was gained just twenty years ago, when a
few of them, gathering over the teapots and muffins,
under the presidency of Henry Fawcett and Edward
Miall, broke up on a side issue what Lord Randolph
Churchill to-day described as the strongest Liberal
Ministry of modern times.   The Radicals of 1893
are the same in spirit as their predecessors of 1873,
and are, numerically, much more in the flesh.   Now,
as then, they are profoundly devoted to the statesman who has done more to carry their principles
into practice than the long line of Liberal Ministers
who preceded him through the century.   But their
attitude towards him is that of Lovelace to Lucasta
" On Going to the Wars.'

> Yet this inconstancy is such
>   As you too shall adore ;
> I could not love thee, Dear, so much,
>   Loved I not Honour more.

The Radical division of Mr. Gladstones army are
always going to the wars on their own account.
Sometimes it is Uganda ; often Egypt ; just now they
are mustering under the flag of Payment of Members.
They would be glad if they could induce their esteemed
Leader to accompany them, even in a subaltern
capacity.   But whether or not, whatever may happen
to the main army, they will go.   Not that they love
Mr. Gladstone less, but they love Honour more—
Honour in this application standing for the fad of the
particular moment.

Who is to Lead?   The prospect slowly darkening round Mr.
Gladstone would be enough to depress the
spirits and damp the courage of an
ordinary man.   It is bad enough, after the hardly-
snatched victory at the General Election, with the
consciousness ever before him of the narrow limitation
of opportunity, to find himself faced in the House of

Commons by such determined opposition as that
which has thrown him on the first round. Still it is
the duty of the Opposition to oppose, and it was
known in advance that the Unionists would dispute
every step on the way towards the accomplishment of
Home Rule. At least the Premier might have confidently counted, through what time is left to him, on
the united and loyal support of his own party. Some
body must lead the House of Commons and be
responsible for the direction of its business. It is
convenient that the direction of affairs shall rest in
one pair of hands. Whose shall they be? Mr
Gladstone's, Mr. Storey's, Mr. Labouchere's, the wrath-
ful Welshmen's, or the Scotch members', inconsolable
for Saturday sittings?

Mr. Labouchere, it seems already forgotten, has to
a large extent had his own way. When, after the
General Election, Mr. Gladstone was understood to
favour the assumption that Home Rule should be not
only the first, but the only, plank in the Ministerial
programme, Mr. Labouchere lifted up his voice,
insistent that, with this lean kine, there should also
herd Reform of the Registration, Shorter Parliaments, One Man One Vote, and Parish Councils.
These, and more, running the whole gamut of the
Newcastle programme, have been adopted by the
Government. Now a new pistol is being presented at
the head of the hapless Premier, and he is p   , not
to say truculently, warned that "the Radical Party
mean to have the principle of payment of members
effectively recognised before the present Session of
Parliament expires."

So they may, if the Session be given up to
the work. In the meanwhile, what is to become
of Home Rule?

When, this afternoon, Mr. Gladstone rose
Sir William
Harcourt. to reply to the questions with which he
was prodded in the back by friendly

hands, he showed no sign of the depression or irritation that ·might have beset an ordinary man in similar circumstances. His face betrayed some traces of his recent illness and confinement to the house, but his mood was even light and airy. In different manner does the weight of circumstances tell upon another eminent statesman seated on the Treasury Bench. Sir William Harcourt, if current rumour is to be credited, enjoys the advantage of relieving a perturbed spirit by privately communicating to malcontents his views of their campaigning methods. When the Welsh members, elate with their success on the Church question, insisted on bringing on their Local Veto Bill, running it in embarrassing contiguity to the Government measure, they are understood to have enjoyed full opportunity of knowing what the Chancellor of the Exchequer thought about them. But there is a vast difference, established with admirable effect, between Sir William Harcourt and the Chancellor of the Exchequer. One is a private individual, a free-born Englishman, who has his views on current events, and a pointed way of expressing them. The other is a statesman, a member of a homogeneous Ministry, above all, the deputy Leader of the House, called on not unfrequent occasions to act as substitute for his chief. What in Sir William Harcourt is but a choleric word would with the Leader of the House be rank blasphemy.

The Chancellor of the Exchequer knows
Dr. Jekyll this, and none more than he deplores the
and
Mr. Hyde. occasional habit of the member for Derby
to run amuck at mutineers. As temporary Leader of the House during the past week his manner and management have extorted the admiration of both sides. His patience has been invulnerable, his tact admirable, his management has reached the highest development of Parliamentary skill. He did not succeed in getting all he wanted;

but in order to realise the full extent of his achievement it is only necessary to reflect on what would
have happened supposing Sir William Harcourt had
been Leader of the House instead of the Chancellor
of the Exchequer.

This is not the first time that, under altered circumstances, the brilliant Parliamentary swordsman
has been transformed into the staid, long-suffering,
but ever-ready Leader. The first indication of possibility of the transformation dawned upon a startled
House at the end of the Session of 1889. At that
time also Mr. Gladstone temporarily retired from
the scene, leaving Sir William Harcourt in the
seat of the Leader of the Opposition. The Conservative Government, then in the plenitude of its
power, brought in the Tithes Bill, with imperative
mandate from Lord Salisbury to have it passed before
the prorogation. The Opposition were, as usual, in a
hopeless minority. But so adroit was Sir William
Harcourt's leadership, so unfailing his resources, that
without anything that deserved the reproach of
obstruction he, at the close of a well-fought week,
compelled the Government to withdraw their Bill.

The House of Commons adjourned at a
25th March.
An All Night
Sitting. quarter-past five this morning, over three
hundred gentlemen going home with the
consciousness that they had deserved well
of their country. There are several novelties about the
obstruction now rampant in the House of Commons.
The first, and really the most creditable, is that the
practitioners are not ashamed of their business.
When the tactics were reduced to an exact science by
the Parnellite members, they shrank with horror from
the charge of obstruction. Mr. Biggar, not being a
sensitive soul, did not particularly mind. But there
was something almost terrible in the emotion with
which Mr. O'Donnell and Mr. Philip Callan resented
the accusation. Many a time when other resources

failed, a good half-hour of a sitting was wasted by
touching appeals of the Irish members addressed to
the Speaker to protect them from charges of obstruction levelled against them by long-suffering members
in other parts of the House.

In the new campaign it is Mr. Chamberlain who,
with characteristic courage and directness of purpose,
first openly avowed the purpose of obstruction. The
Government, master of a small majority, were resolved
to bring in, and drive through the House, a Home
Rule Bill. Very well. The force of numbers must
doubtless prevail in the end. In the meanwhile plain
intimation was given to Ministers that their footsteps
would be dogged and every pace hampered. A
promise handsomely fulfilled, with the early effect of
defeating Mr. Gladstone's cherished intention of read
ing the Home Rule Bill a second time before the
Easter holidays.

An Old Soldier. Mr. James Lowther, a prominent figure
in the House of Commons at a time when
Mr. Chamberlain was as yet scarcely
known in Birmingham, does not find it easy to fall in
with this new Parliamentary manner. In his comparatively young days, when he was fighting the Irish
Church Bill, obstruction was held to be a Parliamentary offence. No one admitted it, and the most
audacious offenders were careful to veil their purpose
under decent Parliamentary guise. To this day the
right hon. gentleman preserves the manner of the
old school.

When, yesterday afternoon, he rose on the motion
for the third reading of the Appropriation Bill and
began to talk of irregularities in the preparation of the
Supplementary Estimates, he had about him a subtle
but unmistakable air of never having heard of the
Home Rule Bill. So effective was his manner, so
convincing his ingenuousness, that for fully ten
minutes the House sat listening with painstaking

endeavour to gather some thread of meaning. Gradually there was audible a restless movement. Members whispered to each other vain interrogation as to the point of the remarks. Amongst new members, more susceptible than others to the imposing judicial air of the Jockey Club luminary, there was a feeling of mental and physical relief, finding expression in a jubilant shout when Mr. Sexton interposed with the remark that the right hon. gentleman was " in the main unintelligible." They had long suspected it. But looking at the Member for Thanet, as with elbow on the box he leaned over the table, in negligent but studious attitude, listening to the inflections of his voice, watching his countenance, almost funereal in its gravity, they felt they must be wrong, and that the apprehension was due to ignorance and in-experience on their part.

Even when the Speaker interposed, Mr. Lowther was unabashed.

" It would," said the right hon. gentleman, appealed to on a point of order, " be unfair and unusual at this stage of the Appropriation Bill to dwell on one particular estimate."

" Yes, sir," said Mr. Lowther, bowing with gracious dignity to his learned brother in the Chair, " that is the rule to which I am particularly desirous of conforming." Then, waving the Speaker down with a sweep of his right arm, he proceeded for another ten minutes, the House again intently listening.

" It is not in order to discuss what is not in the vote," said the Speaker, later.

" That would be so, sir," responded Mr. Lowther, with another bow, not quite so gracious this time. The Speaker must, to a certain extent, be put up with, and should always be treated with a show of deference. But he must not presume on his position, and wantonly interrupt high Parliamentary personages when they are discussing constitutional questions. All this

was implied in the marked frigidity of the bow, and in
the slight frown which contracted Mr. Lowther's fore-
head as he turned towards the occupant of the Chair.

Mark, too, the precise selection of the conditional
mood.   The Speaker had made an assertion, involving
a truism, of Parliamentary rule.   He had put as a
proposition directly applicable to the present case the
axiom that it is not in order to discuss what is not in
the vote.   Had Mr. Lowther given unqualified assent
—as, for example, "Right you are, sir"—he would
have been assenting to the charge personal to himself
implied in the Speaker's remark.   His "That would
be so, sir," was quite a different thing.   It meant that
if the Speaker, being in academical mood, chose to interrupt a statesman offering a few business remarks on
a public Bill, the responsibility rested with him.   The
statesman on his legs might, had opportunity been
fitting, have argued the question out, and perhaps
shown that the Speaker was in error or only partially
correct.   There could be no harm in assenting to a
general hypothetical proposition, and, as it would be
more courteous to do so, Mr. Lowther obeyed the
instincts of a gentleman.   This done, he returned
to the point at which he seemed to have left off,
and, sitting down, was understood to have concluded
his argument.

Obstruction :
New Style.   After this exhibition of antique art the
scene that opened just before one o'clock
this morning and continued till daybreak
was a trifle vulgar.   The new party of obstruction,
improving on the practice of their Irish masters, have
divided the watches of the day and night.   Mr.
Parnell, Mr. O'Donnell, Mr. Biggar, and (in his days of
sin) Mr. Tim Healy used to waste their energies and
minimise their opportunity by all being on the scene
at the same time.   It is true that upon one occasion
Mr. Biggar temporarily withdrew, and, stretching his
form on three chairs in the library, slept for a couple

of hours, returning at six in the morning "like a giant refreshed,' as he genially mentioned. But that was an exception arising in the circumstances of an unusually prolonged sitting. For an ordinary engagement like yesterday, with its interval of two hours between the morning and the evening sitting, the Irish captains would have remained in the trenches on uninterrupted duty. Mr. James Lowther, having agreeably occupied the afternoon, retired at midnight to his couch, and Mr. Hanbury took up the running.

Regarded as an obstructionist, Mr. Hanbury's style lacks finish. He began by going as near to giving the Chairman the lie direct as has ever been achieved since Cromwell took away the Mace. The House having resolved itself into Committee on the Army Annual Bill, the Chairman promptly got to work, and putting the question "That Clause I. stand part of the Bill," declared the Ayes had it. Mr. Hanbury, interposing, began to debate Clause I. The Chairman pointed out that Clause I. had been added to the Bill, and that Clause II. was now before the Committee.

"I am not sure,' Mr. Hanbury shouted from the heights behind the Front Opposition Bench, "that that is a correct statement of the facts."

With Mr. Courtney in the Chair that would have been an end of Mr. Hanbury's participation in the proceedings of the evening. On the threshold of the fight he would have been carried manacled off the field. Mr. Mellor rejoined that he "did not suppose the hon. member meant to contradict him," a pathetically charitable construction of the remark quoted.

From this time forward the still crowded House was in a state of uncontrollable emotion. The spectacle of the meek grey head of Mr. Jesse Collings rising from below the gangway was the signal for such an impetuous roar of contumely that, after feebly beating the air for some minutes, his lips moving in utterance of remarks that might as well have been delivered in the cave under Niagara, Mr. Collings resumed his seat and was seen in the front no more. As the House would not listen to Mr. Hanbury till he had apologised to the Chair, Mr. Gibson Bowles, over-coming a natural tendency towards retirement, rose to address the House.

"I do hope," he said in plaintive tones, "I shall not be interrupted."

Whereupon he was howled down.

That nothing might be lacking to the picturesque-ness of the scene, Mr. Conybeare, in the interests of law and order, moved the Closure. It must have been with strange emotion that the hon. member for Cam-borne found himself fulfilling this part. Time was when he and the lamented Mr. W. H. Smith seemed to be connected by subterraneous machinery. Almost simultaneously with Mr. Conybeare's rising from below the gangway to the left of the Speaker, the Leader of the House was seen upstanding by the Treasury Bench and heard moving the Closure. "Pouncing" the wise called it in those days. In the strange whirligig of time here was Mr. Conybeare "pouncing," accomplish-ing the act with full approval of the Chair.

Two divisions followed, and when hon. members tumultuously returned and resumed their seats, Sir William Harcourt, drawing the sword and throwing away the scabbard, declared that "in view of the intolerable obstruction being practised" the Govern-ment were prepared to fight it out to the bitter end. Old stagers went out and ordered reserve of broiled bones, new members sitting down with the enthusiasm of youth to their first experience of an all-night sitting.

CHAPTER VIII

SECOND READING OF THE HOME RULE BILL.

THE House, resuming its sittings after the
6th April Easter recess, settles down to its work with
the consciousness of a tough fight before
it. Both sides mean business, the business of the
Opposition being obstruction. From what we have
seen before Easter we may easily and accurately
forecast the course of procedure between now and
Whitsuntide. *Ex pede* Jemmy Lowther. We have
seen the length of his foot on the Mutiny Bill, and
can judge what heights he will reach when face to
face with the Home Rule Bill. I have known the
House of Commons pretty intimately for twenty years,
and cannot call to mind any epoch of obstruction
exceeding in deliberation and pertinacity that which
clogged the wheels of Parliament during the past
eight weeks. There have been scenes of more
virulence and of higher dramatic quality. That goes
without saying, since the company of players has, in
earlier times, been composed of Irish members.

It is a curious fact that the Session, as far as it
has gone, has not witnessed the suspension of a single
member. When one calls to mind the performances
of Mr. Hanbury and Mr. Lowther, this abstention on
the part of the Speaker and the Chairman of Ways
and Means seems to imply an increase of forbearance
in the Chair when the obstructionist of the hour is
an English member instead of being an Irish one.
The explanation must, however, be sought elsewhere.

The fundamental and important difference between obstruction to-day and the performance that
concentrated public attention on the Theatre Royal,

Westminster, in the seasons 1880-5, is in the numerical force engaged.   When in February, 1881, the
party of obstructionists were suspended wholesale
it was found that they numbered only 37.   If in the
course of the next few weeks a similar *coup de main*
be rendered necessary, 313 honourable and right hon
gentlemen, with a sprinkling of noble lords, will be
smitten.   These figures not only inspire obstructionists with a sense of confident strength, but they
paralyse the arm of the Speaker when he would use
the instrument for the repression of obstruction
placed at his disposal.   It is one thing to demand
the Closure for the suppression of a minority of 37
or even of 80; quite another when proposal is made
peremptorily to shut up a minority of over 300 in an
assembly of 670.   The realisation of this position
has in the past encouraged the Opposition to go to
extreme lengths, and it will sustain them in the
coming conflict.

One substantial advantage the Government have
in the phase of the fight just entered upon is that
they have succeeded in thoroughly clearing the decks
for action.   They have practically obtained possession of
every working hour for the remainder of the Session,
and may be depended upon stubbornly to peg away.

7th April.
Debate on
Second Read-
ing of Home
Rule Bill.

The Man in the Street working his way
into the Strangers' Gallery of the House
of Commons to-night would naturally
expect to find in this centre of political
action some reflex of the excitement that
throbs through the country at mention of Home Rule.
He has read in the papers how statesmen gave up
their Easter holiday to pursuit of the controversy;
how Ulster had risen in its might and tramped
through the streets of Belfast in procession so far-
reaching that Mr. Balfour, trained though he be in
sitting through long speeches in the House of Commons, was compelled to beat strategic retreat before

half the host had gone by Though probably not
personally feeling any mental convulsion, the Man in
the Street knows that the great heart of the nation
beats tumultuously when Home Rule is mentioned.
To the House of Commons is in the first place, committed the settlement of this momentous question.
Within its walls the concentrated emotion of the
nation might be expected to surge. The Man in the
Street had heard much of the inadequacy of accommodation afforded by the legislative chamber. He
had read Mr. Labouchere's pathetic plea for more
room. He had seen in the illustrated papers pictures
of cataclysmic vigour showing gentlemen, some
apparently in fragmentary condition, making dashes
at seats already occupied three or four deep. He had
heard of Colonel Saunderson's personal encounter with
a Liberal Ulsterman who claimed a seat which the
colonel regarded as his ; who had endeavoured, *more
Hibernico*, to pull the gallant member out by the
scruff of the neck, and who continued the conversation
from a recumbent position under the bench, where the
colonel had gently but firmly laid him.

With these reflections and recollections the
Stranger obtaining the much-prized seat in the
Gallery to-night must speedily have come to the
conclusion that he had strayed into the wrong place.
Instead of the seething multitude fighting for seats,
there was an expanse of empty benches, dotted here
and there by gentlemen, young and old, distinguished
by the common peculiarity of holding a sheaf of
paper in hand. The energy with which these leaped
to their feet when one who had been speaking sat
down was the only sign of life. Sometimes there were
as many as forty present ; oftener the assembly fell
below a score. Twenty or forty, their business was the
same and their action identical. They were there to
"catch the Speaker's eye " and reel off their painfully-
constructed sentences at this favourable opportunity.

For some it is now or never. Next week the Tritons will be back splashing in the pond, and there will be no room for the minnows. The worst of it, regarded from private standpoint, is that the happy thought had occurred to so many. It followed that competition for the Speaker's eye, opening in what seemed exceptionally favourable circumstances, became unusually severe. Worse still, those who succeeded enjoyed their privilege at inordinate length, regardless of gentlemen who sat watchful and waiting, conning their manuscript till even they were sick of its commonplaces.

Yesterday Mr. Gladstone found an hour and a half necessary for moving the second reading of the Bill, a measure of time slightly exceeded by Sir Michael Hicks-Beach in opposing the motion. These were the leaders of parties, and though, perhaps, an hour would have done for them and might have served to better advantage, no one could dispute their exceptional claim to full measure of time. The example unhappily proved contagious, and as far as debate has hitherto gone nothing less than an hour will serve for the delivery of a speech. To-day the debate opened at a quarter to four and closed at midnight. Just eight members of the 670 composing the House of Commons worked off their speeches, a fact leading up to a portentous calculation.

A Fearsome Prospect.

This is not debate. It i preaching, or, rather, prosing. If the proceedings are carried forward on the same scale, and there is no reason in logic or justice why they should not be, a fraction under eighty-four days will be necessary for the completion of the debate commenced yesterday, an arrangement that will pleasantly and agreeably bring the House of Commons up to Tuesday, the 25th of July. Or, allowing for a moderate Whitsun holiday, the end will be reached ten days later. A consideration that makes this prospect not

less alluring is the indisputable and frankly acknowledged fact that the course of debate will not influence
a single vote. Supposing arrangements had been made
to take the division last night at the close of Sir
Michael Hicks-Beach's speech in moving the rejection
of the Bill, the Government majority would have been
to a unit the same as it will prove when, ten days
hence, some eighty or ninety more speeches having
been made (other two or three hundred having been
peremptorily cut off), the tellers march up to the
table to announce the figures. The only consideration
that will avail to vary the result will be the accidental
absence of members owing to illness or other inevitable physical cause, and as between yesterday and
Monday or Tuesday week the incidence of accident
may be taken to balance itself.

Nevertheless, we shall have the speeches, and when
at length human patience, found in its highest
development in the House of Commons, is exhausted
there will still remain scores of members with orations
which after prolonged but vain endeavour they have
failed to deliver on the second reading. For these
will remain the consolation that, slightly recon-
structed, portions may be delivered in Committee, and
of the fragments that remain—seven baskets full or
less—they can be worked off on the Report Stage or
the third reading.

'Tis ever thus. After a full-dress debate in the
House of Commons, as after a storm in the English
Channel, the coast is strewed with fragments of wreck.

The One Man Interested. As far as observation in the House of
Commons goes, there is only one human
mind capable of resisting the influence of
the dreary drip of reiterated assertion that constitutes
a conversation on the question of Home Rule. Only
to Mr. Gladstone is the subject ever fresh and fair.
He alone of trained and intellectual muscle-hardened
Parliament men can sit by the hour listening to the

E

old things said over again in scarcely varied phrase.
Yesterday afternoon he came up quite fresh with a
speech that, as Sir Michael Hicks-Beach, a man not
given to exaggerated language, declared, entranced
the attention of the House, not less that of political
foes than of enthusiastic friends. The exigencies of a
dinner engagement withdrew him from the scene for
an hour or so. But he remained at his post on the
Treasury Bench up to the last moment when he must
needs retire to dress, and hurried back long before
more leisured people had finished their coffee. This
evening he had hastily promised to go off to Brighton,
and, in order to catch the train comfortably, should
have left at twenty minutes past five. This limitation
of prized opportunity was evidently regarded by him
with impatience. Whilst it lingered he made the
most of it, sitting with hand to ear listening to Mr.
Barton as if he were telling a new and enchanting
story. He turned with fresh delight towards Mr.
Stansfeld when that eminent rhetorician rose from
the corner bench behind him. The hand of the clock
had passed the twenty-five minutes. Every additional
moment meant increased rush to catch the train.
Still he lingered, till with a final glance at the clock
he started up and skipped past the Speaker's chair
with the alacrity of young seventeen.

Brighton is a pleasant place in these fair spring
days, with its sunlit air and its rippling sea. To
Mr. Gladstone it is a poor place compared with the
House of Commons, even in the doldrums. For
him no music so pleasing to the ear as the sleepy
murmur of multitudinous commonplaces, or the
shrill shriek of vituperation, on one side or other of·
the Home Rule Bill.

When to-night the Speaker, appealed to
on a point of order, said the word
"satellite," used in debate by Mr. Balfour,
was a harmless word, he probably had in mind a

11th April.
"Satellites."

famous precedent. During the Parliament of 1868 Mr. Gladstone, speaking of Mr. Disraeli, then Leader of the Opposition, referred to the right hon. gentleman's satellites. This was met by an uproar of interruption, which had the unusual result of the Premier losing the thread of his discourse.

" I forget what I was saying," he observed.

" The last word was ' satellites,' " said Mr. Disraeli, half rising from his seat.

11th April.
Mr. Gladstone
and Mr.
Parnell.
In the course of to-night's further debate on the second reading of the Home Rule Bill Mr. W. Redmond loudly protested, with reference to a remark made by Mr. Gladstone, that the Premier was inclined to " put all the blame on Parnell because he's dead." This brought up Mr. Gladstone with an interesting statement. Alluding to the famous passage, quoted by Mr. Chamberlain, that Mr. Parnell was " marching through rapine to the dismemberment of the Empire," he explained that when he had made that remark he was under the impression that Mr. Parnell had been endeavouring to frustrate the effects of the Land Bill. After the Irish leader came out of Kilmainham Mr. Gladstone had reason to believe that his mind had undergone a great change on this point, and since then no word had dropped from him in any speech calculated to give pain to Mr. Parnell or his friends. He had taken an opportunity through a friend of Mr. Parnell's to assure him that thereafter no difficulties would, as far as he was concerned, be thrown in his way, since he believed the course he desired to adopt would be beneficial to Ireland.

12th April.
Two
After-Dinner
Speakers.
I have not chanced to see Lord Rosebery since the New Year opened, meeting him for the first time for more than three months at the dinner given to-night to Sir Robert Duff, on the eve of his

departure for New South Wales. I was much struck with the marked improvement in his appearance, as compared with that presented during the last Midlothian campaign and during the brief Session that resulted in the overthrow of the Ministry of Lord Salisbury. He seems to have recovered all his old alertness and vigour, sapped for a while by the curious inability to sleep that beset him in the autumn.

His speech in proposing the health of the new Governor was marked by something more than his usual felicity. It is a happy accident that in successive Foreign Secretaries in Liberal Administrations the country has found two of the most charming after-dinner speakers of the day. Lord Rosebery's style is much akin to Lord Granville's in respect of grace and delicacy of touch. Where difference comes in is to be found in the circumstance that Lord Granville was more polished and Lord Rosebery is more vigorous. Lord Granville played round the victim of his gentle humour, almost apologetically pinking him with polished rapier. Lord Rosebery will do that sometimes, but occasionally, as the late Lord Brabourne knew, he is capable of delivering a blow straight from the shoulder on the visage of a deserving object. His oratorical style may be described as English, benefiting by application of French polish. Lord Granville's was French, with an unwonted substratum of what we are pleased to regard as British solidity.

13th April.
Lord Cranborne Offers
an Observation
to Himself.

Mr. Asquith spoke on this the sixth night of debate on the second reading of the Home Rule Bill. The vigorous flow of his argument was at one time interrupted by a swift, sudden outburst of passion. He was referring to Mr. Davitt's speech of Tuesday night, and was asking the House to consider all that was meant by the spectacle of this ex-convict, former rebel against the British constitution, won over to constitutional practices by the Bill now before the House. The sentence was interrupted by half-a-dozen members below the gangway, where the Irish members sit, suddenly leaping to their feet, shouting in unison, and pointing with angry forefinger at a member seated at the corner of the gangway. Amid the uproar the voice of Mr. Crilly was heard exclaiming:

"Is that member right in calling Mr. Davitt a murderer?"

The Speaker had risen, and Mr. Asquith resumed his seat. In vain the Speaker called "Order!" The tumult below the gangway irrepressively grew, there being angry shouts of "Withdraw!" "Name! Name!" In a slight lull the Speaker managed to declare that he did not know who was the member indicated. Hereupon a figure on the corner seat half rose, and the hat being removed disclosed the pale face of Lord Cranborne.

"I said it to myself," he hurriedly explained, "but the observation was quite true."

This brought forth a fresh outburst, which the Speaker quelled by observing, amid prolonged cheers from the Irish members, that the remark was a most improper one, and should be apologised for. Lord Cranborne, rising again, said in the same hurried way, "Of course I apologise to the House. The words were not intended for the ears of the House." He resumed his seat amid loud groans from the Irish members, and Mr. Asquith continued his speech.

14th April.
The Mystery of Success in the House of Commons.

What is the secret of success in the House of Commons? It is a question that long ago puzzled Lord Macaulay, and was by him given up as insoluble. Macaulay's own success as a speaker was a mystery, being opposed to all the ordinary canons. He

laboriously prepared his orations as if they were
fresh chapters of his Essays, committed them to
memory, and recited them. It would be interesting to know whether, if he sat for Edinburgh to-
day, he would fill the House of Commons as he
did on the occasions of which graphic record is
enshrined in Sir George Trevelyan's Life of his
revered uncle. If he were a success it would be
an additional triumph, for none other working on
similar or analogous lines can to-day entrance the
attention of the House.

A recent recruit to the ranks illustrates the
peculiarities of the situation. Mr. Blake came over
with a reputation established upon sound basis in
Canada. In that country his admirers were pleased
to regard him as a kind of colonial Gladstone, a resemblance extending even to a shade of Mr. Disraeli
being happily found in his lifelong rival Sir John
Macdonald. When the Irish party, shaken with the
long conflict in Committee Room No. 15, invited
Mr. Blake to come over and help them, it was generally felt that an adroit move had been made.
Acceptance of the invitation seemed to promise almost
compensation for the loss of Mr. Parnell. The ex-
Premier of Canada was not only an old Parliamentary
hand, but a statesman who ranked as an orator in
the Dominion Legislature. To-night the House of
Commons had a second opportunity of estimating the
value of this new addition to its forces. Mr. Blake
found his chance at what is, perhaps, the most
favourable hour for the delivering of an important
speech. Members crowded in refreshed by dinner,
eager to be amused and interested.

He spoke for the hour and a half which has
Mr. Blake. come to be the statutory extension of
speech in the current debate. He was
fluent, evidently well informed. His phrases were
excellent ; the House was determined to be pleased,

and, to tell the melancholy truth, the whole thing was exceedingly wearisome. There was throughout it something subtly but distinctly colonial. The House listened with the sedulous politeness due to his position, character, and the accident of his being in some sense a visitor. But it was unmistakably bored at what partook rather of the characteristics of a lecture than of the life and vigour of a speech.

Mr. Blake is under the fatal disadvantage of having entered the House of Commons too late in life, and is further handicapped by ingrained habits of thought and speech cultured in another world. Without exception that occurs to the memory in rapid review, all men who have made conspicuous success in the House of Commons have entered it when young. Pitt, as Lord Rosebery says, was almost born in the place. Mr. Disraeli, Mr. Gladstone, Lord Salisbury, Lord Palmerston, Sir Wm. Harcourt, Mr. Balfour, Lord Randolph Churchill—the list might be indefinitely extended—all entered it young.

Four Successes. This early apprenticeship is one of the main secrets of the conditions under which success in the House of Commons is achieved. Of course it is not everything, as Mr. Whitbread and some other old stagers still in the House could testify. This week there have been four great speeches each in different style, each illustrating a phase of the honeycombed avenue through which success in the House of Commons is approached. Taking them in order of date they are those delivered by Mr. Chamberlain, Mr. Davitt, Mr. John Redmond, and Mr. Asquith. One was a maiden speech ; two established reputations already to a considerable extent made.

Mr. Chamberlain. Mr. Chamberlain is, comparatively, a veteran, and that, when he interposes in debate, he should command the attention of the House is a matter of course. On Monday he was at his best, a level height from which, indeed, he rarely descends. No man has a keener intuition of what the House of Commons likes to hear and how it should be said. The position in which the development of circumstances has placed him is such as would appal a less resolute spirit and reduce him to silence. Ever his dead self of the years prior to 1886 is being exhumed and carried round public platforms or the benches of the House of Commons. It might be supposed that, of all men, Mr. Chamberlain would be most chary of indulging in the attractive and unfailingly effective device of recalling declarations made by the adversary in former years and in other circumstances. On Monday the most elaborately devised passage in his speech, the one most keenly enjoyed by himself and the Opposition generally, was a string of quotations from the speeches of his former colleagues, once more seated on the Treasury Bench, who had regarded Home Rule and Home Rule leaders from quite a different point of view in the years between 1880 and 1885. That was cleverly done, if not quite original in design. Cleverer still was the fashion in which Mr. Chamberlain ignored the circumstance that the member immediately preceding him had quoted to his discomfiture a passage from a speech delivered at that same epoch in which, in his own incomparable style, he had riddled with ridicule the very Ulster party with which he is now associated.

Mr. Davitt. Mr. Davitt's speech was a success in spite of undue length and some evidence of amateurism. He succeeded in impressing the House with a conviction of his honesty, earnestness and singleness of purpose, a talisman in the way of earning its esteem and securing its attention. The speech was carefully written out and closely followed from the manuscript. That in itself would have been fatal in most cases. Mr. Davitt managed the reading

skilfully, occasionally lapsed into extemporaneous
asides, and was, throughout, delightfully unconventional. Canning used to say, as Macaulay quotes
him in a letter written to Whewell more than sixty
years ago, that the House of Commons as a body
has better taste than the man of best taste in it.
That is true in respect of all good qualities, and is
a faculty that makes it the incomparable assembly
it is. It is more just than the justest man in its
ranks; more appreciative than the most sympathetic;
more generous than the kindest hearted. It was
piqued on Tuesday by the reflection that the tall
dark man with the armless sleeve addressing it had,
not many years before, stood in the dock charged
with treason felony, and had, as he incidentally
mentioned, served a term of over nine years' penal
servitude. He was here returned by his constituents
upon a footing of equality with the best of them,
and the House as a body was resolved that at
least he should be made to feel at home. When
he produced from a recess the fifth package of his
manuscript and proposed to "consider the philosophy
of the question," patience and courtesy were sorely
tried. If he had been a many-acred squire or the son
of a duke this movement would have been marked by
signs of impatience, perhaps cries for the division.
As it was Mr. Davitt, the apology with which he
continued his harangue was greeted with a cheer—
faint, it is true, but distinctly audible.

It is only this Session Mr. John Redmond
has made his mark in the House. It was
scored when he delivered a brief speech
on the Address, the House marvelling to find what
long steps he had taken since—in Mr. Parnell's time—
he occasionally filled his appointed part in the task of
prolonging debates. To-day he strode into the front
rank of Parliamentary debaters. His manner of delivery
is excellent. He has a melodious voice, perfectly under

Mr. John
Redmond.

E *

control. His diction is pure, free from the gaudy colours which come natural to some of his country-men, and yet, as was shown towards the end of his speech, capable of sustained flights of lofty eloquence. These are matters of manner, and it is truer in the House of Commons than anywhere else that manner makes the man. Mr. Redmond's oratorical style, as the House discovered, is based upon a substratum of solid knowledge, sound common-sense, and a states-manlike capacity to review a complicated situation. Circumstances happening within the past three months have devolved upon the Leader of the small Parnellite party the necessity of tacking. Those—chiefly found amongst his own countrymen—most fully acquainted with the exigencies of the hour were most fervid in their admiration of the skill with which to-night the manœuvre was carried out.

Mr. Redmond's speech was a revelation,

Mr. Asquith: Mr. Asquith's was a confirmation and final establishment of a position the brilliant capture of which has no parallel in modern Parlia-mentary history. Lord Randolph Churchill was much longer winning his way to Cabinet rank than the present Home Secretary has been. To some lookers-on these successes will confirm Lord Macaulay's opinion that the House of Commons is the most peculiar audience in the world. A place where Mr. Asquith succeeds and Mr. Chaplin fails; where Sir Ashmead-Bartlett and Lord George Hamilton are dinner-bells; where Sir Michael Hicks-Beach and Mr. Stansfeld, two of the ablest Parliament men, or nearly so, of their time, are thought bores, is surely a very strange place.

17th April. Distinguish Visitors. Every day when the House meets the Speaker walks in procession through the lobby, preceded by the Mace, and accom-panied by the chaplain. To-day the procession was lengthened by the recruiting of the

Lord Mayor of Dublin, who brought with him Mace-bearer and Sword-bearer, together with an escort of the Corporation of the city. Shortly after the Speaker had taken the Chair the Sergeant-at-Arms, advancing towards the table with the usual obeisance, announced "The Lord Mayor and the Aldermen of the City of Dublin." Shouldering the Mace, he returned to the door, where the Lord Mayor was waiting. The bar was promptly drawn out, and the principal doorkeeper cried aloud: "The Lord Mayor of the City of Dublin;" whereat there were loud cheers from the Irish members, who had gathered in considerable number. Mr. T. D. Sullivan, wearing the robes of a Dublin City Councillor, sat within the bar by the cross benches.

The Lord Mayor and Sheriffs standing at the bar, the Speaker rose and said, "My Lord Mayor of Dublin, what have you there?"

Thus challenged, the Lord Mayor announced that he was the bearer of a humble petition of the Municipal Council of the City of Dublin, largely interested in the peace, prosperity, and good government of the country, who desired to see the Home Rule Bill promptly passed. A sort of parenthesis in the petition desired that the House of Commons would specially keep its eye on its financial provisions with the view to giving the future Irish Exchequer a fair start. This aroused a fresh burst of cheers from the Irish members, greeted with some laughter by the Opposition. The Lord Mayor, having recited the prayer of the petition, handed the document to the Clerk at the table, who remained standing at the bar during the reading, and who placed the document in the usual receptacle by the side of the table. The Sergeant-at-Arms, also standing at guard by the bar Mace on shoulder, walked up to the table, replaced the Mace, and the ordinary business went forward.

Eighth night of Home Rule Debate. Lord Randolph Churchill contributed a speech on whose preparation he had evidently bestowed much pains. During its progress—and it lasted two hours—there was witnessed the spectacle, unwonted when he is on his legs, of Members walking out. Mr. Gladstone, after long sitting an attentive listener, produced his letter pad, and took the opportunity of writing a letter.

17th April. Lord Randolph as "a Dinner-bell."

Lord Randolph's main contention was that there is an agglomeration of three causes fatal to the Bill—"a fault running through its construction," as he, dropping into geological terms, called it. The first objection was that the Bill left taxation to the Home Rule Parliament; the second that it separated the Imperial Parliament from the Irish Executive; the third that it presented the unexampled division of the Imperial Parliament by what is known as the in-and-out position of the Irish Members, who, as the Bill proposes, are to vote on some subjects and to retire when others come under consideration. Mr. Gladstone, Lord Randolph said, amongst the few once familiar flashes that lightened up the speech, has been guilty of a philosophic absurdity. He is trying to create one body with two centres of gravity.

The Irish Question in a Nutshell.

Quotation of the definition of the Irish question given by "an old friend," a distinguished Irish judge, much tickled the fancy of the House.

"The Irish question," said the anonymous judge, "lies in a nutshell. It is that a quick-witted nation are being governed by a stupid people."

Lord Randolph Churchill, stopping short of this, admitted that at the present time a quick-witted people are being governed by a stupid party.

It is an open secret that Lord Randolph Churchill's "old friend" is Lord Morris. The noble lord was among the peers in the Gallery, and had an opportunity of noting the effect on the House of one of his many witty sayings.

22nd April.
On the Eve of
the Division.
It was one of the grim satires of the long debate closed this morning that on the twelfth night of incessant talk the Leader of the Opposition and the Leader of the House should have been driven into a corner for lack of time. Between them, these two, whom the House of Commons and the world waiting at its gates really wanted to hear, had allotted to them a space of little more than two hours and a half—to be precise, ten minutes more for the two than Mr. Sexton had thought necessary for deliverance of the thoughts that burned within him. Of what was left Mr. Balfour, though the pink of courtesy, the soul of chivalry, took the lion's share. A little more than an hour must needs suffice the Premier, speaking on a historic occasion, delivering what may prove to be his last great Parliamentary oration.

If Mr. Gladstone felt resentment or disappointment, he carefully disguised it under a manner of unusual buoyancy. If he only knew—the House certainly recognised the fact—he had occasion rather for thankfulness than for regret in this accidental circumstance. Early in the sitting he had been witness of the disaster in which opportunity for prolixity may involve even an adroit Parliamentary hand. Sir Henry James never spoke at such length as he did to-night, and never to so little purpose. His speech had all his worst faults of ingrained manner—the funereal voice, the depressed figure, the ludicrously solemn way of leading up to portentous nothings. Sir Henry is good for a brisk canter of half-an-hour, and, had he been content with so much, might have served his cause and added to his renown. As it was, the blight of two hours' opportunity was over it all, and the Member for Bury, finding the temptation irresistible, lost a great chance.

Like Mr. Gladstone, Mr. Balfour greatly
Mr. Balfour. profited by the circumscribed space within
which he was obliged to talk.   It was a
quarter-past ten when he rose, and it had been made
known to him through the usual channels that Mr.
Gladstone was disposed to speak about eleven.   In
any case it was desirable, in view of the hospital of
invalids and convalescents gathered for the great division, that the end should not be postponed beyond
half-past twelve.   Thus there was no time for exordium or excursion into ancient history.   Any
hitting to be accomplished was to be done by blows
delivered straight from the shoulder.   The condition
exactly suited Mr. Balfour's disposition and habits,
and he acquitted himself in a manner that recalled his
best form when as Chief Secretary he stood at bay
against the Irish Members led by Mr. Parnell.

The scene was one calculated to draw forth the
fullest powers of a capable man.   The House was filled
on every bench.   From the side gallery facing him
two unbroken lines of members looked down eagerly
attentive.   The Prince of Wales sat over the clock, the
centre of a closely-packed peerage on the left, and a
gallery crowded with distinguished strangers on the
right.   Behind the pleasant presence of the *debonnaire* Prince rose tier on tier the strangers who had
the good fortune to obtain admission.   They had been
in their places all the evening; had slept awhile,
soothed by Sir Henry James's monotone; had watched
the hurried procession of members who filled up the
dinner hour breathless with intent now or never to
deliver the long-waiting speech.   Now the Leader of
the Opposition was up business had begun, and the
erewhile jaded mass of humanity piled up to the topmost range of the gallery visibly brightened.

Mr. Balfour had accumulated voluminous notes,
and from time to time referred to them.   But it was
obvious that he discarded whole sheets, the course of

his speech being, in truth, frequently marked out for him by interruption from his old adversaries below the gangway, where though Ministries come and go the Irish camp remains. These he answered with brilliant effect, not once losing command of himself or his audience, cheers and counter-cheers ringing with sharp rattle as one or other of the well-matched adversaries made a palpable hit.

Through some of the tiresome harangues **Mr. Gladstone.** that lengthened the days in the earlier development of the debate Mr. Gladstone had followed the speakers with an intensity physically wearying to himself as it was embarrassing to those near him. As he sat at the end of the Treasury Bench, with hand to ear, drinking in every word of Mr. Sexton's giant speech, he grew visibly older and more haggard. Each one of the five half hours over which the merciless harangue stretched seemed to add a full year to his more than fourscore. To-night, business being at hand, and he having to take prominent part in it, he was almost perfectly at rest. He returned in dinner dress with a flower in his coat, looking quite gay set in the dun ranks of his colleagues, whom a stern sense of duty had restricted to morning dress. Once, when Mr. Balfour was approaching the end of his discourse, he reached forth his hand and, producing the pomatum pot brought into use only on historic occasions, helped himself to a generous dose of its contents. That proved to be rather a matter of precaution than of necessity. The utterance of his opening sentence showed him to be in full possession of the finest notes of his marvellous voice.

Early in his speech he disposed of what he called the copious mass of matter discharged since the debate opened, characterising it in four phrases. The first of the p   fu weapons wielded by the Opposition was bold assertion; the second, persistent exaggeration; the third, constant misconstruction; the fourth, copious, arbitrary, and baseless prophecy. This concise summary might well have sufficed for the occasion. But the Premier proceeded with un-failing vigour for little more than an hour to discuss what he. insisted was the question, "How is Ireland to be governed?" That, he showed, had not been answered by Mr. Balfour or others. Twenty years of firm government was Lord Salisbury's panacea. What had become of that nostrum now? Lord Salisbury had had his chance seven years ago.

"Never again," said Mr. Gladstone, pointing to Mr. Balfour, amid thundering cheers, "will you have a majority of 120 at your back to enable you to coerce Ireland against the wishes of her people."

Even amid the heat of controversy, and driven into a corner by the prolixity of others, Mr. Gladstone found time to pay a warm and graceful compliment to the maiden speech of Mr. Austen Chamberlain. "It was," he said, turning towards his old colleague, who bowed low his acknowledgments, "dear and re-freshing to a father's heart." He spoke for an hour and ten minutes, with unsparing use of his voice, and with animated gestures, including that uplifting of both hands above his head invoked only on supreme occa-sions. Often when he resumes his seat after a great speech he shows unmistakable signs of fatigue, even approaching collapse. This morning he finished almost as fresh as he had commenced, and when the Speaker put the question involving the rejection of Sir Michael Beach's hostile amendment his shout of "No!" rose in full-chested note above the roar of his followers.

He might well have spared himself that ex-penditure of force. It was as if the principal tenor, having sung his solo, joined in the chorus. But an effort more or less was evidently nothing to the lusty octogenarian in this hour of triumph.

For a moment after the House was cleared for the division the centre of interest was diverted from the Premier in quite another direction. Where was Mr. Saunders, and what, after all, was he going to do? Only on the previous night that eminent and impeccable democrat, brought face to face with his irate constituents, had openly defied them, and announced his intention of voting against the second reading of the Home Rule Bill. Would he be as good as his word? or had he at the last moment found salvation? Early in the evening, when Mr. John Burns was observed earnestly engaged in missionary work, doubts as to his powers of resistance found expression.

The Comparative Value of a Lost Sheep.

"I'll bet my shirt," said a well-known and shrewd Conservative, "that Saunders goes with the Ministry."

"Well," said another, gazing reflectively on the velveteen jacket of the member for Walworth, closely buttoned up to the throat over the black stock, "that is not a bet you can make in kind with Saunders."

Had it been booked the Conservative member would certainly have won something, for, as the wave of Ministerialists dashed into the division lobby, it was seen to be bearing on its crest the velveteen coat which but yesterday was to Democracy even as the white plume of Henry of Navarre to the Protestant host on the plains of Ivry.

Anxious Moments.

The Prince of Wales watched with keen interest the slowly developed scene of the division. When the Speaker gave the signal for clearing the House the multitude massed on either side of the Chair rose with one accord and, meeting in turbulent streams midway on the floor, passed each other on the way to the lobbies. There was no doubt within a unit or two how the majority would go. It would certainly be forty. It might be forty-one, and since Mr. Saunders had returned to the fold those who had made exact calculation knew it must be forty-three. Nevertheless, when Mr. Marjoribanks, who had been telling with Mr. Akers Douglas for the "Noes," came back beaming, anxious eyes, turned towards the doorway under the clock, saw, moment after moment, the Ministerial host still streaming in. An uneasy feeling spread over the Opposition benches. It seemed mathematically impossible that the majority could exceed forty-three. Yet why tarried the chariot of the Whips who were "telling" the apparently interminable majority?

All eyes still bent upon the doorway under the clock. Mr. Gladstone was seen slowly making his way through the group which thronged the bar. When those composing it found who it was gently forcing his way, they opened a lane through which he walked with head erect and springy step. At sight of him the Ministerialists with one accord sprang to their feet, waved their hats, and frantically cheered. The cheering was renewed when at length announcement was made that the second reading of the Home Rule Bill had been carried by 347 votes to 304. Behind the rows of excited Ministerialists on the two front benches below the gangway a glimpse was caught of the line of Liberal Unionists, with Mr. Chamberlain at their head, stubbornly seated. Mr. Chamberlain smiled pleasantly as, the thunder of cheers dying away, the voice of Mr. William Redmond was heard calling aloud for "three cheers for Parnell."

Mr. Parnell, however, had his ovation four years ago, when the Liberals, led by Mr. Gladstone, leaped to their feet, welcoming the Irish chief as he entered the House on the eve of the day of Piggot's flight. Now Mr. Parnell is dead and buried, forgotten by all but the grotesque yet faithful Irishman who has planted himself out among the flower of the British aristocracy above the gangway on the Conservative side.

CHAPTER IX.

THE RIFT WIDENING.

SIR WILLIAM HARCOURT this afternoon opened the exposition of his Budget scheme before the smallest audience for many years gathered on a similar occasion. He had, as was speedily made clear, a depressing message to deliver, and his manner was attuned to the occasion. He commenced by casting a regretful glance backward. Up to 1890 the Chancellor of the Exchequer was in possession of increasing surpluses. In 1891 he passed on to a descending plane, and since that time he had been going down at accelerated pace. With few exceptions, all the main sources of revenue showed a decrease. In one of his Budgets Mr. Goschen had spoken of the rush to alcohol. Sir William Harcourt had now to report a stampede from alcohol, with the consequence of diminished revenue from excise. Still, there was a bright side of the picture. The returns of the income tax and of the probate duty supplied irrefragable evidence of the solid advance of the wealth of the nation, and formed conclusive answer to those who affirmed that the country is being ruined by a vicious commercial system.

This position the Chancellor supported by the statement that in the year 1886 a penny in the pound on income tax yielded £1,980,000, while last year it was £2,261,000. He added the interesting fact that in 1842, when Sir Robert Peel first introduced the income tax, the yield per penny was £770,000. If that state of things still existed, it would be necessary, in order to obtain the current aggregate yield of income tax, that

the rate should be fixed at eighteenpence in the pound,
a prospect from which the Committee shrank with
visible horror.

One drag on the Treasury is the unremunerative
returns of the Post Office and Telegraphs. The
country, Sir William pointed out, is, in the increased
expenditure of the Post Office, reaping the harvest of
the complacency with which some years ago increased
charges in the way of wages were forced upon the
House of Commons. As for the Telegraphs, he
reckoned that the loss accruing since the acquisition
of the Service was equal to four and a half millions
sterling. It is going from bad to worse, and with
the competition of the telephone this tendency will
increase.

"A Miserable Mouse of a Surplus." The total expenditure for last year
amounted to £90,375,000, and the total
revenue receipts reached £90,395,000. This
left a balance to the credit of last year of
£20,000, a miserable mouse of a surplus not to be
mentioned when, as the Chancellor of the Exchequer
reminded the Committee, Mr. Goschen's system of
finance had last year involved a borrowing of two
millions in order to give an appearance of making both
ends meet. The increased expenditure of last year
was principally due to excess in two departments,
education costing £310,000 more, and the Post Office
exceeding by £635,000 the expenses of the previous
year. In addition, there was raised by Imperial
taxation a sum of 7¼ millions, handed over in relief of
local taxation. This brought the total expenditure of
last year up to 98¾ millions, a sum dangerously near the
round 100 millions which a few years ago was regarded
as belonging only to periods of war.

Turning to the coming financial year, Sir William
reckoned the expenditure at £91,464,000, for which
he had an estimated revenue of £89,890,000. That
left a deficit of something over a million and a half.

How was it to be provided for ? he asked, and paused for half a moment in his rapid recital of facts and figures.

There was, in truth, nothing left but the income tax. An addition of a penny would in the first year realise a sum of a million and three-quarters. That, Sir William added, will just cover the deficit, and leave a small margin over.

27th April.
Attempt
to Shoot Mr.
Gladstone.

It was only last year Mr. Plunket, then First Commissioner of Works, caused to be let into the floor of the lobby of the old House of Commons a brass tablet showing the spot at which Bellingham lurked, waiting till Prime Minister Percival should pass within sure range of his pistol. On a May evening seventy-one years ago the sound of this pistol echoed through the House of Commons and the Premier fell mortally wounded. People think of the incident to-day when the streets are resonant with the cry of the newsboys announcing extra specials with full particulars of the alleged design for bringing about a fresh turn in the Home Rule controversy by shooting Mr. Gladstone.

This modern Bellingham from Sheffield seems to be a poor crank with such balance as his head at any time maintained upset by reading a succession of speeches by Unionist orators. But there is no mistake about the pistol, with its four chambers loaded, one emptied in the direction of the policeman who had barred his further advance along Downing Street. Townsend may be mad, but, as his actions and the entries in his diary show, there was a nasty method in his madness. If he had chanced to come across the Premier there is little doubt, from the readiness with which he fired when challenged by the policeman, that he would have done his best to shoot him.

Townsend is described, on the authority of his wife, as "a quiet, respectable man of thirty-six," who, it is added, "loses his mental balance now and then."

That is all very well, but even quiet, respectable men cannot be permitted to haunt Downing Street at midnight with loaded pistols avowedly intended for the Premier and incidentally discharged at a policeman.

"The Reason Why." Townsend kept a diary written up in anticipation of his being arrested after having more or less successfully carried out his designs on Mr. Gladstone. It is headed " The Reason Why." The passing of the second reading of the Home Rule Bill by the full Ministerial majority of forty-three, "including that cur Saunders," seems to have brought Mr. Townsend up to the shooting point. "That cur Saunders" is the hon. member for Walworth, who, returned by his constituency to support the Home Rule Bill, showed at the last moment signs of ratting, but found salvation just in time to vote for the Bill.

" All this talking," Mr. Townsend jots down in his diary, " appears not to have made a single convert." However, " It is now time for action. What was the use of the Ulster men howling and calling him (Mr. Gladstone) a traitor? That won't upset the Bill," writes practical - minded, quiet, respectable Mr. Townsend. Accordingly he loads his pistol and prepares to set forth for Downing Street. But here scruple seems to have presented itself to his mind. "There is," he writes, "such a thing as wilful murder." Mr. Townsend would evidently stop at that. " And yet it might be simply and purely justifiable homicide. Now to prove it."

Here is a man, of unsettled mind, meditating murder, but finding it necessary before he undertakes the work to convince himself that it is nothing worse than justifiable homicide. How does he go about the task? He turns to the speeches of the orators and guides of the party of Law and Order. " What said Sir Henry James, one of the greatest lawyers in the land, and yet one of the kindest of men?

What said Colonel Saunderson?" Here for the time the record breaks off. The police-court magistrate, evidently appalled at the vista opening up before him, abruptly stopped the reading of the diary at this point.

Mr. Gladstone's Way Home. Reflection upon the habits of Mr. Gladstone adds seriousness to the possibility of there lurking about men looking him up pistol in hand. He is accustomed when he dines out to walk home unattended. If the house where he has been dining is distant more than a mile from Downing Street the carriage will call for him, but invariably sets him down at some point whence he may take at least a quarter of an hour's brisk walk on his way home to bed. His route generally lies across the space of ground between St. James's Park and the Horse Guards—a lonely waste, favourable for the enterprise of *Messieurs les assassins*.

It was Townsend's ignorance of the Premier's habits that led to his escape last night. He had been dining at Mr. Stuart Rendel's, on Carlton House Terrace, and remained for some time to greet the guests bidden to a reception held after dinner. Shortly after 11 o'clock he left, and, passing down the Duke of York's steps, crossed the Horse Guards' ground, entering No. 1, Downing Street by the back-garden gate. Townsend, who apparently knew the Premier was out dining, naturally came to the conclusion that he would return in his carriage and enter his house by the front door. Thus he skulked about Downing Street, and was arrested by the policeman at the time when Mr. Gladstone, having quietly entered by the garden gate, was in his bedroom.

28th April. A Bloodless Duel. It would be idle to attempt to conceal the fact that for a moment, towards the close of this morning's sitting, the House, speaking of it in its aggregate capacity, held its breath. No one could say whether within the next fifteen seconds Mr. George Curzon would

leap across the table and shake conviction into
the mind of the Chancellor of the Duchy, or whether
Mr. Bryce would make the first move in what seemed
must be the inevitable tussle taking place on the
Opposition side of the table.   Nor might anyone
foretell with certainty the issue of the struggle.
Mr. James Lowther, who before he took his seat
on the judicial bench in connection with the
great Jockey Club case had seen a thing or two,
looked on with critical glance.   Mr. Curzon had the
advantage in respect of height, and, having of late
returned from an adventurous journey in the Far
East, might be supposed to be in good training.   But
Mr. Bryce is wiry and well set, and has not, it may be
assumed, studied for naught gladiatorial episodes in
the history of the Holy Roman Empire.

Amid a scene of throbbing excitement the two
stood, each, with hands resting on the table, craning
forward his neck so as to get as near as possible to the
other.   The attitude could not fail to recall to the mind
of Mr. James Lowther reminiscences of far-off days
when, casually passing by, he may have chanced to
observe the preparations for a cock fight.   What confidences the two exchanged across the table no man
knoweth.   They spoke simultaneously at the top of
their voices.   Unluckily it happened at the same time
everyone else in other parts of the House was shouting (also at the top of his voice), " Order, order! "   At
length, amid the hubbub, the Speaker was discovered
on his feet, and the combatants, regretfully parting,
slowly resumed their seats.

Mystic Incantations.   Strange to say, this happily bloodless
conflict had nothing to do with the Irish
question.   The scene of its origin lay no
nearer Dublin than the shores of Lancashire.   It was
all about the borough bench at Southport and its
alleged composition as divided among political
parties.

"Nineteen, two, and eleven," * was Mr. Curzon's slogan, the last words he flung across the table at Mr. Bryce when he was at length borne down by cries of "Order!" and the increasingly stern interposition of the Speaker.

"Fifteen, thirteen, two," was Mr. Bryce's answering cry.

This retort will, perhaps, convey no intelligence to the mind of the ordinary reader. But its effect on Mr. Curzon may be described by no other word than terrific. Ordinarily his manner is marked by the imperturbability that comes of consciousness of personal superiority. He is able to greet with a smile of mingled geniality and pity attempts from other quarters to set him right on matters of fact or opinion. To-day this mysterious battle-cry uplifted by the Chancellor of the Duchy wrought upon him baneful effect. He was almost beside himself with rage, and but for the presence of the table, which on an earlier and historic occasion kept the peace between two even more eminent men, no one can say what might have happened to Mr. Bryce.

Oddly enough Mr. Curzon's mystic incantation, "Nineteen, two, and eleven," when shouted across the table, had almost equally stirring results upon the Chancellor of the Duchy. Mr. Bryce has long been known to the House as a gentleman of profound erudition and philosophical temperament. He has corrected Mr. Chamberlain's impressions as to the working of the minuter wheels of the American Constitution without departing, in appreciable degree, from the placidity of his ordinary manner. Now the utterance of this Southport Shibboleth strangely moved him, and as it reverberated through the House he was only less excited than Mr. Curzon when there dropped

* Curzon's sentence, with the hiatus filled up, would run—"19 Liberals, 2 Independents, 11 Conservatives." Mr. Bryce averred that there were 15 Liberals, 2 Independents, and 13 Conservatives.

on his agonised ear the evidently effective retort, " Fifteen, thirteen, two."

A Morning Sitting; and Five Minutes for Business. As the Speaker observed, with a moderation and gravity that strikingly contrasted with the excitement at the table, " This is altogether unusual." It was, however, merely an episode in a quaintly ordered afternoon. A morning sitting commences at two o'clock. Whatever debate is to the fore automatically closes at ten minutes to seven, and at seven o'clock the Speaker leaves the Chair, the sitting being suspended for a couple of hours. To-day the main business of the sitting was to make progress with the Employers' Liability Bill. In the four hours that might reasonably have been expected to be devoted to this measure the adjourned debate might have been concluded, and the Bill sent rejoicing on its way. But the Orders of the Day were not reached till a quarter to seven, exactly five minutes of the whole sitting being thus available for legislative purposes.

Two private Bills appropriated the first three hours, and an epidemic of questions did the rest. Mr. Morley has been spending a few days in Ireland, and questions addressed to the Chief Secretary accumulated in formidable heaps. The peculiarity of questions affecting Ireland is that though only one may appear upon the printed paper, it is sure to prove the progenitor of a large family. What actually takes place upon a question relating to Ireland being put to a Minister is a miniature debate. To-day Mr. Sexton opened the proceedings with a formidable bar of iron, which he alleged had been one of the arguments used in recent controversy between Catholics and Protestants occurring in the streets of Belfast; holding it in his hand, he addressed to the Chief Secretary a speech of some length, setting forth in the interrogative form made imperative by Parliamentary rules a narrative from the Catholic point of view of events in Belfast.

From the other side up rose Mr. Arnold-Forster, with a speech nearly equally long, setting forth, also in the form of questions, a statement of the case as viewed from the Protestant standpoint. Mr. Morley made one or two speeches in reply. Mr. W. Redmond gave his view of the question, also clumsily masking assertion in the form of interrogation.

It is a curious game, each one who contributes to it being anxious only to formulate his question, being absolutely indifferent as to whether or not he draws an answer. That it is a gross and inconvenient evasion of a wholesome rule is frankly acknowledged; but that does not affect prevalence of the practice.

Disorderly Questions. According to the standing order, members desiring to obtain information from a Minister on a given subject shall hand in at the table the terms of their question fairly written out. These are considered by the Speaker, and if approved are printed. Even then a member is not permitted to waste the time of the House by reciting his question, but may only call attention to it by quoting its number in the ordered list.

That is an excellent arrangement, conceived in the interests of public business, and is jealously observed. Bearing it in mind, it will be almost incredible to the outsider that, nevertheless, a member may rise and with impunity break every one of the rules that environ the privilege of questioning members. He may not only put a question the terms of which have not undergone supervision by the Speaker, but he may inflict on the House that full recital forbidden to the member who has observed the ordinances that govern business. It is true that if the question is out of order the Speaker interposes; but in the meantime the mischief is done and the object of the member attained.

To-day Mr. Keir Hardie, incited by the example of Mr. Sexton and Mr. Arnold-Forster, managed to get a

side hit at a member of the House belonging to what
he regards as the criminal classes—that is, the
employers of labour.   Thrice the Speaker interposed
whilst he read the terms of what he called his
"question."   It was not answered, and was pronounced by the Speaker out of order, as importing
statements that ought not to appear in a question.
But what of that?   Mr. Keir Hardie had effected his
purpose, obtained a gratuitous advertisement for
himself, and struck at an opponent, the very irregu-
larity of his attack investing it with safety, since
there would be no opportunity of refutation.

It was this kind of thing that irresistibly, and
more or less agreeably, occupied the remainder of the
sitting, leading the House up to a quarter to seven
o'clock, with the already famous five minutes in
which to dispose of the Orders of the Day.   The first
proposed the second reading of the Treasury Chest
Fund Bill.   Sir William Harcourt, by a gesture,
moved the second reading; and in the excitement of
the moment, the House still seething with emotion
consequent on the encounter between the Southport
Chicken and the Ducal Digits, the stage might have
been taken.   But Mr. Hanbury had his eye on the
Treasury Bench, and was quick to arrest machinations
from that suspected quarter.   He was not to be put
off by the raising of the Chancellor of the Exchequer's
hat.   He wanted to know all about the Treasury
Chest, what was hid in its recesses, and what it was
proposed should be done therewith.   It would have
been easy for him to talk out the Bill.   Five minutes
would do it.   But Mr. Hanbury knew better than
that.   By a careful subdivision of time he left the
Chancellor of the Exchequer exactly two minutes in
which to explain.

Sir William was engaged on the task when the
hands of the clock touched ten minutes to seven, and
thus the Minister talked out his own Bill.

The gentleman under whose will Mr. Burt

1st May.
A Windfall
for Mr. Burt.

benefits to the extent of a legacy of £2,000 was the late Mr. Stephens, a well-known member of the Reform Club. He had no personal acquaintance with the Parliamentary Secretary to the Board of Trade, but so much admired his public character and career that he desired to pay this mark of appreciation. The gracefulness of the act was completed by the special direction that the gift should be handed over free of legacy duty.

The House of Commons has been enjoying

4th May.
Domestic
Troubles.

the luxury of an off week. The Home Rule Bill, read the second time a fortnight ago, stands for committee next Monday. In the meantime the affairs of other parts of the still United Kingdom have received an unaccustomed measure of attention. Having only ordinary business to deal with, the proceedings in the Commons have been by comparison dull, exception to the prevalent tone being found in the evergreen Premier. The course of events has brought him face to face with two of the most difficult problems that embarrass his Ministry. One is Egypt, the other the question of the eight-hours day. The difficulty common to these situations is that they divide the Liberal Party. It is easy enough for a Minister with a majority in the House of Commons to deal with the ordinary Opposition. His serious trouble begins when he finds his enemies are those of his own household.

On the Egyptian question the motion calling upon the Government forthwith to fulfil their pledges to evacuate the country was moved by a prominent Liberal and seconded by another. Although the motion was not pressed and there was no sign of general revolt below the gangway, Mr. Gladstone knows very well that a majority of his followers are desirous of seeing the country relieved from the

responsibilities incurred in Egypt. On the question
of the eight-hours day the cleavage is even more
striking, splitting up the Cabinet itself. Mr. Gladstone's own conversion is a remarkable event, and
is characteristically conditioned. He would, he said,
vote for the second reading of the Bill in charge of
Mr. S. Woods, but could not promise what he would
do on the third reading, treating himself to the
unusual luxury of definite declaration to the extent
that he will not be able to support the principle
of coercion. Of course, the Bill without coercion
would convey nothing more than a benevolent
intention.

I have a vivid recollection of sitting by
Mr. Gladstone in the parlour of a manse
in Midlothian one July afternoon in last
year.   It was at a place called Gorebridge, the centre of a populous mining district,
throbbing with interest in the midst of what might
prove the last Midlothian campaign. Mr. Gladstone
had delivered a big speech at Stow, a picturesque
little village almost touching the Selkirk border of
the constituency. He went on to Gorebridge, where
he had another speech to deliver. In accordance
with the pleasant homely custom of the campaign
he accepted an invitation to tea at the manse.
After the meal, served in state in the drawing-
room, he was informed that five delegates, representing the mining community, were waiting to see
him in the dining-room. He knew the nature of
their errand and was fully alive to the embarrassment of the situation. The miners' vote is exceedingly valuable in Midlothian, and the Scotch miners
are in favour of the eight-hours day. But Northumberland and Durham take another view of the question,
and on this very day Mr. Gladstone's colleague, Mr.
John Morley, was fighting Newcastle with his back
to the wall in favour of non-intervention.

[Side note:] Mr. Gladstone and the Scotch Miners.

When Mr. Gladstone entered the dining-room
he found the five delegates standing stiffly in a row,
for the moment speechless. He endeavoured to put
them at ease with beaming smile and hearty hand-
shake. Like Mr. Lincoln when in a tight place, he
had a story to tell them. It was about a public
dinner he had attended a quarter of a century
earlier, where he met an old man who had been
at work in a colliery at the time of the Peninsular
war. His wages, he said, were at the rate of 11s.
a week, whilst wheat was selling at 20s. a bushel,
and the necessaries of life were equally dear.

It was a pretty story, with point and application.
But if Mr. Gladstone thought it would put these
sturdy Scotsmen off the business they had come
about he made a mistake. They wanted the labour
day to be eight hours long, and they wanted Mr.
Gladstone, when he came into power, to pass a Bill
enacting the regulation. It was a striking scene,
worthy of the pa ' brush, to see Mr. Gladstone,
presently seated with his elbow resting on his stick,
his hand to his ear, attentively listening, whilst in
the gloaming in the little manse parlour these five
miners, dressed all in their best, each in turn
addressed the candidate.

Driving back to Dalmeny Mr. Gladstone spoke,
with a twinkle in his eye, of the effective rejoinder
of one of the pitmen. Mr. Gladstone had trotted
out Northumberland and Durham as implacable
against the Eight Hours Bill.

" Yes," said the eldest miner, with his eye steadily
fixed on the ceiling, " but in this affair Northumberland and Durham occupy to the rest of the miners
of Great Britain the position Ulster holds on the Home
Rule question towards the rest of Ireland."

" An admirable point promptly and neatly made,"
said Mr. Gladstone, with generous appreciation of
an awkward rejoinder.

In some of its moods nothing is sacred to the House of Commons, not even the person of one of the editors of Bullen and Leake's "Precedents of Pleading" (Fourth Edition). This Mr. Cyril Dodd discovered when, at the comparatively early hour of twenty-five minutes to twelve to-night, he proposed to take part in the debate on Sir Charles Dilke's amendment raising the question of the appointment of county magistrates.

It is true the House was demoralised by the rapture of deliverance from the boredom of long speeches. Mr. Balfour's services to the country and Parliament are conspicuous; none stands higher than that done to-night. Yielding to the solicitations from some of his supporters, Mr. Gladstone had consented to suspend the Twelve o'Clock Rule. It was all settled. The Twelve o'Clock Rule would have been suspended; three members would have made speeches, which, if only an hour long, would have been moderate measured by the standard established during debate on the Home Rule Bill; there would have been a scramble for the Speaker's eye after midnight; and somewhere between one and two this morning a wearied House would have divided. Mr. Balfour stepped in with the daring suggestion that instead of opening the gates to indefinite talk members should make shorter speeches. He fixed the maximum of his own contribution at twenty minutes, and, as he pointed out, if that average were observed, nine members might take part in the debate at the evening sitting, an unprecedentedly large number. As a matter of fact, thirteen members spoke, and on the stroke of midnight the House was cleared for a division.

This occurrence was accidental, but the accident was too beneficent, and the conclusion too happy, to permit it to pass without grave consideration. It will be admitted by all who sat through the three hours that the debate

was one of the brightest and most pointed that
has taken place in the House of Commons since
the new Parliament met. Not only was the general
effect as regards the thrashing out of the question and the comfort of the audience far happier than
usual, but individual members greatly benefited by
the conditions under which they spoke. Once, as
Boswell charmingly records, he was talking about
Johnson's only half belief in second sight.

The evidence is enough for me, but not for his
great mind," said Boswell. "What will not fill a quart
bottle will fill a pint bottle. I'm filled with belief."

" Are you ? " said Colman ; " then cork it up."

On this question of the appointment of county
magistrates Sir Charles Dilke was filled with facts and
illustrations. There is no doubt that having all the
night before him where to choose, he would, as he did
on Monday night when speaking on the Egyptian
Question, have gone on for a full hour and a half.
To-night, thanks to Mr. Balfour, " Cork it up " was
the watchword. Sir Charles was overflowing with
facts and figures, but, compelled by the exigencies of
the time to be moderately brief, he effectively stated
his case, corking up the redundancy.

Another speaker who vastly profited by the discipline was Mr. Dillon. He can, if need be (indeed,
whether or no), converse with the House in monologue
for a couple of hours. Of all who spoke to-night he was
the only one who transgressed the twenty-minute limit.
But it was only to the extent of five minutes, and Mr.
Dillon will to-morrow morning doubtless be astonished
at his own moderation. If he will only feel assured
of the immense addition to force and point gained for
his speech by compulsory compression he will have
gained an invaluable lesson.

Two Oratorical Styles. To Mr. Asquith the conditions of the
debate were lightly borne, since upon
other occasions they are self-imposed.

F

The Home Secretary rarely exceeds three-quarters of an hour, and prefers twenty minutes, even in making an important contribution from the Treasury Bench to a set debate. Last night he and his department were sharply arraigned by Mr. Havelock Wilson and Mr. John Burns in connection with the action of the naval and military forces at Hull. Mr. Asquith did not occupy more than ten minutes in making reply, and when he sat down it was felt that he had left nothing unsaid. It chanced there was simultaneously supplied for the counsel and guidance of the Parliamentary student an example of another way of dealing with the difficulty. Mr. Mundella was arraigned under the same indictment. Conscious of his own innocence of evil intent, inspired by recollection of the infinite effort he had taken to do the right thing by all men, the President of the Board of Trade, holding a bushel of notes in his hand, threw himself with eloquent vigour into the controversy and talked convincingly for fully half-an-hour. An immediate result was to bring up Mr. Balfour with a speech he avowedly had not intended to make. Mr. Balfour brought up Mr. Gladstone, and if it had not been so near the dinner-hour someone else would have followed Mr. Gladstone. As it was, a good half-hour that might well have been employed in advancing business was appropriated for the delivery of sp   that grew out of the luxurious wealth of Mr. Mundella's language.

Mr. Disraeli's Manner. To-night's experiment, deliberately made and honourably carried out, opens up a new and attractive era in Parliamentary life. It is no new thing to have it demonstrated that, in ninety-nine cases out of a hundred, it is quite possible for a man to say all that is useful to utter on a particular question within the space of twenty minutes. The person chiefly responsible for the disease of verbosity that saps the vitals of the

present House of Commons is undoubtedly Mr. Gladstone. He has the excuse that he can talk continuously for an hour, or even for two hours, and still
charm his audience. That is a gift happily bestowed
on few men. Certainly it was not in the possession
of the late Mr. Disraeli. All his best and most effective debating speeches were delivered within the limits
of twenty minutes, a favourite measure of time with
·him when he was able to consult his taste and inclination. Sometimes it happened that, weighed upon with
a sense of responsibility and of the importance of his
position as Leader on either side of the House, he
thought it proper to speak for an hour or even longer.
Ever in these circumstances there were arid tracts of
more or less g e u commonplace, here and there
lighted up with flashes of the genius which, if untram-
melled, would have sparkled uninterruptedly for
twenty minutes, charming if not convincing.

Mr. Dodd was so delighted with the suc-
Embarrassing Enthusiasm. cess of the new departure in Parliamentary
debate that he felt he could not do less
than take part in it. As mentioned, he seemed to find
his opportunity at a favourable hour. Doing a sum in
mental arithmetic with that rapidity natural to a man
who took a first-class in mathematics at Oxford, Mr.
Dodd perceived that if he spoke for twenty minutes
there would just be five minutes for the Speaker to
put the question and get the House cleared for the
division before the statutory closing hour of midnight.
The member for Maldon had done honour to the
occasion by donning evening dress. Moreover, as he
carried a roll of notes in his right hand and bowed
courteously to the Speaker on rising, the impression
was strengthened that he was about to favour the
company with a song. A flush of pride and pleasure
mantled his brow at his reception. A roar of applause
almost angry in its vehemence greeted him. Members
had evidently been spending the interval between the

morning and evening sitting in studying Bullen and
Leake's "Precedents of Pleading" (Fourth Edition),
and were glad to see " one of the editors " in the flesh.
Mr. Dodd stood beaming and bowing, making acknowledgment of a friendly reception which increased in
warmth and volume. It even grew embarrassing as
there appeared no opening for the setting forth of the
new precedent of pleading with which the hon. and
learned member was evidently charged. He had
been apparently speaking for some moments when
in a lull in the storm he was heard to remark :
" Now let me say one word—"
The crowded House, elate at the prospect, almost
howled in their delight. Mr. Dodd, with his eye fixed
on the Ladies' Gallery, and an expression of anguish
dispelling the beaming glance with which he had first
gazed upon his audience, still seemed to go on talking.
" I will now read—" he was heard to say ; at which
the roar of approval distinctly gained in volume.
" In the division I have the honour to represent—"
was the next remark in his ordered speech that was
comparatively- audible.
There was not much in it, but members on both
sides insisted upon applauding it with such inconvenient pertinacity and enthusiasm that the Speaker
interposed with the stern cry of "Order, order!"
Hereupon there was a lull. But it lasted only long
enough for Mr. Dodd to restate the point at which
his voice a moment ago had been lost in the storm.
" I was saying in the division I have the honour to
represent—"
What he was saying no man knoweth, nor woman
either, albeit Mr. Dodd, with head thrown back and a
strange look in his face as of a drowning man clutching at a straw, still kept his eyes fixed on the *grille*
of the Ladies' Gallery. Apparently, since he unbound
the scroll that had been hastily taken for his music
and held it open before him, Mr. Dodd proceeded to

read something. This conclusion was strengthened when, in a momentary pause on the part of the so-called audience, there rang out the shout, "My correspondent says——"

This prospect of not only having Mr. Dodd on the scene but an anonymous correspondent further increased the enthusiasm that bubbled all around the orator. Once more the Speaker interposed and secured for Mr. Dodd the opportunity of delivering the only completed sentence in a speech that occupied ten minutes in the delivery—

"I recognise the time has gone by for speaking on this matter."

The recognition was a trifle tardy; but as Mr. Dodd hereupon sat down on his hat a wild cheer rang forth, the like of which has rarely resounded in the House of Commons even as a tribute to the eloquence of Mr. Gladstone or Mr. Bright.

CHAPTER X.

IN COMMITTEE ON THE BILL.

COMMITTEE on the Home Rule Bill, com-
8th May. menced to-day, promises to be not only
one of the most important, but one of the
most interesting episodes in Parliamentary history.
It forthwith transformed the House from an indifferent, somewhat idly-disposed assembly, into one
stern of purpose, throbbing with zeal. For the first
time since the new Parliament sat members made
arrangements to be in attendance day after day, and
practically all through each sitting. Dinner pairs are
allowed, but it is a point of honour on both sides to
arrange no other, save in cases of absolute urgency.
For the most part members dine in the House, a sore
strain upon Party fealty, or, being Conservatives, go
across to St. Stephen's Club, where they dine something after the fashion of the Children of Israel at
Passover time, with staff in hand and loins girded.

12th May. There was one thrilling moment in yester-
Mr. Chamber- day afternoon's debate when it seemed
lain Astonishes that a powerful mind had tottered to its
his Friends. fall, that midsummer madness had
attacked one of the coolest intellects of the day. It
happened towards four o'clock, when Mr. T. W.
Russell was on his feet, discussing Clause I. of the
Home Rule Bill in a voice pitched perhaps unnecessarily high. There had just been one of those out-
breaks of angry interruption which frequently mark
Mr. Russell's contributions to debate. He was commenting upon it. Mr. Mellor had interposed in mildest
manner an ordinary inquiry. Then across the suddenly

stilled House was heard a familiar voice sharply saying—

" What the devil are you talking about ?"

With swift pained movement members with one accord turned in the direction of the voice and beheld Mr. Chamberlain leaning forward in his seat, looking straight at the Chairman, with stern even angered expression, his lips firmly closed after utterance of the inquiry here unwillingly quoted.

For an Irish member to flout the authority of the Chair and personally attack its occupant are matters of too common occurrence to excite more than passing remark. For an ex-Cabinet Minister, a leader of debate, a chief among the gentlemen of England, to use language of this kind from his place in the House of Commons, addressed to the Chairman of Ways and Means, was a different matter.

All a Mistake. Happily it turned out that the first impression of the incident, natural as it seemed, was founded upon entire misapprehension. The words cited by Mr. Chamberlain had been used by an Irish member opposite, and were addressed to Mr. Russell. Mr. Vicary Gibbs, anxious that they should not be lost to posterity, had moved " That the words be taken down."

" What words are they ? " asked the Chairman, who last night had plaintively protested there was so much noise he had heard nothing. It was here Mr. Chamberlain had interposed, and was merely citing for the Chairman's information the words, as they reached his ear, floated across the troubled atmosphere of the House.

Then began a mad hunt for the earliest appropriator of the phrase. " Who had used the words ? " the Chairman asked, and Mr. Russell promptly replied by indicating Mr. Swift MacNeill. The member for South Donegal was called upon to plead, and indignantly declared, upon his honour, that he had not used the expression or, as he was particular to add, one word of it. In this assertion he was supported by Mr. Dillon, Mr. Macartney chivalrously coming to the assistance of a lively political adversary and bearing testimony to Mr. MacNeill's innocency.

Had he stopped there all would have been well. But in the mysterious voice that had worked this incantation on a moderately quiet Committee he believed he recognised that of Mr. Sexton. A moment's consideration would have suggested caution in framing this new indictment. Mr. Macartney must have known by long experience that Mr. Sexton is not in the habit of addressing the House with the comparative brevity of the speech cited. In the hurry and excitement of the moment he had not time to reflect on this obvious fact, and plunged into the assertion that Mr. Sexton was the gentleman so anxiously sought for. Mr. Sexton rose and hotly denied the soft impeachment.

Matters were now growing a little mixed.

Apologies All Round. There were at least a dozen other Irish members seated in the quarter whence the mysterious voice had issued. Two had been cited and pleaded not guilty. It would be a simple process to go on naming them one by one till the guilty person was found. Mr. Johnston of Bally-kilbeg turned uneasily in his seat and eyed his compatriots. Mr. Justin McCarthy sat next to Mr. Sexton. He certainly did not look the kind of man to use language of the emphasis that marked the implicated interrogation. But if the thing was to be done at all it must be done thoroughly, and Mr. McCarthy was certainly the next man in line.

Whilst Mr. Johnston hesitated the scene entered upon a new phase. Mr. MacNeill majestically rose and, turning upon Mr. Vicary Gibbs, opened his mouth to fullest extent. In the heat and excitement of the moment a horrible suspicion flashed across the minds of onlookers. It seemed as if a vacancy in St.

Albans was imminent, owing to the proximate disappearance of the sitting member swallowed whole by
the indignant Irishman. But Mr. MacNeill had
opened his mouth with unusual liberality simply to
give fuller volume to the demand that Mr. Gibbs
should offer "a distinct, a humble, and an absolute
apology."

Mr. Gibbs, glad to be let off on these unexpectedly
favourable terms, forthwith apologised. Mr. Macartney
apologised to Mr. Sexton, and Mr. Johnston of Ballykilbeg tried to look as if the glance he had just cast
upon the blameless figure of Mr. Justin McCarthy
had conveyed no half-formed intention.

Here the incident closed, leaving wrapped
in mystery the identity of the offender
Oddly enough, it followed close upon a
similar misunderstanding that had enlivened the preceding sitting. On that occasion it
was Lord Randolph Churchill who was responsible for
the episode. Whilst Mr. Chamberlain was speaking
the noble Lord had suddenly leaped to his feet and
moved that the words be taken down. Here again
rose the bewildered cry, echoed from all parts of the
House, "What words?"

Lord Randolph Churchill Rebukes Sin.

There had been some hubbub among the Irish
members writhing under the lash curled about them
by Mr. Chamberlain. But no one had caught any
particularly objectionable phrase. Lord Randolph,
appealed to, declared he had distinctly heard Mr.
Healy say, "You are knocked up."

The charge was promptly denied by the inoffensive person against whom it had been directed.
But what if it were true? The interjectionary
remark was even dully innoxious. It was the
kind of thing a wife might say to her husband
returning home after spending the evening in Committee on Clause I. of the Home Rule Bill. As
applied to Mr. Chamberlain it was obviously inappro-

F *

priate.   If Mr. Healy had said anything of the kind,
he, as a shrewd observer, might have remarked, " You
are knocking them down."   It turned out that on this
occasion, by rare chance, Mr. Healy had said nothing
at all.   Lord Randolph had heard the clamour of
voices in the Irish camp.   He used in former days to
sit in close proximity with it, and was familiar with .
Mr. Healy's pleasing habit of carrying on a running
commentary.   So, jumping to a conclusion, he convinced himself that " Tim " had been at it as usual,
and that in the interests of orderly debate, of which
his Lordship has always been a distinguished advocate and exemplar, it was his duty to have the words
taken down.

This is fair inference from undisputed facts.   But
the mind goes hopelessly astray when it endeavours
to fathom the depths from which Lord Randolph drew
this imaginary phrase, or to measure the impulses
that caused him to regard it as disorderly.

The mystery is one worthy of being stored
Hopelessly   in company with the other that enshrouds
Mixed.   the identity of the member whose remark
was quoted by Mr. Chamberlain.   Combined, the
incidents bring into strong light the inconvenience
of the situation arising out of the arbitrary mixing
of parties and sections of party that obtains in
the present House of Commons.   Time was, within
recent memory, when political forces were divided
between two great parties, one sitting to the right
of the Speaker, the other to the left.   Now parties,
divided and subdivided, are inextricably mixed,
members, wherever they may chance to sit, finding
themselves environed by the foe.   One consequence
is seen in accidents such as those which yesterday
and to-day bewildered the House.   As Lord Cranborne
earlier in the Session had occasion to reflect, the privilege of thinking aloud may be enjoyed in the House
of Commons only at the utmost peril.   A man may

not murmur " Murderer ! " when a fellow member's social qualities are being catalogued, without finding himself overheard by neighbours who chance to be personal friends of the gentleman in question, and who resent such a remark as calculated to give pain in the domestic circle. Whatever other purpose it may serve, the eccentric distribution of parties on the benches of the House of Commons is fatal to the amenities of private conversation.

19th May.
The Champion
Questioner.

The House of Commons adjourned to-day for the Whitsun holidays. Before the hour of separation struck Mr. Weir managed to fire one last shot. It was a Penn-Deeley patent bolt-head discharged from a Lee-Metford Magazine Rifle, Mark II. pattern now in store. Putting the matter in Parliamentary form, Mr. Weir wanted to know whether all the Lee-Metford rifles are fitted with this particular bolt-head ? Curiosity was contagious, and an hon. member on the opposite benches timidly asked what a Penn-Deeley patent bolt-head might be ? This indicated a degree of ignorance that evidently pained Mr. Weir. Fortunately he was prepared for it. Amongst other ammunition packed about his person there chanced to be a Penn-Deeley patent bolt-head. This he produced out of his waistcoat pocket, and holding it daintily between finger and thumb he in his deepest chest notes, with just a touch of commiseration in their tone, called the hon. member's attention to it.

Mr. Weir is a special and peculiar House of Commons joke it is difficult to make understanded of the people out of doors. The student of the Parliamentary reports will never fail, on looking down the column of any day's business, to find his name appended to from two to six questions addressed to Ministers, and will invariably find the putting of the interrogation marked by " laughter " or " loud laughter." This is puzzling, since the search for

anything comic in the question proves futile. Take the
four which appeared on to-day's paper and consider
whether Joe Miller would have been inclined to include them in his choice volume.   One relates to the
Penn-Deeley patent bolt-head aforesaid.   Another de-
tects the continuance in office, contrary to the Order
in Council, of two district auditors in the employment
of the Local Government Board who have attained the
respective ages of seventy-one and sixty-five.   No. 3,
addressed to the President of the Local Government
Board, inquires if he is aware of the existence of an
excessive up-flow of sewer air at Hampstead.   No. 4
also deals with sewage, which at the present moment
divides Mr. Weir's attention with patent bolt-heads
and district auditors who linger superfluous on the
stage.   It appears that the sewer drain going through
the Nonikiln Burying Ground and a sewer drain of
Nonikiln Steading and House runs into the water
which supplies the town of Invergordon.   Does Sir
George Trevelyan, in his capacity of Secretary for
Scotland, know of these things?

This is evidently no laughing matter, but the
House laughs consumedly, and boisterously cheers the
member for Ross and Cromarty every time he rises.
The secret of this unique Parliamentary success lies
rather in charm of manner than in richness of
humour.   When Mr. Weir rises to arraign the Secretary for Scotland about that sewer drain in far-off
Invergordon he fixes him with glittering eye.   With
solemn sweep of his right arm he produces a pair of
pince-nez, which he deliberately attaches to the bridge
of his nose.   Another glance at the Treasury Bench to
see if the Minister is at attention, and then there rolls
through the House a solemn voice making announcement—

" I beg to ask the Secretary for Scotland question
No. 5."

No verbal description, no form of printed words,

could give an adequate idea of the irresistibly comic
effect of these deep chest notes. It might be done if
this page were capable of illustration by a bar of
music. Failing that, the nearest approach to con-
veyance of idea of the reality is to recall an elder
in some kirk in Ross or Cromarty giving out the first
line of a hymn.

Is He a Humourist? One additional thing that lends interest to
Mr. Weir's interposition is the doubt that
possesses the House as to whether he is
a conscious humourist or something quite otherwise.
Whilst the benches are shaking with laughter he stands
impassive, with wooden expression, waiting till the
uproar has so far subsided that his voice may be heard.
Sometimes when the hilarity is prolonged he slowly
removes his pince-nez, with the assistance of which he
was about to refer to the printed orders, and holding
it between finger and thumb, with elbow reproachfully
bent, turns and regards with haughty stare the benches
opposite, whence the uproar rises with fuller volume.
Whatever happens, he insists on going through the
formula of his question, not hurrying over a syllable,
or uplifting in haste an inflection of his solemn tones.
He may be joking or he may be simply stupid.

Up to this afternoon the secret remained locked in
his breast. Even now it can scarcely be said to be
disclosed, the mystery rather deepening. Having put
his four questions, addressed severally to the Secretary
of State for War, the Financial Secretary to the
Treasury, the President of the Local Government
Board, and the Secretary for Scotland, Mr. Weir was
presumed to have subsided. But when the printed
list of questions was exhausted he was discovered on
his watch-tower below the gangway, and members
knew that his eye was fixed upon the Chancellor of
the Exchequer. Sir William, careless of his doom
played idly with his eyeglass till startled to attention,
by hearing the familiar voice booming across the

almost empty benches. What Mr. Weir now desired
to know was whether the attention of the Chancellor
of the Exchequer had been drawn to the waste of time
consequent on putting and answering questions, and
whether he was disposed to sanction the expedient of
Ministerial answers being printed and circulated with
the votes?

Part of the always subtle humour which envelops
Mr. Weir's movements was discernible in the air of
assumption that he had just hit upon a new idea and
must lose no time in communicating it to the House.
The suggestion is, of course, as old as the incursion of
the Irish members with their illimitable armoury of
interrogation. Looking at Mr. Weir, subdued by the
solemnity of his voice and manner, it was difficult
to believe he had ever heard the suggestion publicly
made, or was otherwise than the originator. As a grave
sort of joke this appearance on the scene of a principal
offender with a proposition, whether original or
borrowed, for the repression of irrelevant and frivolous
questioners was good enough. It requires no rich en-
dowment of wit or humour, and custom has somewhat
staled its piquancy. But the House of Commons is
grateful for any tumbling that will make it laugh.
This would have served as well as anything else but for
the recurrent, bewildering question: Was the member
for Ross and Cromarty deliberately joking, with or
without " deeficulty "; or did he submit this question
in good faith without perceiving how its bearing lay in
the application thereof ?

20th May.
After Eight
Sittings in
Committee.
Mr. Gladstone has gone off to Hawarden
tolerably satisfied with the progress made
in the House of Commons with the Home
Rule Bill. It does not, stated in figures,
amount to much, being only two clauses out of forty-
one. But these two clauses are the backbone of the
Bill. By them the House of Commons has, by unex-
pectedly large majorities, decreed the establishment

ot a Home Rule Parliament and broadly defined its scope and authority. The feature in the whole business which greatly strengthens and encourages Mr. Gladstone is the maintenance of the majority at a pitch considerably above its normal height. It is the first time in Parliamentary history that through an equally long period of storm and stress a Government majority was maintained at such a level. The tendency of a Ministerial majority is to fall away. It can always be beaten up for a great effort It will not stand daily drudgery.

The majority in the present Parliament has in this respect broken the record. Whatever may happen, at whatever hour of the day or night it is called upon, it responds with hearty enthusiasm.

Anyone who closely watches the course of

The Real Leader of the Opposition. events in Committee knows that the real Leader of the Opposition, the life and soul of obstruction, is Mr. Chamberlain. It is he that sets the battle in array, sends out skirmishing parties, and is ever ready to lead an attack in person. The rank and file are already tired of a business that interferes with their social arrangements, keeps them at the House of Commons when they might be much more agreeably employed among the delights of the season. The House of Lords, they say, is sure to throw out the Bill. Why should they toil and moil when that end is inevitable?

Mr. Balfour shows by his languid manner and his hurried speech that he is sick of the whole business. But needs must when Mr. Chamberlain drives. He sits there in constant attendance, relentless, implacable, resolved at any cost to baulk Mr. Gladstone's desire, and destroy a Bill which, as he knows, his old Chief cherishes as the apple of his eye. Mr. Chamberlain may be counted upon to maintain this attitude up to the last, but he will find increasing difficulty in keeping the Opposition nose to the grindstone.

CHAPTER XI.

AT HIGH PRESSURE.

29th May.
Overcrowding. THE unprecedented attendance of members of the House of Commons just now makes wholly inadequate the arrangements in the dining-rooms. Night after night, after the division which customarily takes place before the dinner hour, there is a stampede to the dining-rooms, and those who come in last have to wait an indefinite time. In the meanwhile the dining-room in the House of Lords is practically unoccupied, affairs of State rarely keeping noble lords at the post of duty over the dinner hour. It is suggested that the accommodation of the two establishments should be combined, members of both Houses using them in common.

31st May.
Big Divisions. Twenty minutes is the average time occupied in taking a division in the House of Commons. Since the House resumed after the Whitsun Recess this term has been appreciably extended, more especially when divisions are taken before dinner. At that period of the sitting, when obstruction is going on in the House, all but some fifty or sixty members are engaged outside, the Terrace being a specially favoured resort. An extraordinary sight is presented when members muster in the lobby for division, the crowd extending fully half-way across the lobby, blocking the entrance to the House. The Chairman has to stand for two or three minutes after the sand has run out of the glass, waiting till the doors are closed, a necessary preliminary to putting the question.

Unless discussion on Clause 3 of the
Home Rule Bill be concluded at next
Friday's sitting motion will be made that
the question that the clause stand part of
the Bill be forthwith put. It is Dr. MacGregor who
has undertaken this task, and he will proceed to its
accomplishment, at half-past six "of the clock," as
he puts it, as if he were sentencing Mr. Mellor to
be hanged by the neck until he were dead. Dr.
MacGregor is one of the statesmen the new Parliament brought into political life, and he is, to some
extent, representative of a considerable sprinkling
of the majority. Formerly medical officer and public
vaccinator for Penrith and district, medical superintendent of the Barnhill Hospital and Asylum,
Glasgow, Resident Physician at the Peebles Hydropathic Institution, he entered the House of Commons
with the idea that it was a place of business. To
vary an old Scotch axiom, he would say, "Peebles for
pleasure, but Westminster for work." He has long
been undeceived, and the process has had the effect,
if not of souring his mind, at least of lending a
certain acidity to his manner.

Very early in Committee on the Bill he formed
a habit of abruptly looking in and moving the
Closure, just as he might have ordered an extra
pack for a refractory patient at the Peebles Hydropathic Institute. Accustomed through a long and
honourable career to have his prescriptions forthwith
taken, the Doctor stood for a moment abashed when
Mr. Mellor, having the pill handed to him, declined
to administer it. To see him after such repulse
throw himself back in his seat, lean his head on his
hands, indignantly cross his legs, and shake a forlorn foot, was a spectacle calculated to impress the
beholder with sad thoughts as to the future of the
British Empire.

But there are limits to human endurance. Even

2nd June.
The
MacGregor.

the worm will turn at last, and Dr. MacGregor has
resolved to make an end of the business. "At half-
past six of the clock" on Friday next all will be over
as far as Clause 3 is concerned. What strikes one
as remarkable in this desperate resolve is its extreme
deliberateness. Clause 3 has been under discussion
through the whole of this week with the exception
of Monday's sitting. If it is to have another week
to itself, what is to become of the plan cherished in
Cabinet circles of getting the Bill clear out of the
Commons by the first or second week in July, winding
up other necessary business, adjourning at the end of
July for a two months' recess, meeting again in October
for the despatch of business connected with immaterial portions of the Empire other than Ireland?
If every clause in the Bill is to have a fortnight
allotted to it in Committee, the House of Commons,
sitting continuously, would be well into the new year
before the Committee stage of the Bill is passed.
Evidently, if business is meant, things will have to
move at a rate much more rapid than Dr. MacGregor's
diagnosis suggests to him.

The real drag on the wheels of the Bill is
Irrepressible. the statesman who has given up all his
life and energy to the supreme effort of
passing it. Mr. Gladstone is personally responsible
for the length of the successive debates that have
taken place through the week. It is not only that
upon amendments denounced from the Treasury
Bench as immaterial, or simply obstructive, he has
made long speeches. He has been the cause of
much speech-making in others. The Irish members,
writhing in silence in their camp, watch with
growing dismay the habit of the Leader of the
House. What is the use of a policy of silence, if
the Minister it is designed to support speaks on
every amendment submitted in Committee, rarely
takes less than half-an-hour to do it in, and

sometimes approaches three-quarters of an hour? This would be well enough on a second reading debate. The idea of work in Committee is that points of detail shall be discussed in short, sharp, conversational manner. Five minutes, at the utmost ten, is reasonable and sufficient limit for anything useful to be said in Committee. If the Leader of the House sets the example of delivering set orations on every point that comes up, who shall blame the Opposition if they gratefully welcome his assistance in delaying the progress of the Bill, and follow his example in respect of extended speech?

It happened to-day that, Mr. Gladstone temporarily withdrawing from the Treasury Bench, the leadership fell into the hands of Sir William Harcourt. Mr. Brodrick had moved the third amendment discussed in the course of the sitting. It had struck six "of the clock," and there remained less than forty minutes before the adjournment must take place. Judging by the time occupied by two preceding amendments, not more important in their bearing, there was little hope of discussion on this particular one being concluded before progress must be reported. Probably had Mr. Gladstone been in his place the fatal proportion of discussion would have been observed. In his absence, Sir William Harcourt spoke half a dozen sentences delivered in studiously unprovocative manner. No depths were stirred; no trains of gunpowder fired; no fiery torch was flashed in the half-closed eyes of a Committee disposed, if left alone, to go to sleep, but convinced by the blazing energy with which an amendment was denounced that, contrary to all appearance, there really must be something in it. Within less than half an hour the conversation had flickered out, the Committee divided, and the Government had their customary majority of 40.

There were ominous signs to-day that the
A Self-Denying   Irish members will not much longer be
  Ordinance.   able to resist the influence of evil example
in high places.   Nothing since the date of the Union
has been more remarkable than the attitude preserved
by them from the day the Home Rule Bill was introduced.   On the second reading one or two men selected
by their colleagues took part in the debate.   In
Committee they have hitherto heroically refrained
from speech-making.   This is a self-denying ordinance
prevailing equally in the Radical quarter, where many
members accustomed to take a prominent part in
current proceedings have effaced themselves.   The
debate is carried on exclusively between the Treasury
Bench and the Unionist forces.   This is bad enough for
the ordinary English, Scotch, or Welsh member.   For
the Irish member the torture must be exquisite.   To-
day Mr. Sexton, unable longer to endure, broke silence,
making his first speech since the Bill went into Committee.   As for Mr. Tim Healy, he has survived only
by indulgence in a system of spasmodic blood-letting.
Constantly in his place, attentive listener to Mr.
Chamberlain, Mr. Balfour, and other gentlemen with
whom in happier times he has been accustomed
joyously to wrestle, he has found the situation endur-
able only by the frequent emission of interjectionary
remarks.   This evening he, too, showed signs of increasing demoralisation.   Hitherto his commentaries
have been delivered in a sitting posture.   To-day he
was more than once on his legs arguing points of
order at length.

No great harm has yet been done from this
quarter.   But it is evident the situation is growing
strained.   The Irish members are willing to make
the most costly personal sacrifice in their power if
it results in defeating the tactics of the Opposition
by getting the Home Rule Bill through.   But if the
result is the same in the end, if a whole sitting is

occupied with discussion of a comparatively unimportant amendment, why should they suffer? If other people won't be virtuous, why should they not have their share of the cakes and ale?

It must be admitted that this voluntary retirement of the Irish members into a political order of Trappists invests the daily debate with a certain sadness. Night after night the talk goes on from shortly after four till close upon midnight, for the most part a deadly drip of argument and assertion. The influence of the times and seasons has plainly wrought upon Mr. Balfour. He is in pretty constant attendance and speaks sometimes, but in a studiously indifferent tone and manner, not calculated to excite enthusiasm. It is only when Mr. Chamberlain steps into the arena, and Mr. Gladstone swiftly turns to face him, that benches fill, drooping heads are raised, eyes brighten, the chamber resounds with cheers and counter-cheers, and the dry bones of the debate rattle into strenuous life.

5th June.
A Poor
Practical Joke.
Mr. Labouchere, who has tracked down many designing villains, is still at fault in his pursuit of the ingenious and enterprising person who has during the past few weeks been crowding Old Palace Yard with tradesmen's carts bringing goods the tenant of No. 5 never ordered, and embarrassing his friends with unauthorised gifts. Mr. John Morley is one of those who have benefited by the sudden outburst of generosity attributed to the member for Northampton. On the night before he left London for Dublin there arrived at his residence in Elm Park Gardens a magnificent salmon, with label attached, stating that it was forwarded " With Mr. Labouchere's compliments." Mr. Morley ate the salmon, and now arises the question—Who is to pay for it?

This problem has been submitted (not in Mr. Morley's individual case) to a high legal authority, who unhesitatingly declares that the responsibility lies with the hapless tradesman. It is he who has been duped, not the astute gentleman who was aimed at. I believe in most cases where perishable articles have been forwarded " With Mr. Labouchere's compliments," and have been consumed by the unsuspecting recipient, the tradesman's account has been discharged. But this is entirely an act of grace, he having no legal claim.

6th June.
Hard Times.

Another week has been spent on Clause 3 of the Home Rule Bill, completing nearly a fortnight devoted to its consideration. By this time even Mr. Gladstone must be convinced of the mechanical character of the opposition. There is something quite pathetic in his determination to regard Mr. Chamberlain, Mr. Courtney, Sir Henry James, and even Mr. Bartley and Mr. Gibson Bowles, as really animated in their action by desire to get at the truth, and hammer out of the materials presented by the clauses of the Bill a beneficent Act of Parliament. It requires no specially clear insight to see to the bottom of the little game played by the Opposition. Their only virtue in connection with it is that they openly announce their intention to destroy the Bill. Mr. Gladstone must know this. Nevertheless, when an amendment is moved, he studies it with profoundest attention, follows the speaker with keenest interest, and when he sits down, bends all his unrivalled powers upon the task of pulverising the amendment.

This amiable and honourable weakness is looked upon with growing impatience by the majority of his followers. Parliamentary life conducted on its present terms is no joke. Members are in their place, not only every day, but all through the sitting. A large proportion dine on the premises, in itself a grievous infliction. Those who dine out must find a pair during their absence, which is strictly limited in point

of time. Half-past ten is the usual hour at which
pairs expire, the ultimate limit being eleven o'clock.
If a man is not down at either stipulated hour the
member with whom he has paired is at liberty to take
part in the division, and a vote is lost.

This would be hard enough in ordinary circumstances, but the conditions under which nine-tenths
of the members of the House of Commons live to-day
make the lot more unbearable. They are not expected
to speak, are, indeed, tacitly forbidden to open their
mouths. All that is asked from them is that they
shall be within call when the division bell rings.
This is an irksome thraldom that would be patiently,
even cheerfully borne, if the object for which it is
designed were gained. But it is not. It would be
idle to deny that up to the present time the Opposition, led by Mr. Chamberlain, has triumphed all along
the line. The Home Rule Bill is in a parlous state,
and if matters have to go on through next week as
they have limped along in the present one, it would
be much better to give up the Bill, and either go off
for a holiday or devote the remaining time of the
Session to other measures. There is one other
alternative; that is to meet mechanical obstruction
on the part of the minority with the mechanical force
vested in the majority. Only, if the Bill is to be
saved, this must be done forthwith.

8th June.
A New
Departure.
The practice of unlocking the lobby doors
after a division in the House of Commons
has proved so convenient that it was to-
day extended, all the doors being unlocked
as soon as the counting commenced. Formerly
members were penned up in the lobby till the figures
of the division had been announced from the Chair.
One result of the new arrangement will be to prevent
the overwhelming rush for cabs after late divisions,
members being now able to leave the House in
detachments as they issue from the division lobby.

9th June.
A Morning
Sitting with
the Home
Rule Bill.
Sir William Harcourt is a statesman greatly gifted in debate. But there is no passage in his ordered speech so eloquent as his occasional exits from the House of Commons. Since the Home Rule Bill went into Committee he has not disclosed overmastering tendency to sit through a debate. On the contrary, his prolonged absences have led to conjectural remarks hinting at differences of opinion between himself and his colleagues on the management of the Bill. These are, doubtless, without foundation. No one would allege that the attractions of the ordinary debates on Clause 3 have been such as to command the presence of a member with whom attendance is not compulsory. Sir William has no special connection with the Bill such as would demand his unremitting attendance. Nor, indeed, can that be said to be the case with anyone but the Prime Minister. For him interest in the Bill deepens as the days pass. He has given himself up wholly to the task of furthering its progress, a rate of advance that would probably be increased if his attention were less absorbed. Mr. John Morley has occasionally something to say, and from time to time Sir John Rigby shows how impressive prepositions and the last syllables of unimportant words may be made to appear in the delivery of ordered speech. But these are subsidiary figures. It is Mr. Gladstone who fills the bill, sitting hour after hour insatiably listening, often when debate on a particular amendment is dying out from sheer inanition giving it a fresh start in life by a remark interpolated or a supplementary speech thrown in.

Habitual
Speakers.
It is about this time of the evening that Sir William Harcourt is accustomed to contribute to the debate an eloquent passage towards the back of the Speaker's chair. He has sat for an hour, perhaps more, listening to Mr. Jesse Collings, Mr. Bartley, or Mr. Gibson Bowles.

There is on his expressive countenance a look of patient suffering that should soften the hardest heart. If he might only stand at the table and frankly utter thoughts, the fire of which consumeth him, it would be a relief. But that would mean so much time taken up, with an indefinite period stretching out whilst others replied. So he sits sad and silent. Mr. Gladstone, having made a long speech when the amendment was moved, once more appears at the table, and the drooping debate is revived. Probably Mr. Chamberlain follows, and shows how entirely mistaken is the view of his " right hon. friend." Mr. Balfour thinks it necessary that, since things are waking up, the Leader of the Opposition should be heard. He makes a speech which Mr. Tim Healy accompanies with a fusillade of not obtrusively friendly commentary. Mr. Sexton moves uneasily on his seat, and, finding the temptation irresistible, says comparatively few words. Mr. Jesse Collings uplifts his good grey head, and instantly half a dozen shillelaghs flash forth to strike at it. Admiral Field regards the opportunity favourable for taking a naval view of the situation, and, slinging his glasses into position, roars at the Chairman as if it were blowing half a gale and ordinary men would need a speaking trumpet. Major Rasch rises to state, for the fourth time, that not having made a speech on the second reading of the Bill, and having hitherto observed strict silence in Committee, he really does think that with wheat at twenty-three shillings a bushel and swine fever rampant, the Committee might bear with him whilst he makes a few observations. Mr. Tomlinson usually saves himself for the close of a debate, when he rises with intention to offer the few remarks necessary for carrying the discussion into another sitting. As, however, he is promptly closured, he is not disposed entirely to limit his efforts to that particular epoch of a sitting. The present opportunity

seems favourable for him to show that the issue of
one-pound notes, without being protected by a full
reserve of gold, is sure to be one of the earliest
achievements of the Irish Legislature.

Mr. T. W. Russell, who has made one or two earlier
attempts to catch the Chairman's eye, begins a speech
without that preliminary. Mr. Mellor has called upon
Mr. Theobald, who for a moment mildly disputes precedence. But as Mr. Russell goes straight on, demonstrating that his fellow countrymen are of all nations
in the civilised world the most helpless and hopeless,
Mr. Theobald resumes his seat.

It was when Mr. T. W. Russell's voice
softly floated over the scene that Sir
William Harcourt, shaking himself together, slowly rose and solemnly strode
forth. The action was not that of a man wrought by
long suffering into a paroxysm of impatience. The
long suffering was patent both in face and figure.
But it assumed the form rather of hopeless depression
than of righteous indignation. Without intending it,
the Chancellor of the Exchequer's slow march towards
the door, with one hand lying limp in the recesses of his
waist, his head bent, his eyes half closed, suggested a
funeral. If the Home Rule Bill were already dead,
and he were accompanying it to the crematorium, he
could not have varied his attitude or expression.
Short of that, this new Dead March plainly conveyed
to the looker on the idea that for one mind at least
the limit of patient endurance had been reached, and
that to avoid either a breakdown or a breaking-out it
were well to retire from the scene.

It is curious to observe how the passion
for division is overmastering the Parliamentary world just now. Reference is
not here made to ordinary divisions in the lobby,
though they grow in frequency and length of time in
the accomplishment. Never in the memory of the

*Sir William
Harcourt's
Exit.*

*16th June.
Blocked.*

oldest member have so many hours been occupied in a given week with marching and counter-marching in the division lobby. For this the closure is to some extent responsible. In nine cases out of ten a motion for the closure means two successive divisions, one on the closure, the other on the question closed. With the present muster of members in regular attendance two divisions mean forty minutes, whence it will appear that this athletic method of legislation appropriates a considerable share of a week's sitting.

The lengthened period occupied in dividing is extended by the circumstances under which divisions are called. Some thirty or forty members remain, not to debate a question, but to hear an amendment moved, opposed from the Treasury Bench, and supported by Mr. Balfour or Mr. Chamberlain or both. Then the House is cleared for a division, and the bell throbbing through all the corridors and ante-rooms, clanging on the Terrace, brings in from four to five hundred members ready to vote in favour either of "in accordance with" or "having regard to," according as movement towards either lobby is made from the Treasury Bench. The process of passing four or five hundred men through even a double doorway is not accomplished in five minutes, and till the outer door is closed and locked the Chairman may not put the question. Accordingly he stands, paper in hand, waiting till the wedge of humanity that has blocked the doorway is slowly pressed through. Sometimes Mr. Mellor makes forlorn appeal to members standing at the bar to advance and take their seats, so that those behind may get clear of the doorway. Every member expects his neighbour to observe the injunction, and so the block remains.

The latest division has been effected on the Terrace. In these fine afternoons the Terrace of the House of Commons, with the limpid Thames laving its walls, has become the

Tea on the Terrace.

favourite resort of London society. The practice has
grown up within very recent date, taking root during
the last Parliament when the gentlemen of England
had political ascendency, and their wives, daughters,
sisters, and cousins dropped in for five o'clock tea.
The fashion was firmly established on the afternoon
when Mr. Chamberlain entertained two duchesses,
taking tea at a small round table, whilst Mr.
Labouchere, pale to the lips, and momentarily forgetful of his cigarette, stood prominent in the ring of
Radicals looking on at this final leap of their Lost
Leader.

It was shortly after this social-political event that
the wife of a well-known member issued to a large
circle of friends cards of invitation to " Tea on the
Terrace." It was felt that that was going a little far,
giving too much of an air of business to what should
be a casual occurrence. There was talk of stern
repression. But the storm blew over, and this Session,
favoured by weather more familiar on the Riviera than
by the Thames, the Terrace, as viewed from Westminster Bridge or the deck of a passing steamer, has
become one of the sights of London. From half-past
four to half-past six the broad passage is thronged
with rank and fashion. Even Mr. Keir Hardie has
yielded to the fascination of the surroundings, and may
sometimes be seen with belles from West Ham on
either arm picking his way among the labyrinth of
tea-tables.

It is all very well for young sparks like the Member
for West Ham. For staid Parliamentarians like Sir
Henry Howorth and Sir Richard Temple there is
something incongruous in the appearance of this silken
fringe of fashion on the plain skirts of legislative
labour. The Speaker's attention has been called to
the matter, with the result of promulgation of a stern
edict. From Monday afternoon a hard-and-fast line
will be drawn in continuance of the doorway giving

access to the Terrace. To the left of it only the
foot of man may tread. To the right Paradise will
bloom. Benedick may, an he please, cross over
and visit Beatrix; but the foot of Beatrix may
not, under unnamed pains and penalties, cross the
boundary line.

This is an ordinary business arrangement, but it
cannot fail to lend fresh attraction to the fashionable
resort as promising all kinds of piquant complications.

It is, however, the division in the Minis-
A Momentous terial camp that is of most serious import.
Issue.
It appeared on the horizon this afternoon.
As yet a cloud no bigger than a man's hand, but
threatening presently to obscure the firmament and
break in anything but blessings on Mr. Gladstone's
head. It manifested itself upon the question whether
sub-section 5 of Clause 4 of the Home Rule Bill should
be enlarged by addition of the phrase " in accordance
with," or "having regard to." For all practical
purposes the Committee might as well have divided
upon the question of the conflicting claims of
Tweedledum and Tweedledee, an arrangement that
would have had the additional advantage of
being more intelligible to the public out of
doors. Between the two phrases battled over
by the hour this afternoon there is precisely the
same difference, no more and no less. To the dis-
cerning eye there was much to read between the lines
of controversy. Mr. Gladstone knows all about it, and
might well, with furrowed brow and pale face, sit restless on the Treasury Bench. Mr. Chamberlain is
equally familiar with its true inwardness, and was
ready to make the most of the incident for the
comfort and consolation of his right hon. friend.

No finer piece of high-comedy was played
Breakers on any stage than that going forward
Ahead.
upon this momentous issue. The final
touch to its perfectness was given by the absolute

absence on the part of the actors of trace of consciousness of the real game.   Yet everybody on the stage
knew that it was not sub-section 5 of Clause 4 that
was at stake, with the deep difference that yawned
between " in accordance with " and " having regard
to."   Beyond Clause 4 lie the clauses which are to
settle the financial arrangements between Ireland and
Great Britain.   The Irish members are resolved not
to accept the terms the Government are prepared to
offer.   If Mr. Gladstone thinks they are disposed
to take half a loaf rather than have no bread it
is time he were undeceived.   Hitherto they have
voted steadily with the Government, who have,
accordingly, managed to keep up their majority with
unexpected and unexampled regularity.   But the
Irish members hold the game, and the life of the
Government is in their hands.   They are the pivot on
which Ministerial majorities revolve.   If they refuse
to act the whole machinery will come to a stoppage,
and straightway go to rack and ruin.   To revolt in a
critical division on the financial clauses would be a
desperate device.   This is not a case, common enough
in ordinary times, where a Ministry temporarily at
issue with a section of their followers may, therefore,
depend with confidence upon the temporary adhesion
of the forces of the Opposition.   In a division on a vital
proposal of the Bill upon which the Irish members
were (as twice happened to-day) to vote against the
Government, the masters of Parliamentary strategy
who lead the Opposition would wheel their disciplined
forces round, go into the lobby with the Irish members,
and there would be a swift end of the Government,
and the postponement of the chance of Home Rule
certainly beyond the limits of the present generation.

Comedy and Tragedy.

That is the tragedy which frowned in
rear of the comedy played throughout
this afternoon.   The Irish members had
come to the conclusion it was time to give Ministers

a lesson. So they ranged themselves under the improvised flag bearing the legend "in accordance with," and ground their teeth with stage scorn at the standard which bore the equally proud device "having regard to." In vain Sir Charles Russell with pathetic reminiscence of Mr. Toots insisted that it was "of no consequence." He and his colleagues on the Treasury Bench could be happy with either phrase, whilst from the point of literary style they preferred the clause as it stood. All he desired was peace and concord and some little progress with Clause 4.

It was here Mr. Chamberlain interposed, with that occasionally assumed high comedy manner that causes his old colleagues on the Treasury Bench to regret that he did not follow out that tendency which in early life, as he once told a company of actors, brought him in close connection with the stage. With smiling face, in softest voice, almost literally bubbling over with gratitude, he thanked the Government for the concession just made. It was not exactly in the form originally demanded; but he was aware of the ties that bound his right hon. friend to gentlemen below the gangway opposite. The concession on a most important point gave the Opposition all they had asked for, and he should advise his friends gratefully to accept it as he most humbly and heartily did.

Before utterance of this speech the Irish members might have been content with their protest, shrinking from playing the dangerous game of weakening the Government by open revolt. Mr. Chamberlain had driven a wedge into the door of escape, and they could not get out. He was followed by Sir Henry James gravely insisting on the same lines. Mr. Balfour played back the ball from the other side of the House. In vain Sir Charles Russell, almost angrily, protested that the amendment was absolutely immaterial, and the so-called concession made only to save time.

Mr. Clancy fell into the trap and truculently declared
that the time had come when protest should be made
" against these concessions."   The McCarthyites could
not afford to be behind when the Parnellites took
up the running.   Thus it came to pass that with a
hundred Radicals at their back they trooped out into
the lobby, leaving the Government to be saved by the
Unionist vote.

CHAPTER XII.

THE CLOSURE INVOKED.

20th June. Twenty-fourth night in Committee. NIGHT after night the House of Commons meets, gets to work early on the Home Rule Bill, sits till midnight, works off two or three amendments, and on returning to the task next day finds that two or three fresh amendments are added, leaving the position as it was. The work in the Commons to-day is very much on the same line as the task of our old school friend Sisyphus, and just about as useful.

It is curious to note the almost pathetic confidence Liberals have in Mr. Gladstone's capacity, somehow or other, to get the stone to the top of the hill at last, and to keep it there. His action and attitude are well calculated to inspire this confidence. Whilst men and Ministers find it impossible to repress occasional exhibitions of anger or conceal their impatience, Mr. Gladstone is supernaturally equable. Now and then he has an explosion such as that which on Monday night shrivelled up Sir Henry James. But it takes the form rather of personal attack than of lamentation over the general state of things. Sir William Harcourt makes no attempt to hide his emotion at the waste of time. Mr. Morley occasionally breaks forth in bitter reproaches, whilst the rank and file of the Ministerialists sit and roar "Divide! divide." Mr. Gladstone is in no hurry, treats every amendment as if it was seriously and honestly meant, is ever ready to break butterflies on the wheel.

In appearance he looks younger rather than older as the weeks pass. His voice has gained in richness

G

and vigour, while his mind seems to have grown in activity and resource.

This is all very pleasant to hear and see, but in the mean while the Home Rule Bill sticks in the mud. July is near at hand, the 5th Clause is not yet passed, and among the thirty-five to follow will be found the hardest nuts that have to be cracked.

22nd June.
Samson
Agonistes.

Whilst Mr. Gladstone seems to be renewing his youth, like the eagle, an old foeman is reaching a stage of decrepitude pitiful to see. Lord Randolph Churchill's return to political life, under the wing of his old colleagues on the Front Opposition Bench, was one of the most interesting episodes of the new Parliament. He was welcomed with a fervour which showed how real was his power, how apparently assured his prospects. His first speech, delivered at the table of the House of Commons, from the left-hand side of the Chair, was watched with keen and generally friendly interest. Members who knew him in his young prime, when he was Leader of the Fourth Party, and later, when with development of quite unexpected qualities he led the House, were surprised and pained at the physical change notable in him, and in the evidence of embarrassment that sometimes made his meaning obscure. He pulled up wonderfully when he spoke again in debate on the Welsh Suspensory Bill. Up to the present time that has proved the last successful effort.

This week he made two speeches quite pitiful in their weakness, almost incoherence. It was sad to see him at the table maundering along amid impatient cries of "Divide! Divide!" rising above the buzz of conversation. New members, recalling a famous passage in "Samson Agonistes," ask—

> Can this be he,
> That heroick, that renown'd
> Irresistible Samson? whom, unarmed,

No strength of man, nor fiercest wild beast, could withstand.
Who tore the lion as the lion tears the kid,
Ran on embattled armies clad in iron,
And, weaponless himself,
Made arms ridiculous, useless the forgery
Of brazen shield and spear.

Once — it seems but a few . months back — Lord Randolph commanded the Senate, his winged words waited for with delight by his friends, with apprehension by the enemy. Now there are none so poor as to do him the reverence of listening. Possibly, indeed probably, this week's manifestations have been due to temporary physical indisposition, and Randolph may yet be himself again. In the meantime the impression created is very painful.

**29th June.
The Closure
at Last.**

It had struck half-past five when Mr. Gladstone rose to move his resolution, which proposes to arm the majority of the House with power to resist systematic obstruction to the Home Rule Bill. At this time the Chamber was densely crowded, one of the few notable absentees being Lord Randolph Churchill. Every seat on the floor was taken, the side gallery facing the Treasury Bench being also thronged to its fullest capacity.

The following is the text of the proposals submitted on the part of the Government:—" That the proceedings in Committee on the Government of Ireland Bill, unless previously disposed of, shall at the times hereinafter mentioned be brought to a conclusion in the manner hereinafter mentioned : (*a*) The proceedings on the Clauses 5 to 8, both inclusive, not later than 10 p.m. on Thursday, 6th July; (*b*) the proceedings on Clauses 9 to 26, both inclusive, not later than 10 p.m. on Thursday, 13th July; (*c*) the proceedings on Clauses 27 to 40, both inclusive, not later than 10 p.m. on Thursday, 20th July; (*d*) the proceedings on the postponed clauses, new clauses, being . Government clauses, schedules, and preamble, not later than 10 p.m. on Thursday, 27th July; and, after the clauses, schedules, and preamble are disposed of, the Chairman shall forthwith report the Bill, as amended, to the House; then at the said appointed times the Chairman shall put forthwith the question or questions on any amendment or motion already proposed from the Chair. He shall next proceed, unless and until progress be moved as hereinafter provided, successively to put forthwith the following questions: That any clause or schedule then under consideration, and any of the said clauses or schedules not already disposed of, stand part of, or be added to, the Bill. After the passing of this Order no dilatory motion, nor motion to postpone a clause, shall be received unless moved by a Minister in charge of the Bill, and the question on any such motion shall be put forthwith. If progress be reported, the Chairman shall put this Order in force in any subsequent meeting of the Committee. Proceedings under this Order shall not be interrupted under the provisions of any Standing Order relating to the sittings of the House."

The Premier promised to be brief, and was as good as his word, occupying the attention of the Committee for less than half an hour. Within that time he demonstrated not only the necessity for the action proposed by his Resolution, but its moderation as compared with any precedent. The House has already been in Committee on the Home Rule Bill for twenty-eight days, and it is proposed to allow for the further consideration of the Bill an additional twenty days. The Reform Act of 1831 was passed in a total of forty-nine days, and just the same period sufficed for the carrying of the Land Act of 1881. Thus the Home Rule Bill would have been in Committee within one day of the whole period allotted to these Bills, whilst, assuming it out of Committee on the 27th of July, sixty-four days in all will have been devoted to its consideration, there still remaining the Report stage and the third reading to be dealt with. Beyond the necessity of taking a new departure in order to secure the passing of the Bill, there is the question which underlies the whole foundations of our Parliamentary institutions. Is the will of the majority to prevail, or are the minority to govern ?

30th June. After ¼ Big Debate. Mr. Gladstone's appearance as he entered the House shortly after nine o'clock to-night suggested that he had spent the week at Brighton, dined early, and looked in to spend a quiet evening listening to the seductive eloquence of Mr. Webb and Sir Joseph Pease, who had appropriately chosen opium for their topic. Till he came in, the soporific influence of time and circumstances seemed irresistible. Most of the gentlemen present had been up all night, going home with the milk in the morning. Many had been in their places at two o'clock for the morning sitting, and had remained till seven, taking part in the division on the Closure Resolutions. Only the keenest interest or the most imperative call of public duty would bring a man down again with nose to the Parliamentary grindstone at so particularly inconvenient an hour as nine o'clock. Nevertheless, when the Speaker took the Chair there were considerably more than a quorum present, and, as the division showed, by midnight the number had run up to close upon 300.

This is fresh evidence of the quality patent in the present House of Commons. It is the most faithful in the performance of its duties known to the present generation. The nightly attendance is larger and more constant than Mr. Gladstone can recall in the far-reaching survey it is possible for him to make. This is doubtless due to early training. The yoke of controversy round the Home Rule Bill made itself felt in the infancy of the Parliament. New members

have known no other habit than that of being
constantly in their place, or of pairing if they leave
it for an hour. Old members, whose experience is
more varied, have fallen into the fashion. The
consequence is seen in a succession of division lists
which find no parallel in the journals of the House.
Time was when 600 members in the division lobbies
indicated a Ministerial crisis. To-day it is a matter
of course, twice or thrice in a night, to find over 600
members dividing on a minor amendment.

Mr. Gladstone has never, when in office,
varied from close attendance on the
proceedings of the House, and therefore had not a new habit to form. Still, there
were circumstances concurrent with this particular
case that might well have excused his lingering at
the table where the lavish hospitality of Downing-
street is spread. Almost up to the stroke of two
o'clock this morning he had been on the Treasury
Bench which, since four o'clock on the previous
afternoon, he had quitted but for the interval of a
hasty dinner. He moved the Closure Resolutions in
a luminous speech, an effort trifling in mental wear
and tear compared with the self-allotted task of
listening closely hour after hour to the speech of
others. It was with difficulty he was induced to
withdraw, protesting that he was " not a bit tired."
This he proved by being punctually in his place at
the morning sitting, and in the course of it making
two important speeches and interpolating innumerable
pointed remarks. After twenty-four hours so spent a
younger man might have felt disposed to forego the
pleasure of a debate on the Opium Traffic and find
slumber with more convenient accessories than the
benches of the House of Commons provide. Mr.
Gladstone had his little dinner-party at home in the
interval between the morning and evening sitting,
and, unexhausted by the friendly conflict with the

brilliant wits gathered round his board, posted off on foot to the House.

It should have been Mr. George Russell's
Mr. George Russell's Opportunity. night. That eminent scion of an illustrious house answers for India in the Commons. There stood upon the paper in his name an amendment to the motion, brought forward by Mr. Webb, pointing to the abolition of the opium traffic. Gifted with hereditary Parliamentary aptitude, Mr. Russell might, upon emergency, be able to make an impromptu speech on any subject, as his great kinsman was reputed to be ready at any moment to take command of the Channel Fleet. It is, however, only reasonable to suppose that the Under-Secretary for India had devoted some time and trouble to preparation of the official case he had been told off to present to Parliament. He sat attentive whilst Mr. Webb moved his resolution and Sir Joseph Pease enlarged upon it. A little longer, when gentlemen in other parts of the House had enjoyed the opportunity of expressing their views, he would rise and justify the hopes that centre in him.

And here was Mr. Gladstone, kind enough to hurry over his dinner in order to pay to the nephew of his old colleague and some time leader the compliment of his presence at what was practically his *début* as a Minister. This is an act of graciousness on the part of a leader small in itself, but meaning much. Mr. Disraeli was punctilious in paying the attention to his young friends, and Mr. Arthur Balfour instinctively falls into the habit.

Mr. Gladstone, his mind absorbed in contemplation of bolder strokes of policy, is not remarkable for little *delicatesses* of this kind. It made the exception all the more notable, and the Under-Secretary for India, looking once more over the notes of his speech, blushed with pleasurable pride. These are bad times for

young Ministers anxious to win their spurs. Now and
then a question has to be answered, but there is no
opportunity either of taking part in general debate or
of initiating one on behalf of one's own department.
Everything comes to the man who waits. Mr. George
Russell had waited, and not only opportunity but the
Prime Minister had come.

How it was
Lost.

The Under-Secretary was awakened from
his pleased contemplation by a cheer.
Mr. Gladstone was at the table, addressing
the House. That was odd ; but the narrow limits of
his purpose speedily became plain. The motion on
the Orders of the Day was that the House should
resolve itself into Committee of Supply. Upon this
Mr. Webb had moved, in the form of an amendment,
his proposition for a Royal Commission on the opium
traffic. The Government, whilst not averse—as what
Government is?—to the appointment of a Royal Commission, could not agree to the terms of reference,
which pointed arbitrarily to the suppression of a traffic
upon which the revenues of India largely depend. The
amendment Mr. Russell was charged to move agreed
to the appointment of a Royal Commission, but altered
the terms of reference. A technical difficulty in the
way was that if Mr. Webb's motion were submitted in
the form proposed it must needs be negatived. There
would be an end of the business, and the Ministry
would suffer in the estimation of some valuable friends
by appearing unmitigatedly hostile to inquiry into the
question. What the Old Parliamentary Hand, standing at the table in evening dress with a flower in his
coat and the bloom of eternal youth on his brow, had
to propose was that the motion to go into Committee
should be negatived ; that Mr. Webb's amendment
should thereupon become a substantive resolution
upon which might be grafted the amendment his hon.
friend the Under-Secretary for India was prepared to
submit and support in a conclusive speech.

Probably that was all Mr. Gladstone had intended to do or say when he interposed. But like the reformed gambler who after long interval stakes a napoleon at Monte Carlo and wins, the Premier, having stood for a moment on his feet by the table, said a few words and listened to the welcoming cheer with which he was received, was irresistibly drawn into the vortex of debate. His suggestion being accepted, he rose again, and, carefully avoiding the glance of his hon. young friend seated near him conning the notes of his masterpiece, began to talk around the subject. It was pretty to see how scrupulously he avoided anything like oratorical tone or manner. He was not making a speech on behalf of the Government. That would be done by his hon. friend, the Under-Secretary for India. He was merely talking across the table to Mr. George Curzon and Sir James Fergusson, to whom, as knowing something of India, Mr. Arthur Balfour had left the concerns of the Front Opposition Bench whilst he himself rested from the exhaustive labours of the week. A reference to the late Sir Robert Fowler brought to Mr. Gladstone's mind recollections of what had taken place two years ago, when the matter was last before the House. Two years naturally led him back to thirty, forty, fifty years ago.

"It is to me," he said, "rather a pleasing recollection amongst others less pleasing that in those debates I took what I thought to be the best part in my power."

Here followed a brief history of the China War. Then, taking Mr. Webb's resolution in hand, he found in it a promise of "temporary assistance." That was a very ambiguous phrase. "I object," he said, with a twinkle in his eye belying his grave face and solemn tones, "to that part of the motion as being tainted with the almost mortal sin of ambiguity."

Contemplation of this frailty stirred his deepest depths. So he went on and on through a speech

G *

which Mr. Curzon aptly described as full of charm and argumentative force. When he sat down, lo! three-quarters of an hour, a full quarter of the whole time allotted to the debate, had been appropriated, and when gentlemen on the other side had taken their turn there was no room for the Under-Secretary for India, who, as far as the episode was concerned, "died with all his music in him."

Twenty-ninth sitting in Committee on Home Rule Bill. The flaccid condition of affairs was ruffled by one of the most exciting storms that have recently swept over the House of Commons. As usual, Mr. Chamberlain began it. Having concluded his remarks in support of an amendment moved by Lord Wolmer, he recurred to a speech delivered by Mr. Dillon at Castlereagh in 1887, in which the member for East Mayo was reported to have said that when the Irish Parliament was constituted they would have the control of things in Ireland, and would then "remember" the police and others who had shown themselves enemies of the people.

3rd July.
Mr. Chamber-
lain and Mr.
Dillon.

Mr. Dillon was absent from his place when Mr. Chamberlain resumed his seat. It was rightly surmised that he had gone in search of a report of the incriminated speech, and Mr. T. W. Russell undertook pleasantly to fill up the interval by reciting another passage from Mr. Dillon's speeches on the same lines as that alluded to by Mr. Chamberlain. When Mr. Dillon returned there were loud cries for him, and the House, which had gradually filled up, sat crowded and silent, waiting for the reply. Mr. Gladstone, according to his custom when members below the gangway opposite speak, moved towards the end of the bench, and there sat with hand to ear, attentively following Mr. Dillon's speech.

Mr. Dillon did not dispute the accuracy of the quotation, but urged that the context modified its purport. The gist of his defence—that which manifestly moved the House—was his description of the circumstances under which the speech had been made. It was, he said, a short time after the Massacre of Mitchelstown, where he had seen three innocent men shot down in cold blood, the police acting under an officer so bankrupt in character that even Mr. Balfour had to dismiss him.

"That recollection," he said, " was hot in my mind when I spoke at Castlereagh."

His anger was further swelled by the story told him just before he rose to speak of how inhumanly the police had acted to a mother and a child. It was not, Mr. Dillon said, amid loud cheers from the Ministerialists, fair or just to rake up language used in such circumstances, and never repeated in cold blood. There was renewed cheering when he expressed his regret for having used the language with which the speech had closed.

Mr. Chamberlain was amongst the keenest listeners to this immediately effective harangue. When Mr. Dillon resumed his seat he sprang to his feet, and was received with loud cheers by the Conservatives. At the outset he shot a deadly dart at an old-time enemy. Mr. Dillon had, he said, declared that he had been influenced in his remarks by recollections of what took place at Mitchelstown. But when was the affair at Mitchelstown? It was on the 9th of September, 1887, and the speech at Castlereagh from which he had quoted was delivered on the 5th of December, 1886. A prolonged burst of cheering from the Opposition greeted this statement, and all eyes were turned upon Mr. Dillon, who sat silent, making no sign. Amid renewed cheering Mr. Chamberlain asked how the House could accept the tardy repentance of a man who came down and attempted to palm off a statement of that kind?

Mis-remembering Mitchelstown.

An Earlier
Home Rule
Scheme.
Mr. Harrington, amid tumultuous shouts, cheering, and counter-cheering, gave a new turn to the proceedings. Carrying the war into the enemy's country, he declared that if Irish members were now unfit to be made responsible for the government of their country, they were equally unfit in 1885, when Mr. Chamberlain collogued with them, and sent emissaries to treat with them. Mr. Chamberlain jumped up amid a storm of excitement. As he had refused to give way when Mr. Dillon interposed, Mr. Harrington now made the same answer the member for West Birmingham had then given to Mr. Dillon's claim. He would finish soon, and then Mr. Chamberlain might speak. Mr. Harrington proceeded to give particulars about a gentleman from Walsall who had appeared among the Irish members armed with a letter from Mr. Chamberlain, in which that statesman submitted a scheme of Home Rule for Ireland.

"If we had accepted his model little plan," said Mr. Harrington, "he would have given Home Rule without any of the safeguards of the present Bill."

Shouts of "Order! Order!" and "Question! Question!" roaring from the Opposition ranks attempted to silence Mr. Harrington, but he has a stentorian voice, and was heard above the clamour. Mr. Mellor, appealed to on a point of order, protested he could not quite see what Mr. Dignan, of Walsall, had to do with the amendment. Mr. Chamberlain insisted that, as the name had been dragged in, Mr. Harrington should continue his statement, and that he should reply. Prevailing over the Chairman's scruples, Mr. Chamberlain explained that Mr. Dignan, "not a friend, but a political acquaintance," having gone to Ireland on his own errand, wrote to him giving an account of what he had seen, whereupon Mr. Chamberlain replied, broadly sketching a scheme of local government in the nature of National

Councils, something akin to that which, with the approval of Mr. Gladstone, he had later brought under the notice of Mr. Parnell.

Reminiscences of the Round Table Conferences. Sir William Harcourt's appearance on the scene, as promising further sport, was hailed with cheers and counter-cheers. The Chancellor of the Exchequer remembered very well the period of December, 1886, at which time the incriminated speech of Mr. Dillon was made. The Round Table meeting, arranged at the instance of Mr. Chamberlain, was in process. Sir William Harcourt, amid sharp interruptions from Mr. Chamberlain, and cheers and counter-cheers from the crowded and excited House, was proceeding into detail about the Round Table, when Sir Michael Hicks-Beach interposed on a point of order, asking whether these observations had anything to do with the amendment.

"I suppose," said Mr. Mellor, "that the right hon. gentleman is coming to the amendment," a delightfully naïve answer, which almost brought the House back into good-humour.

When the uproarious laughter had ceased, Sir William Harcourt put his case into a sentence, declaring that three weeks after the speech made by Mr. Dillon, which now so shocked Mr. Chamberlain, that right hon. gentleman was ready to give the Irish members as full a control of the police as was provided in the Bill before the House.

Mr. Chamberlain and Mr. Lough rose together. There were loud cries of "Lough! Lough!" Mr. Chamberlain declined to give way, and at length succeeded in saying "I rise to give to that statement an absolute contradiction."

Mr. Lough having read a few extracts from Mr. Chamberlain's speeches in 1885, Mr. Balfour interposed, and, with a bitterness that recalled old conflicts, brought the debate back to Mr. Dillon, upon whom he heaped contumely and scorn. A division, in which 196 voted for Lord Wolmer's almost forgotten amendment, and 230 against, happily rounded off the succession of scenes in time for members to get off to a delayed dinner.

As soon as questions were over Mr. Dillon rose and claimed permission to make a personal statement. The House was at the moment pretty full, Mr. Chamberlain, likely to be concerned in the incident, being a notable absentee. Mr. Gladstone was in his place, and gave to the scene that followed anxious attention. Mr. Dillon frankly admitted that he had yesterday made a mistake in his reference to Mitchelstown, and offered the House his fullest apology. He thought it impossible even for his bitterest enemy to suppose that, as Mr. Chamberlain had put it, he had deliberately attempted to palm off a story which carried on the face of it its own refutation.

4th July. Mr. Dillon Explains.

"I deny," Mr. Dillon emphatically said, "that I entertained the project attributed to me of revenge against those who were opposed to the people of Ireland."

"Oh! oh!" cried some of the gentlemen of England seated above the gangway.

"1 deny it," Mr. Dillon sternly repeated, turning upon them. "No fair-minded man can find in the six hundred speeches I have delivered in this time of tribulation grounds for the imputation."

As happened yesterday, Mr. Harrington followed Mr. Dillon, and was proceeding to read the terms of the letter addressed by Mr. Chamberlain to the gentleman from Walsall at the time, according to the statement of the Irish members, when that right hon. gentleman was negotiating with them a scheme of Home Rule.

Lord Randolph Churchill rose to order, asking whether in the absence of Mr. Chamberlain it was

competent for Mr. Harrington to refer to the subject.
Mr. Harrington proceeding with the reading, Mr. Balfour asked whether it was not desirable that the statement should be made in the presence of the gentleman
chiefly concerned. The Speaker ruled Mr. Harrington in order, and he proceeded to the end, showing
how Mr. Chamberlain, writing in 1885, had declared
that he was ready to go further on the Home Rule
line than the step of conferring upon Ireland municipal
government. He was prepared to see the establishment of an Irish Legislature empowered to deal with
education and the land.

"Cheer that!" cried a not unfamiliar voice below
the gangway, as the Conservatives listened in comparative silence to this disclosure.

Mr. Courtney rose to put the House in possession
of the real facts. Whilst he was struggling against
the indisposition to hear him Mr. Chamberlain entered, his arrival being hailed with loud cheers by the
Conservatives. Promptly interposing with the remark
that he had not had an opportunity of making himself acquainted with what had taken place during his
absence, he said he would simply read a telegram
received from Mr. Dignan, the Macchiavelli of Walsall.

"I have," that diplomatist telegraphed, "read your
statement in *The Daily Post.* It is true and singu-
larly accurate." ·

There was some disposition to smile at this way of
putting it, as if Mr. Chamberlain's accuracy was so
little habitual that it might be described as singular.
Mr. Chamberlain added no word to this reading, and
the episode abruptly closed.

It was followed by another scene. Mr.
Mr. Conybeare Tritton called attention to a letter in the
and the *Daily Chronicle,* in which Mr. Cony-
Speaker. beare, defending himself against a charge
of inopportunely moving the Closure, unmistakably
implied that the Speaker, in refusing, "with curt

severity," to put the Question, had acted in a manner strongly contrasting with his complaisance in analogous circumstances in June, 1887.

"But then," Mr. Conybeare added, "a Liberal Home Rule Bill is not to be compared with a Coercion Bill."

The Speaker observed that he had not read the letter, and had not been made aware of the intended procedure of Mr. Tritton. The proper course for a member desiring to review his conduct was not to write to a newspaper, but to bring the matter under the notice of the House by resolution.

"I hope I may venture to say," the Speaker added in ringing voice and with indignant sweep of hand and arm, "there is not another man in this House who, whatever my failings and shortcomings may have been during a period of ten years, can accuse me of having been partial on one side or the other."

The declaration was approved by loud and enthusiastic cheers. The Speaker added that he must leave the matter in the hands of the House. The only part he could play was to deprecate any harsh conduct they might be disposed to take in view of the proceeding of Mr. Conybeare.

Like the Speaker, Mr. Gladstone had no notice of what was forthcoming. But he seized the occasion to deliver one of those loftily-toned speeches to which he is moved when anything is done calculated to lower the standard of Parliamentary life. Amid a fresh burst of cheering he paid a high compliment to the conduct of Mr. Peel in the Chair through a period of unexampled difficulty. Mr. Conybeare, he said, had been guilty of a most grave and serious error, but since the Speaker had deprecated further action he thought the House should not further pursue the subject. In this view Mr. Balfour concurred, and, Mr. Conybeare not being present to carry on the conversation, it here closed.

CHAPTER XIII.

THE CLOSURE AT WORK.

6th July.
The First
Weekly
Closure. WHILE all London is making holiday on this the wedding-day of the Duke of York and Princess May, the House of Commons met at its usual time, and proceeded with its familiar business as if no marriage-bells were ringing. The full attendance (lacking only the Speaker, Mr. Mellor temporarily taking his place in the Chair) and the concentration of interest testify more than anything that has gone before to the commanding interest in the Home Rule Bill. To-night it is intensified, since the first date of the application of the Closure has been reached, and at ten o'clock the blow will fall.

As early as twenty minutes past four the House got into Committee, taking up the amendments to Clause 5, on which it has been many days engaged. In view of the festal day and the pending fall of the guillotine, the debate was carried on with surprising vigour. But everyone was waiting for ten o'clock, when the crisis was due. Shortly after nine members began to return, and by twenty-five minutes to ten, when Mr. Gladstone arrived, the House was crowded. Members coming later found seats on the gangways or in the side-galleries, those later still standing massed at the bar. Seven or eight peers occupied their gallery, being joined during the first division by Sir Richard Webster, who, being paired, could take no other part in the division than that of a spectator. The amendment under discussion when ten o'clock struck was one of Lord Wolmer's. At a

quarter to ten the Solicitor-General sat down after
briefly opposing it.   Mr. Balfour followed, his appearance being hailed with a loud cheer from the
Opposition.   He commenced a lively speech by an
allusion to the " perfunctory and preposterous arguments " advanced by the Solicitor-General.

"I presume," he said, glancing up at the clock,
"that the right hon. gentleman thinks we have now
reached a period of discussion when arguments are
wholly superfluous, when the appeal is not to be to
law, not to reason, not to precedent——"   Here
the sentence was interrupted by loud cheers from
the Ministerialists, cries of "Coercion!" and "June,
1887!"   Mr. Balfour, when his chance came, concluded—"but to such majorities as the Government may be able to command."

Further remarks drew up the Solicitor-General
with an explanation, interrupted by cries of "Speak
up!"   The interruptions were so persistent that Mr.
Gladstone indignantly rose and with outstretched
arm made an appeal to the Chairman, whose reply,
as far as it could be caught amid the uproar, was to
the effect that "it was unworthy of the House."

As ten o'clock drew close at hand cries of
"Time!" were heard.   Mr. Balfour had no intention of overstepping the limit, and punctually as the
finger pointed to the hour resumed his seat.   Simultaneously the Chairman rose to put the question.
As Mr. Gladstone walked out to vote against Lord
Wolmer's amendment the Irish members rose in a
body, cheering and waving hats till the Premier
passed under the doorway.

The Liberal Unionists persistently kept their
places till this demonstration was over.   When Mr.
Balfour returned from the division lobby the
Opposition greeted him with a similar manifesta-
tion, this time the Liberal Unionists rising and
waving their hats.

Lord Wolmer's amendment being rejected by a majority of 38, the Chairman put the question "That Clause 5 stand part of the Bill." There was a sharp cry of "Aye!" answered by a prolonged cry of "No!" accompanied by shouts of "Gag! Gag! Gag!" As the House divided there came the now accustomed shouts as Mr. Gladstone and Mr. Balfour passed out on either side. Mr. Courtney, on his way to the "No" lobby, paused for a moment at the table and spoke to Mr. Mellor. The Conservatives above the gangway, suspicious even in this quarter, cried "Leave the Chair to itself!" The Clause was agreed to by a majority of 35—324 voting in its favour and 289 against.

When the figures were announced in the division on Clause 6, showing that. in a House of 615 members the Ministerial majority had been reduced to 15, the Opposition were wrought to a pitch of excitement not seen in recent years. Mr. Johnston, of Ballykilbeg, was so profoundly moved that he rose and defiantly wagged beard and forefinger at the Treasury Bench. In the excitement of the moment the Chairman forgot to repeat the figures announced by the Whips, and was reminded of the omission by excited cries of "Numbers! Numbers!"

Disregarding this interruption, he put the question "That Clause 7 be added to the Bill." Sir James Fergusson, remaining seated with his hat on, the House having been cleared for a division, said there were blanks in the Clause, and wanted to know what they were voting about. To which there came jubilant response "That doesn't matter." Mr. Mellor sturdily putting the question, the House divided amid fresh scenes of excitement. The Clause was added to the Bill by a majority of 36, a return towards the normal Ministerial majority, at which there was much cheering. Mr. Gladstone, returning from the division lobby after voting for

Clause 8, was hailed by the Ministerialists with enthusiastic cheering. On this division the numbers were—For the Clause, 323 ; against, 291—a majority of 32.

It was now twenty-five minutes past eleven, and the work appointed for the Committee being concluded, Mr. Gladstone moved to report progress. A storm of cries of " No ! no ! " rang through the House. Mr. Mellor discreetly met this fresh and unexpected outburst by leaving the chair, being pursued in his retreat by shouts of contumely.

Mr. Gladstone took up his box and walked out, the Conservative Opposition hooting him as he passed between the Treasury Bench and the table. At the first break of this fresh insult, the Liberals and Irish members angrily leaped to their feet and, waving hats and arms, enthusiastically cheered the Premier, who, with head erect, walked out apparently unconscious of either demonstration. The Speaker having taken the chair, Sir William Harcourt thought it would be now agreeable for the House to adjourn. At half-past eleven the assembly, excited beyond even recent custom, streamed forth, joining the crowd still keeping holiday outside.

It is a truism established by a multitude
7th July.   of cases that the House is invariably the
A Breach of
Privilege.   chief sufferer from any attempt to put
in operation the archaic rules that deal
with breaches of privilege. Thanks to the bearing of the Speaker, the Leadership of Mr. Gladstone, always fine at these crises, and the admirable manner of Mr. Balfour, the dignity of the House was splendidly vindicated when this afternoon the question of Mr. Conybeare's newspaper attack on the Speaker again came up.

It was a delicate undertaking for Mr. Tim Healy to appear on the scene, in some sense as the advocate of Mr. Conybeare. The patience of the House longsuffering in measure unknown to ordinary assemblies, had broken down. Mr. Gladstone, after generously and skilfully endeavouring to let Mr. Conybeare down gently, gave up the attempt, and amid a ringing cheer moved that the letter which was the head and front of the offending was a breach of privilege. Mr. Balfour seconded the motion, and the House having long had opportunity for studying the exhibition presented by Mr. Conybeare was no longer in a mood to be trifled with. Mr. Healy's ordinary contributions to personal debates are not framed in manner successfully designed to soothe angry passions. Now Tim cooed the House of Commons like a sucking dove. He was respectful to his audience, deferential to the Speaker, and, above all, careful to dissociate himself from the slightest sympathy with Mr. Conybeare's action. It was to that gentleman he personally directed his remarks, suggesting that " his dignity would not suffer " by making the apology the House demanded.

Members smiled at this way of putting it; but Conservatives joined Liberals in cheering Tim when he finished his speech, Mr. Chamberlain paying a handsome tribute to the delicacy of its tone. Probably nothing that passed gave the Speaker more pleasure than to hear this truculent personage with ordinarily ungovernable tongue now declare in broken accents how in times past "the Irish members, then a persecuted minority, frequently felt the shelter of your protection."

Mr. Conybeare makes a Personal Explanation By this time it must have been borne in upon Mr. Conybeare that he had made a mistake. Incredible as it appears, he had deliberatel come down to the House prepared to flout its judgment and have a fresh fling at the Speaker. This state of mind, even when developed by Mr. Conybeare, was so inconceivable that the House listened to him for fully a quarter of an hour before realising the situation. When he asked leave to make a personal explanation it was readily granted on the natural assumption that, however tardily, he desired to offer an apology for the conduct questioned on the previous Tuesday. The House of Commons is almost absurdly ready to receive an apology. A member may go to utmost extremes of personal abuse or disorderly conduct. If only, under whatever pressure, he will apologise, he is cheered as enthusiastically as if he had accomplished some meritorious action. It is the old, old story of the joy over the one sinner who has repented. The member for Camborne has not succeeded in establishing for himself a position of personal popularity in the House. But had he this afternoon occupied three minutes with frank apology all would have been forgotten and forgiven. At least for the rest of the night (assuming he held his tongue) he would have been a prime favourite.

His voice and manner, it is true, were not particularly gracious. His black brows met in a forbidding scowl, and his voice was unpleasantly harsh as he complained that when on Tuesday he chanced to be absent when a charge of breach of privilege was brought against him "none of my hon. friends" thought it worth while to rise and suggest that the absence might be due to accident. This unfortunate manner might be due to habitude, training, or some natural cause beyond his control. It is not given to every man to be graceful. Only men of fine breeding and nature can comport themselves with winning grace when making an apology. Members showed some signs of growing impatience as the speech lengthened and approach to the apology grew more remote. Still, it must come, and the best must be made of the unfortunate manner of its presentation. It is an ancient axiom that you cannot make a silk purse out of a sow's ear.

When Mr. Conybeare had disposed of **No Apology.** those men in buckram, his " hon. friends," presumedly ready to take up the cudgels in his behalf, he turned to demolish Mr. Gladstone and the Speaker. These high authorities had on Tuesday night agreed that proper procedure for a member having a charge to make against the Speaker was by resolution, not by attack in the columns of a morning newspaper. Now, was that so? Mr. Conybeare proceeded to ask, turning over fresh leaves of the sheaf of manuscript with which he had provided himself. He differed from the right hon. gentlemen, and would presently show they were altogether in the wrong.

At this proposal the crowded House almost gasped for breath. Instead of apologising, Mr. Conybeare was justifying his position. Instead of withdrawing the charge against the Speaker, he was repeating it. Mr. Cohen rose to order, but was so terrified at a gesture made by the Speaker, and a glimpse caught of the terrible face set in the broad-bottomed wig, that he gratefully resumed his seat without submitting the question of order he had in his mind. Mr. Conybeare went on in harsher voice, with blacker scowl, citing passages from the Speaker's ruling on Tuesday and the Premier's remarks in supporting it.

Then Mr. Gladstone interposed, and with voice, manner, and turn of phrase that made more painful by contrast the exhibition from which they temporarily relieved the House, pointed out that the limits of a personal explanation had been already exceeded. This gentle manner, misunderstood as a sign of weakness, only encouraged Mr. Conybeare to continue. Mr. R. T. Reid more sharply raised the question whether this sort of thing was to be permitted to go on much longer.

That was the signal for a magnificent **The Lion Roused.** outbreak from the Chair which almost alarmed the House. The lion was loose,

and its roaring made even innocent men tremble.
On Tuesday, when he alluded to the printed charge,
the Speaker displayed an emotion a little out of proportion, some thought, to the intrinsic importance of
anything that might be said or done by Mr. Conybeare.
This fresh departure was more than Peel flesh and
blood could stand.   Trembling in every limb with
indignation, uplifting his voice to thunderous heights,
the Speaker turned full on the figure seated below the
gangway, with head hung down and arms sullenly
folded.   He recited a considerable list of attacks, of a
kind similar to that now under consideration, made
upon the Chair by Mr. Conybeare.   Incidentally he
mentioned that in 1887, Mr. Conybeare having
brought against the Speaker a charge of the most
outrageous character, a member had put in his hands
a motion for his expulsion, and abandoned his intention of moving it only at the Speaker's earnest
entreaty.   These attacks had been repeated by Mr.
Conybeare, "and now, forsooth," said the Speaker,
" under the guise of performing a public duty, he
charges me with the grossest offence possible to a
man in my position."   He hoped the House would
excuse him if he had shown some warmth, " but,"
he added, amid a prolonged burst of sympathetic
cheering, " I would be scarcely human if I could sit
unmoved under such imputation."

Such an outburst of splendid wrath would
have withered up an ordinary man.   It is
questionable whether it singed a hair of
Mr. Conybeare's beard.   There was a bad five minutes,
when it seemed that, after all, he would have the satisfaction of leaving the House of Commons in a ludicrous
position.   It having been unanimously agreed that the
letter was a breach of privilege, there followed, as a
natural consequence, the passing of the sentence.   The
Speaker, generously anxious to give the culprit a last
chance, suggested that he might even now apologise

A Surly
Apology.

for his offence against the authority of the Chair and
the dignity of the House.   But Mr. Conybeare had
withdrawn, and no one could say where he was at the
moment.   Mr. Storey and Mr. Caine went in search of
him, and for fully five minutes the House sat uncom-
fortably conscious that it was in a ridiculous position.
Just when this had grown unbearable, the member for
Camborne slouched in, and almost inaudibly mumbled
an apology that had obviously been prepared for his
use by mediatory hands.

"Something in the nature of an inadequate apology," Mr. Balfour described it, "wrung slowly and
painfully from the reluctant lips of the member
for Camborne."

Such as it was, the House was glad to accept it as
the price of getting rid of Mr. Conybeare.

CHAPTER XIV.

STORM AND STRESS.

PARTY feeling runs higher in the House
of Commons just now than has been the
case since the epidemic of Jingo fever.
It centres chiefly round Mr. Chamberlain, who, to
do him justice, makes no special effort to smooth
ruffled feelings. The House is much in the condition
of a habitually volcanic mountain. Through a sitting
there are spaces, sometimes two or three hours in
length, when debate goes forward in humdrum style.
Suddenly, without warning, there is eruption, and
down the slopes of the erstwhile placid pastures there
rolls a torrent of flaming lava.

The change that has gradually come over the
scene is strongly marked in the case of Mr. Gladstone.
When the Session opened he was so immovably
placid in his manner as to aggravate some of his followers spoiling for a fight. No provocation from the
other side or from the more potent source of irritation
in the camp where Mr. Chamberlain sits was successful
in rousing him. He could not be induced to take the
strong measures for coping with avowed obstruction
forced on his attention by impetuous followers. He
was always hoping that to-morrow and to-morrow
things would be better, and that patience would accomplish its perfect work Of late he has altered his
mien. If Mr. Balfour, Mr. Chamberlain, or Mr.
Goschen trail their coat before him, be sure he will
jump upon it with passionate energy marvellous in an
octogenarian. His yielding to the hot passion of the
hour has been the withdrawal of the last breakwater
that stemmed the rush of Parliamentary passion.

12th July.

This, the second night of recurring closure,
resulted in the addition of a batch of
clauses to the Home Rule Bill. Under
the special resolution there is no opportunity for speech-making. The only thing to be done
to testify to patriotic feeling is from time to time to
walk all round the House through the division lobbies
back to a seat that may or may not be found. That
is a kind of exercise which, started punctually at ten
o'clock, and pursued through two hours of a summer
night, is apt to pall upon body and soul. Mr. Villiers
early retired from the contest. Mr. Gladstone, looking
fagged, stayed on to the last, judiciously seizing the
opportunity for twenty winks whilst members returned from the division lobbies, waking up to chat
and laugh with Sir William Harcourt, who bubbled
over with good humour. Sir Isaac Holden, another
octogenarian, saw the fight through, apparently without (using the phrase in a Parliamentary sense) turning
a hair.

13th July. "After Supper WalkaWhile."

The last division showing a falling off in the attendance, there were cries of " Agreed ! agreed ! " when
Clause 23 was put from the Chair. But the Opposition
were determined to die hard, and went out once more
on the dreary round.

A member, desirous of making the best of
the necessity of frequent walking through
the lobby in connection with the Home
Rule Bill, has carefully measured the distance achieved
in completing each division. He finds it to be as
nearly as possible two hundred yards. Hence it follows that members who took part in the ten divisions
challenged to-night had the satisfaction of knowing
that in the best interests of their country they walked
an appreciable distance over a mile.

Legislation by Mileage.

No one, least of all Mr. Chamberlain,
would like to see Sir William Harcourt
marching to the stake ; but there ` are

14th July. A Martyr Minister.

times when, looking upon him in the House of Commons, it is borne in upon the reflective mind that, if such should unhappily prove his fate, he would bear himself with singular appropriateness of manner. When contumelious remarks are addressed to him he has a way of drooping his eyelids, bending his head, and meekly folding his hands upon his stricken breast, which recalls familiar pictures of the early Christian martyr walking to his doom. The effect of the attitude is not the less impressive since it usually follows upon some particularly aggressive action. He has wantonly cracked some skull, prodded someone under the fifth rib, and, reprisals being made, suddenly assumes this attitude of superhuman meekness. With a "Well, well," he protests he is really very sorry, nothing having been further from his intention than to introduce controversial matter into the conversation.

Sir William had most of this morning's sitting to himself, and the House enjoyed full opportunity of considering this phase of an interesting personality. For weeks, even months, he has observed that vow of silence imposed upon all good Home Rulers. What he must have suffered hearing Mr. Balfour and Mr. Chamberlain incessantly talk and he forbidden to reply will probably never be known. The agony has been patiently borne. Even when an ingenious mind might have found excuse for romping in and having fifteen minutes of fearsome joy, Sir William has been able to resist the temptation. To-day his opportunity came, but it was sorely handicapped by circumstances. In the first place, it was a morning sitting, and at the Theatre Royal, Westminster, morning sittings have that depressing effect upon pit and stage that Miss Ellen Terry, according to confidences made to her friends, finds prevalent even at the Lyceum at a morning performance. At Westminster, moreover, there is lacking the advantage of

darkened windows and artificial light. Business,
commenced at an unaccustomed hour, is carried on
under the chilling influence of daylight.

Thunder and Rathbone. How much atmospheric conditions have
to do with Parliamentary success was
shown on Wednesday afternoon, when
Mr. Rathbone, of all men, raised the standard of revolt
against his revered leader. Mr. Rathbone, though
an amiable man, is not an impressive orator. On
Wednesday when he, with broken voice and curiously
flattened bodily aspect, as if he had literally been sat
upon, protested that thirty years' faithful following
had been checked by Mr. Gladstone's light-hearted
treatment of the question of Irish representation in
the Imperial Parliament, the very heavens were
moved. The sky suddenly grew black. Through
the darkened chamber the lightning flashed, and peal
after peal of thunder echoed the plaint of the member
for Carnarvonshire. Standing at the corner seat
behind the Treasury Bench, looking down upon the
guilty Minister who feigned sleep on the Treasury
Bench, Mr. Rathbone's figure assumed heroic proportions. His voice, not ordinarily his strongest
point, reverberated through the ghostly chamber till
members, tremulously listening, were not sure at
particular moments whether it was the thunder or
Mr. Rathbone that spoke.

Marriage of the Duke of York. That was a rare scenic effect Sir William
Harcourt might well envy his long faithful
friend. There was neither thunder nor
lightning to-day, only a prosaic July
afternoon. Proceedings opened with a sort of anti-
climax to recent rejoicings round a Royal marriage.
Mr. Gladstone moved, and Mr. Arthur Balfour
seconded, congratulatory addresses to all nearly concerned in the happy event. This is a ceremony
which always has a depressing effect upon the
spirits of the House of Commons. Spontaneity is

the soul of congratulation, and inevitably spontaneity must be absent from the formal proceedings of a deliberative assembly. The moderate number of members present were chiefly anxious to watch how Mr. Gladstone would tread afresh the well-worn ground, and how Mr. Balfour would comport himself in this new experience as Leader of the Opposition.

That Mr. Gladstone acquitted himself well goes without saying. It is a truism of Parliamentary criticism that on these occasions, whether they be ushered in by wedding-bells or by muffled notes from the belfry of St. Paul's, he says the right thing in the right way. Mr. Balfour's speech, in respect of loftiness of tone and felicity of expression, was a worthy second, adding fresh evidence to that accumulated with sudden access during the past three weeks of his aptitude for the high office to which he has been called.

It is, nevertheless, a melancholy fact that the chief interest of the House was centred in the prospect of the counter-demonstration hinted at by the Premier in the opening sentences of his speech. Few knew who was the member who had privately intimated his intention of varying the unanimity of the proceedings. It turned out to be Mr. Keir Hardie who had rattled his pea-charged bladder in the Premier's face and alarmed the House of Commons with the prospect of breaking in on the congratulatory pæan with discordant note.

But nothing came of Mr. Keir Hardie, as nothing hitherto has come except the wearing of a tweed travelling cap under the eye of the Speaker, and a succession of abortive attempts to move the adjournment of the House. The Address of Congratulation was moved in time to leave Sir William Harcourt full opportunity of delivering his speech. Beyond this prelude and other depressing influences of the hour there was its subject-matter. He had undertaken to explain what he called "the simple outlines" of the financial scheme of the Home Rule Bill.

Depressing Moments. To tell the truth, however the great heart of the nation may glow in presence of the theme, the House of Commons is sick unto death of the Home Rule Bill, and an excursion into figures, however colossal, was not an exercise calculated to release it from a state of torpor. Sir William Harcourt, excelled by no man in the quickness and accuracy of his Parliamentary instinct, was aware of this fact, and attuned his voice and bearing to the situation. He pitched his voice in a low key, monotonously maintained through a speech of considerable length. Of his scanty audience it is probable that only Mr. Gladstone, Mr. Goschen, and Mr. Sexton thoroughly understood the subject. From time to time Mr. Chamberlain reminded the House of his presence on a back bench. For the most part the Chancellor of the Exchequer addressed his observations across the table to Mr. Goschen, occasionally replying "That is so" to an interjectionary speech made by Mr. Sexton.

Sometimes the Old Man—not Mr. Gladstone, but the other and older Parliamentary Hand alluded to by Mr. Wallace in a speech that establishes his reputation as the most vigorously original speaker in the present Parliament—got the upper hand, and Sir William slyly prodded Mr. Goschen or, accidentally as it were, beat Mr. Chamberlain's hat over his eyes. The manner in which it was done, though of course undesigned, added to the aggravation, and brought up in succession his two right hon. friends with angry retort that temporarily awoke the attention of the slumbering House. Nothing could be more immediate or complete than the Chancellor's contrition. Mr. Goschen complained that he had attributed to him advocacy of a certain policy, whereas he had been merely stating a hypothetical case.

"Very well," said Sir William in a cooing tone, as a motherly nurse soothes an intractable child, "I will not call it a policy but a hypothesis. It is only a syllable longer."

The milk of human kindness with which he overflowed was not to be soured even by Mr. Chamberlain's remark snapped across the House, "You are running away, as you did last night." Had that remark been addressed to Mr. Sexton, it would have been the end of ordered business for the sitting. He would have capped it by retort more unparliamentary still. Mr. Bartley would have risen to insist on withdrawal. The whole House would have broken into uproar. Mr. Mellor would vainly have repeated his famous and familiar dictum, "All disorderly words are undesirable"; and at ten minutes to seven the morning sitting would have lapsed. Sir William Harcourt folded his hands with pathetic meekness, protested he had not meant to irritate anyone, and members went to sleep again, soothed by the murmur of innumerable figures.

19th July.
Mr. Michael
Davitt.

The accident by which Mr. Michael Davitt has been prevented from re-entering Parliament is regretted on both sides of the House of Commons. That the disability should have been imposed on him is a last misfortune in a very hard case. His seat for North Meath was vacated on petition, owing to the indiscreet and unsolicited advocacy of his cause by certain parish priests. Bankruptcy followed on his inability to pay the costs arising out of the proceedings in connection with the petition. It is no secret that money to meet the charges was offered him from more than one quarter. But Mr. Davitt would not be beholden to charity in this or other form. The Act of Bankruptcy left him incapacitated for Parliamentary service unless he had a certificate of discharge. This in the circumstances would have been forthcoming as a matter of

course. But the Judge's holiday being due, his
Honour went off to take it, leaving Mr. Davitt uncerti-
ficated, and therefore unable to accept the invitation
pressed upon him to occupy the safe seat vacated by
Mr. Deasy.

Mr. Davitt will probably be less troubled by this
turn of affairs than anyone else. He has never been
attracted by House of Commons life, though, being
there a short time, he made one of the few marks
scored by new members. Still, according to his
habitude, he would have yielded personal inclination
to the claims of his country, and would have stood for
West Mayo if the Bankruptcy Judge's holiday had
chanced to be taken at a less inconvenient time.

21st July.
Mr.
Chamberlain.
This is the forty-fourth sitting in Committee on the Home Rule Bill. Mr.
Chamberlain resumed the debate in a
speech notable among other things for
breaking, as far as he is concerned, the silence of a
full week. Up to last Thursday, particularly on that
day, he was in the van of the fight. Tireless,
resourceful, he might ever be counted upon to be in
his place ready for a tilt with Mr. Gladstone.

This week he has sat silent on his dismantled
watch-tower behind the Treasury Bench. A beaten
army, at Metz and elsewhere, is always ready
to turn and rend the captain who, whilst the issue
was yet uncertain, they enthusiastically followed.
The Tories, who never trusted or liked their ancient
but transformed enemy, now gloomily reproach Mr.
Chamberlain with being the chief cause of their
crushing defeat at the very moment when they had
counted on victory. If, they say, he had refrained
from speaking at a critical moment, the Government, if not actually placed in a minority on the 9th
Clause, would have been paralysed by the smallness
of their majority. Mr. Chamberlain, certain that the
long-delayed hour of triumph was at hand, let himself

H

go, and delivered a speech the jubilant malignancy of which turned the waverers in the Ministerial ranks, driving them back into Mr. Gladstone's arms.

That is the story as told on the Terrace **His Position in the House.** and murmured in the smoke-room. It is useful as indicating the peculiar position Mr. Chamberlain holds in the House of Commons. He has undoubtedly earned the distinction of being the best-hated man who sits on its benches. Oddly enough, he has through the vicissitudes of a remarkable political career always, in certain degree, held this high position. Sir William Marriott and Lord Randolph Churchill will recall a time, following close upon the Aston Park Riots, when they had but to mention the name of Mr. Chamberlain to raise a roar of execration among the gentlemen of England seated at that time to the right of the Speaker. It then seemed impossible for any public man to be held in more bitter detestation by his fellow kind than was the Radical Chief by the Conservative party. The only parallel case known was that of Mr. John Bright. It came to pass that that one-time terror of Toryism appreciably benefited by Mr. Chamberlain's emergence into political prominence. No party seems capable of cherishing at the same moment bitter hatred for two men. Thus it came to pass that Mr. Bright gradually won upon the esteem of the Conservative party; the clamour, for which in earlier days his uprising in the House of Commons had been the signal, being reserved for his younger and even more aggressive colleague.

This feeling of personal animosity, rarely evoked in English political life, seemed then to have reached its fullest possible development. But compared with what actually exists at the present day, with Mr. Chamberlain still the object of attack, the evil humours of that epoch are as moonlight unto sunlight, as water unto wine. When in these days of

newly ordered conflict Mr. Chamberlain rises to discuss
a clause or amendment in the Home Rule Bill Mr.
Byles cannot contain himself. Hot Yorkshire blood
has doubtless much to do with the ebullitions that
from time to time disturb the serenity of the ecclesiastical precincts below the gangway. But the
member for the Shipley division of Yorkshire is,
with a difference, typical of the personal attitude of
a large section of the House of Commons towards
Mr. Chamberlain. Mr. Byles actually heaves the
oratorical half-brick at sight of the stranger. They
threateningly turn it over in their pockets, glance
at the Speaker, and find relief for their overcharged
feelings in anguished howls and more or less inarticulate murmurs.

"Cool as a Cucumber." In striking contrast with this seething sea
of hatred, malice, and all uncharitableness
is the almost benign presence that evokes
its upheaval. It is terrible to think what would happen in the House of Commons if Mr. Chamberlain
were not richly endowed with the priceless gift of
imperturbability. As he observed the other day in
the midst of one of the recurrent outbursts of storm,
he is always cool as a cucumber. The fiercer the
storm rages the milder he grows, the more genial
is his smile, the more dulcet his tones. Always
supremely good in debate, he is at his very best
when he stands with his back to the wall, beating
off, with what seems a dangerously slight rapier, the
forest of shillelaghs that rage round his head.

It is well that it should be thus. Of all men in
public life Mr. Chamberlain has the least right to
claim immunity from attack, or to go whimpering to
the Speaker when rude words are spoken about him.
In political warfare he has never hesitated to shoot;
and though it is a curious phase of human nature,
noted in journalism not less than in the Parliamentary
arena, that a man habitually engaged in prodding at

others indignantly resents any chance puncturing
of his own skin, it is well to have a conspicuous
exception.

Mr. Chamberlain's speech this afternoon was
marked by the full measure of his dialectical skill. It
was an elaborate and merciless criticism of the latest
edition of the financial proposals of the Home Rule
scheme. It seemed natural he should be followed
by Mr. Gladstone, who had sat attentive. Probably
that was part of Mr. Chamberlain's plan of campaign in interposing at this juncture. Had the
Premier followed, there would have been a slashing
speech which would have sustained and increased the
heat to which Mr. Chamberlain had worked up the
Committee. Mr. Balfour would inevitably have followed, and by the time he had concluded the morning
sitting would have slipped away. It would have been
magnificent, but not business.

What actually took place was one of those little
moves more familiar when Mr. Disraeli was Leader of
the House than has been the case in later times. Mr.
Henry Fowler was put up to reply, and effected his
task in a manner that distinctly added to his Parliamentary reputation. In the way of tactics nothing
could have been better than to oppose to the brilliant
swordsman this matter-of-fact business man with his
full knowledge, his lucid method of exposition, and his
sturdy fashion of sticking to the text. Mr. Fowler
instantly brought the excited audience down to the
wholesome level of a deliberative assembly, and
effectually prevented any fresh development of the
extraneous.

CHAPTER XV.

THE STORM BURSTS.

27th July.
A Memorable
Scene.

As the history of the last twenty years testifies, the House of Commons has not been unacquainted with grief in the way of disorderly scenes. At least, it has been able to boast that in one extreme development they manage these things worse in France. Up to to-night there has never been actual personal conflict, on the floor of the House. It is true that on the eve, or, to be more precise, on the morning, of the introduction of the Home Rule Bill there was a scrimmage in which Colonel Saunderson, one of the heroes of to-night's riot, prominently figured. But at the moment he laid low the Irish member who accused him of sitting on his hat the House was not actually in session. It was still early morning, and the mêlée arose in the process of securing seats whence Mr. Gladstone's speech on introducing the Home Rule Bill might be conveniently heard. To-night the riot raged midway through the sitting, interrupting the deliberations on one of the most momentous measures ever submitted to the judgment of Parliament.

It began, as most memorable scenes in the Commons do, after a long interval of deadly dulness. As usual in these later times, it was Mr. Chamberlain who fired the unsuspected train. In the dramatic arrangements of the Opposition campaign it was his turn to be interrupted by the application of the closure.

"King Herod."

He was evidently determined to make the most of the opportunity, and succeeded beyond his wildest expectations. It was a

quarter to ten when he rose, and the House, deserted
through the drear night, was rapidly filling up.   Mr.
Gladstone was in his pla   , and though he sat reposeful
on the Treasury bench, with face upturned so that the
light falling on it showed his closed eyes and appearance of placid sleep, Mr. Chamberlain knew very well
he was wide awake, intently listening.   Cheers and
counter-cheers punctuated the vitriolic sentences that
dropped from the corner of the third bench below the
gangway.   With his eye on the clock, noting the
speeding moments, Mr. Chamberlain kept his dead-
liest dart for the last.   After scornfully describing the
Ministerialists as slavishly obedient to Mr. Gladstone's
varied moods, saying "It is good" when he called
an object black, crying "It is better" when he
described it as white, he quoted the line from the
terrible picture portrayed in the Acts of the Apostles,
when King Herod, going down from Judæa to Cæsarea
upon a set day, arrayed himself in royal apparel, sat
on the throne and made an oration to the men of
Tyre and Sidon.

"And the people shouted, saying, It is the voice of
a god and not of a man."

Up to this moment Mr. Chamberlain had not mentioned by name the iniquitous king over whom, even
in this moment of apparently final triumph, the Angel
of the Lord stood with uplifted sword.   It was not
because he was afraid to push the illustration to its
utmost point.   There was a cry of "Judas!"
and a sudden disturbance in the Irish camp.

Judas.

Mr. Chamberlain waited till there was a lull,
and then, his clear voice ringing through the House,
he added, "Never since the time of Herod have there
been such slaves to such a dictator."

That was the last completed sentence spoken for
the next twenty minutes, through which there raged
in the House of Commons a scene Donnybrook
Fair in its prime could not excel.   Mr. Chamberlain's

comparison of Mr. Gladstone to King Herod at the moment preceding the awful fate brought down upon him by a reign of unrelieved wickedness seemed natural enough to good Conservatives. They madly cheered the reference. But when the Irish members, not to be outdone in force of Biblical allusion, greeted Mr. Chamberlain with cry of "Judas! Judas!" articulate words could not give expression to the Opposition's outraged feelings and their jealousy for the maintenance of decent order in debate.

At this point Mr. Chamberlain was inter-
The Closure. rupted by two of his political friends, Mr. Johnston and Mr. Vicary Gibbs, simultaneously on their legs. Their voices did not rise above the clamour. The shouts were varied by cries of "Ten o'clock! ten o'clock!" and, the hand of the clock now pointing to that hour, the Chairman rose amid deafening shouts. He proceeded to put the question, but what it might be was not heard amid the stormy cries. Mr. Vicary Gibbs, seated with his hat on, was heard to call attention to the fact, patent enough, that someone had called out "Judas!" He mentioned Mr. T. P. O'Connor as the offender. The Chairman rose with vain cry of "Order! Order!" Mr. Vicary Gibbs, still seated, shouted out his accusation against "the hon. member for the Scotland Division of Liverpool." He moved that the "words be taken down."

The Chairman declared that the expression had not reached his ears, at which there were cries of "Oh, oh!" from the party of Law and Order.

"It reached mine!" shouted the indomitable Vicary Gibbs. "I move that it be taken down."

Mr. Hanbury came to the assistance of his neighbour, whereupon the Chairman insisted upon putting the question, and, the order given for the House to be cleared, some members rose, making for the division lobby.

But the Conservatives sat still, answering to the word of command, " Don't move ! "

It is one of the quaint regulations of procedure that, when the House has been cleared for a division, members desiring to address the Chair may do so only when seated with their hats on. On various benches members in this attitude were seen, with hand to mouth, yelling at the perturbed Chairman, who stood at the table, forlornly wringing his hands and calling out "Order ! Order!" as if it were an incantation.

Mr. Hanbury now took up the running, and insisted upon the Chairman taking down the words Mr. Vicary Gibbs was still strenuously reciting. Mr. Mellor, again on his feet, vainly appealed for order. Mr. Gibbs, running down the gangway, planted himself on the Front Opposition Bench, whence he more conveniently shouted something meant for the Chairman's ear, its purport drowned by the uproar that filled the Chamber. Members who had left for the division lobby streamed back, and, amid increased excitement, the floor and benches were filled.

While Mr. Gibbs was still bellowing at A Free Fight. the Chairman, Mr. Mellor crying "Order! Order !" Mr. Logan rushed over from below the gangway towards the Front Opposition Bench, making straight for Mr. Carson, who was shouting something at the top of his voice. He seated himself in quite inadequate space between Mr. Carson and his neighbouring colleague, and they angrily shouted and gesticulated at each other. Sir William Walrond appeared on the scene as a peacemaker and induced Mr. Logan to retire. As he was going, Mr. Hayes Fisher and Sir E. Ashmead-Bartlett assisted his departure with violent hands. Mr. Fisher seized Mr. Logan by the back of the neck and thrust him forward. The strangers in the gallery privileged to witness this new legislative departure testified to their feelings by loudly hissing.

The Irish members, seeing a friend in trouble, rushed forward in a body to the rescue. They were met at the gangway by Colonel Saunderson, Mr. Burdett - Coutts, and Colonel Waring. Hats were knocked off in all directions. The House filled with uproar. In the gangway a tumultuous mass of men clutched at each other's throats. In the vortex of the maëlstrom Mr. Tim Healy was seen struggling. Colonel Saunderson, his coat half torn off his back, struck out right and left. The first blow fell on Mr. Crean, who in the rush was separated from his assailant. Forcing his way back again, he dealt the Colonel a terrible blow on the face. Mr. Tommy Bowles, sitting down with both hands to his mouth, yelling at the top of his voice, attracted the special attention of Mr. Tim Healy. Hissing, booing, yelling roared through the House. A mass of fully forty members—what is known in quieter times as a quorum—were still inextricably mingled below the gangway. One member was knocked down and dragged out of the scuffle by the heels. For fully five minutes the scrimmage lasted, hats being blocked, coats torn, and faces bruised.

Someone had the happy thought of calling out, "Send for the Speaker!" The cry was taken up in various parts of the House. All the while Mr. Gladstone sat on the Treasury Bench, pale to the lips, profoundly moved by this Parliamentary experience, new to a veteran of more than fifty years. The Sergeant-at-Arms appeared in the *mêlée* and tried to part the combatants, an effort in which he was gallantly assisted by Sir William Walrond and Mr. Herbert Gladstone. A fresh movement was made by the Liberals, led by Mr. Gladstone, walking out of the House, the fight still going on around the almost coatless Colonel Saunderson. One Tory member was heard to shout out: "Mr. Mellor, I shall not leave the House till the Speaker arrives." A group, including

H *

Mr. Balfour, Mr. Chamberlain, Sir J. Gorst, and Lord
R. Churchill, gathered round the Chair in animated
conversation with Mr. Mellor. They had passed out
into the division lobby, where echoes of the combat
reached their ears, and they with some difficulty
struggled back to the table. Mr. Gibbs, who still
retained his newly-assumed post on the Front Opposition Bench, attempted to still the storm by crying
aloud that the Chairman had taken the words down.
Mr. Hanbury, anxious to have this point settled,
questioned the fact, and was eagerly assured by Mr.
Gibbs that it was all right. Mr. Balfour, seated, and
wearing somebody else's hat, addressed the Chair, but
what he said no man out of arm's length knoweth.

The Speaker
Arrives.

It was now twenty minutes past ten, the
uproar having been in full force for
twenty minutes. The Speaker had been
sent for, and his appearance instantly calmed the
scene. The Chairman, standing at his right elbow,
reported that he had taken down the words of an
anonymous member, though he was careful to say
they had not reached his ear. Mr. Vicary Gibbs
named Mr. T. P. O'Connor as the offending member.
The Speaker appealed to whomsoever was guilty on
his honour to take the responsibility. Mr. Healy
showed a disposition to argue the matter, urging that
the point of disorder upon which the Speaker had
been sent for was the refusal of the Conservative
members to leave the House when the signal was
given by the Chairman. The Speaker appealed to
the Leaders of the House to assist him in coming to
a conclusion. Mr. Gladstone and Mr. Balfour succeeded each other with an eloquently halting narrative. Eventually Mr. T. P. O'Connor owned up and,
at the instance of the Speaker, apologised. The
tumultuous scene closed, and members went out to
the strangely delayed division.

There followed a series of divisions on the new

clauses and schedules, but the proceedings partook of the character of an anti-climax. Everyone was glad when it was over; and, amid loud cheers from the Ministerialists, the Home Rule Bill passed through Committee.

29th July. Colonel Gunter's Simple Story. Nothing has been told in connection with the riot in the House of Commons on Thursday night equal in heartrending effect to the simple story of Colonel Gunter. Unlike twenty-one colleagues seated in various parts of the House, who have been induced by an enterprising evening paper to record their impressions of the scene and their personal experience of its episodes, the gallant Colonel reserves his epic for the ear of his friends. Like the annals of the poor, it is short and simple. Ten o'clock having struck, the fatal hour for the condemned amendments, the Colonel heard Mr. Mellor put the question from the Chair and subsequently order the House to be cleared preparatory to a division. Thereupon the member for Barkston-Ash, trained in the tented field to habits of obedience, rose from his accustomed corner on the fourth seat above the gangway behind ex-Ministers, squared his shoulders, and began to march down the gangway steps.

Before he had advanced two paces he received an Irish member full in the pit of the stomach. During twelve years' active service, much of it spent in the Crimea, the Colonel has grown used to alarums and excursions, but candidly confesses that he was never so much surprised in his life. The inconvenience was not to be slighted, the Irish member arriving head first—and so soon after a hasty dinner, too! The situation is complicated by the fact that to this hour the Colonel does not know who the projectile was. He suspects Mr. Crean, but that may be an after-thought consequent on subsequent observation of that hon. member's active and eccentric proceedings.

Apart from the immediate consequences of the ramming process, the attention of the Colonel was distracted by the circumstance that the unceremonious visitor, whoever he might be, commenced vaguely but vigorously to thump him with his fists. Thereafter, in the tempest that suddenly surged down the gangway and over the benches adjoining, he disappeared in the throng.

Colonel
Saunderson.

This uncertainty of the identity of persons more or less prominently engaged is one of the notable peculiarities of this amazing outbreak.   There is, for example, the mystery which surrounds Colonel Saunderson's participation in the proceedings.   His earliest conviction that something was wrong was borne in upon him by discovering an hon. member tumbling over the back of the bench on which he was seated and, to a certain extent, dispersing himself over him.   There is no standing order or written injunction against that method of moving about the House.   But it is unusual and inconvenient.   Taken in conjunction with what Colonel Saunderson saw going on two benches below, where Mr. Hayes Fisher had hold of Mr. Logan by the back of the neck, and Sir Ellis Ashmead-Bartlett was apparently pummelling him in the region of the shirt-front, it conveyed the impression that things were in an abnormal state.

Colonel Saunderson, though constitutionally p to the pathways of peace, could not but regard this almost burglarious procedure as an act of war. Accordingly, having assisted the intruder to his feet, and recognising in him Mr. Crean, the Colonel aimed a blow at him straight out from the shoulder and hit Mr. Austin on the left jaw.   It is a question which was the more surprised at this, Colonel Saunderson or Mr. Austin.   With opportunity for calmer consideration it would have been recognised as fresh evidence of the general topsy-turvyism prevalent. But opportunity for calm reflection was limited. Before Colonel Saunderson could explain the little mistake that had occurred Mr. Crean, whose activity was catapultic, gave Colonel Saunderson what Dick Swiveller's friend, the Marchioness, was accustomed to describe as a "wonner" on the right temple..

This made discrimination impracticable, and the Colonel hit out right and left, a lurid light seeming to flash up and down his white waistcoat as glimpses were occasionally caught of it through the surging mass. It was merely the reflection of the gaslit roof. To the overwrought mind of on-lookers it lent a new terror to the scene.

How the Battle Began. This battle royal by the gangway was the Waterloo of the campaign. Quatre-Bras had immediately preceded it. That engagement took place on the Front Opposition Bench, and was the precursor of all that followed. It is strange to reflect upon the triviality of circumstances that sometimes lead to momentous issues. Had Mr. Logan chanced to be voting in the other lobby, he would have passed out by the doorway under the clock. Not skirting the Front Opposition Bench, Mr. Carson would not have called out "Yah!" to him, nor would Mr. Hayes Fisher have observed "Bah!" That being so, Mr. Logan would not have loftily remarked—

"Mr. Carson, I did not speak to you, and you have no business to address such an impertinent remark to me."

Mr. Carson, in the circumstances alluded to, would not, however appositely, have responded, "Get away; you are a gang of gaggers."

. Mr. Logan would not thereupon have sat partially upon Mr. Carson and, to some extent, upon the Front Opposition Bench. Mr. Hayes Fisher would not have clutched him by the back of the neck whilst Sir Ellis Ashmead-Bartlett ministered to him in front. The Irish members below the gangway would not have rushed forward in a body with intent, as Mr. Harrington later explained, to assist the Sergeant-at-Arms in keeping order. That being so, Mr. Crean would not have rested under strong suspicion of being the projectile that momentarily took away Colonel Gunter's breath. Nor would he thereafter have rolled over the back of the bench upon the knees of Colonel Saunderson. Colonel Saunderson, hitting out at Mr. Crean, would not have struck Mr. Austin, and the general scrimmage which followed might have been avoided.

All this shows how careful we ought to be in considering and ordering the most trivial actions of our daily life.

Peacemakers. Amongst the prominent martyrs of the misunderstanding that prevailed were the Irish members. Even Dr. Tanner did not escape the prevalent influence. When at the height of the scrimmage he was observed advancing rapidly in the direction of the Front Opposition Bench it did not occur to anyone that he was bent on pacific errand. Several of his own compatriots even intercepted him, gently, but firmly, turning his steps aside. It was the same with Mr. Tim Healy. Observing the incident on the Front Opposition Bench, he has told the world how " I went towards Mr. Fisher, having my hat in my hand." That is a piece of evidence introduced with the skill of a trained advocate. If Mr. Healy had had a shillelagh in his hand, it would be easy to understand what followed. "Some of the Tories objected to my passing down their bench," Mr. Healy writes, "and one of them, Mr. Harry Foster, rushed at me." Finding his signal of peace not understood, Mr. Healy placed it on his head, and, as he gently puts it, "was borne from the gangway,'

and looking back saw " a tangle of men on the gangway striking at each other. I saw no one hit."

That is still another peculiarity of the
More Frightened than Hurt. great fight. The spectacle Mr. Healy
looked upon from his position of retreat
must, it seemed, inevitably lead to the
serious disabling of at least a score of legislators.
One could see the teeth set, the eyes flashing, faces
aflame with wrath, and a thicket of closed fists
beating about in wild confusion. Yet, including
Colonel Gunter's misfortune, there were not more
than four men who bore about them marks of the
fight. When it was over, Colonel Saunderson, an
old campaigner, walked out with a bunch of keys
held to his bruised cheek—a simple remedy so
efficacious that when he appeared on the scene next
day only a slight scratch showed what might have
been. The appearance amid the throng of the
Sergeant-at-Arms was portentous, and seemed to show
that things were desperate indeed. But Mr. Erskine's
sternest remonstrance was addressed to a member
standing up below the gangway, watching the fight.

" I beg your pardon," said the Sergeant-at-Arms
gently, "but you're standing up with your hat on,
which you know is a breach of order."

The conscience-stricken member dropped down
on the seat, and the Sergeant-at-Arms passed up the
House on his message of peace.

Mr. Gladstone, seated on the Treasury
At the Bottom of it all. Bench, watched the scene throughout
with wofully troubled visage. He heard
Mr. Chamberlain's comparison of himself with King
Herod on the eve of his tragic downfall. He heard
the answering shout of " Judas! Judas!" that rose
from the Irish camp. Short of sight and hard of
hearing, as he pleaded when summoned as witness
by the Speaker, he could not have been blind to
the free fight going on opposite, nor deaf to the

clamour that accompanied its progress. Once he rose and took a step as if about to cross over, but promptly resumed his seat. To all appearances he was wholly unconscious of his personal responsibility for a scene the parallel of which was not to be found in his more than fifty years' experience of Parliament. Yet from time to time Mr. T. W. Russell shouted it at him from behind. Sir Ellis Ashmead-Bartlett roared it at him across the table. It was reserved for Mr. Fisher in the comparative quietude of the Library of the House of Commons to put the accusation formally and deliberately. After describing Mr. Logan's incursion on the Front Opposition Bench, Mr. Hayes Fisher writes, "To put a stop to his aggressive conduct I immediately seized him by the neck and forcibly ejected him on to the floor of the House. This was the signal for a general scrimmage." That seems clear enough and frank enough. But Mr. Fisher proceeds: "In my opinion, the responsibility for the discreditable scene of last night rests even more with Mr. Gladstone than with Mr. Logan." This is delightful as presenting Mr. Hayes Fisher in the hitherto unsuspected character of a humorist.

Colonel Gunter, over whose woes of Thursday night the House is still laughing, is a member of the eminent family of purveyors whose headquarters are appropriately fixed in the aristocratic neighbourhood of Berkeley Square. One of his forbears lives in history as having been the occasion of George the Fourth's saying a witty thing. Like the Yorkshire member, this earlier Gunter was in the Army. One day, riding in the suite of his Sovereign, his horse became embarrassingly restive.

31st July. An Earlier Gunter.

"Very sorry, your Majesty," he said, "but my horse is awfully hot."

"Ice him, Gunter, ice him," said Merry King George.

CHAPTER XVI.

THE BILL REPORTED.

AFTER throbbing with life through three months, culminating in the historic outbreak distantly alluded to by the Speaker as " the regrettable incident of Thursday night," the House has been in a state of almost complete collapse. The only exception to the prevalent depression is found in the person of Mr. Tommy Bowles. It would be misleading to say that this eminent jurist has fully preserved through the week that virile form which is the delight of the Senate and the sustentation of the Empire. But, considering the subtle predominant influence, he has been remarkably active. At the outset of his Parliamentary career Mr. Keir-Hardie acquired a habit of apparently posting letters to himself. Corners of envelopes peeped out from every pocket, whilst in both hands he carried an overflow supply. He did not seem to answer the letters, or even to open them, for the quantity did not appreciably diminish, nor his appearance through a long sitting greatly vary. As he walked about the House and corridors thus letter-laden he seemed to be engaged in the process of taking in his correspondence at the pores, as Joey Ladle in the recesses of his employer's cellar used to imbibe his spirituous liquor. Either Mr. Hardie's correspondence has decreased in bulk, or by long practice he has acquired a habit of more rapid absorption. He is rarely now seen without a few letters stuck in his waistcoat pockets. But his resemblance to an overladen and peripatetic pillar-box is less striking than of yore.

4th August. Collapse.

Mr. "Tommy" Bowles. Mr. Bowles acquired analogous habits, with the difference that, instead of stocking himself with letters, he loads himself with Blue-Books, Parliamentary papers, and odd volumes of Grotius, Kent, and other authorities on international law. To the stranger in the gallery there are few incidents more impressive or better calculated to convey a sense of the importance of Parliamentary affairs than to see the member for King's Lynn walk up the floor of the House with two arms full of Blue-Books. These set down on the bench where he is accustomed to sit are, in full view of the House, carefully studied and arranged, and then Mr. Bowles goes out for more. Sometimes, especially when he happens to select white papers to load himself withal, his movements are to the imaginative mind reminiscent of a magpie coming and going twig laden, intent on building its nest.

Mr. Bowles apparently does not make use of all the papers he studies, but their effect upon Sir Edward Grey, Mr. Mundella, or whomsoever may chance to be the Minister immediately under his attention, is prompt and effective. Mr. Mundella is an old Parliamentary hand, and manages with some success to dissemble his apprehension. Sir Edward Grey, though full of promise, is still young, and has not learned to restrain his feelings or check his emotions. When Mr. Bowles, after brief absence, returns with a Blue-Book that looks like Siam or Morocco, the Under Secretary for Foreign Affairs moves uneasily on the Treasury Bench, rather overdoing the effort to appear indifferent.

A Poser for the President of the Board of Trade. What makes Mr. Bowles so formidable as a critic is the range of his special information. Mr. Curzon knows something of Siam, and Sir Richard Temple, as he told the House on Wednesday, has the map of that remote country "distinctly imprinted on his brain." Mr. Bowles knows everything. As was written in a now almost forgotten book about Theophrastus Such, "in relation to all subjects he has a joyous consciousness of that ability which is prior to knowledge." Siam may be his *forte ;* omniscience is his foible.

Thus it comes to pass that no Minister is safe from him. The other night, having tackled Sir Ughtred Kay Shuttleworth with inquiry as to whose duty it was to call up the engineers and stokers when the *Victoria* was sinking; having floored Sir Edward Grey in questions about the slave trade in Tripoli ; having settled Siam and mediatised Morocco, he suddenly swooped down upon the President of the Board of Trade, insisting upon his straightway explaining to the House the bearings of the new rules of the road at sea. This was a fearful dilemma for Mr. Mundella, not accustomed to find himself in a position in which he must confess ignorance. With anyone else in front of him he might have got out of the difficulty with vague remarks about always turning to the left. Mr. Bowles was not to be trifled with.

"Suppose," he said, fixing the unhappy Minister with glittering eye, " the right hon. gentleman were at sea in heavy weather close hauled. If he met a fleet bearing down upon him on the weather bow what was he going to do ? "

Mr. Mundella looked pleadingly across at Admiral Field, but that friendly tar was too far off to lend a hand.

"Would he put his helm up ? " the inquisitor sternly continued. One could see the phrase half formed on Mr. Mundella's parched lips. "Up what?" he would like to have asked, but wisely said nothing.

"Would he put it down, then ? " Mr. Bowles continued. " Or " — giving the wretched Minister one more chance—" would he reef his foresail ? "

To get away from this terrible inquisition Mr. Mundella would probably have done anything. But the middle-aged mariner opposite, still fixing him with glittering eye, held him to the end, and then, gaily casting off the painter, turned upon Sir E. Grey with swift sudden inquiry as to what Russia was doing in the Pamirs?

11th Aug.
Last Stage of the Home Rule Bill.
Last Monday the Opposition returned to their task with loyal fervour. They mustered in surprising numbers, considering it is the second week in August, and showed every sign of readiness to renew on the report stage the desperate resistance offered to Home Rule on earlier passages of the Bill. But the first division taken, showing the Government majority steadfast at forty, damped their ardour, which ebbed away as successive divisions proved that that figure, actually above the normal level as matters stand to-day, was the minimum majority. If it had fluctuated at anything below forty, if it had haply touched thirty, the course of events through the past week would have been different.

But what is the use, Unionists ask themselves, of ever climbing up the climbing wave? Why should they stay in town in close attendance at Westminster if the only result of the self-sacrifice is to strengthen the position of the Ministry by demonstrating the steadfastness of their followers? Even Mr. Chamberlain now fails to stir the stagnant pool. Time was, but a few weeks past, when night after night he stood the centre of an excited audience, the Chamber filled with the roar of cheers and counter-cheers. Through this week he has been not less constant in attendance, not less persistent in attack, not one whit less bitter in speech. But the seed he has abundantly scattered has fallen upon stony ground. A whole week has passed, and there has not been anything approaching a scene. Even when Mr. Gladstone and Mr. Chamberlain come to grips the scanty audience looks on unmoved. What the House chiefly desires is to see an end made of the business, and so home to bed.

It is one of the curious episodes in the tiresome drama that as it reaches deeper depths of dulness Mr. Arthur Balfour grows sprightlier. At no time since the Bill was introduced has he shown to more advantage as Leader of the Opposition than through the week which has now worn itself out. His speech last night, interposed in the debate arising on the Habeas Corpus clause, was a masterpiece of effective attack masked under light raillery. Again to-night, in the difficult and delicate situation arising out of Mr. Gladstone's proposal for a conference on the question of single-member constituencies, he comported himself in a manner that delighted his supporters.

The Leader of the Opposition.

For some time at the commencement of the campaign it seemed as if the real Leader of the Opposition sat at the corner seat below the gangway on the Ministerial side. Conservatives observed with chagrin, not always successfully hidden, that their titular leader was disposed to play second fiddle, the first place in the orchestra being assumed by Mr. Chamberlain, for whom, as Mr. Gladstone suggests, their admiration as a powerful ally is in excess of the inveterateness of their love for the individual. However true this may have been through the Committee stage of the Bill, it has certainly not been the case in the first week on the report stage, throughout which Mr. Balfour has, apparently without effort, assumed and sustained his proper position of predominance.

It was pretty to see him watching Mr. Gladstone to-night when the old Parliamentary Hand played that strange lead about the single-member constituency. The Premier was himself a delightful study. Probably

"Will you Walk into my Parlour?"

if he had in six sentences proposed to adopt the successful precedent of 1884 in relation to the distribution of seats, and hold a friendly conference of the two Front Benches with a view to settling this branch of the Irish question, a simple answer accepting or declining the proposition would have been forthcoming. But Mr. Gladstone, in his anxiety to disclaim any ulterior intention, overdid it. His manner was so serious, his sentences so involved, his whole attitude so suggestive of a conspirator who never missed attendance upon any possible religious observance, that there was spread over the benches opposite a subtle atmosphere of distrust. It was a dangerous position for a young statesman to stand in. There was a vague but strongly felt idea that Mr. Gladstone's speech was a much elongated paraphrase in prose of the metrical invitation of the Spider to the Fly. The Leader of the Opposition could not assume that to be the case ; yet it would not be well to advance too close to the parlour door. Mr. Balfour must say something in reply, and he said nothing with exceeding skill. Uncompromising Mr. Courtney, from his watch-tower on the other side of the House, cried aloud that he would have nothing to do with the business, and good Conservatives, finding light at last, heartily cheered this determination.

14th Aug.
Mr.
Labouchere.

In the last Parliament there were few private members who exercised a measure of influence equal to that of Mr. Labouchere. His interposition in debate, frequent and wide in range of topics, always filled the House. Apart from that, he from the smoke-room and other places of political resort pulled strings to which many important-looking puppets danced. His position a short thirteen months ago is indicated by the fact that in speculation as to the formation of a Liberal Ministry his name was never omitted from competitive lists. Moreover, he was invariably named for Cabinet rank, the only difference of opinion being as to the post he would best fill. Another line on which speculation ran was as to whether or not, if office were offered him, he would think it worth while to barter his position of independence for Mr. Gladstone's shilling.

As matters turned out, this problem was never solved, since the necessity for deciding it was not cast upon Mr. Labouchere. But the marvel created by his being overlooked in the dispensation of Ministerial posts, and the apologies and explanations volunteered for the omission, almost supplied compensation for disappointment as testifying to his personal importance. In some quarters doubt was openly expressed whether Mr. Gladstone, on the threshold of his new career, had not made a fatal step by leaving Mr. Labouchere out of the Ministry. Not only, so it was said, had the Premier lost the collaboration of a shrewd politician and an influential publicist, but he had made an enemy who, advantageously posted on his flank, might be counted upon incessantly to harass him.

This was the forecast with which the Session opened. Mr. Labouchere to some extent justified it by taking in his weekly journal a bold and independent line on the question of the Ministerial programme, with some indications of restiveness on the important points of the Home Rule Bill. He was expected to be as mischievously active in the matter of foreign policy as in home affairs. If he did not worry Mr. Gladstone to death on the Egyptian question, he would make it uncommonly hot for him in Uganda.

Not only have all these things come to naught, but so has Mr. Labouchere. From being the most important and influential private member in the House he has sunk to a position amongst the least considered. How this strange thing has been brought about is an interesting problem that would require more space for study than is here allotted. It must suffice at present

to indicate one of the most striking personal features
of the new Parliament.

It is triumphant testimony to the influence
of party discipline and the feeling of
patriotism that pervades the House of
Commons that at the present time, in
mid-August, with grouse on the wing and reports of
one of the finest seasons for many years, there is an
average attendance of 350 members. Their self-
denial is the more creditable since, whilst there are
irresistible attractions out of town, the House has
absolutely none to offer. There are no scenes, nor
prospect of any. Both sides have settled down in
dogged attitude, each bent on tiring out the other in
purely physical effort. The House meets at 3 o'clock
and sits till after midnight. Through all that time
talk is going on, varied by an occasional division.
But nothing is said with hope or expectation of
influencing the issue ostensibly before the House.
The Opposition, inspired by Mr. Chamberlain, keeps
the thing going with the cynically avowed intent of
compelling Mr. Gladstone to adopt the Conservative
device of the guillotine introduced by Mr. W. H.
Smith on the report stage of the Coercion Bill in
1887. Mr. Gladstone shrinks from the expedient now
as he did when the Bill was in committee. Everyone knows that recourse to it is inevitable, and that
the only consequence of further hesitation will be
the prolongation of the Session to a date that will
make it inconvenient, if not impossible, to have an
autumn Session in order to make progress with
English measures.

Meanwhile, accepting this situation and
its wholly mechanical necessities, hon.
members have unreservedly turned their
thoughts in the direction of suitable dress for
exceptional times. Looking round on the House on
any afternoon of this week its appearance recalls

*18th Aug.
Playing for
the Closure.*

*Summer
Dress.*

rather a garden party than a legislative assembly such as is known in these climes. In the matter of dress the House of Commons is ridiculously conservative. There is an idea, the growth of centuries, that a member should not appear in his place in clothes other than what would be found suitable for church. Up to a date that does not go further back than twenty years, a man would as soon have thought of walking up the floor in his shirt sleeves as of carrying into the House any headgear other than the sacred cylindrical "topper." When Mr. Joseph Cowen was in 1874 elected member for Newcastle-on-Tyne, the hat question loomed large before his philosophic mind. He had never worn a topper in his life, and no one had ever crossed the lobby of the House of Commons on his way to his seat in a felt hat, whether soft in texture or of the unyielding "bowler" type. Mr. Cowen, though a man of strong principles, unswerving from any position or attitude he believes to be right, is, personally, one of the gentlest and most unassuming of men. It was no light thing for him to go to Westminster and flout the usages of Imperial Parliament. Still, he could not, on his conscience (or on his head), wear a top hat. He compromised the matter by entering the precincts of the House in a broad-brimmed soft felt hat, comfortable to wear and comely in appearance. But he never wore it in presence of the Speaker, as is the quaint custom in the House of Commons when members are seated in their places.

Another billycock hat that was an embarrassment to its owner was the property of Mr. Broadhurst, whose proud boast it is that from the position of a working mason he made his way to become a Minister of the Crown. Whilst the two positions were yet unbridged, Mr. Broadhurst's uncompromising billycock was no trouble to him. Returned to the House as member for Stoke, he adopted Mr. Cowen's expedient

of coming down in his ordinary headgear, but refrained
from wearing it in his place below the gangway.   When
he was invited to take a seat on the Treasury bench
he felt that something—a topper to wit—was due
to his exalted position.   He accordingly bought a
silk hat, but kept it exclusively for House of Commons use.   He might be seen any day the House
was sitting hastily crossing the lobby, crowned with
a billycock, presently to return at more leisurely
pace with a shiny hat on his head.   This he kept in
his locker, returning it when the business of the
sitting was over and he was free to walk home.

These are reminiscences of older time.   It has now
come to pass that members—chiefly for Irish constituencies, it is true—go about under the shade of billy-
cocks, brown and black, none daring to make them
afraid, even though they sit covered in the presence of
the Speaker.   This week a new and long step has been
taken on the downward path.   I have known the
House of Commons pretty intimately for twenty years,
and up till Monday last I never saw a member within
the precincts of Westminster wearing a straw hat.
On Monday one made its appearance in the lobby,
and as nothing happened the example was on the
next day followed by two other members.   They were
punctilious to leave the things in their lockers when ·
they entered the House.   But easy is the descent to
Avernus.   Last night the Speaker was conscious of
two members, one immediately on his right hand,
another below the gangway in the Irish camp, wearing
straw hats.   After this anything may happen.

Something has happened.   Since Lord
22nd Aug.   Wolmer, now Earl Selborne, resolved to
More
Innovations.   withdraw from the useful avocation of a
Whip and to devote his life to the, perhaps,
higher walk of statesmanship, he has from time to
time succeeded in looming large on the public view.   He
has even been made the occasion for a case of breach of

privilege, and has moved several amendments in successive stages of the Home Rule Bill. These episodes in an honourable career will, doubtless, be proportionately dealt with by the historian. But Lord Wolmer is most likely to be known to posterity as the man who first wore a kamarband in the House of Commons.

Only those long intimate with the place can fully realise the courage requisite for such an accomplishment. There is no written sartorial law in operation, but there are certain broad principles instinctively recognised and religiously obeyed. One of these is that when the Speaker is in the Chair members, in whatever part of the House they may be seated, shall wear a waistcoat. So deeply rooted is this tradition that members even ostentatiously indifferent to authority shrink from flouting it in this particular respect.

A curious evidence of this was forthcoming at to-day's sitting. The House was seething with excitement in anticipation of a fresh pitched battle. Mr. Gladstone had intimated that on Monday he will adopt a resolution which, as he smilingly said, Mr. Balfour is familiar with, ordering that at eleven o'clock on Friday next the process of closuring the report stage of the Home Rule Bill shall commence. Mr. Chamberlain promptly met this with an amendment, the terms of which he chanced to have in manuscript in his pocket. Mr. Tim Healy on his watch-tower below the gangway so far yielded to prevalent fashion as to be sitting at the moment with his waistcoat open. It occurred to him that someone might be made uncomfortable if he interposed the inquiry, " Who is leader of the Opposition ? " As he sprang to his feet on this errand he was reminded of his state of *déshabille.* He could not afford to lose the opportunity of saying this pleasant thing, and if he waited to dress the chance would have fled. . So, even as he leaped to his feet, he seized his waistcoat and hastily adjusted it, with the

result that members turning in the direction whence
the interruption came beheld the hon. member with
his waistcoat all askew, the topmost button having in
his haste become attached to the middle buttonhole.
The effect was comical, but the impulse creditable,
conveying a silent rebuke to Lord Wolmer, and to
those worse than he who, having left off their waistcoat, had not even put on a kamarband.

There have through all time been
eccentricities of dress in the House of
Commons. But never was beheld in
presence of the Mace such an aggregate
spectacle as was witnessed to-night. It seems a period
adjoining the Middle Ages when Mr. Monk, at the
time member for Gloucester, used to act the part of
the Parliamentary swallow. He possessed a suit of
dusty white, crowned by a white hat a generation of
legislators had grown familiar with. It was never
authoritatively settled whether Mr. Monk adopted
the principle which governs the heating of railway
carriages in the United States, ordering the fires to
be lighted and extinguished upon certain fixed dates
in autumn and spring, however the temperature may
vary. Some members alleged that was the case,
others asserting that whilst he, to some extent, was
guided by dates in the almanack, Mr. Monk exercised
deliberate judgment in fixing the time when summer
had set in. However that might be, no member,
wherever he sat, presumed to put on obtrusively
summer garb until Mr. Monk was observed walking
up the floor of the House in his dusty-miller suit,
swinging in his right hand the well-known hat. The
day after the House of Commons, with one accord,
blossomed into summer dress.

The change was wrought decently and in order.
Men took off their black waistcoats, but they put on
white ones, and did not rise to address the Speaker waistcoatless, or with their more or less slim waists bound

The Parliamentary Swallow.

about with gaily-coloured sashes, as if they had just
looked in from a bull fight. Sir Charles Wetherell
used to obstruct the Reform Bill of 1832 with a wide
waste of shirt visible between the lowest button of
his waistcoat and the band of his trousers.

"His only lucid interval," said the Speaker of the
day, who had heard all his many speeches.

But the old Recorder of Bristol at least wore a
waistcoat, and in his gloomy prophecies of the depth
of degradation to which the Mother of Parliaments
would descend when it had got rid of old Sarum and
the rest, never ventured to picture Parliament with
the Speaker in the chair—not yet, it is true, in
pyjamas—facing a straw-hatted, waistcoatless House,
wantonly fanning itself.

As it was Lord Wolmer who introduced
Dress on the Front Benches. the kamarband, so, it must be admitted,
it was Sir John Gorst who brought in the
first fan. He will probably   that it was deftly
constructed out of a copy ofprinted Orders of the Day.
That, though possibly a mitigation of the offence,
is not full extenuation, nor does it relieve him from
the responsibility of his example. It should be said,
to the credit of the two front benches, that their occupants had hitherto kept strictly within the bounds
of older Parliamentary licence in the matter of
summer garb. None have gone beyond a white
waistcoat, combined efforts in this respect of Sir
William Harcourt and the Solicitor-General (Sir
John Rigby) giving to the Treasury Bench the
fantastic appearance of slowly forging ahead under
full-bellied sail. Mr. Gladstone and Mr. Arthur
Balfour keep up the dignity of the situation, combined with a moderate amount of comfort, in suits
of modest grey.

Mr. Courtney was at one time accustomed to
dazzle the House by appearing in a suit of jean,
aggressively yellow in hue. This, though, in its

earlier career, worn contemporaneously with Mr. Monk's historical suit, did not compete with it. It was a thing apart, as completely defined as an electoral area under a scheme of proportional representation. In those days it was thought a bold thing to walk abroad in such attire. To-day it is naught. All can grow the flower now since all have got the seed, though, happily, the blossom does not, as a rule, take precisely the hue that finds favour with Mr. Courtney's æsthetic taste.

25th Aug.
The Bill
Reported.

To-night being the fourteenth sitting in discussion of the Report of the Home Rule Bill, the Closure finally bundled it through that stage.

It may be interesting to place on record the fact that throughout the Committee stage—from May 8th to August 25th—there were 192 divisions. Of these, sixteen were considered to be of sufficient importance for over 600 members to be present at them. In no fewer than ninety-five between 500 and 600 took part; in forty-five between 400 and 500 voted; and in thirty-one between 300 and 400; while in only five divisions were there less than 300. The total votes recorded in these divisions were 95,282.

CHAPTER XVII.

READ A THIRD TIME.

WHILST Mr. Gladstone was moving the
third reading of the Home Rule Bill the
House presented an appearance for which
there is no parallel on a Wednesday
falling on the 30th of August. It was ten minutes
past twelve when the Premier, with springing step,
walked in from behind the Speaker's chair. He was
in summer dress, with a rose in his coat, and smiled
brightly at the loud cheer with which he was
received. At this moment the House was not what
passes for crowded, though unusually full for noontide
on a Wednesday. Mr. Balfour followed the Premier
at an interval of a few moments, the Opposition
cheering him. A curious haze filled the House, in
strange contrast with the brightness of the summer day
outside. Even this was speedily dispelled under the
magnificence of a speech which in respect of cogency,
lightness of touch, felicitous illustration, and irresistible argument will rank amongst Mr. Gladstone's
highest efforts.

Mr. Gladstone, on rising, was received with another
rousing cheer. It was evident at the outset that
he was in remarkably good voice. He spoke his
piece, which lasted just over an hour, without even
once having recourse to the glass of water that stood
by his side. He took the trouble at the outset to
controvert a statement made by Mr. Chaplin as to
Cavour's opinion on the relations of England with
Ireland. Mr. Chaplin had said Cavour approved the

Union. The Premier quoted a passage in which the
Italian statesman distinctly condemned it.

"But there are other passages in which he said
things quite different," said Mr. Chaplin across the
table.

"Oh," said Mr. Gladstone, with outstretched hands
and a comical air of surprise; "then Cavour con-
tradicts himself!"

Turning to estimate the results of the
seventy-eight days already devoted to the
consideration of the matter, Mr. Gladstone

Time Table of
the Debate.

found they had secured the passing of the Bill and
the residue of the Session for devotion to British
legislation. This had been obtained partly by the
unbounded sacrifices made by members, and partly
by the use of the Closure, which latter he regarded
as an evil. At this admission there was a burst of
cheering from gentlemen opposite.

"I am glad to find," said Mr. Gladstone quietly,
"that some of its authors also disapprove of the
Closure"—a shaft that went straight home.

If, as appeared probable, the House divides on
Friday on the question of the third reading, eighty-
two days will have been appropriated for discussion
of the Bill, a debate prolonged over all precedent.
This assertion Mr. Gladstone demonstrated by citation
of leading cases, going back for more than a hundred
years. Of the longest periods in recent times there
was the Reform Bill of 1831, which occupied forty-
seven days; the Irish Land Bill of 1881, which took
forty-six days; and the Coercion Bill of 1887, got
through in forty-two days. Entering more minutely
into the details of the building up of the debate, he
showed that the total number of speeches made in
Committee on behalf of the Bill was 459. "An awful
roll," he said, looking across at the quarter whence
interruption usually besets his speech. Grown wary
by their former rebuff, hon. gentlemen in the corner

Mr. Mellor is not able to see made no sign. That was well, since the next statement set forth that against the Bill 913 speeches had been delivered. This statement was greeted with laughter by the Ministerialists and some bold cheering from the Conservatives.

"I will give you a little further material for cheering," said Mr. Gladstone in one of his merry asides. It was provided in the statement that whilst the speeches in favour of the Bill had occupied $57\frac{1}{4}$ hours, those against it had required not less than $152\frac{3}{4}$ hours. Thus whilst the speeches against and for the Bill were as two to one, the time occupied was as nearly as p   three to one.

Hideous and Monstrous Falsehoods.

Inossible of this unprecedentedly long discussion, it was said that the main provisions of the Bill had not been dealt with. It was true that whilst eleven clauses had been discussed, twenty-six had not. At this admission the Opposition loudly cheered.

"That is about the proportion," Mr. Gladstone added, "or rather better, of the Coercion Bill of 1887." At which effective retort the cheering came from the other side.

The eleven clauses discussed had, he showed by citation of the subjects dealt with, contained the great and cardinal principles of the Bill. The Premier found there were seven pleas upon which the Unionists supported their opposition to the Bill. The list began with "Separation," and concluded with affirmation that party controversy within the walls of the House of Commons would, in the new state of things, become intolerable. These affirmations Mr. Gladstone characterised as hideous and monstrous falsehoods, though he was careful to explain that he gave members opposite full credit for sincerity in the views they expressed. If they were true, how terribly the fact would recoil upon this country! After seven hundred years of the domination of England over Ireland, the result was alleged to be that Ireland cannot undertake without danger and ruin duties which in other countries have been found within the capacity of the people, and their accomplishment fraught with happy results. Recalling a phrase by Lady Mary Wortley-Montague—to the effect that at the time she wrote the common practice was to take the word "not" out of the Commandments and put it into the Creed—Mr. Gladstone applied the system to the table of the seven pleas he had cited. He would put in the word "not" where they affirm a thing, and remove it where they deny.

The Premier closed his speech with an eloquent passage in which he indignantly repelled the charge that the brand of incapacity has been laid by the Almighty on the Irish race.

The
Blessedness
of Brevity.

It is the fashion in the House of Commons to say of Mr. Gladstone's last speech that, if not his greatest, it will take its place in the front rank of the brilliant collection of his orations ranging over half a century. This habit is in itself, even admitting it to be exaggerated, a marvellous testimony to the Premier's vitality of mind and body. It was not wont to be said of Mr. Disraeli in his last years, nor of Lord Palmerston, of Earl Russell, Lord Brougham, or of any statesman who had passed the limit of threescore years and ten. Probably critics are affected by the glamour of the personal fascination of Mr. Gladstone fresh upon them whilst they speak. The effect of the latest effort is sharp, whilst the impressions of speeches of yester-year are dulled by lapse of time.

Making this allowance in fullest measure, it must be said that only Mr. Gladstone's self can parallel the qualities of this historic speech. It had the immense advantage, one Mr. Gladstone is little disposed to secure for himself, of compression. He was on his

legs only five minutes over the hour, and he seemed
to have left nothing unsaid. From a great master the
effect of an hour's speech, first upon the audience and
thereafter upon mankind listening round the doors of
the House of Commons, is more than twice as valuable as a speech of two hours' duration, six times as
effective as one that has run, with whatever stately
course, through a period of three hours. Mr. Gladstone, in the lustiness of youth, once took five hours
to expound his Budget scheme. It is a happy sign
of his unfathomable capacity for learning that of
late he has fallen into the way of saying all he
has to say within the maximum limit of an hour
and a half.

Last night I had the good fortune to meet
Mr. Gladstone at dinner at the house

31st Aug.
After a Hard
Day's Work.

of one of his colleagues in the Cabinet,
and was more than ever amazed at
his tremendous personality. It was a small party of
less than a dozen, a circle easily brought within range
of his voice in conversation. It was reasonable to
suppose that, after a day such as he had passed
through, a man of half the Premier's age would have
been grateful for opportunity to dine quietly at home,
or if an engagement of long standing had taken him
out to dinner he might have been expected to have
literally observed the Scriptural instruction and let
his conversation be "Yea, yea, and Nay, nay." The
speech on moving the third reading of the Home
Rule Bill, an effort which standing alone would suffice
to make a man's reputation, was but an item in a long
day's work. Since he left his bed in the morning the
cares of the Empire had rested upon him. There is
rumour of trouble abroad, whilst at home he finds
himself on the eve of a conflict with the House of
Lords that may have momentous consequences. If
there were nothing the matter in Siam, and Parliament were in recess, there is the ordinary hourly task

imposed upon the head of the Government, to which
Mr. Gladstone adds a private correspondence for the
range of which no subject is too large nor any topic
too small.

Yet to see and hear him at the dinner table last
night one would imagine he had spent an idle
day, and was grateful for opportunity of meeting
some ordinarily intelligent persons in conversation
with whom he might break its arduous inanity. He
talked on all subjects, from the history of the Poor
Law Bill to the limits of caricature, from Dante to
Omnibuses, on which latter subject he displayed
an intimate knowledge that would have amazed a
veteran driver or a consummate conductor. Whatever subject he touched upon it was for the moment
the most interesting in the world, not only to his
audience but to himself, a theme to be discussed
au fond, enriched with picturesque illustration,
lightened by those touches of humour the capacity
for which some critics, whilst admitting all else, in-
scrutably deny him.

Next to Mr. Gladstone's oration, the most
interesting episode in the debate on the
third reading of the Home Rule Bill was
the maiden speech of Mr. Coningsby Disraeli. It
carries one back to old times to find the name " Mr.
Disraeli" following that of "Mr. Gladstone" in the report
of a day's proceedings in Parliament. The member
for Altrincham has established a claim upon the consideration of the House by the deliberation that has
marked the preparation of his maiden speech. There
is a case in the present Parliament of a member who,
taking the oath and his seat one day, on the next
favoured the House with his views on current topics.
Coningsby Disraeli, as a new member bearing a name
the House of Commons will not willingly let die,
might at any time have caught the Speaker's eye.
He has wisely waited a full twelve months, a sign

of grace which, other things apart, would commend
him to the favourable notice of the House. He
is a young man—in his twenty-fifth year—with a
pleasant appearance and hereditary self-possession.
He observed the precaution of bringing with
him voluminous notes, but had conned his lesson
well, and for the most part was independent of his
manuscript.

It was evident he has studied only one model
of Parliamentary oratory, and has caught some of its
tricks and turns of phrase. Speaking of the action of
the Government with respect to the retention of the
Irish members, he described it as " a policy of drift,
with Age at the Prow and eighty Irish members at
the helm." That has the true Disraelian ring about
it. His great kinsman might have said it, and
certainly would had he been alive just now and had
the idea occurred to him.

Another echo of the uncle is heard in the sentence, " This measure was born in deceit, nurtured
in concealment, swaddled in the gag, and is now
forced upon the country without the sanction of the
people."

It is Disraeli, but D'Israeli the Younger. The
world knows what he grew into, and both sides of the
House will watch with friendly interest the career of
the inheritor of his name and estate.

It happened that Mr. Gladstone was temporarily
absent from the House whilst young Disraeli was
speaking, an accident I know he regretted. Few
things in his disposition are more charming than his
quick sympathy with youth trying its callow wings in
Parliamentary debate. This new-comer, bearing his
ancient foeman's name, would have lent a peculiar
interest to the occasion. Sir William Harcourt and
Mr. Balfour also chanced to be away at this interesting
moment. It was pretty to see Sir James Fergusson
and one or two other occupants of the Front Bench

turning round in their seats to watch this appearance
of a new Disraeli on the Parliamentary horizon.

For an assembly that has been notoriously
and shamefully gagged it must be admitted there has been a good deal of talk
in the House of Commons through the
eighty-two days during which, at one stage or other,
the Home Rule Bill has been before it. In this last
week the growing sense of weariness that has sapped
the energies of the House has naturally increased in
force. Had decency permitted, there is no doubt
members would gratefully have divided on Wednesday as soon as possible after the Premier had
moved the third reading. That was not to be.
Wednesday was occupied up to the last moment.
Thursday was droned through in most melancholy
mood. To-night members trooping back in hundreds
from moor and link and sea joined the emaciated
band who have kept watch and ward at Westminster
whilst they have shot or golfed or fished. Looking
down the serried ranks waiting for the division and
deliverance from the nightmare of fourscore days,
it is easy to distinguish between those who have
stayed uninterruptedly at Westminster and the gayer,
bronzed-cheeked throng who, having paired to the
eve of the third reading, now look in to make a brave
show in the division lobby.

It was a notable, unique crowd to find
peopling the floor of the House of Commons on the 1st of September. Whilst
Mr. Chamberlain spoke, and, in fuller degree, whilst
Mr. John Morley was declaiming the last phrases in
the long controversy, the appearance of the Chamber
suggested rather a pending division on the Address
than the final full-dress division of an unusually long
and arduous Session. But though the benches were
crowded, and in the last ten minutes there was that
movement which indicates a time of high excitement,

Side notes:
1st Sept. After Many Days.

Hopelessly Bored.

there were plainly visible signs of ineffable, hopeless
boredom. The trail of eighty-two days' talk was over
it all.

For those who remembered the effect wrought by
Mr. Chamberlain's speech on the second reading, still
more the memorable riot that followed on his last
speech in Committee, the contrast whilst he spoke was
strongly marked. Here was a crowd scarcely less in
numbers. Here was the same debater, merciless in
criticism, pitiless in point. But there was lacking that
electrical condition of the atmosphere through which
winged words flashing leave trails of lurid light.
Probably Mr. Chamberlain's speech of to-night when
studied in *Hansard* will bear comparison with any
of his earlier orations that inflamed the House with
passion. There were, of course, cheers at certain
passages. Once, when he lapsed into the confidence
rarely permissible in Parliamentary debate, and summarised the correspondence that had privately passed
between himself and Mr. Gladstone when the Ministry
of 1886 was formed, members pricked up their ears,
and there was that rustle that presages a scene. But
it came to nothing.

Mr. Chamberlain was himself weighted by the
depressing influence of the hour. He spoke throughout with a quietness of manner unfamiliar in this
most bitter controversy. Even more eloquent than
his polished phrases were the look and attitude
of the audience. They must needs be there, since
three days had been appointed for this concluding
stage of the prodigious debate. But they were bored
to death, and the sooner 'twas over the sooner to sleep.

Mr. Arthur Balfour, prime favourite on his own
side, esteemed and admired on the benches opposite, found the circumstances overpowering. He
had to speak, and, replying as Leader of the Opposition on a first-class debate, he must occupy at least
an hour. What was a man to say on such a well-

worn topic ?   There were moments when beneath the
clear, ringing tones of his argument and denunciation
was heard the chilling sound of whispered conversation on the part of what should have been the
audience.

Mr. John Morley had evidently made great preparation worthily to fill the final part allotted to him in
the long-drawn-out drama.   The closing passages of
his speech resounded with stately eloquence—heights
to which he has never before risen since he stood on
either side of the table.   Delivered three months ago,
these choice passages of the English language, pure
literature infused with the fire of oratory, would have
been heard in rapt silence by a charmed House
waiting for opportunity to applaud.   To-night it was
with difficulty the Chief Secretary worked his way to
the sonorous end, the passage being marked by un-
mannerly interruptions from a group whom in ordinary times the obscurity of their corner under the
gallery would not have shielded from swift and angry
rebuke by an indignant House.

It was well-meant but mistaken kindness
The Courage of Youth.   that brought Sir Edward Grey into prominence on such an occasion.   Grandnephew
of the Earl Grey who was Premier in the Reform
Cabinet, grandson of the Sir George Grey who was
Mr. Gladstone's colleague through many years, the
Premier was naturally anxious to give him a run.   It
was regarded in advance as a great opportunity, and
the young Under-Secretary not only laid himself out
to make the most of it, but actually succeeded.   It
was a good speech, and would have made a distinct
mark had it been delivered on the second reading.
Served up to-night it was necessarily composed of
funeral baked meats.   With the courage of youth
Sir Edward assumed that the House had assembled
with virgin mind, ready to be impressed with elementary ideas on the wrongs and rights of Home

Rule, the bearings of this particular Bill, the iniquity of the Opposition, and the righteousness of Ministers. Everything he said was well conceived, admirably expressed, and nicely delivered. But, alack! the House had heard it, or something fatally like it, before, and every man in the audience had, months ago, irrevocably made up his mind as to which way he would vote in the pending division. Sir Edward's enterprise was akin to that of an adventurous mariner who should put forth from the Mersey, steer westward, and come back with news that he had discovered the Isle of Man. The Isle of Man is indisputable. But we have all known it so long.

It was reserved for Colonel Nolan to invest
An Unreported Speech. the proceedings with the only touch of originality that lightened the slow progress of the dawdling hours. When, at approach to eleven o'clock, Mr. Balfour appeared at the table and was welcomed with a rousing cheer, in which party fidelity and personal liking were appreciably reinforced by gratitude at this sign of approach to the end, Colonel Nolan was discovered on his legs by the Cross Bench fronting the Chair of the Sergeant-at-Arms. His interposition at this juncture was greeted with a shout of execration. But the member for North Galway was not in the Royal Artillery for twenty-five years for nothing. He is accustomed to stand fire in the House of Commons and elsewhere. Now folding his arms, planting his right foot out firmly before him, bending his head and closing his lips, he prepared to await the coming of the time when gentlemen opposite and around him should tire of shouting, and he might commence operations. He was awakened from his reverie by hearing the Speaker quietly call on " Mr. Balfour," who forthwith proceeded with his speech.

Limbering up, the Colonel resumed his seat and bided his time. He was up again when Mr. Morley rose to follow Mr. Balfour; but that was only a feint.

It was when the Chief Secretary had concluded his speech, and the crowded and excited House had dropped into silence awaiting the putting of the qu - tion, that Colonel Nolan once more came to the froæt, resuming his defiant attitude. The roar that went up to the glass roof resembled nothing so much as that uttered by a famished tiger which sees half a sheep placed within reach of its paws and suddenly withdrawn. Colonel Nolan looked as if he were saying something. His lips moved, his head wagged, he changed his position from one foot to another, folding and unfolding his arms as if, finding it impossible to be heard above the din, he had resolved to communicate his views on the Home Rule Bill by semaphore signals. After a while the growing tempest was stilled by the interposition of the Speaker, whose command over the House, even in its most turbulent moments, was testified to afresh.

"I won't keep you seven minutes," said the Colonel, looking up at the clock, apparently hesitating whether, since he had the Speaker on his side, he might not have made it ten.

He was even better than his word, and having with incredible speed gabbled more in five minutes than an ordinary man could speak in fifteen, he subsided, and the crowded House melted away into the division lobbies.

2nd Sept. Division on the Third Reading. At a quarter to one this morning the House divided. In the interval, whilst members strayed back from the division lobbies they amused themselves by cheering the leaders. Mr. Gladstone, sprightliest of the three hundred who went into the Ministerial lobby, came back with the first flight and, the House being nearly empty, took his seat without recognition. Mr. John Morley coming later was cheered, as was Mr. Justin McCarthy by his party, and louder still, since he came later, Mr. Balfour.

At five minutes past one the tellers from both lobbies had returned and stood in a line at the table. But there was no Speaker in the Chair. There they stood till the Speaker, disdaining appearance of hurry, arrived and cried "Order! Order!" in a dignified voice that convinced the House it was not he who had been in default. Mr. Marjoribanks, reading out the figures, made known that the amendment for the rejection of the Bill had been negatived by 301 votes against 267, a majority of 34, hailed with prolonged cheers and counter-cheers.

The Speaker having repeated the figures said, "The question is that the Bill be now read a third time."

There was a loud shout of "Aye," answered by a feeble cry of "No." The Speaker's assertion that "the Ayes have it" was not challenged, and so, amid a fresh burst of cheering, the Home Rule Bill passed the Commons and sped across the corridor to the waiting Lords.

The assembly forthwith broke up, Mr. Gladstone remaining seated on the Treasury Bench, toying with the red despatch box upon which he had just written his letter to the Queen. After a while he pulled himself together and walked out, the Irish members and Liberals—those who had been passing out halting, those who were seated leaping to their feet—cheering and waving hats and handkerchiefs.

The Men in the Street. Probably in recognition of the importance of last night's division, the crowd gathered in Downing-street and at Parliament Yard in anticipation of the gathering of members was far in excess of anything yet seen. The Premier, accompanied by Mrs. Gladstone, left Downing-street shortly before four o'clock in the afternoon. Although he was in a closed carriage, he was speedily recognised and loudly cheered all the way to the entrance to Palace Yard, where the welcome was taken up with a ringing cheer that followed him into the House.

His departure from the House this morning was made the occasion for a remarkable demonstration. An immense crowd had assembled at all the approaches to Palace Yard. When, at a quarter-past one, the Premier was seen driving out, he was hailed with a prolonged cheer, the people running after the carriage, following it into Downing-street, where another crowd was in waiting.

CHAPTER XVIII.

THE BILL IN THE LORDS.

5th Sept. THIS afternoon, Lord Spencer having undertaken to move the second reading of the Home Rule Bill, there was a gathering such as is never seen in the House of Lords save when questions are at issue touching either the Land or the Church. Although London is "empty," a crowd of peeresses and the daughters of peers adorned the side galleries. Members of the House of Commons forsook their own place to listen to the Lords. The more fortunate obtained seats at the end of the gallery by the bar. The rest were penned up in standing room at the bar. On the steps of the Throne, where Privy Councillors are privileged to resort, was seen the tall figure of the Chancellor of the Exchequer, made more prominent by a generously developed white waist-coat. Half-a-dozen Bishops, including the Bishops of Ripon and Chichester, the latter older than the Prime Minister, were in their places. Like the Irish members in the other House, whilst Governments come and go the Bishops keep their seats. In the present disposition of parties they chance to be stationed on the Liberal side, and did something to fill up the gaps. But even with the full gown and lawn sleeves it did not come to much. Far more eloquent than any speech delivered on either side was the contrast of the scattered groups on the benches to the right of the Lord Chancellor and the serried ranks where the Conservatives sit.

Whilst Lord Spencer was speaking the only peers

present on the Front Ministerial Bench were Lord Kimberley, the Marquis of Ripon, Lord Oxenbridge, and Lord Carrington. On the Bench immediately opposite the portly figure of Lord Salisbury was plainly incommoded by the crush of colleagues. When Lord Spencer had been on his legs for a quarter of an hour the Duke of Cambridge arrived and took his seat in the judicial quarter of the cross-benches.

The New Stage. There is no doubt that, regarded as a spectacle, the House of Lords is far more attractive than its Cinderella sister. The Chamber is more spacious, loftier, and dowered with stained-glass windows. The House of Commons, preferring utility to ornament, long ago deliberately disfigured itself. Few members suspect that above the glass roof, through which a flood of gaslight falls upon their heads during night sittings, there rises a stately carved ceiling which need not shrink from comparison with the possession of the House of Lords. It was much admired when the Commons first took possession of their new home; but it was speedily found to be murderous in its effect upon speech. After many experiments it was decided that the ceiling must be sacrificed. Accordingly, across its costly carving, burying it for ever from human sight, was spread a tombstone in the shape of a false ceiling.

This, made of glass, serves the double purpose of lighting the House by innumerable gas jets, the heat generated being utilised for the ventilating apparatus. The result is admirable, the House of Commons now being, in respect of acoustical properties, the most perfect debating chamber in the world. The House of Lords have kept their carved ceiling, and the world loses much of the peers' eloquence and words of wisdom. There are probably less than a dozen who can be heard all over the Chamber with ordinary ease. For the rest, the beginnings and endings, sometimes the middle of their sentences, go rolling round the ceiling, up and down the lofty stained-glass windows, behind the Throne, out into the passages, anywhere but into the Press Gallery. And thus the world knows little of some of its greatest men.

But if the strangers in the Gallery cannot hear every word uttered by noble debaters, they are at least privileged to look upon a striking scene. To the eye accustomed to the House of Commons, with its cramped passages, its absence of colour, its stunted proportions of length and breadth, the House of Lords is fair to see. It may be less businesslike, but it is more magnificent. Within the last two years it has been illumined by electricity. From the lofty roof slight rods are pendant, the electric light branching starlike from their extremities. It possesses two other decorative adjuncts forbidden to the House of Commons. One is the Bishops, the other the Ladies. The Bishops, white surpliced and lawn-sleeved, sit together in a group between the Ministerial bench and the rails that circle the Throne, spreading over the House a charming air of innocence. The ladies, in this always-summer time gowned in frocks of daintiest hue, fill the long galleries on either side, encircling the scene as it were with a garland of flowers. Members of the House of Commons standing at the bar of the Lords, or cooped up in the odds-and-ends of the gallery allotted to them, think regretfully as they look on the scene of their wives and daughters imprisoned behind the impenetrable grille of the Ladies' Gallery at the other end of the Palace of Westminster.

In the House of Lords public business **Earl Spencer.** commences at half-past four, though their lordships meet a quarter of an hour earlier. On the stroke of the half-hour Lord Spencer appeared at the table, being welcomed by a quiet little cheer from the something less than thirty friends scattered over the benches behind. Beginning at the beginning he reviewed the history of Ireland since the Union, summarising the effect of the various Acts which had in the meantime been passed for the amelioration of the lot of the Irish people. The immobility preserved by their lordships was broken for the first time when Lord Spencer remarked that if the Bill brings contentment to the Irish people there will be less danger than now exists of Irish members coquetting—to use Mr. Goschen's word—with political parties. Lord Spencer was not able at the first attempt to conclude this sentence, it being broken in upon by laughter which Lord Halsbury led. The ex-Lord Chancellor almost physically bubbled over with merriment at the prospect of contentment ever dawning upon Ireland.

Having once heard the sound of their own voices, the Conservative peers broke out into a really respectable cheer when Lord Spencer observed that the Liberal party are accused of handing over the government of Ireland to men of the worst character. The applause increased when he further alluded to them as "men who had sometimes been called murderers." But if it were a heinous crime to bestow the government of Ireland upon the men who would be elected by the free constituencies, how, he asked, was it less heinous when the Government of Lord Salisbury proposed to legislate in favour of giving local government in the counties of Ireland? Here Lord Spencer proposed to quote a familiar passage from Lord Salisbury's famous speech at Newport. But although it was only six o'clock it was too dark to read, and Lord Spencer after making a vain effort apologised for his inability.

"Oh, never mind," said Lord Salisbury, across the table, "it is not worth reading."

Lord Spencer concluded a speech that occupied an hour and forty minutes by a simply-spoken but eloquent appeal to noble lords to pause before they took the step expected of them. It was a great opportunity of freely making concession to Ireland. There was peace abroad, and no turbulence in Ireland. They might now, without suspicion of submitting to pressure, realise the hope that dawned over Ireland, dispelling the long period of despair.

"Hope encourages peace; despair engenders discontent."

The Duke of Devonshire.

The Liberals again did their best to cheer Lord Spencer, the gentle sound lapsing in the fuller cheer from the Ministerialists that welcomed the Duke of Devonshire as he strolled up from a bench below the gangway towards the table. The curious arrangement, familiar in the Commons, whereby the bitterest opponents of the Government sit on the same side of the House at least stops short of Mr. Chamberlain or Sir Henry James standing at the table in front of the bench where Ministers sit. The Lords are above little prejudices of that kind, and to-night the Duke of Devonshire delivered his speech from the very spot where his parted colleague had stood, and by which he now sat.

The Duke did not appear nearly so profoundly moved in presence of the Bill as some of his commentaries upon its iniquities would seem to make natural. There were, indeed, in the course of his speech, moments when the most pressing question in the mind of onlookers was whether the Duke would fall asleep first or whether precedence would be taken by the audience.

At the close of the first half-hour there was a welcome movement on the part of members of the House of Commons, who, a division being signalled from the other House, unceremoniously dashed forth. A little later, among those returning, came Mr. Balfour and Mr. Chamberlain. They took their places at the steps of the Throne, accidentally but significantly supporting it on either side. From this coign of vantage they heard the Duke of Devonshire denounce Home Rule as the policy of a single man, not a policy emanating from a party or approved by the country. They also heard him assure noble lords that many members of the other House, knowing the fate that awaited the Bill at the hands of their lordships, had voted in its favour, not because they believed it was a desirable measure, but in order to avoid unpopularity with their party.

In the House of Commons a statement like this would have been greeted with shouts of "Name! Name!" Noble lords took it for granted, and the Duke of Devonshire plodded along.

It was eight o'clock when the Duke con-
Tired Already. cluded his speech by moving the rejection of the Bill. By this time the House had lamentably emptied, alike on the floor and in the galleries. Lord Zetland followed in a speech in which he bemoaned the prospects of the Civil Servants and Constabulary under a Home Rule Bill. To him succeeded Lord Powerscourt; Lord Brassey, who made a vigorous defence of the Bill; the Duke of Norfolk, who, in spite of Roman Catholic sympathies, declared against the Nationalist members; Lord Massereene and Earl Cowper, who argued that the Bill was not to be seriously considered, since it had been carried through the Commons by a small majority controlled by the Closure. Lord Ribblesdale made a lively speech in support of the Bill, Lord Cadogan winding up the debate from the Conservative side.

Lord Salisbury, with what personal sacrifice will probably never be known, sat out to the end a debate which was dolorous in the extreme, suffering from the irresistible influence of anti-climax to the real fight that went on in the Commons. It was arranged in advance that the debate should go on to midnight. But at twenty minutes to twelve human nature, even in the Lords, succumbed, and the debate was adjourned.

Lord Lawrence having moved the adjournment of the debate on the second reading
of the Bill last night, it was understood
he would at to-day's sitting resume the
debate.   It turned out that he had merely acted in
the interests of the Duke of Argyll, who, worn out
before the Duke of Devonshire concluded his prodigious discourse, retired from the scene.   When,
promptly at half-past four, the Duke of Argyll rose,
the House was full, though not quite so crowded as
last night.   The falling away was rather on the Conservative side, there not being much margin for such
movement in the Liberal camp.   On several benches to
the right of the Woolsack there were some new comers,
including Lord Rosebery, who had the satisfaction of
hearing a phrase of his quoted with approval by the
Duke of Argyll—a rare indulgence on his Grace's part.
Lord Rosebery nearly missed it, having been temporarily called out of the House by a message conveyed
in the red box of the Foreign Office.   He came back
in time to hear the remark and to conceal his satisfaction.

Again, as yesterday, members of the Commons
filled all the space allotted to them.   Those who as
peers' sons or Privy Councillors had the privilege of
standing within the steps of the Throne availed themselves of it.   The Duke of Devonshire, following an
example long familiar in the House of Commons on the
part of the Marquis of Hartington, arrived half-an-hour
late.   His Grace has taken up a position at the corner
of the Front Opposition Bench below the gangway in
close proximity to his old colleagues in a former
Administration.

The Duke of Argyll, not dallying with
topographical niceties, has now gone
boldly over to the Tories, and delivered
his speech this afternoon standing at the feet of
the Marquis of Salisbury.   He began in moderately

(Marginal notes: 6th Sept. The Mac-Cullamore. — Hopelessly Bad.)

good form, but as he proceeded with a speech that occupied an hour and fifty minutes in delivery, his voice sorely failed, making it difficult to catch the full course of his sentences. By way of exordium, he went straight for the Bill, belabouring it with a succession of carefully prepared phrases. It was, he said, a Bill which effected revolutionary changes in the Constitution; it reached the House of Lords by the employment of revolutionary means; it had been sent there by a majority of only five per cent. of the whole House of Commons; a majority of the British representatives were against it on every important point; and, lastly, it had never been before the people. In these circumstances the nation looked to their Lordships at least to give them time to think. It was not only open to them to reject the Bill; it was expected and demanded of them that they should do so. If they missed the opportunity, the country would be filled with feelings of absolute dismay, indignation, and shame. If the Bill passed, nothing in the Constitution would stand—not the unity of the Empire, nor the dignity of the Crown, nor the purity of public life, nor the liberties of the people, nor many other things in a catalogue magnificently reeled off.

Much of a speech listened to with signs of marked approval by the Conservative Opposition was devoted personally to Mr. Gladstone, whom the Duke relentlessly pursued with bitter accusation. In one of these more acrid attacks a curious incident happened. Through the open windows there came the sharp yelping of a dog in the courtyard, the uproar threatening for a moment to drown the other voice within the Chamber. The person assailed, after long suffering, finally fell upon the dog, and hounded it out of hearing. The Duke of Argyll went on with no other interruption, showing afresh by new instances how hopeless is the depth of degradation to which his former chief had sunk.

" Was there ever such folly ? " he exclaimed, citing a proposal he attributed to the Premier.

Save for the occasional huskiness of voice noted, delivery and speech were in most ways very good. The Duke is a picturesque figure, with his black stock and the indescribable cut of the early English gentleman about his clothes. As a work of art, and as an effective argument, the oration was spoiled by the personal animosity displayed towards Mr. Gladstone. Once the Duke, with fine effect, dragged in his headless ancestor, whose blood, running in his veins, prevented him, as he said, being an advocate of the doctrine of passive obedience. That was but once, whilst the head of Mr. Gladstone was dragged in even oftener than that of Charles the First in the Memorial of Mr. Dick. Whenever it appeared under the Duke's left arm, be sure it was being pummelled with the other fist.

Probably in anticipation of a speech
7th Sept.
Lord
Selborne.
from Lord Rosebery the gathering in the House of Lords this afternoon showed an increase even on the first day. This was more particularly noticeable in respect of the Bishops and the ladies. The half-dozen of the former present on the first day increased to sixteen, filling entirely the three benches where they sit flanking the Woolsack. In the gallery, to the left of the Woolsack, the red fez of his Excellency Rustem Pacha advantageously appeared between two pretty bonnets. The members of the House of Commons again filled up all the spaces open to them, Lord Wolmer listening to his father's speech from the gallery over the bar. If he heard it all, he was more fortunate than some of his neighbours.

Lord Selborne, like the Duke of Devonshire, a later seceder from Mr. Gladstone's councils, so far observed earlier habits as to speak from the Liberal side. This had a comical and unpremeditated effect. The ex-Lord Chancellor, rising promptly at half-past

tour, commenced his speech with considerable vigour,
uplifting his voice to shrill heights, and driving home
his arguments with open hand striking the table. All
his gestures and glances were full of righteous anger,
and, as he was immediately faced by the crowded
bench of ex-Ministers, he seemed to be scolding Lord
Salisbury, innocent at least of any complicity in the
Home Rule Bill. It must be said of this speech, as far
as its purport could be gathered from the front row of
the Strangers' Gallery, that it was entirely free from
the personal animus displayed yesterday by the Duke
of Argyll, the noble lord seriously, almost devotion-
ally, devoting himself to the task of assailing the Bill
by argument.

"The noble and illustrious earl," as Lord Rosebery
called him in the graceful sentence with which he
opened his speech, spoke for one hour and three-
quarters. Through the last thirty minutes only the
monotonous murmur of a voice reached the gallery.

"A Chamber of Death." Lord Rosebery was almost stridently
cheered by his few political friends when
he appeared at the table, standing in the
same place whence Lord Selborne had denounced the
Bill. Of that speech Lord Rosebery remarked it
was of exactly the same kind which had been made
against every great measure—from Catholic Emancipa-
tion to Reform. After some happy bantering of the
Duke of Argyll and the Marquis of Londonderry, Lord
Rosebery announced that he did not propose to follow
the discussion in so far as it had not criticised the
Bill. It had been an interesting academic but
purposeless discussion, unreal in every part. Not
one of the noble lords facing him had entered the
House with other than preconceived resolution how
they would vote. They were not to be moved by
argument from one side or another.

"This is not a dissecting-room," Lord Rosebery
said; "it is the chamber of death itself."

What was at stake was much more important and far-reaching in its consequences than any Bill. It was not a Bill, but a policy that was at issue. What were the Lords going to do? The responsibility of the situation weighed with them more heavily than with the Commons, since they were masters of the situation. An opportunity—"which, I suppose, you are going to throw away," Lord Rosebery parenthetically remarked, with a gesture towards Lord Salisbury—presents itself of settling this question, or at least of declaring and defining the Conservative position in regard to Ireland. They might have read the Bill a second time, and in Committee could have done what they pleased with it, a course which would have led to a conference between the two Houses that might have had happy results.

When, just after half-past seven, Lord Rosebery sat down, at the close of an incisive speech that lifted the debate out of the academic groove he had deplored, the brilliant audience which had filled every space of the Chamber almost with one accord moved out.

Lord Waterford. Two hours later the Marquis of Waterford gave a new and more cheerful turn to the proceedings. He spoke just after the dinner hour, when the House began to fill again. It was drawing on to eleven o'clock, and the Bishops, not used to be out so late at night, had fled; only three remaining. There were but a dozen ladies in the gallery, still in morning dress. Lord Spencer ran Lord Salisbury close as the peer most constant in attendance. The Marquis of Waterford, privileged by physical infirmity—of which no testimony was found in his vigorous speech—is permitted to address the House seated. This variation from custom lent a new and cheerful aspect to the sitting. Lord Waterford's oratorical style is colloquial, and finding him at his ease, with an air cushion at his back, the proceedings took on something of a post-prandial air, in welcome contrast with the portentous sermonising of the first hour and a half of the sitting.

Lord Waterford's style is so successful as to suggest that, after all, the best Parliamentary attitude is that of a member seated. He demonstrated that this unusual attitude does not enforce restriction on the movements of the arms, the vigour of the voice, or the general liveliness of demeanour.

Lord Cranbrook followed with a breathless
Lord Cranbrook. oration. He had at least the credit of pleasing his audience, his fluent denunciation calling forth from the Conservative peers even louder cheers than had approved the onslaughts of the Duke of Argyll. For them the old tags about degradation of the Empire, breaking-up of the Union, betrayal of Ulster, the demoralisation of the Irish people, and the like, seem to have perennial freshness. There was no light and shadow in the speech. Wherever the Bill touched finance, land, police, the powers of the Lord-Lieutenant, or the action of the veto, it was hopelessly bad. It was pretty to hear Lord Cranbrook, of all men, conclude his speech by an approving citation of a passage from "that great tribune, Mr. John Bright." But then it was taken from a speech delivered in the declining years of the statesman who, when he sat opposite Mr. Gathorne Hardy in the Commons, was to him Anathema.

The Lord Chancellor, stepping aside from the Woolsack, now took his turn in the debate, delivering a speech which for weight of argument, grace of elocution, and charm of delivery formed a pleasing contrast to what had immediately gone before. Almost the only bitter touch in it was the paraphrase of the position assumed by the Unionists towards the Bill; namely, that it was the work of a despotic fanatic who had lost his head, assisted by colleagues who have lost their principles. Lord Herschell put this forward a little timidly, as if he were going too far in the direction of burlesque. A reassuring cheer from some of the Conservative peers put him at rest on that score.

Just after ten o'clock Lord Salisbury rose, **Lord Salisbury.** and was hailed with what was, for the House of Lords, a prolonged cheer. For half-an-hour previously the galleries and the space before the Throne had been filling up as by the slow incursion of the tide. The House was crowded when Lord Rosebery spoke; it was packed when Lord Salisbury began to address it. The Lord Chancellor, seated on the Woolsack, seemed a mere speck amid the crowd that surrounded him, with a background of the throng before the Throne. Peers coming in late after dinner, accustomed to an embarrassment of riches in the way of seats, found every one occupied, and were fain to remain standing through the hour and a quarter the Leader of the Opposition spoke. These late-comers were chiefly in dinner dress, one prominent exception being Lord Morris, to whom the Irish question is a matter too serious for indulgence in the frivolity of dinner. The side galleries were filled with ladies, many in evening dress. Rustem Pacha was still faithful to his post of observation.

Lord Salisbury, in spite of constitutional deference to the House of Peers, was evidently impressed with a sense of the presence of the larger audience listening at the doors, their habitation limited only by the area of the English-speaking race. Frankly turning his back upon the Lord Chancellor, he faced the Press Gallery and spoke up to it throughout his brilliant speech. It scarcely needed this special attention, since his resonant voice filled the chamber. Doubtless right hon. gentlemen within the rails by the Throne, and peers behind the Woolsack, heard every word he said. He used no notes beyond a square of paper about the size of an ordinary envelope, and that was rarely referred to. From time to time, when

he came to a fresh subject, he took a pull at a glass
of water and went on afresh with the flow of
perfectly-constructed and modulated sentences.

A Policy of Despair.

He poured contumely and scorn on the
retention of the Irish members, upon
which question in 1886 his colleagues
among the Dissentient Liberals broke away from
their party. That an incursion of eighty foreigners
should have the special isolated distinguished privilege of determining the issues of an Imperial Government was, he protested, a proposal such as had never
been suggested in favour of the Colonies. The Bill
was the outcome of a policy of despair.

"You have failed," he pictured Mr. Gladstone
saying to the Conservatives, "and we must try something never before attempted."

But had the Government the right to work this
policy of despair, to risk the prosperity of a large
minority of the Irish nation? What reason was
given for this experiment, whose details no one
would defend, whose results none could foretell?
Lord Salisbury, without using a phrase which a predecessor in his Leadership of the Conservative party
had introduced on an historic occasion, denounced the
Bill as a leap in the dark. Did the House know
who were the men who would administer the Government in Ireland the Bill proposed to set up? They
were the respondents branded by the report of the
Parnell Commission. Thirty-eight men now members
of the House of Commons were numbered in the list,
"and remember," said Lord Salisbury, in an aside
which drew forth loud cheers from his friends, "the
third reading of this Bill was passed by a majority of
thirty-four." Is it not well to fight against such an
enemy? "Would you not," he asked, turning for a moment from the irresponsive Press Gallery to the throng
of peers behind the Ministerial bench, "fight to the last
to prevent your interests falling into such hands?"

"I think the Contents have it."

It was the voice of the Lord Chancellor sounding through the crowded chamber just after midnight. The scene was one seldom witnessed in this august, but not always entertaining, assembly. The floor was packed with peers occupying every bench on either side, irrespective of party camps. They swarmed round the Woolsack till the Lord Chancellor, upstanding and desiring to glance around with intent impartially to judge how parties were divided before pronouncing on the issue submitted to him, craned his neck in almost undignified fashion. Behind the rails of the Throne, against which the crowd of peers pressed, was another throng made up of Privy Councillors and sons of peers privileged to assemble here if peradventure they could find room. From both side-galleries bright eyes rained influence. Members of the House of Commons, forsaking their own Chamber, flocked into the Lords, shouldering each other in a dense mass by the bar, filling the odds-and-ends of the gallery which the Lords assign to them in acknowledgment of a somewhat similar provision made for peers in the other House.

The great debate was over. Four days had sufficed for an ungagged House of Lords to dispose of a matter the gagged House of Commons had talked round for more than fourscore.

"The question is," said the Lord Chancellor, "that this Bill be now read a second time. Since which an amendment has been moved to leave out all the words from 'now,' and insert 'this day six months.' The question that I have to put is that the word 'now' stand part of the question. Those who are of that opinion say 'Content.'"

Here there was a faint, shy murmur from the benches to the right of the Lord Chancellor. The Liberal peers were content, so steeped in contentment

that they were loath to break the peaceful moment
by noisy cry.

"The contrary, 'Not content,'" added the Lord
Chancellor.

At which signal there came from the crowd to his
left, from the throng behind the Woolsack, from the
white-winged Bishops clustered above the Ministerial
Bench, from the group below the gangway behind the
bench on which the Duke of Devonshire sat, an almost
angry roar of " Not content ! "

The Lord Chancellor paused a moment, as if
weighing a nicely-balanced problem. Then in a low,
clear voice, looking straight before him, he repeated :
" I think the ' Contents ' have it."

It is said by some who stood close to the
Woolsack that when Lord Herschell committed himself to what, if the speaker
were not the Lord Chancellor, might be
described as this " whopper," a faint blush stole over his
ingenuous countenance. That is, however, testimony
probably warped by personal feeling and desire to save
the credit of an amiable and upright man. There was
certainly no tremor in the voice, no flinching in the
attitude, as the Lord Chancellor, called upon to give
his opinion as to the side on which, in the House of
Lords, preponderance in favour of the Home Rule
Bill declared itself, affirmed it was demonstrated on
behalf of the second reading. There was nothing for
it but to submit the question to the arbitrament of
the division. With a burst of almost merry laughter,
their lordships rose to their feet and began to pass
out into the lobbies.

The phrase is used in the plural for fuller accuracy.
Watching the multitude slowly making its way down
to the bar it seemed as if all were going into one lobby.
In ordinary times the Whips stand by the wicket and
" tell " members as they pass through. Although undesigned, there was not lacking something of dramatic

*The Lord
Chancellor
Blushes.*

effect in Lord Salisbury's proposition that this usual course should be departed from. Such a gathering would never be so marshalled till the night was far advanced. Better let them pour through into the outer hall, and there be counted.

Clearing
the House.
So it was arranged, and the memorable gathering of peers, spreading out the full breadth of the floor, pressed slowly onward towards the passage by the bar into the division lobby. With them went the Bishops, their white lawn looking like flecks of foam on the eddying current swirling outwards. Lord Kimberley, Lord Spencer, Lord Rosebery, and other Ministers seated on the front bench made early retreat, lest peradventure they should be swept away by the stream passing between the table and the Ministerial bench and carried off to vote against the Home Rule Bill. There was something pathetic in the position of their few followers seated on the benches behind. Some had risen to go out, but found their way blocked first by the Bishops, not yet dispersed, and beyond them the solid phalanx of peers who had been standing before the Throne. If they had chanced to be going the other way, towards the bar, motion would have been easy enough. They might have drifted out with the tide. To go against the tide was quite another matter, and after vain effort they gave up the attempt, resuming their seats, and sitting patiently whilst the great majority swept past them. By-and-by the pressure was removed from the upper end of the Chamber, and the minority, fit, few, and forty-one, made haste to escape.

The
Returning
Tide.
In the House of Commons when a great division takes place there is one moment when the House is absolutely empty, save for the presence of the Speaker, the Clerks at the table, the Sergeant-at-Arms, and the messengers attendant. The Sergeant-at-Arms,

advancing to the bar, glances keenly round to see that
there are no lingerers, and then signal is given to
lock the doors. After the cheers and counter-cheers
that mark the close of the debate, with the bustle
of departing crowds stilled, a strange quietness falls
upon the place. The interval is to be counted only
by seconds until the doors are unlocked, and one
stream enters from beneath the gallery, the other
from behind the Speaker's Chair. There is no
parallel to this in similar circumstances in the House
of Lords, there being, in fact, no locked doors by the
passages outward on either side of the throne. So
far-reaching was the throng of " Not Contents," that
almost before the rear had straggled out of the House
by the bar, the vanguard entered from the other side.
The benches rapidly filled up. The Peers seemed to
come in more quickly than they had made their
way out. But fully forty minutes elapsed between
the signal to start and the announcement that all
was over.

Here, again, the House of Commons, in some
respects less spectacular than the Lords, has the
advantage. In the Commons, when a division is
completed, the tellers, having handed in their report of
the figures, range themselves in line facing the Mace on
the table, and he who represents the winning side
receives from the Clerk the paper setting forth the
result. The floor of the House is a clear space, save
for the presence of the four tellers. They retire a
few paces, and, with obeisance thrice made to the
Chair, advance to the table, where the teller for the
victorious side proclaims the result of a contest upon
which, perchance, may rest the fate of a Ministry.
It is obvious that here is fine opportunity for what on
the stage is known as business. Lord Randolph
Churchill will not forget that night in June eight
years gone by when the paper containing the doom of
Mr. Gladstone's Ministry was handed to Mr. Rowland

Winn, Whip for the Opposition. As the Whips marched backward to take up their position for advance, there was time for noble lords and hon. members to leap on the benches, wave their hats in triumph, and shout themselves hoarse, whilst Mr. Rowland Winn, the fateful paper in his hand, stood impassive, awaiting opportunity to advance and announce the result.

Thrown Out. This morning, as Big Ben was sounding the third quarter of an hour past midnight, there was no space on the floor of the House of Lords for tellers to march up and down. Four hundred and sixty marquises, dukes, and a' that, Old Nobility and New, Bishops and the Master of the Buckhounds, were gathered within the four walls. There was no room for them on the benches, and, these filled, noble lords stood round the Woolsack, an almost impenetrable mass, threatening asphyxia to the panting Lord Chancellor.

Presently a noble lord was seen making his way through the throng, handing a piece of paper to the Lord Chancellor over the shoulder of a peer who could not get further out of the way. A great silence fell upon the assembly. Without assistance of the token, possible in the Commons, of the paper being in the first instance handed to the Ministerial or Opposition teller, no doubt existed as to the way the aggregate of votes had gone. It is true the Lord Chancellor, forty minutes earlier, had uncompromisingly declared that the Contents had it. Even a Lord Chancellor may be mistaken. Still there remained disclosure of the precise figures by which the fate of the Bill had been sealed. Amid the hush the voice of the Lord Chancellor sounded with clarion clearness—"For the second reading, 41 ; against, 419."

So there had been a mistake somewhere, and, after all, it was the " Not Contents " who " had it."

CHAPTER XIX.

A NEW FOURTH PARTY.

11th Sept.
A Unit of
the Majority.

THERE is a gruesome story current alleging that the triumphant majority of the House of Lords against the Home Rule Bill was swelled by the temporary appearance on the scene of a noble lord, brought over from a private lunatic asylum in charge of his keepers, who waited till his lordship had gone chattering through the lobby with his peers, and straightway took him in charge again. An attempt has been made to establish the fact by a question put in the House of Commons. As might have been expected, the Speaker declined to be a party to so painful an incident, and the question was not put. But the object of the ardent inquirer was gratified, since the terms of his question found circulation in the newspapers.

Everyone knows at whom the finger was pointed, and laments a sad case. The peer in question is still in the prime of life, as far as years are counted. Whilst still a boy he succeeded to one of the oldest peerages in the United Kingdom, and is representative of that exceedingly limited ring of our Old Nobility which, in his hot youth, the present Duke of Rutland fervently prayed might be spared, even though Wealth and Commerce, Laws and Learning died.

A Case in the
Commons.

Had the question been put, the Lords might have retorted that in such a matter the hands of the Commons are not clean. An analogous case certainly took place in the Parliament of 1874-80, through which, for the first time in his career, Mr. Disraeli governed as well as reigned. It was in the memorable division that bestowed upon the Queen the proud title of Empress of India. Mr. Disraeli was particularly anxious that his gift to his Sovereign should be approved by an overwhelming majority. Remote parts of the world were scoured for errant legislators. Sick men were brought from their beds to totter round the division lobbies. One member, whose vagaries had made him notorious in the early Sessions of the Parliament, had for some time disappeared from the scene, withdrawn by friendly hands which, cruel only to be kind, had placed him under restraint. To everyone's surprise, when the House was cleared for division, his tall figure was seen in the crowd at the bar, and his familiar stentorian voice swelled the chorus of "Aye" that hailed the Queen Empress. He voted straight—straighter than he usually walked—and again withdrew, never to be seen again in the House of Commons. Shortly after, he succeeded to the peerage.

**13th Sept.
The Union
Jack.** Mr. Shaw Lefevre informed the House of Commons to-night that the Queen had consented to an application made to her by the Lord Great Chamberlain that the Union Jack might be hoisted on the Victoria Tower when Parliament is sitting. The satisfaction with which this announcement was heard by the faithful Commons was tempered by the further announcement that the cost of the display would be £25 a year. Twice a day men will have to climb the seven hundred steps that lead to the top of the tower, first to haul up the flag, next to haul it down.

**16th Sept.
The Irish
Constabulary
Vote.** The House of Commons having adjourned at twenty minutes to three this morning, after a sitting extending almost round the twelve hours, met again at noon, and has spent the Saturday half-holiday in pegging away at the Estimates. This is its usual way of dealing with appointed business. There being in the

Estimates an aggregate of 185 votes, it spends thirty-five days, spread over the Session, in disposing of eighty-five, and scrambles through the odd hundred in a fortnight. Last night the Irish votes, including that for the Constabulary, came on. The shade of Joseph Gillis Biggar, if it revisits the glimpses of Big Ben, must have stood aghast at the scene. There was a time, whilst the former member for Cavan was yet with us, when the Constabulary Vote was merrily made to last over three sittings, generally carried on all night. Now the Irish Nationalist members sit and look on quiescent, what time £732,249 are voted for the sustentation of their natural enemy the Royal Irish Constabulary.

For the most part Irish members did not even take the trouble to look on. Mr. Tim Healy, amongst others, is enjoying the comforts of his island home, having paired till the Autumn Session with no other than Mr. Carson, some time Solicitor-General under the administration of Mr. Balfour. Mr. Dillon is here, and walks fitfully about. Perhaps with old recollections thronging upon him he finds it too much to ask that he shall be actually in his seat in the House whilst the Vote for the Constabulary is agreed to. But he looks in occasionally, and has full opportunity, if he were so disposed, to lift up his voice in protest or denunciation, as yesteryear was his wont. Mr. Sexton, uncheered by reminiscences of prison life, sits through the debate, even offering an occasional observation congratulatory of the change wrought in the land under the administration of Mr. John Morley.

It is instinctively felt it would never do to let the Constabulary Vote pass without some show of debate. Accordingly, the loyal Irish rush in where the Nationalists no longer desire to tread. They make a poor substitute for the " bhoys " who, in earlier Parliaments, worried this vote as a hungry dog attacks a long-withheld bone. Mr. T. W. Russell is a keen debater, whose influence would be much greater if his advocacy were made less cheap.   He is a little out of it upon the Constabulary Vote, while Sir Thomas Lea, the decorous but doleful Mr. Dane, and even Mr. Macartney—usually a sprightly speaker, to-night depressingly loquacious—in no sense, save by contrast, recall the brave days of old, when Mr. Dawson, a modern "Malachi, wore the collar of gold he won from" the suffrages of citizens who make Lord Mayors of Dublin.

The Three Musketeers.   In truth the week has been dolorous in the extreme, the only flutter of interest showing itself when conversation pointing to the precise day of the adjournment has been going forward.   This state is the less gracious since the House was promised much sport in these closing days.   Mr. Hanbury and his trusty lieutenants, Mr. Bartley and Mr. "Tommy" Bowles, undertook to make an Autumn Session impossible by indefinitely prolonging Committee of Supply.   It was to be done by an elaborately-worked-out system of relays, whereby some two hundred good Unionists were to be kept constantly on the spot, one hundred going into country quarters with the definite object of recuperating, so that a fortnight later they might take their turn at the mill, relieving another hundred.   But the plan has come to naught.   It has been liberally construed in the direction of the "going into country quarters."   Not one hundred, but three hundred Unionists have gone away for the purpose of recuperation, omitting only the adoption of arrangements for returning.

Perhaps the Three Musketeers who have attempted in the new Parliament to revive the traditions of the Fourth Party were scarcely the men for the task. Without wishing to say anything rude (as Lord Rosebery observed when in the Home Rule debate he asked Lord Muskerry what Ireland knew about *him*)

it may be suggested that, with varied capacities and
abundant good qualities, Mr. Hanbury, Mr. Bartley, and
Mr. Bowles are scarcely on a level with Lord Randolph
Churchill, Sir Henry Wolff, and Sir John Gorst—not
to mention Mr. Arthur Balfour, the odd man of the
Fourth Party, who, scrupulously playing up to the part,
was usually "out" when there was drudgery to be done.

There was a time when Mr. Hanbury was
Mr. Hanbury. a promising young man.   It seemed
certain that he would be absorbed in the
Ministry, and, from an Under-Secretaryship, would
work himself up, probably, to be Postmaster-General.
Somehow successive Ministers overlooked him, and
he fell into a state of depression that excited the
concern and sympathy of his friends.   In the peculiar
circumstances of the new Parliament he thought he
saw his chance for a new departure.   He was a
member of the Parliament of 1880–85, a witness to
the wondrous things wrought in it by Lord Randolph
Churchill and his two colleagues.   Why should he
not in a Parliament to which Mr. Gladstone had
returned as Leader revive the ' ancient tradition?
There is no monopoly about a Fourth Party.   What
Lord Randolph Churchill did was simply to organise
and develop a House of Commons tendency, older
even than the time when D'Israeli the Younger set
himself to undermine the power of Sir Robert Peel.
The opportunity seemed even more favourable than
that ready to the hand of Lord Randolph Churchill,
since Mr. Gladstone's majority was not much more
than a third of that which seemed to make him
impregnable when he met Parliament in 1880.   Then
there were Mr. Bartley and Mr. Bowles ready to hand.
Mr. Bartley we have had long with us.   Providence
seems to have had a special eye on potentialities when,
at this particular juncture, Mr. "Tommy" Bowles, defeated in earlier encounters at the poll, was returned for
King's Lynn.   Here was not only the hour, but the Men.

It is sad to have to record the utter rout
Mr. Bartley. of an enterprise which began under
auspices so fair. It is sadder still to
reflect that the brunt of the failure rests with the
general in command. Mr. Bartley has a grave and
serious air of inestimable value in such a combination.
No stranger in the Gallery, looking at him whilst he
is addressing Mr. Mellor, would venture to think he
was merely talking against time. Rather would the
unaccustomed ear laboriously strain itself, for an hour
or more, in endeavour to grasp the point towards
which he was evidently advancing. In addition to
fluency of speech and Parliamentary experience, Mr.
Bartley has a certain grave humour, sometimes
unconscious, as when on Monday night he observed
to an applauding House: "I know nothing about
cordite or anything else."

Mr. Bowles brings to the councils of the
"Tommy" Bowles. new party the sprightliness of mature
youth. He knows a great deal about
everything, except the House of Commons. He
could give Mr. Mundella points in distinguishing
between a handsaw and a marlinspike. He has a
pretty wit, reminiscent, perhaps, of a worthy alderman, one Waithman, whose speeches in debate in
Committee on the Reform Bill of 1831 will be found
as plentifully sprinkled through the *Hansard* of the
time as are Mr. Bowles's in the enlivening volumes
that record discussion on the Home Rule Bill. Praed
marked the worthy alderman and did his familiar
speech into verse, as thus:—

> "I do not rise, I never will,
> To make a speech about the Bill;
> I only want to urge once more
> What I have often urged before;
> It can't be doubted or denied
> That members on the other side
> Are talking, talking day by day
> Just for the purpose of delay."

All unconsciously Mr. Bowles paralleled this in prose when rising one night this week in Committee of Supply, and being greeted with a howl of execration, he put on an air of injured innocence.

"Why these remarks?" he said. "I do not often speak or interfere with the privilege of gentlemen opposite in talking for the purposes of delay."

"Tommy" has capacity; and if he were better advised, kept better company, and, above all, sat silent through a Session, he might gain a position in the House.

18th Sept.
Lawyers in
the House.

The acceptance by Sir Horace Davey of the seat on the Judicial Bench vacated by Mr. Justice Hannen has given unqualified satisfaction at the Bar, where the merits of this great lawyer are best known, and therefore most esteemed. It is a high position into which Sir Horace steps, and he pays a large money fine upon its acquisition. For many years his income at the Bar has exceeded £10,000 a year. The salary of a Lord Justice of Appeal is just one half of that amount.

There are compensating advantages in the way of dignity, leisure, the prospect of a pension, and the release from temptation to ineffectual striving in the political arena. For years Sir Horace Davey has been a striking example of the occasional failure of the highest capacity at the Bar to "catch on" in the House of Commons. The value of his advocacy in a court of law has long been appraised by the best judges at a height that justified him in demanding a special retainer of £50 before he opened his mouth in any Court. In the High Court of Parliament, when the great lawyer has opened his mouth, the doors have simultaneously gaped, and the audience has strolled forth.

It was much the same on the platform when Sir Horace offered himself to various constituencies.

Whilst some glib, noisy spouter enchanted the audience, this fine intellect, this highly cultured mind, a storehouse of learning, seemed, when he spoke, physically to wither the audience, who either melted away or remained to interrupt with loud conversation or irrelevant remarks.

Whilst Sir Horace Davey is, by the height of his capacity and the ab ss of his failure, a notable instance of the ingrainedy unsuitability of lawyers for the air of the House of Commons, he does not stand alone among his contemporaries. If there is any man who, judged in advance, might have had foretold for him a brilliant success in the House of Commons, it is Mr. Frank Lockwood. He is almost irresistible with a jury, and what is the House of Commons but a larger jury, selected over an area more fully representative of humanity? A clear thinker, a lucid and attractive speaker, Mr. Lockwood enjoys in large degree the priceless gift of humour, for flashes of which, whether conscious or unconscious, the House of Commons is almost abjectly grateful. On the rare occasions when, in these latter days, he speaks, Mr. Lockwood is listened to. But no one can say he is a House of Commons' success, as are other men of far less capacity, oratorical ability, knowledge of affairs, and, judged by other standards, general attractiveness.

What is here noted of Mr. Lockwood applies in measure to that greater advocate, Sir Charles Russell, to Sir Richard Webster, and to the present Solicitor-General, Sir John Rigby.

"It's an odd thing," said a well-known Chancery barrister, when, one night towards the close of the debate on the Home Rule Bill, there arose the familiar mocking cry, "Rigby! Rigby!" "that a man who can any day earn a hundred guineas by fees at the Bar should be a laughing-stock in the House of Commons."

22nd Sept.
A Cholera
Scare.
The House adjourned to-day for a brief recess, but not till another charwoman has been sacrificed. The earlier discovery of cholera on the premises was regarded with some suspicion in the Conservative Whips' room. There was a disposition to look askance at Sir William Harcourt, who was thought capable of any device calculated to frustrate obstruction. Whatever Conservatives may have thought or suspected, they hastened their departure from Westminster, and thus the hapless charwoman did not die in vain.

For a second time the announcement " Cholera in the House of Commons " flames on the bills of the evening papers. It turns out on inquiry to be something quite other of which the second charwoman died. But there is something uncanny about the whole business, and the House has through the week presented an appearance of deepening depression. So low have attendance and spirits fallen that Mr. Chamberlain, after due consideration, abandoned the intention of making the second reading of the Appropriation Bill the occasion for a parting fusillade on Mr. Gladstone and all his works.

CHAPTER XX.

THE PARISH COUNCILS BILL.

LOOKING round the House of Commons
3rd Nov. to-night, listening to the papers read,
chiefly by elderly gentlemen, on the sub-
ject of Parish Councils, it is difficult to believe it can
be kept together far into the month of December.
The attendance on Thursday surprised everyone. It
testified in striking manner to the determination of
members, more especially on the Ministerial side, to
make the most of a possibly fleeting opportunity.
The life of the present Parliament is predestined to
be short. Therefore, says the new member, let us
talk, vote, and be moderately merry, for to-morrow is
the dissolution.

On Thursday, when, after barely six weeks' holiday, the business of the Session was resumed, not
only were the benches crowded, but there was in
the air that buzz of excitement which in ordinary
circumstances presages an outburst. There were
various things that, being started, might have shown
sport. Matabele, the great Coal Strike, the Labour
Question; or, failing these, the general iniquity of
Her Majesty's Ministers. That something would be
done or said, by way of giving a lively send-off to the
Winter Session, was a conviction in everybody's mind.
Whilst members looked round wondering who was
going to begin, Mr. Henry Fowler was discovered at
the table moving the second reading of the Parish
Councils Bill—an estimable measure, an able Minister,
but a concatenation of circumstances not conducive
to exhilaration, much less to excitement.

J*

Had there been any prospect of serious fight on this stage of the Bill, Mr. Fowler's method and manner of dealing with it would have extinguished the smouldering fire. It was admirably done, a performance that has appreciably strengthened the Parliamentary reputation of the President of the Local Government Board. The effect was almost soporific, and, but for the fact that some twenty or thirty members had occupied the recess in preparing speeches to be delivered on the second reading, the stage might forthwith have been accomplished.

"The Man from Shropshire." To-night the House is still steeped in the dolour in which it was cunningly enveloped by Mr. Fowler. Mr. Stanley Leighton made spasmodic but ineffectual efforts to rouse it from the depths of lethargy. The Man from Shropshire, as Sir George Trevelyan long ago happily dubbed the member for the Oswestry division of that county, is one of the few relics of an old school of oratory left to the House of Commons. Like many others, he served his apprenticeship at the Oxford Union, but then and later he pursued his studies with the help of a private tutor and a cheval glass. He is the sort of man who, being on his legs before an audience, looks as if he were saying something useful in the choicest language. He has a good presence, a flexible voice, and a convincing way of wagging his forefinger at the Treasury Bench. He has also a ponderous humour, as witness his terrible wigging of Mr. Harry Lawson. Him he accused of being a Cockney, and told how, addressing a rural audience among his constituency in hardly-won Cirencester, he, chancing to be stationed under an elm tree, described himself as "standing under this spreading oak."

"What," Mr. Stanley Leighton asked, wagging his finger at Sir William Harcourt, who sometimes lives in the New Forest and ought to know better, "can the hon. member for Cirencester know of Parish Councils ?"

Mr. Stanley Leighton comes of a good old Tory stock, and likes his stories, as his mutton, old. This particular electioneering joke dates back, certainly, to the reign of George IV. It is neither an oak, nor an elm ; it is a chestnut. But Mr. Leighton liked it all the better for that. A new story is always a dangerous thing. You never know how it may be taken. One mellowed with age is safer and more suitable for use at quarter sessions and in the House of Commons. So Mr. Leighton bore aloft this hoary denizen of the forest as if it were a young sapling, and could hardly carry it round the House for laughing at the force and freshness of the humour it embowered.

It was on the approach of midnight yesterday that this rollicking joke was appropriately made. Mr. Leighton was so pleased with it and himself that he determined to give the House a little more. Having talked up to midnight, when the debate stood adjourned, he had the privilege of resuming it in the freshest hour of to-day's sitting, and he liberally availed himself of the opportunity. For a while his exuberant delight in his own speech was contagious. That curious gift, already alluded to, of looking as if he were saying something pointed, deluded young members. They stayed on listening, but finding the sentences led no whither presently departed. It seemed as if the sitting must collapse, and the second reading of the Bill be taken from sheer mental exhaustion on the part of the few members present.

A Minister in Mufti.

At this stage Mr. George Russell appeared at the table, and within a few moments the scene had changed. Members half asleep on the benches woke up, wondering what the Under-Secretary for India did in this galley. Soon there was laughter and cheering, ironical and otherwise, which brought in loungers from the lobby.

Amongst the audience were Mr. Gladstone and Sir William Harcourt, whose faces were watched with keen interest from the opposite benches, as Mr. Russell, taking the bit between his teeth, bolted, with Mr. Henry Fowler sitting dazed on the box. The Under-Secretary for India, though a statesman of almost reckless courage, is not disposed lightly to break up a Ministry in which he holds an honoured place, or wantonly to spoil the chances of an important measure committed to the care of a colleague. He felt that the speech he was about to deliver, standing at the Ministerial box, required a preface, and it was the delivery of this singular exordium that fastened attention upon him. Though he rose from the Treasury Bench, and literally stood at the feet of the Premier, Mr. Russell was not, he assured a listening senate, taking part in the debate in a Ministerial capacity.

A member of a Government is, after all, human. He has his feelings, sympathies, and convictions, and though it is certainly not usual to volunteer their exposition to the possible embarrassment of colleagues, exception may be made in favour of certain highly marked individualities. Divesting himself for the evening of Ministerial associations or responsibility, Mr. Russell discussed the squire, the parson, and the peasant, as a private member, " one whose natural home is rather below the gangway than above it."

The effect of this breezy speech upon Mr. Jesse Collings was indicative of the sensation it created among the landed classes and the aristocracy generally. The member for Bordesley was so moved that, speaking in low, hesitating voice, he addressed the Speaker as " Mr. Mayor." Sir Richard Webster, with that fuller command over his feelings which becomes an ex-Attorney-General, smartly belaboured Mr. Russell, and expressed the keenest desire to know what Mr. Gladstone thought of the speech he had listened to.

A Changed Man.

The Premier is, however, not just now in communicative mood, and made no sign in response to this invitation. The change wrought in the aspect of the House as compared with the period of the Session when the Home Rule Bill was under discussion is nowhere marked so strongly as in his manner. Day after day, week after week, month after month, whilst the Home Rule Bill made its weary way through the House, Mr. Gladstone was on the Treasury Bench, alert, resourceful, accustomed to deliver two or three speeches in a sitting if necessary, sometimes when to onlookers necessity did not seem to be imperative. Quite a different personage sits now in the place of Leader, an unemotional elderly gentleman, who evinces no desire to take part in the conversation, and is seen glancing at the clock at the approach to the dinner hour—he who in the Summer Session could hardly tear himself away long after the hand of the clock had pointed to the mystic figure eight.

The Premier is evidently resolved to make partial holiday through this abnormal Session. Whether he will find rest and refreshment in the new condition of affairs is a question. Better suited to him is the storm and stress of incessant action. A Home Rule Session that nearly killed some people left him in better health of mind and body than he had been for years.

6th Nov. "In my Early Days."

Mr. Arthur Balfour spoke for an hour in further debate of the Parish Councils Bill, a weighty speech listened to with marked interest by Mr. Gladstone and a moderately full House. The Leader of the Opposition began with pointed reference to the speech of Mr. George Russell, delivered on Friday night, which has seriously fluttered the dovecotes of the squirearchy. It was, he said, a platform speech, born out of due season and delivered in the wrong place. " Exaggerated rubbish," he described Mr. Russell's declaration of the agricultural labourer as at best a cipher and at worst a serf.   Unmindful or forgetful of the fact that the Under-Secretary for India commenced his speech with precise disclaimer of speaking otherwise than as a private member, he remarked that he would not have paid much attention to the speech had it not been delivered from the Ministerial box.

Harping on this point, he drew from Mr. Gladstone an interesting interruption.   The Premier reminded him and the House that in former times—" in my early days "—it had been the habit of members of the Government not in the Cabinet, and not belonging to the particular department concerned in the question before the House, to speak with the full liberty of private members.   He regretted that of late the custom had fallen into desuetude.

Mr. Balfour was glad to have drawn from Mr. Gladstone a disclaimer of Mr. Russell's views—a way of putting it met by a shake of the head from the Premier.   Then, if he did not disclaim Mr. Russell's views, he did not associate himself with them ?   At which Mr. Gladstone again shook his head, and Mr. Balfour went on to denounce the Bill.

The second reading of the Parish Councils
7th Nov.
The Love of
Hodge. Bill was taken amid a chorus of congratulation that should presage swift and easy passage through Committee.   It is astonishing how active is the interest of the politician in the welfare of the rural population.   Liberal, Conservative, or whatever they be, they are each all one in their love for Hodge, more particularly since he now has a vote.

Mr. Goschen presented himself to the favourable notice of the House as the real father of the Bill, since, as he claimed, he had made the earlier movement towards the establishment of Parish Councils.   That said, he proceeded to urge the Government to destroy their bantling by dividing it in twain, leaving out the portion that deals with the Poor Law. This drew from Sir William Harcourt the happy retort that, bearing in mind the judgment of Solomon, the House would see who was the true parent of the Bill. It certainly was not the one who assented to the proposal that it should be cut in twain.

It must be sorrowfully admitted that the

10th Nov.
In Bullying
Mood.

House of Commons with its many admirable qualities shares the tendency to cowardice that ever distinguishes a mob. Its sure instinct tells it whom among its members it may bully, and of whose stubborn insistence it would do well to take account. The game was fought over a long period during the early development of the Irish Home Rule party. When between 1874 and 1889 these strange people invaded the select enclosure at Westminster, they seemed to have devoted themselves to a hopeless fight. But they pegged away, and, as all the world knows, finally won. In those far-off days when Mr. Parnell was accustomed to arise from the side of the faithful Joseph Gillis he was howled at, sometimes for a quarter of an hour by Westminster clock. He stood with hands and teeth clenched, facing the turbulent House, filling up partial pauses in the uproar with savage retort, and when they were tired out, concluding his speech at the precise length originally intended. Soon the House came to learn that it was no use buffeting this rock. Later in the 1874 Parliament when Mr. Parnell rose to take part in debate he was not any the more welcome. But he was much less interrupted.

Mr. Biggar, following in different way on the same lines, reached a platform of equal supremacy. His famous four hours' speech did more than anything else to tame the spirit of the House of Commons. A man that would do that would do anything. It was evidently no use attempting to drown such a voice with clamour. Thus there grew up possibility of that spectacle which many members seated in the present Parliament have watched with awe-struck eyes—Joseph Gillis rising at the choicest hour of a debate, and, peremptorily waving down other aspirants for precedence, taking it for himself, just as if he had been Prime Minister or Leader of the Opposition.

A Victim. These things are recalled for the comfort and consolation of Mr. Percy Melville Thornton, who represents in the House of Commons the young-bloodedness of Battersea and the untarnished respectability of Clapham. Mr. Thornton does not often interpose in debate, and had the right to expect a better reception than he met with to-night. He had something to say on the vexed question of contracting out of the Employers' Liability Bill. What it exactly was remains unknown, since Mr. Thornton, pitching his voice a little too high for the unequal contest with four hundred gentlemen shouting for a division, did not succeed in fully conveying his impressions.

It was partly his modesty and non-obtrusive habit that led to this catastrophe. It was twenty minutes to twelve when he, after long effort, caught the Speaker's eye. Many times earlier in the sitting he had risen, but so had half-a-dozen other members, and Mr. Thornton courteously gave way. Now was his opportunity or never. At midnight the debate must needs stand adjourned. If any attempt were made to carry it on to the next sitting the Closure would inevitably be moved. If he did not speak now, Battersea would be for ever abashed and Clapham humbled in the dust. Long ago, both at Harrow and Jesus, Mr. Thornton was renowned as a half-miler. The race before him was analogous in point of brevity. If he got an opening he must work his speech off with a spurt, and reach the goal before midnight sounded.

He started off on a high note, at which the House roared with angry shout that, to those unaccustomed to the grim humour of Parliament, would seem to suggest bloodthirsty intention, if members only get at the mild-looking gentleman struggling with adversity. As the noise chiefly came from below the gangway on the Opposition side, Mr. Thornton, turning his back on the Speaker, faced it, and, with shrill voice, either supported or opposed the amendment. All that the Speaker and members above the gangway could see was a back view of the hon. member waving his arms as he screamed at the laughing and shouting crowd below the gangway.

It was a contest that could have only one conclusion. In the quiet and leisure of his study facing the glades of Clapham Common Mr. Thornton has, among other Literary Essays, produced one bearing the engaging title "The Recovered Thread of England's Foreign Policy." It is easy enough for gentlemen on the edge of Clapham Common to direct the destinies of the Empire, and Recover Threads which have baffled the keen sight and nimble fingers of Lord Salisbury and Lord Rosebery. Things are quite different in the House of Commons, when, patience exhausted by hour after hour of dull talk, members clamour for the division. After long battling with the storm, Mr. Thornton dropped the Thread of his carefully-prepared speech, and after forlorn attempts to Recover it subsided, panting and much more breathless than he had been on many glorious occasions when he came in first after the spurt over the half-mile course at Harrow.

This experience might have been expected
A Second. to daunt all other men, and the House, apparently not ashamed of its triumph over an unprotected member, now looked forward to the division. With a gasp of amazement it discovered

standing in the breach a middle-aged young gentleman in evening dress, with carefully tended moustache
and notable shirt-cuffs. He presented himself from
a corner seat below the gangway, on the Opposition
side. This is the headquarters of the Irish party;
and this elegant person, nervously arranging his shirt-
cuffs, did not look like an Irish member. On closer
scrutiny he turned out to be Captain Naylor-Leyland,
who usually watches over the Empire from a seat in
the centre of the benches behind the Opposition
Leaders.

When the astonished and freshly aggrieved House
recognised the personality of the new intruder it
raised a shout more thrilling even than the prolonged
roar that had snapped the thread of Mr. Thornton's
oration. It was no use attempting to speak against
this thunderclap. Captain Naylor-Leyland, recognising that Life is short and Art is long, seized the
opportunity to give some finishing touches to a
costume which ordinary people were inclined to
regard as complete. He readjusted his right cuff,
and carefully examined the link on his left cuff.
Finding it a little awry he gave it a few deft touches.
Then he thrust both hands in his pockets and looked
round on the animated scene. As there was no
immediate prospect of cessation of the uproar, with
concurrent opportunity of his stating his views on
the contingencies attendant upon contracting out of
the Employers' Liability Bill, he withdrew his hands
from his pocket and gave a few careful touches to
his well-brushed hair. This members on the benches
opposite seemed to regard as a personal affront. They
roared with blood-curdling ferocity, a demonstration
which had a curious effect on the gallant Captain.
Again thrusting both hands deep into his trousers
pockets he abruptly withdrew them, and letting both
arms fall at his side went through a process of raising
and drooping his shoulders as if he were at work

upon one of those portable gymnastic apparatus by
means of which muscle is developed by raising
scientifically-adjusted weights.

Even this did not mollify the House. Members
angrily glanced at the clock, and yelled "Divide!
divide!" Giving up the gymnastic performance as a
failure, the Captain did his hair over again, narrowly
examined his shirt-cuffs, and, dexterously interposing
in a comparative lull, shouted, "I won't keep you
more than five minutes!"

The House, generous in instinct even when blood
is hottest, hereupon partially subsided. It was ten
minutes to twelve. Now that the Captain had
completed his toilet, there would be no harm in
giving him five minutes for his speech. It was quiet
solely by comparison with the uproar that had lately
filled the House. Only here and there could a
sentence be heard. From these it was apparent that
Captain Naylor-Leyland wished to remind the House
that there was another railway company besides the
London and North-Western, of which so much had
been heard. There was the Great Eastern, with
access to some of the most beautiful scenery near
London—perhaps a little flat in average level, but full
of topographical and historic interest. The gallant
Captain was evidently only coming round to the
Employers' Liability Bill when the hand of the clock
pointed to five minutes to twelve. Members had
been watching for this, and without six seconds grace
they raised again the roar, "Divide! divide!" The
Captain, who was apparently approaching some
interesting details about Saturday-to-Monday trips,
looked round with anxious face. But it was no use
striving against such forces.

"I thank the House for the indulgence with
which it has heard me," he said meekly, and, check-
ing an impulse to do his hair over again, resumed
his seat.

A quarter of an hour later it was made known
that in a House of 453 members the Government had
escaped defeat by a majority of nineteen.

16th Nov.
The Uses of
Grand
Committees.

The fact that the report stage of the
Employers' Liability Bill has been disposed of in five sittings has uplifted the
heart of those who hope to have something like a Christmas holiday. This feeling shows
that the House of Commons has come to be thankful
for small mercies. At one time, not very far distant,
it would have been regarded as a monstrous thing to
occupy five sittings with discussion of the report
stage of a Bill, however intricate. This particular
measure was, during the summer, taken in hand by a
Grand Committee, carefully selected so as to be representative of all sections of party, with special infusion
of experts. It was, in fact, a microcosm of the House
of Commons, better suited for the work assigned to it
than the larger institution.

What has happened through this week has been
that, having delegated Committee work to this body,
the House of Commons has gone over all the work
itself, clause by clause, line by line. The time may or
may not have been well employed. Obviously it dis-
poses of the assumption that the invention of Grand
Committees is a time-saving process.

CHAPTER XXI.

SOME ORATORS.

WHEN from a back bench above the gang-way on the Opposition side there rose a well-groomed young gentleman with avowed intention of putting to the Chief Secretary for Ireland a question "of which he had given him private notice," few knew that this was Mr. John Kenelm Digby Wingfield-Digby, member for North Dorset. He is among the violets of the Conservative party, living a coy life on a bank under the shadow of the Gallery, in his legislative capacity content to cry "Hear! hear!" or "Oh! oh!" according to circumstances, and to vote in the opposite lobby to Mr. Gladstone. Yet he is not new to Parliamentary life. Returned for Mid-Somerset in March, 1885, he was present during the turbulent scenes of that Session, and was in the House on the famous night in June when Lord Randolph Churchill leaped on to his seat at the corner of the bench below the gangway and waved his hat over the fall of Mr. Gladstone's Government.

He liked the experience so well that at the dissolution he offered himself for another division of the county. But merit, especially when unassuming, does not always meet with recognition, and the many-syllabled Digby—for brevity known among the Dorset (Queen's Own) Yeomanry Cavalry as The Digby Chicken—was left at the bottom of the poll. He was returned for North Dorset at the last General Election, and took his seat on a back bench, he and the House all unconscious of the fame that awaited him.

That Mr. Wingfield-Digby, though still young in years, is free from the tendency to the haste that besets youth, is p a proved by consideration of the deliberateness which his action to-night was founded. On Nov. 8 Mr. John Morley, speaking at Manchester, delivered, his soul against the House of Lords. On the next day the speech was reported in the morning papers, and, either in the morning-room at the Carlton, in his castellated home in Dorset, or amid the glades of his stately park in Warwickshire, Mr. John Kenelm Digby Wingfield-Digby read the scathing passage. An Irish member feeling similarly aggrieved would have been down on the Chief Secretary on the afternoon of the day when his wanton words still buzzed in the public ear. An Englishman might have approached the subject on the following day. A Scotchman would not have permitted the week end to pass before he overcame precautionary habit and advanced to the attack. It was only on the eighth day after the report of the speech appeared in the public journals that Mr. Wingfield-Digby took action.

This remarkable deliberation on the part of the young statesman gives colour to the report current in the House to-night that when on Monday Mr. Chamberlain comes back, he will find a note from Mr. Wingfield-Digby giving him private notice to ask, Whether he is correctly reported, speaking at Denbigh on Oct. 20, 1884, to have said "the House of Lords is a club of Tory landlords which in its gilded chamber has disposed of the welfare of the people with almost exclusive regard to the interests of a class."

Probably Mr. Wingfield-Digby will be content with his success of to-night. It was startling and overwhelming. When he announced that the extract challenged referred to the House of Lords, hon. gentlemen below

Marginal notes:
Mr. John Morley denounces the Institution.

The Liberal Party Approve.

the gangway opposite and members in the crowded Irish camp ominously pricked up their ears. The passage hitherto had not excited particular attention. In the flood of objurgation on political platforms outside the House which makes Wednesday evenings pleasant eras in the week, this particular passage had been forgotten. It was left to Mr. Wingfield-Digby to rescue it from oblivion. It had been the phrase of an individual; now it was to be endorsed by the assent of a Party.

" You are dealing," Mr. Wingfield-Digby read from the manuscript with which he had provided himself, " with a vast, overwhelming preponderance, a huge dead-weight of prejudice and passion——"

Here the crowd on the Ministerial benches, gathered by the attraction of the question hour, broke in with a mighty cheer. Mr. Gladstone, who, probably like many others present, had the passage brought to his notice for the first time, leaned forward with hand to ear eagerly listening. When the cheer interrupted the reading of the quotation his face relaxed into a beaming smile, which grew into a chuckle as the cheering again and again stormed forth.

" —of bigotry," Mr. Wingfield-Digby continued, a note of hesitation in his voice contrasting with the confidence with which he had commenced the citation. Another cheer, sharp and jubilant.

This was awkward, as appeared from the perturbed face with which the reader, forcibly interrupted, gazed round at the animated crowd before him and on his left hand below the gangway. But he had commenced and must needs go through with it.

" —of party spirit—(another cheer) impenetrable to argument—(a shout of delighted acquiescence) immovable by discussion—(a roar of applause) beyond the reach of reason—(a perfect yell of delight)— to be driven from its hereditary and antiquated

entrenchments, not by argument or by reason, or by
discussion, but by force."

Here followed a thunder of cheers, which, rolling
across the corridor, must have reached the House of
Lords, at the moment placidly considering in Committee the clauses of the Savings Banks Bill. If at
this critical moment Mr. J. A. Picton had risen in his
might and made his way towards the House of Lords,
there is little doubt his banner would have been
followed by a turbulent throng, and the question
whether the House of Lords is to be ended or mended
would forthwith have been settled. But the member
for Leicester made no sign, and the rest were content
to hail with another rasping cheer Mr. Morley's
unblushing acceptance of responsibility for the words
quoted.

As for Mr. Wingfield-Digby, he with characteristic
deliberation formally gave notice that " next week "—
probably towards the end of the week—he will ask
the First Lord of the Treasury a further question in
connection with the subject.

24th Nov.
Mr. Keir-
Hardie.

There is no doubt that Mr. Keir-Hardie in
his House of Commons relations has turned
out a failure. This is largely due to the
fact that he began badly. In these days
it is hard for a member of the House of Commons to
live up to a brass band, a waggonette, and an escort of
seedy persons breathing extreme Socialist doctrines.
When to this is added an unkempt head of hair, a
tweed cap, a jacket and trousers obtrusively short, the
difficulty is increased tenfold.

Nature has not endowed Mr. Keir-Hardie with the
gifts necessary to fill so large a part. He is really a
modest, unassuming man, whose tongue cleaves to his
mouth when he rises in the majesty of the People to
beard a plutocratic House of Commons. His personal
manner is entirely free from the swagger associated with
the brass band and accessories that introduced him to

Palace Yard and Parliamentary life. He rarely, in ordinary debate, obtrudes himself on the notice of the House, speaks to few, and few converse with him. Apart from the feeling of antipathy the tactics to which he is avowedly devoted creates in the mind of an assembly such as the House of Commons, he has not succeeded in securing the confidence of the other Labour members. It is true that this is a community a little exacting in their relations with each other. When in anticipation of the opening of the new Law Courts the judges met to draft a word of welcome to the Queen, it was found to commence with the phrase : "Conscious as we are of our own infirmities." Discussion arose as to whether this was not striking the note a little too low. It was stilled by the soft voice of Lord Bowen suggesting the variation : " Conscious as we are of each other's infirmities." The Labour representatives, whether on the public platform or in the House of Commons, do not yield even to her Majesty's judges in the capacity of consciousness of each other's personal shortcomings.

None Other Genuine. The member for West Ham at the outset selected a false position. He assumed the character of the Only Genuine Working Man returned at the General Election. In token whereof he flaunted in the face of the Speaker the tweed cap aforesaid, and in moments of exceptional exaltation declined to wear a necktie. He would take no counsel with men like Mr. Fenwick or Mr. Cremer, suborned, as he held them to be, by the attractions and attentions of a plutocratic Chamber. Still less would he regard with friendly eye Mr. Burt, who had sold his birthright for a mess of pottage at the Board of Trade. Let apostates like these sit on the Ministerial benches. James Keir-Hardie, of Lachnorris House, Comnoch, Ayrshire, would be throned apart on the Opposition side.

From that quarter he rose in the earliest days of

the new Parliament sounding the first note of discord in the nominal Ministerial majority by giving notice of an amendment on the Address. This movement created a thrill of pleasurable excitement in Conservative circles. Lord Randolph Churchill in particular was seized with sudden excitement of hope. Here already, as the band was tuning up, was the little rift within the lute that, widening, should presently make mute the Ministerial music. There was quite a rush of members into the House when it was known that " Keir-Hardie was up." But he was not up long, the Speaker ruling out of order the ill-drawn amendment he submitted.

This first failure in his new career has never been retrieved. He has always been going to do something desperate, and has ever feebly and ineffectually fizzled out. There is hardly anything easier of accomplishment for a member, however personally inconsiderable, than to obtain leave to move the adjournment in order to discuss any question that may have occurred to him as being of urgent public importance. He is the more certain of success if the interruption of public business comes from the Ministerial side. It is Mr. Keir-Hardie's sole Parliamentary distinction that, having several times within the space of twelve months made the attempt, he has invariably failed.

His performance to-night shows why
Moving the this conclusion is inevitable. He associ-
Adjournment. ated himself with a subject which, with ordinary approach to intelligent management, could not fail to insure success. The privation of the unemployed appeals to every man, with increased force if he happen to be representative of a constituency in which figure large groups of working men. Even if a course proposed be ill-considered and not likely to have practical result, to stand up in one's place in the House in order to provide

opportunity to get it talked about is a cheap and attractive form of philanthropy. To refuse to move is to incur the odium of lack of sympathy with a body of citizens who, if they have no bread, have votes.

Mr. Keir-Hardie is perhaps the only man in the House of Commons who could have failed in the task he to-night allotted to himself. He took every possible step to avoid success. A first condition of carrying such a proposal in the House of Commons is that it should have the support of the whole body of working men representatives. If they hang back, how is the outside member to know which section is really representative of the working men? Mr. Keir-Hardie has managed to estrange himself from his co-workers, and, though they did not take the extreme course of remaining seated when challenged for support of his request to move the adjournment, they were known to look upon it with suspicion.

Mr. Keir-Hardie had his game, such as it was, to play, and proceeded with quiet obstinacy. As soon as questions were over, he moved the adjournment, "in order to discuss as a definite matter of urgent public importance the widespread destitution among large masses of the working class due to so many being out of employment, and to the inadequacy of the measures adopted for dealing with it." The Speaker before putting the question made the customary inquiry as to whether it was the pleasure of the House that leave should be given. Two rows of members rose from the benches below the gangway on the Ministerial side, and one or two Irish from the camp behind which Mr. Keir-Hardie sat. According to the Standing Order, forty assenting members are necessary in order to sanction further proceedings. Were there forty on their feet? The Speaker, looking round, hesitated, and then began to count. There were only three dozen, all told, and the proposal fell to the ground.

Curious
Conclusion
of the
Matter.

Once before, in analogous circumstances, Mr. Keir-Hardie suffered a similar rebuff. He had then accepted it, forgetful or ignorant of one other card the magnanimity of the House, mindful of the interests of minorities, had left in his hand. The Standing Order provides that a member moving in this matter may, if he please, demand a division. Never, since the Standing Order was passed, has this privilege been claimed, largely for the reason indicated, that the failure to obtain permission to move the adjournment is of the rarest occurrence. Mr. Keir-Hardie remembered now this last shaft in his quiver, and promptly discharged it. It was all very well for members in the security of uncatalogued numbers to snub the working man and ignore the claims of starving families crying for bread. How would they like to see their names recorded in the journals of the House, for reference on suitable occasions in coming times ? He accordingly claimed the right to take a division, and when the numbers were declared it was found that, lo! a strange thing had happened. When members had been privileged to remain seated, unrecognised individuals in a mass refusing assent to the claim put forward on behalf of the unemployed, only thirty-six stood up with Mr. Keir-Hardie. When the division was invoked, with a prospect of a printed division list, there were forty-four—four more than was necessary to inaugurate the debate had they, a quarter of an hour earlier, taken the same view of their public duty.

1st Dec.
Two Young
Statesmen.

The House of Commons has through the week been deprived of the presence of Mr. Arthur Balfour, and the Opposition have been poorer for lack of his counsel. The occasion, which all regret, is useful in showing how large is the place the still young Leader fills in the historic assembly. If he were only there to be gazed upon, it would be something gained. His graceful presence, bright looks, pleasant voice and ready smile, are something to be thankful for amid the arid pastures of the Parish Councils Bill. There are two comparatively young men in the House, both advanced by leaps and bounds into foremost positions, both certain, if they live, to attain the highest pinnacle, who are curiously dissimilar in manner. Mr. Balfour is, according to the almanack, four years older than Mr. Asquith. In manner the Home Secretary is at least forty years older than the Leader of the Opposition. No one seeing Mr. Asquith answering Mr. Darling on the subject of Anarchist meetings in Trafalgar Square, or replying to Mr. John Redmond as to his intentions with respect to the dynamite prisoners, would imagine that a gleam of humour ever irradiated his mind or lighted his pathway. Those who know him off the bench are aware that this is a misapprehension. Mr. Asquith's supernaturally grave manner on the Treasury Bench is, like Hamlet's inky cloak, an outward semblance, proper to the occasion. His humour, even in lightest moments, is perhaps a little grim. It certainly is not lacking. Mr. Arthur Balfour, on the contrary, ever bubbles over with lighthearted humour, a sunny nature breaking through all the clouds that cares of State may bring. This natural gift is one of inestimable value to a Leader in the House of Commons. Like the quality of mercy, it is twice blessed.

In Mr. Balfour's temporary absence, Mr. Goschen naturally assumes the position and functions of Leader of the Opposition. It is curious to note how he avoids any formal assumption of the part. The Leader's place is opposite the brass-bound box upon which one night Mr. Joseph Gillis Biggar leaned and genially addressed a paralysed Ministry. Mr. Goschen has through the week been content to find a place much lower down, not even advancing to the box when on rare occasions he has risen to take part in conversation opened by Mr. Gladstone.

Monumental Gravity. This excess of modesty has been the less embarrassing since Mr. James Lowther has dropped into the seat of Leader, and remains there by the hour, a monument of impassive gravity. If Mr. Lowther never said anything, simply sat and stared at the brass-bound box, he would be an invaluable ornament and assistance to the Constitutional party. There are many wise men in the House of Commons, but none who look so wise as the right hon. gentleman whom the Isle of Thanet has given back to the Legislature. New members gazing respectfully upon his recumbent figure cannot realise the "Jemmy" Lowther of the Parliament of 1868, when, coupled with the lamented Cavendish Bentinck, he hunted Mr. Gladstone over courses marked by the Irish Church Bill and other revolutionary measures. In his Parliamentary time he has heard so much of the chimes at midnight and after, that now he is all for getting to bed at twelve o'clock. When ardent young fellows like Sir Albert Rollit desire to put in an hour or two after midnight, in order that progress may be made with private Bills, in succession to the Government measures, it is Mr. Lowther who stands in the breach and protests against such unconscionable extension of working hours.

He likes, now, the plodding humdrum discussion, and at any sign of disorder in other parts of the House, more especially below the gangway opposite, his eye flashes with some of the old familiar fire. But it is indignation, not mischief, that burns within him. To-day, Law and Order know no sterner or more uncompromising advocate than the right hon. gentleman, whom it seems a desecration to allude to by his once familiar appellation. Indeed, so jealous is he of order that he has been known to wrangle with the Chairman of Committees when he suspected that functionary of unwittingly overstepping its limits.

Opening for a
New Fourth
Party.
It is not advancing age nor failing force
that is accountable for this more mellow
mien. Mr. Lowther looks almost as
boyish, and is quite as active, as he was
twenty-five years ago. It is the surroundings that
have wofully changed, the personal associations that
are sadly varied. In the new Parliament Mr. Lowther
has found a group of men who would willingly take
service under him and follow him to the death in
circumventing the iniquitous design of the perennial
Premier. Mr. Gibson Bowles would not serve under
Mr. Hanbury, whilst recollection of the fate that
befel Mr. Gibson Bowles's pilot off Algiers is sufficient
to dissuade even a man of Mr. Hanbury's courage
from submitting to the leadership of the member for
King's Lynn. Mr. Tomlinson has the greatest respect
for Mr. Stanley Leighton as a country gentleman of
good birth, fixed views with regard to Mr. Gladstone,
and a charming incoherency of speech. Mr. Stanley
Leighton, from the heights of the back benches,
resists an instinctive tendency to look down upon
Mr. Tomlinson as a borough member, recognising in
him a high-minded statesman with a singular gift of
explaining intricate points arising upon amendments
to the Parish Councils Bill. But neither could
bring himself to acknowledge the supremacy of
the other.

If Mr. James Lowther would only set up in business
for himself, these four, sinking minor difficulties and
prejudices, would hasten to rally under his flag, and
the House of Commons might see the new birth of a
Fourth Party, beside whose career the achievements of
Lord Randolph Churchill's faction would pale. There
was a time when Mr. Lowther seemed to be attracted
by this prospect. Possibly close contemplation of the
means and instruments at his disposal have something
to do with the chastened mood in which, to-night, he
sits and broods in the seat of the Leader of the

Opposition. However it be, he has made no sign, and the forces on the bench behind him are wasted for lack of concentration and guidance.

Had he been otherwise disposed, Mr. Lowther might have done much to uplift the debate on the Parish Councils Bill from the Slough of Despond through which it has slowly moved. None save those whom duty to their Queen and country compel to sit it out from hour to hour know how depressing is the experience. That it should germinate influenza to an extent that threatens to decimate the ranks on both sides seems a natural consequence. Mr. Arthur Balfour, parodying a well-known deliverance, is reported to have said that he has tried Committee on the Parish Councils Bill and confinement to his bedroom with the influenza, and prefers the influenza. Those who have suffered both experiences will recognise a certain similarity of effect in the extreme lassitude of mind and body which supervenes.

There are only two men in the House whose rising in Committee on this Bill causes a flutter in the dulled pulse. One is Mr. Chamberlain, the other Sir William Harcourt. Mr. Chamberlain's command over the attention of the House of Commons was never more triumphantly vindicated than to-night, when, on word going round that he was on his feet, members taking refuge from the Bill in the lobby, the smoking-room, or the reading-room, trooped in to listen. He brought up Sir William Harcourt, and to him enter Sir Michael Hicks-Beach. It seemed for a moment as if there would be a wholesome breeze stirring the sluggish atmosphere and dispelling the saddening vapours. All three did their best, especially Sir William Harcourt. But the task was beyond their united efforts, and Mr. Stephens, Mr. Wingfield-Digby, Mr. Alphæus Morton, and Major Rasch filing in, the debate slumped down

Rival Epidemics.

Mr. Chamberlain.

again to a level at which it was mercifully cut off by
the glad clamour of midnight.

8th Dec.
"Rigby!
Rigby!" To-day, as happened yesterday, the House
of Commons was afflicted by an epidemic
of conundrum. Members are always
athirst for information, and the question
hour is frequently one of the most interesting epochs
in a sitting. But there has not been anything of precisely the same fashion as that which suddenly asserted
itself on Clause 13 of the Parish Councils Bill, and
prevailed through the two closing nights of the week.

It is Sir John Gorst who is primarily responsible for
the phenomenon. Sir John Rigby's presence on the
Treasury Bench has from the first had curious effect
in the direction of exciting in members opposite the
instinct of interrogation. Whenever they see him
they want to ask him something. It is quite a
common thing for this thirst for information to find
outlet for its agony in cries of " Rigby! Rigby!"
But the movement has been vague, undisciplined.
Upon Sir John Gorst there dawned last night the happy
thought of drawing up a question for the Solicitor-
General with all the care and precision bestowed upon
a Protocol. Whilst the cries of "Rigby! Rigby!"
resounded through the House, and the Solicitor-
General, serene and gold-spectacled, sat looking as if
he had never heard of such a person, Sir John Gorst,
taking up a slip of paper, wrote out on his knee the
following conundrum:— " Suppose the case of a
member of the Church of England who after the
passing of this Bill desires to vest a charity exclusively
in the officers and ministers of the Church. *How is
he to do it ?*"

Sir John
Gorst's
Conundrum. The italics only feebly mark the emphasis
with which Sir John Gorst, standing at the
table, hurled the conundrum, as if it were
a catapult, at the portly presence of the
Solicitor-General, affecting a reposeful attitude on the

K

bench opposite. He did not spoil the effect by an additional word. Having said what he had to say, he, like the parson who won the approval of the Northern Farmer, " coomed awää "—that is to say, he promptly resumed his seat. A ringing cheer from the Opposition told how the bolt had sped. The Solicitor-General, inured to these evidences of restless desire for his opinion on moot points, did not immediately rise. But his capitulation was only a matter of time. He was brought to his feet by Mr. Arthur Balfour's threat to report progress. That was merely the final stroke that toppled over the wall of resistance. The foundations were dislodged when Sir John Gorst propounded his conundrum.

Mr. Harry Lawson Puts it Simply. Infected by the epidemic, in its way as resistless as the influenza, Mr. Harry Lawson to-night produced his conundrum. Mr. Cobb's amendment to Clause 13 of the Parish Councils Bill was under discussion. To this Sir Michael Hicks-Beach had moved an amendment. Mr. Griffith-Boscawen proposed an amendment to Sir Michael Hicks-Beach's amendment to Mr. Cobb's amendment to Clause 13. Mr. Grant Lawson, not to be left out of such choice development, submitted an amendment to Mr. Griffith-Boscawen's amendment to Sir Michael Hicks-Beach's amendment to Mr. Cobb's amendment to Clause 13. Whilst the hapless Chairman rose and fell in his seat, clutching papers right and left, reading part of an amendment, finding it belonged to something else, taking up another slip of paper just handed in, and halting hopelessly before a hieroglyph, enter Mr. Harry Lawson with inquiry:

" Is it in order to move an amendment to an amendment to an amendment upon an amendment amending a clause ? "

That is a question which, suddenly sprung upon a man, might, unless he were phenomenally vigorous, be expected to reduce him to a state of coma. Mr.

Mellor has had time and opportunity to grow case-hardened. He answered sadly but swiftly, "I am sorry to say it is," and proceeded to devote himself to the solution of a tangle, the public disclosure of which is useful as throwing light upon the difficulties of the Chairman's position in Committee on an intricate and fiercely-fought measure like the Parish Councils Bill.

Happily, deliverance came from an unexpected quarter. Mr. Grant Lawson, finding himself faced by the necessity of explaining his amendment, supposing he succeeded in having it put from the Chair, shrank in affright and begged leave to withdraw it. He was met by an angry cry of "No!" from gentlemen opposite, who do not view with especial favour the persistent efforts of the members for Tunbridge and Thirsk to lead discussion on the Parish Councils Bill. It was bad enough on the Employers' Liability Bill to have Mr. Tomlinson and Mr. Hanbury constantly to the fore. But they are members who have sat through several Parliaments, and the House has grown accustomed to their appearance and idiosyncrasies. There is a deeply-rooted sentiment in the House of Commons that new members, as is written in nursery text-books about little boys, should be seen but not heard. Mr. Griffith-Boscawen and Mr. Grant Lawson have been heard a great deal in Committee on the Parish Councils Bill, the former bringing to the discussion the voice and intonation of a curate preaching his first sermon, with a measure of appreciation of its convincing qualities not shared by the congregation.

A Dilemma. This secret resentment found voice in the refusal to permit Mr. Grant Lawson's amendment to be withdrawn. In such case there was the alternative of its being negatived, or, more probably, with the angry spirit evoked, of a division being taken. In either case it would be necessary for Mr. Mellor to recite the amendment, and state the

exact place at which Mr. Griffith-Boscawen's amendment to Sir Michael Hicks-Beach's amendment to
Mr. Cobb's amendment to the 13th Clause would
come in.   Mr. Mellor would doubtless be equal to the
task.   But there was no disguising the anxious look
with which he surveyed the turbulent House.

Mr. Chamberlain came to the assistance of the
Committee, naturally assuming for the moment the
position of Leader of the House.   In a few clearly-
cut sentences he admitted the inconvenience of piling
up amendment on amendment, a process that might
be illimitably extended.   But the remedy was in the
hands of the Ministerialists.   Mr. Grant Lawson had
offered to withdraw his amendment.   There had been
some cries of "No!"   These were probably uttered
under a misapprehension, and if the question were
put again would not be repeated.

It must have been wormwood and gall to gentlemen below the gangway to accept the guidance of
Mr. Chamberlain.   But his logic was irresistible, his
manner irreproachable, and Mr. Mellor, again putting
the proposition that the amendment be withdrawn,
leave was given, and Mr. Grant Lawson, grateful for
the escape, temporarily subsided.

Pardonably jealous of the success of Sir John
Gorst, Mr. Balfour was to-night to the fore with his
own conundrum.   Mr. Pecksniff, pursuing his educational processes, was accustomed to stir the minds of
his pupils with profound questions abruptly put.

"Will Mr. Chuzzlewit," he would say, "be so good
as to give us his opinion of the structure of a wooden
leg?"

There is nothing of Mr. Pecksniff about Mr. Arthur
Balfour.   Still, this episode returned to the mind as,
standing at the table, the Leader of the Opposition,
with head slightly posed on one side, an insinuating
smile illuminating his countenance, looked across the
table, and said in softest voice:

" Will the Solicitor-General oblige us with a definition of a parochial charity ? "

" Baiting
Rigby." Sir John Rigby's reception of these complimentary attentions supplies the finish-
ing touch to a little comedy, the unfailing
success of which is probably a puzzle to the outsider.
Sir John entered the House dangerously late in life,
coming to it with a reputation at the Bar equalled by
few. Accustomed to command the almost reverential
respect of court, it must seem to him a harum-scarum
place. The closest parallel to the circumstance is to
be found in Mr. Bultitude's journey with the boys
on their return to school, he being, all unconsciously,
transformed. The House of Commons, as keen as
a lot of schoolboys for anything in the shape of
" a lark," discovered what a treasure they possessed in
the Solicitor-General when, making his first appearance at the table, he replied to a question. It was a
simple matter the purport of which does not dwell in
the memory. But no one present will ever forget the
effect wrought upon the House by the Solicitor-
General's reply—his grave appearance, his slow enunciation, the excruciating emphasis he places upon
prepositions, and the terrific meaning he imports into
the concluding syllable of any word ending in "ing."

For greater accuracy he had written out his
answer, which took the form and style of an Opinion
upon a Case, and probably had it been sought in the
usual way through the agency of a solicitor would
not have been forthcoming under fifty guineas. A
ripple of laughter broke in upon the third completed
sentence. As the Solicitor-General went on, more
impressive than ever, the laughter grew, and when he
made an end of reading he sat down amid a burst
of hilarious cheering that lasted several moments.

It was all a puzzle to him, and has probably
remained so to this day. The outbreak was distinctly
lacking in trace of those good manners which, with

rarest exceptions, control the high spirits of the House. Since then this kindly, unobtrusive gentleman, whom the Bar recognise as among the leading jurists of the day, has found himself in the position of the butt of the Opposition. "Baiting Rigby" has come to be one of the recognised diversions of a sitting. Last night the game went fast and furious for more than two hours. To-night there were signs of determination to play it over again.

The Solicitor-General meets the ordeal with a patience and quiet dignity which will inevitably have their reward in landing him in a position of a prime favourite. In the meanwhile some members are inclined to ask whether the game has not been carried on long enough, whether it is worth the candle—here represented by the reputation of the House of Commons for courtesy and good manners.

CHAPTER XXII.

LORDS AND COMMONS.

THE House of Commons is just now without a Speaker, and is not supported by the presence of the Sergeant-at-Arms. Both are on the sick list, and Mr. Mellor has become more indispensable than ever. He takes the chair at three o'clock, and remains till the House goes into Committee, when he has the satisfaction of seeing Sir Julian Goldsmid or some other Deputy-Chairman seat himself on the cushion, every thorn in which Mr. Mellor knows.

These are occasions which serve to convince the House of the immense advantage that lurks behind wig and gown, more especially when they clothe a stately presence like that of Mr. Peel. Daily accustomed to see him in the Chair, it is not without a shock members find inadequately filling its recesses a slim, elderly gentleman with a kindly face, a slight stoop, and a white necktie. The Speaker withdrew from the scene after Monday night's sitting. He was in his place on that day, apparently in his usual health. When he woke in the morning he found himself practically voiceless. That is an affliction which, developed in some parts of the House, might be borne with equanimity. Obviously a Speaker who could not raise his voice above a whisper would be a failure. Mr. Peel accordingly kept his room, where it speedily became clear that what is the matter with him is influenza.

Almost simultaneously the Sergeant-at-Arms was attacked and withdrew from the scene. Right hon.

gentlemen who sit on the Front Benches in the neighbourhood of the Chair have an uneasy sense that that particular locality is infested with the dreaded microbe. Just before the Speaker was stricken two of the messengers, whose station is behind his chair, and whose duty it is to convey messages to occupants of the Front Benches, were knocked over by the influenza. But, though this seems a favourite hunting-ground, the microbe does not exclusively settle there. It manifests itself in all parts of the House, including the Press Gallery, where there has this week been one fatal case. On the floor of the House, both above and below the gangway, members are cut off in twos and threes. At the present rate of devastation, in addition to having neither Speaker nor Sergeant-at-Arms, the House of Commons will soon lack a quorum.

New Year's Day, 1894. The news that Mr. Gladstone is suffering from a defect in his eyesight which threatens to take the serious form of cataract comes as a surprise upon those familiar with his personal appearance. The most noteworthy feature in this remarkable personality is the brightness of his eyes. As a rule, when men approach fourscore, however straight their back, sprightly their gait, and vigorous their mind, their eyes grow dim. To this day, when he becomes animated in private conversation, Mr. Gladstone's eyes flash with wondrous light. In the House of Commons, when moved by remarks made by honourable or right honourable gentlemen opposite, he leans across the table and almost literally scorches the adversary with the flame of his eyes.

When Lord Beaconsfield was in the House of Commons he used to bring with him a single eyeglass, which upon occasion he, with curiously elaborate process, screwed under his right eyebrow, and through it regarded distant parts of the House. He rarely used it, and it had an embarrassing way of disposing itself about remote parts of his person. When his particular friend and crony, Lord Barrington, was raised from the Irish peerage to the status of a peer of Great Britain, and people asked why, the explanation was proffered that he had earned the undying gratitude of Lord Beaconsfield by the certainty and dexterity with which he could find the Premier's eyeglass when it had got round somewhere about the small of his back.

Mr. Chamberlain, when addressing the House of Commons, stonily regards it through an eyeglass —by preference held over his right eye, by long practice equally at home in either. To more than one generation Mr. Bright was made familiar in the pages of *Punch* because of his eyeglass. Which was odd, since he never wore one any more than Lord Palmerston went about with the little bit of twig between his teeth invariably provided for him in the *Punch* cartoon. Mr. Balfour wears a very becoming pair of *pince-nez*. Sir William Harcourt, addressing the House of Commons, finds his glasses twiddled between finger and thumb indispensable to the delivery of his best jokes. Mr. Gladstone, oldest and noblest Roman of them all, uses glasses only when he has occasion to quote either from manuscript or small print. Whether walking, talking, or going about the ordinary business of the day, he is free from the tyranny of glasses.

The House, still in the Session that opened on the 31st of January in last year, met again to-day after a month's recess. As members had only four days' holiday at Christmas, this interval can hardly be regarded as an excess of luxury. The Parish Councils Bill has been passed after thirty-five sittings in Committee. The Lords, in something less than as many hours, have recast the measure in some important clauses. As

12th Feb.
The Interminable Session.

K *

for the Employers' Liability Bill, the Lords having incorporated with it the principle of contracting out, the Government, if they stand by their declarations, must drop it.

16th Feb. The Busy Lords.

The last touch necessary to complete the dolour of the scene in the House of Commons to-night was supplied when the Duke of Devonshire took his seat in the Peers' Gallery and, resting his head on his hands, incontinently yawned. Torn between conflicting attractions, his Grace had, after an interval, been drawn into the House of Commons. He began the afternoon cheerfully in the Lords with consideration of the Commons' amendments to the Lords' amendments to the Sea Fisheries (Scotland) Registration Bill. Their lordships, running amuck at most things, had not omitted notice of this modest measure. When it came before them in the ordinary course of legislation they, to use an appropriate word not unknown in the fish market, gutted it. The Commons patched the thing together again, sent it back, and their lordships ruthlessly ripped off the bandages.

There was something that might have touched a heart of stone in the spectacle of Lord Playfair standing at the table pleading that at least a shred might be left of the original Bill. But the Scotch lords were ruthless. The others knew nothing about it, and when divisions were called instinctively went out to vote against the Government. The Duke of Devonshire sat and looked on, the gangway and many other circumstances separating him from his old colleague Lord Rosebery. When divisions were called he shook himself together and slowly strode forth to assist in deciding the issue whether there should be eight representative members on the Scotch Fishery Board or whether some other number should be substituted. This process could not go on for ever. A deaf ear being turned to Lord Playfair's plaintive prayer that a new clause inserted in the other House dealing with the rating powers should be accepted, crisis came.

"See what a rent the envious Casca made," said Lord Playfair under his breath. Then, glancing reproachfully at the Earl of Camperdown, he gave up the ghost of a Bill.

Mr. Chamber-lain shows his Teeth.

This experience might be supposed to have satisfied average human hankering after depressing surroundings. An ordinary man would gladly have sought change of scene at home or at his club. The Duke of Devonshire is not an ordinary man, and having assisted at the obsequies of the Scotch Fishery Bill in the House of Lords, he bent funereal steps to the House of Commons to watch the tinkering of the Parish Councils Bill. Had he looked in last night he would have found the scene worth a visit. The same Bill was under discussion, and, in the main, the same members were talking round it. But whilst to-night the debate is in a condition indicative of coma, at yesterday's sitting the air was charged with electricity and the crowded benches indicated something approaching a crisis.

Mr. Chamberlain, standing below the gangway in a position nearly corresponding with that on the opposite side whence he had made his maiden speech, startled his audience by speaking disrespectfully of the House of Lords. Lord Cranborne, alone among the Conservatives, had uncompromisingly defended an amendment passed in the other House at the instance of Lord Selborne, with the assistance of two archbishops and thirteen bishops, refusing the use of schoolrooms for meetings in connection with elections to Parish Councils, thus, as the Ministerialists asserted, literally opening the door of the public-house. Sir William Harcourt beat Lord Salisbury's son about the head with extracts from a speech delivered in other circumstances a short time back when he advocated a directly opposite view.   That was awkward, but easily borne in comparison with Mr. Chamberlain's brief, almost contemptuous, intimation that if the noble lord insisted on taking a division he should go into the lobby against him.   From this personal reference Mr. Chamberlain went on in his incisive manner ruthlessly to describe what he called the absurdity of the position in which the Bill would be placed were the Lords' amendment agreed to.

The Conservatives sat in appalled silence whilst the Liberals greedily listened.   They would not permit themselves to cheer Mr. Chamberlain, even when he had momentarily relapsed into something approaching his earlier attitude towards the House of Lords.   But the smile that illuminated their countenances showed how keenly they appreciated the situation.

A Legal Argument and its Consequences.   This and other incidents helped to make last night's sitting lively.   But there was not sufficient stock of vigour to last over a second sitting.   The first settled the fate of the Lords' amendments to the Parish Councils Bill, and there was no longer that element of possible surprise which is the salt of Parliamentary debate. The conclusion was inevitable, and the approach to it monotonous.   For the greater part of the sitting the members whom Mr. Disraeli used grandiloquently to designate " the gentlemen of the long robe " took the floor, and with a vigour that found no sympathising cord in the audience argued at length round the principle of compensation for injury or inconvenience in respect to the management of a farm, if resulting upon compulsory purchase.   That blessed word "severance" was wrangled over by the hour.   Deep answered unto deep, Sir Richard Webster calling upon the Solicitor-General, Sir John Rigby answering Sir John Gorst, and Sir Henry James interposing to put right his hon. and learned friends briefed in the case whether for the plaintiff or defendant. In the tenth clause on which this argument arose the draftsman, unconsciously imitating Mr. Silas Wegg, dropped into poetry. Much turned upon

> The right to take or carry away
> Any gravel, sand, or clay.

This couplet, a gem of poesy embedded in the arid prose of the clause, was repeated by the learned counsel in varying tones of assurance, doubt, indignation, approval, suspicion, hesitation, exultant triumph, or withering scorn.

The Duke of Devonshire, seated up in the Gallery, caught the refrain as it rose and fell on the flood of talk about severance, arbitration, compensation, compulsory acquisition, and the Land Clauses Consolidation Act. His lips slowly moved as he repeated the couplet; his head gently rocked with the soothing cadence:

> The right to take or carry away
> Any gravel, sand, or clay.

His Grace of Devonshire happily slept.

20th Feb.
Mr. Gladstone and the House of Lords. Mr. Gladstone is always a centre of attraction when found in his place in the House of Commons. He has doubtless grown used to the condition of life. Otherwise it must be irritating to feel how closely and narrowly he is watched by hundreds of pairs of eyes. This week the interest has quickened owing to circumstantial stories current about failing health and coming retirement. His speech to-night in moving the rejection of the Employers' Liability Bill created profound disappointment amongst the young men of the Party, who are longing to whet their spears in the blood of the House of Lords. Called together by a rarely peremptory Whip they assembled in full force, prepared to be led into battle. When Mr. Gladstone stood at the table they cheered madly for

several moments. A few words said by him would have inflamed them beyond control, and the Lords, who crowded the portion of the gallery allotted to them, would have witnessed an instructive sight.

Possibly it was consciousness of the inflammable material surrounding him that made Mr. Gladstone particularly moderate in manner and careful in the choice of his words. He undoubtedly succeeded in temporarily damping the enthusiasm of the embattled host, the application of the *douche* being complete when the Opposition declined to challenge a division. Some men say in their haste that this incident is final proof of Mr. Gladstone's breakdown. By chance the night before supplied opportunity for proof that he is as adroit, as supple, and almost as vigorous as ever. The speech he last night unexpectedly interposed to the discomfiture of Sir Richard Webster showed him at his best. That was an unpremeditated outbreak. To-day's address followed upon long cogitation, and indicated that, rightly or wrongly, he has come to the conclusion that the hour has not struck for pitched battle with the Peers.

23rd Feb. Business Ways in the House of Lords. The proceedings in the House of Lords to-night for a while touched the loftiest heights of comedy. That nothing should be lacking to the completeness of the entertainment the piece of the evening was preceded, as is the custom on other stages, by a little farce. Lord Fortescue provided this by his unaided efforts, and it proved as tiresome as are most *levers de rideaux*. At half-past four public business was understood to commence. The particular business named on the Orders of the Day was consideration of the Commons' treatment of the Lords' amendment to the Parish Councils Bill. Everything seemed in order and in readiness. The Lord Chancellor was on the Woolsack ; Lord Kimberley was in his place with a copy of the Bill in hand ; Lord Salisbury sat the centre of a phalanx of colleagues. The benches behind them were crowded, bringing into melancholy relief the red cushions opposite.

A Dark Mystery. Lord Fortescue carefully prepared himself for the part he had undertaken. He, so to speak, brought with him a book of the words, and, scorning the assistance of the prompter, read from it when, as frequently happened, he dropped the thread of his discourse. How he came to the front nobody knows. As has been said, there was a moderately crowded House waiting to take up the business of the evening, which dealt with a critical stage of the Parish Councils Bill. And here was Lord Fortescue standing by the Cross Benches reading a paper, possibly on protoplasms, peradventure on periwinkles. He had no notice of amendment on the paper, and, as far as was observed, had not been called upon by the Lord Chancellor. Nevertheless, here he was, very much in earnest, with a bundle of uncompromising foolscap in his hand, evidently resolved to read every word it contained.

At the outset their lordships looked on with something almost approaching a movement of curiosity. At least it would be well to know on what subject he was discoursing. After a while this emotion fluttered out, and the peers made general the conversation which Lord Fortescue had initiated.

The threescore members of the House of Commons clustered below the bar and seated in corners of the gallery above it looked on in amazement. Had such an incident been possible in their House it would have proceeded to swift determination under quite other circumstances. The elderly gentleman reading a paper by the Cross Benches would have had his monologue broken in upon by stormy cries of "Divide! Divide!" before which he must have subsided. The manners of the House of Commons notoriously have not that repose which marks the

caste of Vere de Vere. The House of Lords is too
well-bred, too punctiliously polite to be guilty of such
conduct. Regarded as an orator, there is certainly
something lacking to the perfection of Lord Fortescue.
As a counsellor on affairs of State he has not succeeded in impressing the assembly with a sense of
commanding force. Moreover, as hinted, not a single
consecutive sentence of his harangue was audible.
But he is the third earl of his line, which in these
days, under pressure of the accelerated process of
making opportunities of introducing new blood into
Ministries by squeezing out effete drops upon the
House of Lords, is a status of quite respectable
antiquity. So noble lords talked to each other in
an undertone, whilst Lord Fortescue remained on his
legs for twenty minutes by Westminster clock.

He might have sat down earlier if he had read his
manuscript straight away. He had, however, committed it to memory, and insisted upon the attempt
to recite it. When memory failed he turned to the
manuscript, and having invariably lost his place, a
minute or two was occupied in finding it. Which
done, he went on again as before, till again he came to
a full stop, and noble lords looking up from their
conversation found him placidly turning over his
manuscript.

He was absolutely unembarrassed. The ignorant
public outside were under the impression that the
House of Lords had brought itself to the edge of a preci-
pice where one fresh false step would lead to portentous
consequences. Everything depended upon the utterances which within the next hour Lord Salisbury and
the Duke of Devonshire might make. There was
much to be done. Time was precious; the task
elaborate; necessity urgent. Yet if Lord Fortescue
had been reading morning prayers with the servants
seated on a bench at proper distance he could not
have turned over the leaves of the book with greater

deliberation, or with a fuller sense of the responsibility and authority of his position. To the Commons it was a marvellous, a chastening spectacle, disclosing, as in a flash, the great gulf fixed between the two assemblies.

When Lord Fortescue had got to the last folio of his manuscript he did not immediately sit down. He was in no hurry, and no one would presume to hurry him. Accordingly he stood till he had adjusted, folded, and pocketed his manuscript, and then slowly sat down with the air of a man who had settled a great controversy.

A Little Comedy.

It was only then the Duke of Devonshire lounged up to the table and with a sympathetic yawn began his speech. It was a pretty part he had to play, perhaps a little too finely drawn to suit his somewhat cumbrous manner. To him had happed the lot of preparing the fall of the majority, who, swearing they would ne'er consent to some forty things insisted upon by the Commons in the structure of the Parish Councils Bill, were about to consent to many of them. The leading idea of the comedy was that Lord Salisbury was inclined, had indeed resolved, not to abate one inch of the position taken up by him in Committee. At all hazards, in face of all threats, with a full knowledge that Bermondsey was bristling with indignation and had recklessly voted £15 towards the expenses of a meeting in Trafalgar Square, the majority of the Peers would vindicate their independence and assert the privilege of their House. To him entered a trusted friend, a prized and invaluable ally, who, whilst admitting that right was on the side of the Peers, counselled them to refrain from going the full length of their disposition and opportunity, and, rather than inflict upon the country the loss of a measure which had something good in it, sacrifice their own feelings and magnanimously yield to the Commons. Lord Salisbury,

having this view of the situation suddenly and
unexpectedly presented to his mind, was to start
with surprise, cross the stage to the right, fold his
arms, ponder awhile, and then, for the sake of the
country, yield.

Lord Salisbury when he received the cue acquitted
himself admirably.   Through the Duke of Devonshire's halting speech he listened with that intentness
and with some of those little starts of surprise, indignation, and growing conviction with which when Mac-
beth has been played for a hundred nights Macduff
hears that all his pretty chickens are slaughtered.
When he commenced his reply ladies in the gallery,
unfamiliar with the wiles of man engaged in politics,
felt convinced that all was lost, that the Marquis would
turn a deaf ear to the peaceful counsels of the Duke,
and that war to the knife would be declared between
the House of Lords and the House of Commons.
Perhaps the transition from this angry mood of
indignant irreconcilability to that of concession and
compliance was a little abrupt.   Another rehearsal
or two would have trimmed the approach and the
exit.   But on the whole it was admirable, happily
contrasting with the undesignedly artistic ruggedness
of the Duke of Devonshire's manner.

CHAPTER XXIII.

EXIT MR. GLADSTONE.

1st March.
Mr. Glad-
stone's Last
Speech in the
Commons. FOR a man reported to be sick unto resignation, Mr. Gladstone looked pretty well when, close upon half-past three, he briskly stepped in from behind the Speaker's chair, and amid a cheer from his friends, eagerly on the look-out for his coming, took his seat on the Treasury Bench. He did not wait for the approach to the Orders of the Day before taking part in the proceedings. A disposition being shown to talk around the instructions drawn up by the Speaker arranging the new process of balloting for places, Mr. Gladstone interposed and, with more peremptoriness than is usual with him, pointed out that the work could be better and more conveniently done in private communication with the Speaker.

At twenty minutes to four o'clock, the Speaker having read the first of the Lords' amendments to the Parish Councils Bill, Mr. Gladstone stood at the table. A ringing cheer broke forth from the Ministerial ranks, and was maintained for several moments, the Premier meanwhile standing waiting, with one hand resting on the brass-bound box. The House was at this time crowded, a notable absentee being Mr. Chamberlain. A double row of lords filled their benches in the Gallery. The Duke of Devonshire had the Prince of Wales's seat over the clock, with Lord Rowton, who has recently displayed a loyal affection for it, just behind. Lord Rosebery and Earl Spencer sat together, and occasionally exchanged a remark.

When the cheering subsided Mr. Gladstone commenced with a slight huskiness of voice that soon wore off. He spoke for just over the half-hour, without a single note, and, contrary to the habit of younger debaters, without the assistance of a glass of water. Early in his speech came the statement of opinion, emphatically delivered, that the operation of sending the Parish Councils Bill backward and forward between the two Houses had continued long enough—a declaration approved by an almost fierce outbreak of cheering.

The growing enthusiasm was momentarily checked when Mr. Gladstone set forth the alternatives of insisting on disagreement with the two amendments still at issue, and so sacrificing the Bill, or accepting them under protest, with intention of finding an opportunity—" which," he added, " I hope will be an early one "—of amending the Act in these particular respects. It was true the Government had acquiesced in the loss of the Employers' Liability Bill. That was because the amendment insisted upon by the Lords vitiated the whole measure. In the case of the two amendments to the Parish Councils Bill made yesterday by the Lords they, though serious, affected only isolated clauses. In these circumstances the Government had come to the conclusion that it would not be well to complete the wreck of the Session. With this exception all the principal Bills had been wrecked, a reminiscence which evoked another angry burst of cheering from the portion of the audience that had lapsed into low spirits at discovery that actual battle was postponed.

The revival grew as Mr. Gladstone proceeded in solemn tones to declare that the repeated rejection of Bills by the House of Lords raised a question of the gravest character. It was an old question, as was shown by a record published in 1880, setting forth what had been done during the previous fifty years by the House of Lords. A study of that work left upon the mind the conviction

"A Declaration of War."

that the case was, upon the whole, grievously unsatis-factory. Since then the situation had been more acute, a stage having been reached at which the House of Lords showed itself ready, not to modify, but to annihilate the work of the House of Commons.

"In our judgment," said Mr. Gladstone, slowly and emphatically, "this state of things cannot continue."

Hereupon followed a stirring scene, watched with unaffected interest by noble lords. Some members below the gangway sprang to their feet; many waved their hats; all along the Ministerial ranks there ran a thunderous cheer, the sound of which again gave the orator long pause. It was renewed when he went on to declare that the contest once raised must go for-ward to its issue. That would be settled by a higher authority than the House of Commons, the authority of the nation. The time when its arbitration would be invited was a matter for the Executive Government to determine.

"For me," said Mr. Gladstone, in a passage the possible significance of which did not escape the densely-crowded audience, "my duty terminates with calling the attention of the House to the fact which it is really impossible to set aside—that in considering these amendments, limited as their scope may seem to some to be, we are considering a part, an essential and inseparable part, of a question enormously large, a question that has become profoundly acute, a question that will demand a settlement, and must at an early date receive that settlement from the highest authority."

The Gage Picked Up.

The Premier concluded by formally moving acquiescence in the Lords' amendments. Mr. Balfour's rising gave an opportunity, gratefully accepted by the Opposition, of making a counter-demonstration to that evoked on the other side by the Premier's speech. He commended the action taken by the Government with respect to the Lords' amendments, holding that it would have been grotesquely absurd to sacrifice the measure because, as he cleverly if not accurately put it, the Lords have adopted in modified form an amendment placed upon the paper by the Minister in charge of the Bill. As to the second and more important part of the speech, he discovered behind the dignified language Mr. Gladstone always has at his command nothing less than declaration of war (here the Ministerialists loudly cheered) against the ancient constitution of these realms—a dexterous turn of phrase upon which the Opposition took their turn at cheering. For the first time, he said, in a passage declaimed with energy and loudly applauded from the benches behind him, the people of Great Britain have become aware that their interests are not safe in the hands of a party majority unless that majority be controlled by another assembly whensoever it betrays the interests of the nation. Mr. Gladstone had thrown down the challenge.

"Let me tell him," said Mr. Balfour, by way of a parting shot, " that we look forward without dismay to the fight, and that we are not perturbed by these obscure threats."

Mr. Balfour, by his vigorous speech and, his joyously fighting manner, maintained the interest of the House at the high pitch to which Mr. Gladstone had wrought it. When Lord Randolph Churchill presented himself to continue the debate the benches rapidly emptied, the bustle of departing members making strange accompaniment to the speech of a man who was once wont to hold the House of Commons enthralled.

2nd March. Historic Exits from the Commons : Mr. Disraeli's. The House of Commons has an instinctive sense of the approach of a great moment in its history, and bears itself accordingly. Only once in modern times has this instinct conspicuously failed. It did not know on that August night, now more than seventeen years dead, when Mr. Disraeli stood at the table and talked to it, that it would be the last time he might ever speak from the familiar place. He knew it, of course, and it was possibly not by accident that the final word spoken by him in the ear of the House of Commons was "Empire." The speech attracted little attention from a by no means crowded House. The Session was old, members were weary, debates on Foreign Affairs had come to be something of a bore. The Premier spoke after dinner, and sat for a while silent with folded arms and head bent down. When the question in discussion of which he had joined was disposed of midnight struck, and the business of the sitting was approaching completion. He rose and shook himself together with the action which in those closing years he found a necessary preparation for stately march under observant eyes. Had he followed his ordinary habit and passed out behind the Speaker's chair, one would not have noticed, even been aware of, his departure. On this particular night he walked the full length of the floor, turning as he passed the Mace to make obeisance to the Speaker. He halted again on reaching the bar, and stood there for a moment silently regarding the House, less than half filled, wholly unconscious of this silent farewell. Then he crossed the bar, never more to return to the scene of his one historic failure and his many brilliant successes.

Mr. Gladstone's.

When last night the House of Commons, crowded to its fullest capacity, listened to Mr. Gladstone it did not surely know it was attending to the last speech he should deliver as a Minister of the Crown. The air was full of rumours, but the immediate effect of the speech was to discredit the supposition that resignation was imminent. That it had been decided upon, and must take place at an early date, was accepted as inevitable. Looking on the upright figure standing by the brass-bound box, watching the mobile countenance, the free gestures, noting the ardour with which the flag was waved leading to a new battle-field, it was impossible to associate thought of resignation with the Premier's mood.

The situation, one of difficulty not unfamiliar to the Leader of the Liberal Party, was approached and mastered with a skill peculiar to Mr. Gladstone. Faced by serried ranks of opponents, he was hampered on the flank by malcontents within his own camp. As usual at political crises, there was a body of states-men below the gangway who knew much better how to set the battle in array than did the veteran commander. They thirsted for the blood of the hereditary legislator. They would be satisfied with nothing less than Lord Salisbury's head brought in on a charger by the Sergeant-at-Arms. When, on the threshold of his speech, Mr. Gladstone plainly declared that the conflict between the two Houses had con-tinued long enough they vociferously cheered. When he proceeded to explain the plan of campaign, in-volving temporary suspension of hostilities, they relapsed into sullen silence. When the speech was over they, thirty-seven strong, went out into the lobby to vote against their chief, who in the last division he will ever figure in as Leader of the House of Commons found himself walking shoulder to shoulder with the men who had defeated his cherished Home Rule scheme, and who now fell in line to support him against a revolt of a section of his followers.

A pretty and appropriate episode this in a long and illustrious career through which it has often come to pass that Mr. Gladstone has suffered most grievous hurt in discovering that his foes were among those of his own household.

This pitiful proceeding was the only thing that marred a historic scene. The audience was worthy of the occasion. Closely packed, from the benches on the floor to the topmost range of the Strangers' Gallery, it sat watchful and intently listening. Of the members who have taken prominent part in recent stirring Parliamentary history only Mr. Chamberlain was absent. Had he been there he might have spent an interval of proud, if pained, reflection on the unfulfilled. Had he not, for conscience' sake, separated himself from the bulk of the Liberal Party at the cataclysm of 1886, there would have been no occasion for the controversy that has, though within a limited circle, raged during the last few days as to who shall be Mr. Gladstone's successor. " *Vous l'avez voulu, vous l'avez voulou, George Dandin!* " Mr. Arthur Balfour, a young elegant hardly known to the House, and not at all to the country, when Mr. Gladstone began his Ministry of 1880, now faced him, Leader of the Opposition, with an established reputation whose daily growth has been watched by none with keener pleasure or more generous satisfaction than by the veteran against whose shield he has tilted. On Mr. Balfour's right hand sat Lord Randolph Churchill, who, within the same space of fourteen years, has found time laboriously to build and abruptly to wreck a unique position. In the gallery over the clock sat the statesman who nearly twenty years ago succeeded Mr. Gladstone when, "at the age of sixty-five and after forty-two years of laborious public life," he first thought himself entitled to retire. At arm's length from the Duke of Devonshire, with head resting on his hands, Lord Rosebery looked on at a scene the secret of whose full import he shared with the few who knew how peculiarly close was his personal interest in it. Between them, bolt upright, sat Lord Spencer, to whom the turn affairs had taken must

Faces among the Audience.

have been the strangest of all. Had the event
which culminated to-day taken place ten years ago,
upon Lord Spencer, not Lord Rosebery, all eyes
would have been fixed in search of the successor
of Mr. Gladstone. His high character, his long
services to the Liberal Party, crowned by his personal
devotion, priceless in Ireland in the troublous times
between 1882-85, marked him out for the office.
But events move rapidly in politics, and some men
insensibly move aside. It has come to pass, when
to-day Mr. Gladstone finally quits the scene, Lord
Spencer's name has not even been mentioned in the
running for the succession.

It seems, to men familiar with the House
After?   of Commons these twenty years and more,
that it cannot possibly be itself with this
majestic figure withdrawn. For those of sentimental
mood the pity of it is that presently, almost immediately, things will go forward much as they did
heretofore. No man, not even Mr. Gladstone, is
indispensable. When Mr. Disraeli vanished from the
scene it was felt that an irretrievable blow had been
dealt at its attractiveness and personal interest. But
the Speaker took the Chair as heretofore, the Clerk
proceeded to read the orders of the day, the Fourth
Party leaped into existence to make things lively, and
members straying over to the House of Lords on
occasional field nights marvelled to discover how dull
Lord Beaconsfield had become. Happily, though the
dignified presence may be withdrawn, and never more
will be seen on the Treasury Bench the figure which,
seated there, became the cynosure of every eye, there
will ever remain with the House of Commons the
precious possession of memory. Men, in this respect un-
divided by political opinion, momentarily free from party
asperity, will be thankful that, though they never saw
Pitt in the flesh, never heard Canning's voice, they have
sat through successive Parliaments with Mr. Gladstone.

5th March.
Prorogation.

In the Session concluded to-day the House of Commons held 226 sittings, about ninety more than the average for the last fifteen years. Ten days were given to the debate on the Address, eighty-two to the Home Rule Bill, forty-six to the Local Government Bill (the same number as served for the Irish Land Bill of 1881), thirty-eight to financial business, and more than a dozen to the Employers' Liability Bill, also dealt with by a Standing Committee. The work of nearly a hundred days on the Home Rule Bill, the Employers' Liability Bill, and the Scotch Sea Fisheries Bill, was nullified by the action of the Lords.

CHAPTER XXIV.

SESSION 1894.

A BAD BEGINNING.

12th March.
The Third
Session.
To the profound regret of members assembled for the opening of the new Session it was made known that, owing to indisposition, the Speaker would not be in his place. Mr. Mellor, the Deputy-Speaker, accordingly headed the procession of members to the other House to hear the Queen's Speech read and the opening of the Session proclaimed. Mr. Mellor again took the Chair at four o'clock, when the business of the sitting actually commenced. At this moment the House was nearly empty, though the ticket on the back of every seat intimated that members tarried only because they were sure of their places. Sir William Harcourt arrived shortly after the stroke of four. Members were now streaming in, and the new Leader of the House was greeted from the Ministerial side with a ringing cheer, which testified to personal popularity greatly strengthened by the part played by Sir William Harcourt in standing aside for Lord Rosebery to pass to the Premier's seat. A few minutes later Mr. Arthur Balfour arrived, the cheers being now taken up on the left of the Speaker's chair.

In accordance with the beneficent arrangement made last Session by the Speaker, the House was spared the dreary time-wasting process of public ballot for precedence in the bringing-in of Bills. It is, however, still necessary for members to hand in their notices at the table during the sitting on the first day of the Session. A long line of members was thus engaged. Amongst them came Mr. Labouchere, the necessity for reading his manuscript to the bewildered Clerk, staring forlornly at the hieroglyphics, creating some delay in the forward movement of the *queue.* Gradually the House filled up, till, when the customary formal resolutions and Standing Orders were reached, the place presented a bustling aspect.

These preliminaries over, the Deputy-Speaker called on members having notices of motion. Sir William Harcourt, leading the way from the Treasury Bench, was again cheered, the applause being renewed when it was made known that the measure he proposes to introduce on Thursday is one dealing with the registration of voters and other matters connected with the law of Parliamentary election. There followed a list of notices from the Treasury Bench, which dispels any lingering idea that the Session opened to-day is to be conducted on half-time principles. Mr. Asquith has in charge a Bill disestablishing the Welsh Church; Mr. John Morley will bring in one restoring the evicted tenants to their holdings in Ireland, a prospect loudly cheered by the Irish members; Sir George Trevelyan has in hand a Bill dealing with local government in Scotland; Mr. Shaw Lefevre one for the equalisation of rates in London; Mr. Mundella one for the settlement of labour disputes, and another consolidating the law affecting merchant shipping; whilst Sir William Harcourt's deliberate enunciation of the formal title of his Local Veto Bill led to a burst of merry laughter and ironical cheering.

The New Leader.

Lament for the Old.

In debate on the Address Mr. Balfour early charmed the crowded House by his lofty lament over the blow struck at the fame and position of the House of Commons by the withdrawal from the scene of the great example of all that

was most splendid and most vivid in its proceedings.
In tone and manner that bore testimony to the
genuineness of the tribute, the Leader of the Opposition declared that every member of the House owes
a debt of personal and public gratitude to Mr. Gladstone, inasmuch as he had maintained the high standard of public life and Parliamentary conduct established in an elder age. This passage was loudly cheered
from both sides. Sir William Harcourt supplemented
it by another tribute even more warmly couched. At
one time, when he came to refer to Mr. Gladstone's
personal relations with his colleagues, he broke down.
It was some moments before he was able so far to
overcome his emotion as to proceed with the sentences
glowing with affection for the man and admiration
of the Minister. As he spoke in low, saddened,
occasionally broken tones, the House sat silent, now
and then a murmur of cheers approving some
felicitous phrase.

This personal matter, dealt with from either side of
the table in a manner worthy of the theme and of the
occasion, did something to minimise the fierceness of
party conflict. After standing together by the empty
seat of the great orator and statesman whom one
had followed and the other fought through their
respective Parliamentary careers, it was difficult for
Sir William Harcourt and Mr. Balfour to gird at each
other in more familiar way. Mr. Balfour accordingly
deferred detailed criticism of the Ministerial programme
till the Bills promised were before the House.

Debate on the Address resumed. Mr.
Labouchere proceeded to attack the House
of Lords as a Parliamentary institution,
moving an amendment to the Address
praying the Queen to withdraw their power to veto
Bills. Sir William Harcourt, replying in a House
more than decimated by the approach of the dinner-
hour, agreed that the state of things dealt with in

13th March.
Defeat of the
Government.

Mr. Gladstone's last speech could not be maintained. He criticised the terms of the amendment, which, he pointed out, called upon the Crown to put an end to the existence of the House of Lords. To do that would require the creation of 500 peers. Was Mr. Labouchere ready with a list ?

Mr. Labouchere airily accepted this challenge, whereupon the Chancellor of the Exchequer, lapsing into more serious mood, asked the House to leave it to the Government to consider the manner in which Mr. Gladstone's declaration of war might be practically followed up. Mr. Labouchere, an old Parliamentary hand, perceiving the weakness of the Government, owing to the withdrawal of members from both sides in search of dinner, made no effort to carry on the debate, and a division was called. It was seen from the almost simultaneous entry of the Whips that the issue was very close. Mr. Labouchere assumed that the victory lay with him, and advanced to take the paper from the hand of the Clerk, who hesitated to hand it till, again consulting the figures, he found that the Government were in a minority of two, 147 voting for the amendment and 145 against. The result was received with hilarious cheering from the Radicals and from the Irish members, who had largely contributed to it.

14th March. "The Predominant Partner." It is not the least striking of the compliments paid to Lord Rosebery that in the inner circles of politicians opinion is divided as to whether his stumble on the threshold of his Premiership was accidental or deliberate. Making his first speech as Premier, replying to Lord Salisbury's remarks in the debate on the Address, he let fall the remark that he entirely concurred with the noble lord in his view that until a majority of the representatives in the House of Commons of English constituencies — " the predominant Partner "—were prepared to vote for Home Rule, attempts to pass a Bill would be futile.

It is long since so brief a remark was followed by such swift upheaval. The Irish were aflame with suspicion, the Liberals were puzzled, the Conservatives jubilant, and on the next night the new Government, only twenty-four hours launched on what promised to be a prosperous voyage, found themselves in a minority on a critical division. What did Lord Rosebery exactly mean by his remark, and with what purpose was it introduced ? The general public regard it as a slip, and many newspapers have set up a standing headline, " Lord Rosebery's Indiscretion." There are others, with closer knowledge of the young Premier, who insist that he is not the kind of person to commit an indiscretion, verbal or otherwise. They see in the statement sign of deliberate purpose to make known to whom it may concern that he is not so blindly enthusiastic in the Home Rule cause as to sanction the present House of Commons knocking its head against the wall of the House of Lords, wasting time that might be better employed in achieving domestic legislation urgently desired by Great Britain.

What Lord
Rosebery
meant. Last night, after the brief sitting of the House of Lords, and before catastrophe befell the Government in the Commons, I had a long chat with the Premier, in which he discussed the Home Rule question and his relations with it in perfectly frank manner. Lord Rosebery is as sound on the Home Rule question as any of his Liberal colleagues, not excepting Mr. Gladstone. But he is a hard-headed man of business, and recognises the absolute impossibility of passing a Home Rule Bill against the will of the strong majority of representatives returned by English constituencies. Had Mr. Gladstone been younger and stronger, able to carry on the fight for another year or two, he would undoubtedly, after the interval of the present Session devoted to arrears of British work, have brought in a Home Rule Bill again, let the Lords throw it out a second time, and then go to the country, hoping to win Home Rule amid the storm of popular wrath that would rage round the heads of the unpopular Upper House. It is certain that Lord Rosebery will not take that course. We shall have no fresh Home Rule Bill during the existence of the present Parliament. But that does not mean abandonment of the cause by the Liberal party. It is merely a change in the plan of campaign.

Lord Rosebery dwells upon the significant fact that whilst in 1886 the majority of members returned by English constituencies adverse to Home Rule was 215, in 1892 it was reduced to 71.

"Let Ireland," he says, "remain quiet. Let the Irish members in the present House of Commons loyally work with the English Liberals in bringing up the arrears of legislation demanded by the English electorate, and the conversion of England to Home Rule, which has already advanced by leaps and bounds, will go on to the end, obliterating the remainder of the overwhelming anti-Irish vote which in 1886 hurled Mr. Gladstone from power and swamped the Liberal party. If, on the contrary, the Irish members, not being able to get their own way in exactly their own time, play into the hands of the Conservatives, and so turn out the Liberal party, who have sacrificed everything for their cause, and if agrarian outrage becomes again rampant in Ireland—well, there is an end of Home Rule for the present generation."

I ventured to suggest that, as happened in the case of the Reform struggle of 1867, the Conservatives, being in power, might endeavour to secure a long lease, dishing the Liberals by giving Home Rule to Ireland, even as Mr. Disraeli gave household suffrage to the Radicals of 1867.

"If Mr. Disraeli were still alive and in power," said Lord Rosebery, "anything in that direction would be possible. The Conservative party of to-day, under the leadership of Lord Salisbury and Arthur Balfour, cannot concede any scheme of Home Rule that would be acceptable to the Irish people or to the Irish vote. They must get Home Rule from the Liberal party or not at all."

Sir William Harcourt, having last night reproved Mr. Labouchere for the levity with which he approached a great constitutional question, to-day presented himself in most portentous mood. In solemn tones, with slow enunciation, he insisted that it would be impossible for the Government to offer to their Sovereign an Address with a single portion of which they could not agree. Mr. Labouchere's amendment, added to the Address last night by a majority of two, he had at the time criticised, and now repeated the objections taken against it. These were partly literary criticisms, but principally a protest against the attempt to force the hand of the Government, driving them on a course they were, at the proper time, fully inclined to take. Amid cheers from a much larger number of Liberals than had backed up Ministers in the division on the previous night, the Chancellor of the Exchequer claimed that in this matter the Government should be trusted by their supporters with absolute freedom of choice of time and opportunity. A responsible Government could not approach the question in the light and airy manner of Mr. Labouchere. If the matter is to be approached—" as," Sir William added in a parenthesis much cheered, "in my opinion it must be approached" —it will be in a different manner. If Ministers of the House of Commons tender advice to the Sovereign on the question, they must tender it in no ambiguous form. What he proposed was that when the Address in its present form, loaded with Mr. Labouchere's amendment, was put from the Chair, the Government would meet it with a negative. For it would be substituted another Address, differing only in its general

Two Addresses and a Single Speech.

terms from the tenor of that originally proposed, and containing no reference to the House of Lords.

The opportunity was a tempting one for Mr. Balfour, and he made the best of it. From the outset he assumed an air of generous superiority which greatly delighted his friends. He approved the grave manner with which the Chancellor of the Exchequer had approached consideration of an unexampled position in Parliamentary history. He confessed that after the statement, shrouded in language of prophetic obscurity, he did not understand now better than he had before what was the policy of the Government with respect to the House of Lords. The Chancellor of the Exchequer had yesterday been more fortunate in convincing his opponents than in carrying with him his friends. In the division ninety Conservatives ("Unionists" was a better word suggested *sotto voce* by Mr. Goschen, and immediately adopted by Mr. Balfour) had supported Ministers, whilst only thirty Home Rulers had by their vote expressed their confidence in the Government of their choice. The only question now was, How might the Government give their followers an opportunity of eating the—— "No," said Mr. Balfour, with outstretched hands and apologetic air, he was not going to say anything rude, and substituted for the too-obvious reference, "of showing" how they could most conveniently say on Wednesday precisely the reverse of what they had declared on Tuesday. For himself, and he thought he spoke for his friends, who approved with hilarious cheer, he desired to give the Government every assistance, and would to-day renew the support extended yesterday.

"The Government," he added, in a final passage from a high-comedy part admirably played, "may count upon us now, as upon all other occasions, to support the ancient constitutional usages of this House."

Mr. Labouchere, who had been diligently making notes, defended his amendment from the critical attacks of the Chancellor of the Exchequer. But, really, he did not care anything about the Address. His amendment, having been passed, would remain as the deliberate opinion of the House of Commons, and could not fail to have its effect upon the policy of the Government. He repeated his suggestion that 500 or so of peers should, if necessary, be made to bring about the extinction of the House of Lords.

"Send up 500 dukes," he said, looking with winning air of entreaty towards the Chancellor of the Exchequer, on whose face there was no indication of response. "I will undertake to find the men."

After some conversation, there being, as the Deputy Speaker pointed out, no question before the House, Sir William Harcourt rose with solemn mien to move a new Address in reply to the gracious Speech from the Throne. It was a novel experience, the creation of a precedent in Parliamentary history, and Sir William Harcourt is the very man worthy to fill the part. His stately figure seemed to swell, his sonorous voice pealed through the listening chamber.

"I rise, Mr. Deputy Speaker," he said.

At the moment Colonel Saunderson (who, everyone was glad to observe, does not carry any trace of the wound over the right eye he received in the great Parliamentary engagement of the summer Session) simultaneously rose—"rose to a point of order," as he, quite superfluously, said. The Chancellor of the Exchequer paused and glowered over his pince-nez at the intruder. It was a supreme moment at which to suffer interruption. But the occasion was novel, and no Parliamentary precedent was ever established without discussion. So, having overcome an earlier impulse to snap off the head of the intruder, Sir William slowly resumed his seat, taking the extreme edge, so that, as soon as Colonel Saunderson had made his point, he might get on his legs without a moment's delay and demonstrate its inapplicability.

The shade of vexation that crossed Sir William Harcourt's expressive countenance when Colonel Saunderson interrupted was nothing compared with the thunder that clouded his brow when he gathered the exact purport of the point of order on which this strict disciplinarian moved. Was it proper, the Colonel wanted to know, for the Chancellor of the Exchequer, being charged with the time-honoured duty of moving the Address in reply to the most gracious Speech from the Throne, to present himself to the notice of the House in ordinary morning attire? So anxious was the Colonel to maintain Parliamentary traditions and meet the convenience of the Leader of the House that, assuming as a matter of course the Deputy Speaker would rule the point of order in his favour, he intimated his readiness to move the suspension of the sitting for twenty minutes whilst the Chancellor of the Exchequer arrayed himself in uniform suitable to his rank.

Across the fancy of the crowded House there flashed a vision of Sir William Harcourt, in his private room, getting into the uniform of a colonel of the militia, or, peradventure, donning the frock coat of an admiral of the line, with fevered consciousness that the House of Commons was sitting waiting for him to move the Address.

A roar of laughter burst forth, irreverent but irresistible, not to be hushed by the angry rebuke of the outraged Chancellor of the Exchequer, shocked beyond measure at the levity with which gentlemen opposite, self-styled pillars of the Constitution, apostles of Law and Order, could thus make merry over the process of direct communication between the House of Commons and the Sovereign, the humble instrument being Sir William Harcourt.

The new Address, seconded by Mr. Morley, was agreed to without debate or division—another incident in which the present Session beats the record.

CHAPTER XXV.

THE TWO LEADERS.

ALL trace of the Ministerial crisis of last
19th March. week has disappeared from the Parliamentary scene. There are some who have
convinced themselves that, on the whole, the episode
is not to be regretted. It is, they plead, useful as
showing that even at the risk of damaging their own
friends the Radicals will seize every opportunity of
girding at the Lords. The position need not be
disputed if only the sort of thing does not take place
again. From that point of view the episode has
another claim upon friendly recognition. Ministers
have privately intimated to whom it may concern that
any more little games of this kind will lead to serious
complications.

In the meantime, there being no fireworks in the
air, business has progressed at exhilarating pace. It
is like old times in far-off days to have the Supplementary Estimates passed at a single sitting. At one
moment it seemed as if similar good fortune would attend Sir Ughtred Kay-Shuttleworth in charge of the
Navy Estimates. Still, two nights cannot be grudged
to debate on what is practically the whole state of the
Navy and its general management. When, on Saturday, the House adjourns for a brief Easter recess it
will have been only a fortnight in Session. In the
pre-Easter section of last year the House sat exactly
two months, and when it adjourned had done no more
than has now been done in two weeks, save the introduction of two or three Bills. The debate on the
Address alone occupied ten days—a fuller period than

this year has sufficed for passing the Supplementary
Estimates, the Army and Navy Estimates, not to
speak of considering two Addresses. This idyllic
state of things is, of course, chiefly due to the fact
that there is no Home Rule Bill in the near distance.

20th March.
The Leader
of the Oppo-
sition.

Mr. Arthur Balfour has now finally settled
in the saddle of Leader of the Opposition,
and rides well. There was a time when it
seemed as if he were loath to stay, finding
the drudgery of leadership uncongenial. He came
late, went away early, and when he took part in debate
displayed an air of aloofness and indifference that was
very curious. That is all changed now. He sticks to
his post, and is always on the alert for a chance of
conducting operations against the enemy. In the
short stretch of Session already passed he has found
opportunity of making three speeches, each different
in its way, combining to establish his Parliamentary
position on a firm basis. One was on the Address,
when he' paid an eloquent tribute to Mr. Gladstone ; the second on the Ministerial crisis, when
he played his part with great skill ; the third on
Monday, when he found himself placed by Lord
Randolph Churchill in a difficult position, since he
could not support his motion against Lord Rosebery,
and would not throw over a friend. He managed to
dance among the eggs with a vigorous grace that
delighted the House.

A Wraith.

To old members there is something pathetic in the sight of Mr. Arthur Balfour
following or preceding Lord Randolph
Churchill in debate. They recall a time, not parted
by many years, when Lord Randolph, strong, vigorous,
irresistible, was the leader, Mr. Balfour, languid, sometimes lackadaisical, following him at respectful distance. On Monday Lord Randolph stood at the table,
sad wreck of a man, attempting to read a carefully-
prepared manuscript in a voice so strangely jangled

that few could catch the meaning of consecutive sentences. As soon as he rose members began to move towards the door. When he sat down he had talked the place half empty—he at whose rising eight years ago the House filled to its utmost capacity.

Beside him, strong, smiling, debonnaire, with perfect command of himself and over the House, sat his old subaltern, now Leader of the Opposition, a statesman trusted by the House of Commons, adored by his party. Lord Randolph, with flashes of his old courage, doggedly fronts the empty benches and struggles against physical disability. But it is a painful sight to those who remember what he was and still esteem him.

22nd March.
Mr. Glad-
stone's Empty
Seat. The House of Commons has settled down to its work as if there had never been such a person as Mr. Gladstone. He is still member for Midlothian, and probably may some day look in and take the corner seat behind the Treasury Bench, a place that will have for him many recollections. When a statesman of first rank retires from a Ministry this corner seat is reserved for him. Here Mr. Forster sat when he was driven out of Mr. Gladstone's Government of 1880. Hence he rose on the memorable night when he disclosed and denounced the Kilmainham treaty. There Lord Hartington sat on quitting Mr. Gladstone's side when his old leader unfurled the flag of Home Rule. He was presently joined by Mr. Chamberlain, and there had its birth the Dissentient Liberal Party, which has played so prominent a part in English political history during the last seven years. Here Lord Randolph Churchill encamped when, having played his last stake, he stepped down from his high position in the Conservative Cabinet, walking forth never to return.

All these figures, interesting and important, will be eclipsed by an infinitely greater personality when Mr. Gladstone, after what in a letter published this morning he speaks of as "more than sixty years of highly contentious life," drops into the historic seat. It would be impossible to exaggerate the influence he might wield if upon occasion he chose to interpose. Some day, doubtless, he will present himself, and, addressing the House from this corner seat, will add one more to the many famous pictures in Parliament of which he has been the central figure. But there is no reasonable expectation that he will observe anything like a regular attendance on his Parliamentary duties.

He came up to town from Brighton yesterday and underwent a careful examination at the hands of an eminent oculist. It was placed beyond doubt that a cataract is present in both eyes, and that an operation will be necessary. This involves confinement to the house for a considerable period, practically covering the whole of the Session. Before next Session has far advanced the dissolution will be upon us, and Mr. Gladstone is not likely to offer himself for re-election. In all probability his last speech in an assembly which his voice and presence have filled for more than sixty years was delivered on the Thursday afternoon preceding the prorogation, when he took up his parable against the House of Lords.

30th March. "A Spit-to-Win'ard Admiral." That the member for Lynn Regis, in spite of a stately manner and an intimate acquaintance with the Law of Nations and the lay of a ship's rigging, should be familiarly known as "Tommy" speaks volumes in his favour. No one in the House would think of referring to Mr. Robert Hanbury as "Bobby." That is a diminutive reserved for quite another personage, a pillar of Her Majesty's Court and a stay of Her Majesty's Government.* Mr. Bowles is, in truth, a man of wide knowledge, considerable ability, gifted withal with a pinch of that most precious

* Mr. "Bobby" Spencer, brother of Earl Spencer.

L *

savouring—humour. If he only thought he knew less, his success would be much greater. It is said of him that he is one of three members who addressed the House of Commons on the day he took the oath and his seat, the other two being Irish representatives. That only shows how misleading is memory, and with what ease tradition establishes itself in a popular assembly. As a matter of fact, it was not till the second day of his appearance on the scene that the House of Commons found itself being instructed by the member for Lynn Regis, and he has been talking ever since.

Even with his personal friends and political supporters this habit is prone to engender resentment. When, just before the adjournment for the Easter Recess, the Navy Estimates came under discussion Mr. Bowles instinctively took charge of the ship. There were some right hon. friends on the Front Bench below him whose ex-official position seemed to qualify them to take the lead in debate on behalf of the Opposition. Lord George Hamilton was in his place. Mr. Forwood had mustered, and that gallant seaman from Sheffield, Sir Ellis Ashmead-Bartlett, trod the deck with firm, springy step. But "Tommy" piped the crew to quarters and proposed to direct the manœuvres.

"Won't *you* say something?" he asked Mr. Penrose Fitzgerald, who, cradled on Corkbeg Island and some time a member of the Cork Marine Board, is well up in seafaring matters.

"No," said the member for Cambridge, turning in his cheek an imaginary quid; "I'm not going to sail under spit-to-win'ard admirals like you."

That was hard, but was nothing more than the ebullition of a racy nature, and may be forgiven for the delightful picturesqueness of the phrase. It does not affect the main fact that the House recognises in "Tommy" Bowles a good fellow.

6th April.
Ministerial
Difficulties. The Opposition have tasted blood and will not be content until they have run the quarry down. Last night a private Bill, approved from the Treasury Bench by the head of the department directly concerned, and supported by a full muster of Ministerialists, was, after an exciting division, defeated by a majority of one. Later in the sitting Ministers, ineffectually attempting to make progress with public business, were not only baulked, but had their majority reduced, first to eighteen, then to fifteen.

No Ministry, however strong, can afford to have misfortunes, and the Government of Lord Rosebery, which is not strong, has been at least twice since the brief Session opened terribly unfortunate. The Liberal Party in office can least afford the assault of such accidents as have befallen it this week. The immediate effect of such a course of events, had they happened to the Conservatives seated on the Ministerial side, would have been to draw their ranks closer together, with impulse to offer a united front to the common enemy. The Liberals in office are always ready to blow up themselves and, more especially, their esteemed leaders.

What will happen on Monday, when motion is made to appropriate the time of private members, is looked forward to with keen interest. What actually happened to-day when this new manœuvre in face of the enemy was announced was a clamour of protest from Liberal members who chanced to be personally interested in particular Tuesdays. A meeting of the Radical Committee was promptly summoned for Monday, and no secret was made of the intention of applying a pistol to the head of a Government already staggering under well-planted blows delivered in the front. If Sir William Harcourt will consent to vary the proposed rule by making special exception in favour of the body of his supporters who have secured

Tuesday week for a motion assailing the House of
Lords, they will support him in suppressing the
equally established rights of other private members.
If not, they will join the Opposition in voting against
the Ministerial proposal.   -

Thus they loudly talked to-night. Probably
opportunities of reflection provided by the
interposition of the Sabbath Day may lead
them to modify their conclusions.   If they vote
against the Government the Ministry will resign, and
a dissolution will inevitably follow, either at the
instance of Lord Rosebery or on the insistence of Lord
Salisbury, who would naturally decline to attempt to
carry on the Queen's Government with the present
House of Commons.   Probably Sir Charles Dilke or
Mr. Labouchere, disinterested, not to say enthusiastic,
supporters of the Government, would not hesitate
to face even this contingency.   They, above all
things, stand for the right, and their seats are quite
safe.   They have no private scores to play off against
friends on the Treasury Bench.   At the same time
they feel that their opportunities of furthering the
public good would be enlarged if they were left with
free hand in Opposition against a Conservative
Government with probably only a bare working
majority.

Ministers will carry their proposal on Monday
night.   But it will be too much for them to hope that
they will be strengthened and sustained in debate by
the assistance of a unanimous party.   It is possible,
even probable, that their majority, perilously diminished by the defection of the Parnellites and the
flickering enthusiasm of the Nationalists no longer
on the Home Rule war-path, may be diminished
by deliberate abstention of a few English Radicals.
That will be a gravely critical step.   When, on the
Address, Mr. Labouchere defeated the Government
by a majority of two, it is no secret that an influential

*Crisis
Approaching.*

section of the Cabinet, looking ahead with a foresight that was justified on Thursday night, protested it was no use attempting to carry on in these circumstances. They were appeased only by promise that any repetition of similar wantonness of mutiny should be the signal either for resignation or Dissolution. Three weeks have elapsed since the Ministry were first wounded in the house of a friend. Any opening of the wound afresh must inevitably and promptly prove fatal.

A Bleak Prospect. To tell the truth, there is nothing in the near prospect that for them makes life particularly worth fighting for. To an Opposition ably led, united by firmest bonds, full of life and spirit, there is fronted a wavering line of Ministerialists, divided and subdivided by faction, every man knowing better than his Leader how affairs should be directed. Apart from discouragement below the gangway, hapless Ministers are harassed by discords within the Irish camp, upon whose steadiness everything depends. The open defection of Mr. Redmond is serious enough in view of a majority that has fallen below forty. It might be disregarded if the larger body of the Nationalists were well in hand, and might be counted upon whenever the division bell rang. That this is not the case was demonstrated on Thursday. There is no significance in the absence of the nine unpaired Nationalists beyond the serious one of the evidence it supplies of insubordination and indifference. In common with the main body of the Ministerialists they received the urgent Whip claiming their attendance in anticipation of a critical division on the Scotch Grand Committee resolution. Had the question at issue touched the Home Rule Bill they would have been in their places, as they were regularly throughout last Session, maintaining the Government in the sufficiently strong position held by a working majority of thirty-six or thirty-eight. They would have been in their places on Thursday even at some personal inconvenience if they had known the Government stood in peril.

But with a watchful, wary Opposition a Government that can at best command a majority of a trifle over thirty is in hourly peril. The only way to sustain it is for every man of the army to be within sound of the trumpet summoning him to the ramparts to repulse sudden attack. The Irish Nationalists will fulfil that condition only when the Home Rule Bill stands as the first Order of the Day. As that is not a condition of the present Session, no one can tell what a day may bring forth.

Five years ago, or even less, anyone contemplating the possibility of Sir William Harcourt succeeding to the Leadership would have felt doubt as to his capacity to meet one indispensable condition of full success. He is such a brilliant talker, delights so unrestrainedly in buffeting the adversary, there might well be apprehension that he would find it impossible to resist the human temptation to bring down the oratorical shillelagh when, casually passing by, he observed a head protruding from under the folds of a tent. He has not long filled the seat vacated by Mr. Gladstone, and already he has shown that the apprehension was groundless. As Leader of the House he has become thoroughly imbued with the conviction that his sole duty is to advance the business of the day. Talk, he now perceives, is fatal to work. Therefore, whilst deprecating the passion on the part of others, he will, as far as possible, hold himself guiltless.

With the proverbial enthusiasm of a pervert he carries conviction to extreme limits. Once this week he has had occasion to make an important Ministerial announcement. Twice he has been called upon to take prominent part in a set debate. One can easily imagine at what length, in what tortuous sentences,

13th April. William the Silent.

with what hedging and ditching of eloquence, Mr.
Gladstone, had he still been Premier, would yesterday
have announced that the Liberals, having when in
Opposition loudly denounced the policy of annexing
Uganda, had, being in office, resolved to undertake
its protectorate. Mr. Gladstone's sensitive conscience
would not have been at rest till it had been publicly
convinced, by word of his own mouth opened in
presence of the House of Commons and within
hearing of the listening universe, that whilst with
respect to a particular and unchanged course he
had been right in 1891 in saying "I won't," he was
equally right in 1894 in saying "I will."

For Sir William Harcourt the position
Uganda. personally was not less delicate and
difficult than it would have been for Mr.
Gladstone. He had been especially prominent and
uncompromising in his opposition to the action of the
Government of Lord Salisbury when, on the entreaty
of the East Africa Company, they were drifting into
the occupation of Uganda. Now, going further than
Lord Salisbury had three years ago proposed to step,
the Liberal Government were making it exceedingly
awkward for Her Majesty's Opposition of the Session
of 1891. The right-about-face must needs at some
time be explained. Yesterday it was absolutely necessary to get certain votes in the Navy Estimates, if
possible leaving a margin of time for dealing with
the Army Annual Bill. It would be time enough
when a vote on account of Uganda was asked for to
show that the present Government had been literally
correct alike when they said white was black and
when they averred the absolute error that underlay
the assertion. For the present the Chancellor of the
Exchequer, plaintively deprecating untimely discussion, contented himself with setting forth in a
single sentence the determination of Her Majesty's
Government to establish a regular administration

in Uganda and declare the territory under British protection.

Whilst Sir William Harcourt has thus, with even unnecessary vigour, conquered the old Adam which incites him to oratorical triumphs or smart but costly repartees, he is not yet inured to the condition of affairs which requires a Leader of the House always, or nearly always, to be in his place on the Treasury Bench. A noble infirmity of temper makes him impatient of a bore. He is not gifted with that apostolic sweetness of disposition that enabled St. Paul to "suffer fools gladly." Before he was weighted with responsibility of the Leadership he had an eloquent way of walking out, in the midst of a speech from the other side, much more effective by way of rejoinder than would have been half-an-hour's pointed reply from another member. That a man, not being the Speaker or the Chairman of Committees, finds himself unable to sit for nine hours listening to average talk in the House of Commons is an indictment not to be wantonly brought. It is an ordeal few can stand, a continual feast of "thrice boiled colewort," the mere contemplation of which used to frenzy Carlyle.

It is strange to reflect that within recent memory the men most successful in performing the duty without outward sign of weariness or ultimate penalty of early death were two of the brightest intellects of the age. When Mr. Disraeli was Leader of the House of Commons he took his seat when questions began and, with the briefest possible interval for dinner, did not quit it till the Orders of the Day were disposed of. He did not even, as far as observation went, lighten existence by the occasional oblivion of a few moments' sleep. With folded arms, crossed legs, head bent down, but eyes roving over the bench opposite, and ears alert to every sound, he sat on silent through the dull hours.

Mr. Gladstone observed the same close, continuous attendance, with the difference that, instead of sitting quiescent, he was, through the dull night, in constant state of excitement, relieved now and then by the refreshment of a long speech. Up to the last Session of the 1880-85 Parliament, he was on the Treasury Bench practically throughout the whole of a sitting. When Mr. Balfour came into the Leadership this burden of attendance, whether anything was worth listening to or not, was more than he could bear. He is in better training now, and sits through long stretches of dreary talk. Preparation for the Budget, and last week a domestic affliction which all regret, have hitherto deprived the House of Commons of the full companionship of its new Leader. These are temporary causes the coming week will see removed. Sir William Harcourt is too old a Parliamentary hand not to know that the House of Commons is a team that may be successfully driven only by an undeputed coachman always on the box-seat.

6th April. "The Bonnie Pit-boy." The will of Sir George Elliot, Bart., just proved, should be as useful as a supplementary chapter of Mr. Smiles' "Self Help" in encouraging youth of humble birth, surrounded by adverse circumstances, to press forward and upward. His personal estate has paid probate duty upon a sum reaching within a mere trifle of half a million sterling. Sixty years ago Sir George Elliot, Bart., ex - M.P., late of Park Street, Grosvenor Square; the Carlton Club; Houghton Hall, Durham; Aberaman House, Glamorgan; and Belle Vue, Newport, Monmouthshire, was a pit-boy, hard at work in a Durham colliery that later became his own property. It was one of the many good traits about Sir George that he was not ashamed of his origin, though of late years it grew so remote he did not think it worth while to lead conversation in that direction.

There were times when it might be useful, and then Sir George—who, behind a manner of beaming geniality, scarcely hid one of the shrewdest minds, the canniest natures known to men—was ready to take advantage of the accident of birth. When he contested North Durham, a constituency largely made up of working miners, his agents were careful to placard the walls with invitations to support " The Bonnie Pit-boy." They did this only fitfully, returning him in 1868, rejecting him at the general election in 1874. He got back again on a bye-election in this same year (1874), was out again in 1880, re-elected in 1881, and finally parted with the seat in 1885. In that year he unsuccessfully tried another division of the county, and found a refuge in Monmouthshire, also a mining district. At the general election of 1892 Monmouth preferred a Home Ruler, and at the time of his death Sir George was out of Parliament.

He was not a strong politician, but a seat in Parliament fitly crowned the edifice of his career. As in this country frequently happens in the case of men who have won their way from indigence to great wealth, he joined the party of the nobility and gentry. They were glad enough to have him, for he was a man of generous disposition, paid handsomely for his footing at the Carlton, and was occasionally able to win a seat which otherwise would have been captured by the enemy. Mr. Disraeli, with his customary shrewdness, made much of Sir George Elliot. He used to invite him to spend from Saturday to Monday at Hughenden —a rare mark of favour. There was a story current eighteen years ago at the Carlton that Sir George, lunching *tête-à-tête* with the Premier, threw himself back in his chair and, genially regarding his host, said, " Now, Mr. Disraeli, tell me what you think about Mr. Gladstone."

Another story that connects his name with Mr. Disraeli is certainly true, for he told it me himself.

At one time during his Premiership Mr. Disraeli, discussing at a public meeting the conditions and prospects of trade, let fall the remark that the demand for chemicals had suddenly and appreciably increased, adding that that was an infallible indication of reviving trade. This was regarded by the ordinary newspaper reader as one of Dizzy's epigrams, reminiscent of an earlier speech, when he mystified the farmers of Buckinghamshire by a display of erudite research on the science of cross-breeding sheep. Better-informed authorities vindicated the Premier's prescience, showing that the use of chemicals largely entering into innumerable processes of manufacture, a comparatively slight increase in the demand infallibly indicated a healthy growth of trade. This was a great success for Dizzy, the respect engendered being increased by consciousness that at first there had been an ignorant disposition to laugh at the conceit.

Years afterwards Sir George Elliot told me this was his thunder. He had accidentally mentioned in conversation with Dizzy the movement in the chemicals market, and had indicated its bearing on the question of trade. Dizzy betrayed no special interest in the topic at the moment; but later it was brought out brand-new, hall-marked as his own, and proved an immense success.

CHAPTER XXVI.

THE DEATH DUTIES BUDGET.

WHEN Sir William Harcourt rose to introduce his Budget the House had filled to its utmost capacity, a measure quite inadequate for the accommodation of members on the benches on the floor. The crowd massed here was more conspicuous from the circumstance that every member held in his hand a copy of the paper setting forth the main figures in the financial statement. Once or twice in the course of the speech these were heard as well as seen, a mighty rustling noise interrupting the Chancellor of the Exchequer as he proceeded from page to page in exposition of the situation.

Members who could not find seats on the benches camped out on the gangway steps. The Strangers' Galleries were crowded to the topmost tier, camp stools being introduced to enlarge the seating accommodation below the gallery.

Sir William Harcourt commenced with an interesting disquisition on the incidence of the liquor trade. Rum, which had done so much for Mr. Goschen, had failed the Treasury at this crisis. The revenue from spirits generally had appreciably decreased, but the wind was tempered to the shorn Chancellor of the Exchequer, inasmuch as the run upon beer, consequent on the sultry summer, had practically balanced the account. The Chancellor paid a hearty compliment to the permanent officials at the Treasury for the remarkable precision of their estimate of the revenue made in cloudy forecast of an exceptional year. On a revenue, including advances to local bodies, of ninety-eight millions, the realisation varied from the estimate by only one-half per cent. That, Sir William said, amid responsive cheers, was remarkable testimony to the stability of the revenue and to the sagacity and experience of the staff. Although it had been an ill-starred year, there was no sign of reduced power of purchasing the necessaries and even the luxuries of life, whilst the savings banks returns showed that the people were still able and willing to put by for rainy days.

In the coming financial year the Chancellor of the Exchequer was faced by the problem of meeting a total expenditure, including local subventions, of £102,700,000. As compared with the demand upon his predecessor of twenty years ago, that showed an increased expenditure of £23,823,000. As compared with last year, it was an addition of four millions, £3,126,000 being represented by an increase of naval expenditure. The estimated revenue was £90,956,000, being £177,000 less than the actual receipts of last year, facts which demonstrate the Chancellor's assertion that expenditure is increasing more rapidly than revenue. The net result of the column of figures here summarised was that the House found itself faced by the necessity of providing for a deficit of £4,502,000.

A Mighty Deficit. A deep sigh resounded through the crowded House at this confirmation of the most doleful expectancy. How is the deficit to be met? Sir William asked, with outstretched hands that suggested they might be expected to receive at least an additional twopence on the income-tax. "Not by borrowing," said the Chancellor, and the House heroically cheered. Nor would he consent to meet the emergency by abandoning the provisions for the reduction of the National Debt. But there were debts and debts. There was a new debt

bequeathed from the last Government on account
of Imperial and naval defence. This amounted to
£5,745,000, and the revenue of the year was loaded
with the charges on this account. He gratefully
recognised an admission made by Mr. Goschen in
course of debate on the Navy Estimates, wherein the
Chancellor of the Exchequer responsible for handing
on that burden to his successors declared that had he
foreseen the fact that the charge would not be exceptional, and that it would have to be met at a period
of depression, he would have made other arrangements. Fortified by this authority, Sir William Harcourt announced as the first foundation of his Budget
that he intends to apply to the liquidation of this
legacy the new Sinking Fund established for dealing
with it. By that means, and by the saving of the interest on the Suez Canal shares allocated to the
clearing off of this debt, the deficit would be reduced
by a sum of £2,379,000.

This quite unexpected and startling disclosure of
the secret of the Budget led to a buzz of conversation
which interrupted for several moments the interesting
story.

How to Meet It. When there was a pause there came again
the question, "How is this balance to be
met?" Mention of the death duties
brought forth a ringing cheer from the Liberals,
renewed when Sir William observed that, even if it
were not made necessary by existing circumstances to
grapple with this question, it would be his duty to
attempt it. He proceeded to explain the mysteries
of the death duties, five in number, understanded
not of the people, but, as Sir William slyly observed,
fondly familiar to lawyers highly paid to grapple with
their intricacies. The present state of the law, he
said, amid loud cheers, is unjustifiable and intolerable.
He proposed to alter it by establishing a single duty
of the probate type, to be called the Estate Duty. It

would be a charge according to the principal value of all property, whether real or personal, settled or unsettled, that passes on the death of the owner. There was some gasping for breath on the back Conservative benches when Sir William adventured the statements that the Dead Hand is a creation of the law, that no person has any right to property beyond the term of his natural life, and that the State has the right to set forth under what conditions his property shall pass. The indignation was smothered when Sir William quoted from a speech by Mr. Goschen in which he had upheld this doctrine.

As Mr. Goschen later, with plaintive exaggeration, complained, fully a quarter of the Chancellor's speech was made up from quotations of his earlier heresies, spoken when other times had enforced other manners of logic. Throughout the something more than two hours and a half Sir William Harcourt spoke, unassisted even by the refreshment of the traditional glass of water, there was nothing on view more interesting than the face and figure of Mr. Goschen as unexpected ghosts of dead speeches embodying sound Liberal finance, uttered by him in former days, rustled through the House at the call of the Chancellor of the Exchequer.

The New Estate Duty. Amidst breathless attention Sir William Harcourt proceeded to catalogue the graduated scale of the new Estate Duty which is to supersede the present charges of the probate class. For small estates up to £1,000 the charge will be lower than now. Up to £10,000 it will remain unaltered. Thereafter a graduated scale will be established till estates of over a million pay duty at 8 per cent. A loud cheer greeted the announcement that this revision of taxation will yield an additional income of between three and a half and four millions. That seemed to settle the Budget as more than covering the deficit. But the first of several surprises came when the Chancellor explained that only a small part of this treasure trove will flow into the Exchequer this year. He could not estimate the amount in excess of a million, which left over two millions still wanting. An additional penny clapped on the income-tax, raising it from sevenpence to eight-pence, would yield £1,780,000. Even that was not fully available to meet the deficit. Having taxed the landed classes, Sir William Harcourt proposed to comfort them by an allowance under Schedule A, amounting to a deduction of one-tenth for land and one-sixth for houses.

" That," he said, scanning the benches opposite, intent on catching the eye of members likely to leave large properties to their heirs, " is a boon to the living owner. The death duty will be a tax on his successor."

This arrangement will, in the coming financial year, withdraw seven hundred thousand pounds from the increment of the increased income-tax. Having done something for the landowner, Sir William Harcourt was not forgetful of the struggling professional man and the moderately well-to-do tradesman. He proposes to increase up to £160 the abatement on incomes under £400. This is an addition of £10 on the current arrangement. A quite new relief is provided in the case of incomes between £400 and £500, which are to be assessed after an abatement of £100. The widely appreciable result of this boldly-conceived plan will be that no citizen with an income under £500 a year will pay as much under the new eight-penny income-tax as he did under last year's rate of sevenpence.

This exposition of what at first hearing seemed to clear the deficit at a bound reduced the gain from the added penny on the income-tax to the immaterial sum of £330,000. That left still lacking more than a million.

"The addition I get," said Sir William Harcourt, making only one bite at two cherries, "from sixpence a gallon on spirits and sixpence a barrel on beer."

By this time the House should have got pretty well accustomed to surprises. This dramatic disclosure served to take what modicum of breath remained. There was a wild rush for the fresh air of the lobby in which the telegraph office is situated. Again Sir William Harcourt had to pause amid the hum of conversation and the bustle of departing members. Those who remained heard him effectively plead that no one could accuse him of robbing the poor man of his beer, since the added tax meant only the addition of the twenty-fourth part of a penny to a gallon. On spirits it reached the extent of three farthings a bottle.

"How," he asked, "was that to be meted out to the consumer on a glass of whisky or a quartern of gin?"

This added impost would yield a revenue of £1,340,000, the sum total of the whole intricate but lucidly explained transaction, leaving him the proud possessor of a surplus of £291,000.

19th April. The Speaker's Dinner. The Speaker, though not in robust health, has so far recovered as to be able to sit out his turns in the chair, an inestimable advantage for all concerned for the business of the House of Commons. Last night he gave his first Parliamentary dinner, and a fortnight hence will hold his first levée.

There are two curious things underlying the prosaic appearance of the list of the Speaker's guests officially communicated to the newspapers. One is the fact that, whilst it includes the name of Mr. Warner, who moved the Address, that of Mr. Fenwick, who seconded it, is absent. This is doubtless owing to the circumstance that the dinner was full dress, and the wardrobe of the member for the Wansbeck Division of Northumberland does not

include that costume. The difficulty first arose upon
the motion for the Address, when, in accordance with
immemorial custom, both the seconder and the mover
were expected to present themselves in what Colonel
Saunderson, anxious for the proprieties in the case
of Sir William Harcourt, spoke of as "the uniform
suitable to their rank."   Mr. Warner masqueraded in
the uniform of the 4th Oxfordshire Light Infantry.
Had Mr. Fenwick been disposed, he might have made
effective and picturesque appearance arrayed in the
clothes he wore when he worked in the Bedside
Colliery. With lantern in hand and pick on shoulder,
he would have beaten the record in the matter of
uniforms.   Mr. Fenwick is constitutionally averse to
anything sensational, and would consent to second
the Address only if he were permitted to wear his
ordinary morning dress. This was granted. But at
the Speaker's Parliamentary dinners the rule is inex-
orable. No full dress, no dinner. So Mr. Fenwick
quietly dined at home.

The other peculiarity of the list is the fact that it
appropriately opens with the name of "the Right
Hon. Sir William Harcourt."   Next come "the
Hon. Arthur Brand, Mr. George Leveson Gower, and
the Hon. C. R. Spencer," three of the junior members
of the Ministry who act as Whips. After them the
carefully-edited list lapses again into the catalogue of
mere Cabinet Ministers, proceeding in due course till
it reaches the Lords of the Treasury. The explanation of this is simple, but significant. That eminent
statesman, "Bobby" Spencer, is Vice-Chamberlain;
Mr. Leveson Gower is Controller of the Household;
Mr. Brand has just stepped into another office about
the Court, and, consequently, though in his Parliamentary relation he is the very Junior Whip, he at
the Speaker's dinner takes precedence of ordinary
Secretaries of State for War and the Home Office,
also of nonentities like the First Lord of the

Admiralty, the Chief Secretary for Ireland, the President of the Board of Trade, and the President of the Local Government Board.

The Juniors hugely enjoy this annual
The Whitebait Dinner. opportunity of taking precedence of those who on the Treasury Bench haughtily sit as their superiors. There is an analogous case at the end of the Session, or used to be, when whitebait dinners were still in vogue. At that festival the President's chair is taken, not by the Premier, should he be present, or, in his absence, by his right-hand man on the Treasury Bench. It is the newest, and, therefore, generally the most inconsiderable Minister of the year, who presides. In the Session of 1881 Lord Rosebery joined the Government as Under Secretary for the Home Department. As such he presided at the whitebait dinner. His speech in proposing the toast of the evening is to this day talked of among his colleagues as a marvel of audacious humour. To some it was the first revelation of a capacity since so rapidly matured that the Under Secretary of 1881 is, in 1894, Prime Minister.

Since the day when Job sat himself down
20th April. Mr. Balfour Bowed Down. amid the dust of the land of Uz and covered his head with ashes the world has not seen so anguished a figure as Mr. Arthur Balfour presented to the view of the House of Commons to-night whilst Lord Randolph Churchill was championing the claims of the Duke of Coburg. With head bent to the level of his knees, both hands tightly clasped around the back of his neck, he sat abashed, abased, as if desirous of shutting out all sights and sounds. This extraordinary evidence of physical and mental suffering presented to the gaze of a perplexed Gallery certainly could not have arisen from consideration of his own unworthiness, or of any untoward event following upon his personal action. Also like Job, Mr. Balfour

is "a man perfect and upright, one that fears God and eschews evil." On the whole, things are going very well with the Opposition, a condition of things largely and directly attributable to the skill and capacity of their leader. Nothing has been more remarkable in the still young Session than the advances made by Mr. Balfour in the esteem of the critical assembly in which he holds a prominent place. The fierce light that beats upon the two Front Benches in the House of Commons has finally revealed in him a leader who in every way satisfies its unsparing demands. There was a time early in his new career when Mr. Balfour shared the doubts of his best friends as to whether he was exactly fitted for the post to which the dilemma of his party had called him. Its trammels irritated him, and, above all, the duty of remaining in his place hour after hour through dull nights bored him. He came late, went away early, and when there were signs of restlessness among his following he intimated that, if they did not like it, he would gladly leave them.

What Might Have Been. When soon after the death of Mr. W. H. Smith Lord Randolph Churchill reappeared on the scene and took up his place in obtrusively friendly contiguity to the Treasury Bench, wistful eyes were turned towards him, and good Conservatives thought of what might have been. Had Lord Randolph at this juncture plotted and manœuvred, it is probable he might have dispossessed the Leader who had but just crossed the saddle and was by no means comfortable in his seat. Lord Randolph in times not long past had shown the House of Commons sport, and that is a quality which, as Lord Palmerston once shrewdly observed, it above all things likes in a Leader. Through five years he, with a numerically insignificant party, had daily striven with the greatest Parliamentarian of the age, at the head of an overwhelming majority.

Discountenanced and distrusted by his own leaders, he had pegged away till the stately structure of Mr. Gladstone's second Administration, riddled through and through, toppled into the dust. Having reached the highest pinnacle to which sheer merit can lift a man, Lord Randolph had wilfully—wantonly, it seemed to outsiders—leaped off, suffering a mighty fall that would have shattered some men. He was physically and mentally unhurt, and after brief retirement returned to the scene of his earlier triumph.

Perhaps Mr. Balfour, as he sat with bowed head, clasped fingers nervously twitching and feet spasmodically beating the floor, was thinking of this epoch, or even of an earlier one when, attracted by the clear vision, tactical skill, vigorous speech, and dashing courage of the Leader of the Fourth Party, he had humbly joined its ranks in something of the capacity of a supernumerary. Perhaps he was not thinking of any of these things, his depression arising from a feeling of sympathy with his *collaborateur* in the Leadership.

Sir W. Harcourt. Sir William Harcourt's position is, truly, one that may be maintained only by a man of infinite patience and dauntless courage. Had a kind fate chanced to have drawn him into the Conservative camp, he would to-day have been installed in a position of almost reverential regard. At the commencement of the Session claims upon his party, established by long and brilliant service, were crowned by an act of self-abnegation which in modern political history finds its nearest, but not complete, parallel in an episode of the late Lord Granville's career. The Liberal party may find leisure to consider where they would have been suppose Sir William Harcourt had encouraged the schism that resented his exclusion from the post for which, at a time when Lord Rosebery enjoyed the privilege of serving under him at the Home Office, he seemed

destined. Sir William Harcourt not only stood aside
when the interests of the Party were assumed to
demand the sacrifice, but loyally and heartily accepted the situation and a secondary post in its
direction.

Radical
Revolt.

With any other community save the
congeries of faction that calls itself the
Liberal Party this sacrifice would have
established a claim to respect and consideration that
would have made its object almost autocratic. As a
mere matter of fact, one of Sir William Harcourt's
earliest experiences in the Leadership of the House
was to find himself and the Government placed in a
minority of two by the action of his own friends.
Since then the Chancellor of the Exchequer has
established a fresh claim upon the gratitude of his
party by meeting a serious crisis with what is admitted to be at once the adroitest and soundest
Budget of modern times. That happened on Monday. On Tuesday the country rang with applause at
this masterpiece, and to-night (Friday) the Leader of
the House was obliged to invite the assistance of the
Opposition to avert possible defeat arising out of the
action of a section of his own followers. It is true
that here he obtained a victory, the magnitude and
completeness of which does not appear on the face of
the figures in the division lobby. Mr. Dalziel protested that if the question of continuing the annuity
of £10,000 to the Duke of Coburg had not been made
one of confidence in the Ministry, not five members
on the Liberal benches would have voted against the
motion for the cessation of the payment. That only
sixty-seven should have been found to go into the
lobby in support of Mr. Morton's resolution is, under
the circumstances, a token of confidence which should
cheer Sir William Harcourt in moments of direst
depression.

CHAPTER XXVII.

RUMOURS OF RESIGNATION.

23rd April.
Thorns in the
Treasury
BenchCushion.
THE unparalleled pressure weighing down Ministers just now is illustrated by the fact that twice within a week Sir William Harcourt's ordinarily angelic temper has broken down. Once he turned and rent Mr. Chamberlain, who was harping on the string of the occasional withdrawal from the scene of the Leader of the House. The second time it was Mr. Bartley, who, munching the same remainder biscuit, was seized by the throat by the harassed and irate object of the petty attack. It would, of course, have been better had Sir William Harcourt been able to treat these unjustifiable and undignified attacks with the scorn they deserve. But, after all, he is, as it is fabled he once admitted, almost human, and the provocation, though mean in conception, was irritating in effect.

The British workman who insists on limiting his daily labour to eight hours is in a happy position compared with Her Majesty's Ministers through the Session. For them a day's work rarely means less than fourteen hours' incessant labour. After the day at the office desk comes the night at the House of Commons. Even assuming that the sitting is over soon after midnight, Ministers must be in their places at half-past three, prepared to be heckled, and thereafter may not leave the premises till the cry of "Who goes home?" echoes through the lobbies. In the present nicely balanced state of parties Ministerial office means almost total withdrawal from that social life that makes London bright from April to July. Ministers are not only compelled to decline dinner invitations on Mondays, Tuesdays, Thursdays, and Fridays, but must, perforce, dine in the House—a terrible experience to suffer night after night through a long Session.

In the case of Sir William Harcourt this strain, mental and physical, falls upon a temperament naturally explosive. A member of the House, whose recollection goes back over thirty-four years, recalls an incident connected with the Leader dating back to the almost prehistoric time when he was Mr. Vernon Harcourt, earning a living at the Parliamentary Bar. In one railway case he had a difference with the Chairman of the Committee, who had called him to order on a particular point.

" Oh, very well," said Mr. Harcourt hotly, " if I am not to be heard, it is just as well the fact should be made known."

" Clear the room," said the Chairman, quietly.

The order having been obeyed, counsel, witnesses, and the general public withdrawing, the Chairman appealed to the Committee to say whether in his remarks he had been personally offensive to the counsel, or had in any sense exceeded the limits of his authority. The answer being unanimously in the negative, the doors were reopened and the public readmitted. With them came Mr. Harcourt, wondering what the proceedings might portend. He was not long left in doubt. The Chairman quietly said:

" Mr. Harcourt, before you proceed with your address, it will be necessary for you to apologise for the remark you last addressed to the Chair."

For all answer, the learned and irate counsel flung down his brief, and with head erect strode out of the committee-room.

In the House of Commons regret at the withdrawal of Sir Charles Russell on his elevation to the Bench is universal. At the Bar natural emotion is modified by

25th April.
Lord Russell
of Killowen.

the consideration that the transmigration of the great advocate will lead to a flow of business in other channels. For many years Sir Charles has monopolised the best business at the bar, enjoying princely revenues. The other night conversation arose among some authorities on the subject as to what Englishman drew the largest professional income. Three names were mentioned, but it was unanimously agreed that Sir Charles Russell stood first.

His acceptance of a seat in the Court of Appeal means a serious pecuniary sacrifice. The salary of a Lord of Appeal is £6,000 a year, and necessarily represents the full professional income of the incumbent. The Attorney-General has a salary of £7,000 a year, besides fees. In 1886–87, the last return available, these amounted to £5,109. Thus the Attorney-General exceeded by £2,000 a year the official salary of the Lord Chancellor. In addition he has his private practice, which, though limited in the terms of the minute agreed upon when the present Government came into office, must be considerable. Certainly Sir Charles Russell's professional income cannot be less than £14,000 a year. To drop to £6,000 a year on being raised to the Bench is a pretty considerable sacrifice for a man still in the prime of life.

It is suggested that the new Lord of Appeal should take the title of Lord Epsom. This is, of course, a sly hit at Sir Charles Russell's well-known predilection for the turf. It has the further recommendation that he has a charming country residence, Tadworth Court, situated on the fringe of the breezy Downs. Here he breeds prize pigs and costly Alderney cows. This fair land of ours presents no more idyllic scene than is presented at Tadworth Court on quiet Sundays in summer, when Sir Charles, fresh from his labours in Parliament or some great triumph in the Law Courts, tramps about the meadows or the farmyard in shooting coat and felt hat, looking wondrous

M

wise at the points of an Alderney, or poking with
forensic forefinger the fat ribs of a prize porker.

Mr. Herbert Gladstone has not long held
the office of First Commissioner of Works,
but has had time to discover that the
pathway is not so easy to tread as people
were induced to believe from observation
of Mr. Plunket's sunny face whilst he walked it. One
of his earliest difficulties clung about the flagstaff on
the Victoria Tower. For half a century this pole has
stood there naked and ashamed. On the rare occasions when the Queen has opened Parliament in person
the Royal Standard has floated from the tower, but
the aggregate duration of these opportunities would
not exceed the limits of a winter's day. On the mind
of Mr. Arnold-Forster, musing over the destinies of
the Empire, there dawned the happy thought that it
would be well if from this high vantage-ground the
Union Jack flaunted in the breeze, in sign that the
Parliament of a still United Kingdom was in Session.
Mr. Shaw-Lefevre, consulted whilst he was First Commissioner of Works, said it would cost fifty pounds a
year, an insuperable objection. When Mr. Herbert
Gladstone succeeded, Mr. Arnold-Forster approached
him on the subject, and was not disappointed.
Young, enthusiastic, his soul unseared by the hot
iron of office, Herbert consented, and to-day the
meteor flag of England flies from the Victoria Tower.
It is true that, seen from the roadway, it looks a trifle
small. But everything must have a beginning, and
by-and-by, peradventure, the folds may widen. In
the meanwhile, it is a speck of colour to be thankful
for in the dim atmosphere of London.

Hardly had this difficulty been settled
when another, even more embarrassing,
confronted the Minister scarcely settled in
the chair at the Board of Works. For
many years there has been spasmodic eruption of

27th April. The Union Jack on Victoria Tower.

The Grille in the Ladies' Gallery.

desire in some quarters that the *grille* in front of the Ladies' Gallery should be removed. It is understood that impetus to the movement comes from the advocates of woman's rights. They object on principle to the distinction between male and female visitors to the House. Whilst the men sit in full view in the Strangers' Galleries over the clock, why should the women be shut in behind iron bars which a prison make over the Speaker's chair?

Apart from that, it is undesirable as a matter of tactics. On nights when Lord Wolmer or Mr. Walter M'Laren succeed in bringing to the front the claim of women to the Parliamentary suffrage, the Ladies' Gallery is thronged with the sisterhood who take a prominent part in the campaign. It is felt that if, whilst the debate was going on, the secretaries and other leaders of the movement were in full view—soft eyes raining influence on the crowded House—it might be not without effect in the division lobby. Sir Richard Temple is not the only member susceptible to a spell of this kind. Even Sir Henry James might modify his objection to this extension of the franchise if, whilst he listened to Lord Wolmer, his gaze, upturned to the Ladies' Gallery, rested upon

> " A rebel in the softest silks,
> A kind of muslin Mr. Wilkes."

It is a small matter beside the great issues at stake. But a wise general omits no advantage, and this particular one is annually lost to the Woman's Rights party.

The succession to the Board of Works of a Minister young, able, good-looking, *galant*, was an opportunity not to be missed by the Old Parliamentary Hands of the male sex who are permitted to think they direct the Woman's Rights movement. Without a thought of this pitfall, Mr. Herbert Gladstone placed on the paper a resolution for the appointment of a Select Committee to consider the accommodation of the House. Forthwith that *preux chevalier*, Mr. Conybeare, swooped down with an amendment enlarging the instruction to the Committee, ordering them to take into consideration the structure of the Ladies' Gallery. Nothing was said about the obnoxious *grille*. But no secret was made that the proposal was founded upon desire for its removal. The First Commissioner, hemmed in by Youth and Beauty—Mr. Conybeare on one side, the Dames of the Woman's Rights Association on the other—suggested a compromise. Suppose he were to remove the iron fretwork from the centre part of the gallery, leaving it standing before the two-thirds space to right and left where ladies who preferred seclusion might blush unseen?

This concession was jumped at by the astute persons conducting the negotiation.

Confidence.

They perceived it was what an hon. member once described as "opening the door to the thin end of the wedge." The First Commissioner was equally delighted. After all, with a little common-sense and some quickness of intellect, it is not so difficult to take part in the government of one's country. Had he stubbornly said "No," his resolution for the appointment of a Committee would have been blocked, and the larger inquiry demanded by a strong party in the House would have been burked. If he had yielded to full extent, there would have been uproar in the House. This happy thought of the removal of the centre *grille* seemed to meet every objection. Possibly, when it was so arranged, there would be uncomfortable crowding behind the *grille* on the part of the prettiest women in the newest frocks and the daintiest bonnets. But that was their affair. Let them settle it amongst themselves with as little breach as possible of the order which obtrusively and superfluously enjoins "Silence!" in the Ladies' Gallery.

With a light heart the First Commissioner of Works stepped across Palace Yard on his way to the Treasury Bench. It was a fine spring afternoon, and the Union Jack on Victoria Tower was sporting in the breeze. That it should have the opportunity was a work sufficient of itself to immortalise his tenure of office. Now he had approached and, he had reason to believe, successfully grappled with a question even more difficult and delicate. When the time came he, replying to an innocent-looking question put by Mr. Walter M'Laren with almost feminine grace, confided his intention to the House.

Despair. Hardly had he spoken than there went up an angry roar, comparable only with what may be heard at the Zoological Gardens when the tiger observes the keeper going by with the lion's dinner, the tiger's cloth having not yet been spread. The First Commissioner had, so to speak, fallen off the grill into the fire. In all parts of the House, above and below the gangway, members sprang to their feet with catapultic force, and almost literally grabbed at the Speaker's eye. Lord Randolph Churchill, being nearest, caught it, and in a voice choking with emotion asked the First Commissioner if he was aware that in former days this cuestion had been the occasion of many divisions. Was it now to be settled on the *ipse dixit* of a First Commissioner of Works? Sir Donald Macfarlane, his white beard bristling with a fierceness that seemed incompatible with its length, suggested that the matter should be referred to a Select Committee. Mr. Tomlinson tumbled in breathlessly with a protest that many ladies instinctively preferred to be separated from mankind by a grating. The prophetic soul of Mr. Johnston, of Ballykilbeg, beheld a vision, which he communicated to the House, of the First Commissioner torn to pieces in the conflict between occupants of the Gallery as to who was to bask in the

lamplight and who to sit in the shade. Mr. Bartley,
always anxious for the dispatch of business, saw
his opportunity, and proposed to the unresponsive
Chancellor of the Exchequer that he should give a
day for discussion of the matter.

Mr. Herbert Gladstone, as his proposal showed, is
a man of courage. He is, moreover, an athlete of renown, ready to enter upon engagement to swim a mile,
run a mile, walk a mile, and hop a mile with any man
in the House bar Mr. Tommy Bowles. But his spirit
quailed before this unexpected outbreak. In quaver-
ing voice he protested that really he had meant
nothing, was, in short, only funning. The House
might rest assured that till its desire to the contrary
had been distinctly made known the *grille* in the
Ladies' Gallery should remain untouched.

For many years Mr. Gladstone has been
accustomed to pay an early visit to the
Academy on private-view day, under the
guidance of Mr. William Agnew. Begin-
ning at the first room, he diligently went through to
the ninth, a terrible undertaking for a man of half
his years. To-day he has intermitted the almost
lifelong custom. Apart from the bodily fatigue, the
condition of his eyes precludes the possibility of
peering upon a thousand canvases. He is just now
vegetating at Dollis Hall, a suburban residence placed
at his disposal by Lord Aberdeen. Yesterday he came
forth and, for the first time since he walked out of
the House of Commons after delivering a memorable
defiance to the House of Lords, he addressed a public
meeting. The occasion was the furtherance of a
memorial to his old friend and doctor, Sir Andrew
Clark. He delivered a charming speech, perhaps the
most eloquent point being the circumstance that he,
craving the indulgence of the audience, remained
seated.

That is a confession of physical weakness to be

[margin note:] 3rd May.
Mr. Gladstone
Breaks Silence.

wrung from him only by importunate necessity. It is only two months and two days since he made his last appearance at the table of the House of Commons. He then remained on his feet for just over the half-hour, delivering a momentous speech without a manuscript note, and, contrary to the habit of younger debaters, without the assistance of a glass of water. Yesterday he spoke for twenty minutes, but found it undesirable to attempt to stand. He sat with both hands resting on a stout stick, his face aglow with animation, his voice musically resounding to the utmost recesses of the crowded hall.

4th May.
Rumour of
the Speaker's
Resignation.
The past week has seen the birth of two rumours which, though evidently based on nothing surer than shrewd surmise, have appreciably contributed to the feeling of vague uneasiness that possesses the House of Commons. Mere mention of the prospect of Mr. Peel quitting the Speaker's chair is enough to chill the marrow. His incomparable fitness for the post would at any time be admired. In existing circumstances, with a resolute, alert, well-led Opposition, and sore lack on the Treasury Bench of the control over affairs which accompanies knowledge that behind it is a strong united majority, his value to the State is incalculable. If the assertion positively made be verified, and at the close of the present Session Mr. Peel retires from the Speaker's chair, the House of Commons might as well, for all practical purposes, put up the shutters, close the legislative shop, and await in silence the coming of the inevitable General Election.

Happily Mr. Peel has not formed the definite determination attributed to him. The labours of a Session of unprecedented length have told upon a physical frame not herculean in its strength. He has also suffered in mind and spirit by some phases of modern Parliamentary life. Those personally intimate with him say he has never been quite the same man since the scene that shamed a summer night last year, when a free fight took place on the floor of the House. There is no doubt that if he followed the impulse of private convenience and personal desire he would take the earliest opportunity of enjoying the dignified leisure earned by a memorable career in a position on which there beats a fierce light more searching than that which does not always glorify the Throne. Mr. Peel's first instinct is that of public duty, which, combined with sentiments of loyalty to ancient friends and old colleagues on the Treasury Bench, will certainly keep him at his post as long as he is physically strong enough to stand by it.

Of Sir William Harcourt's.
The rumour of Sir William Harcourt's early resignation appeared some hours too soon for its perfect success. It was current when the House met yesterday. It would have been much more effective had it been published immediately after the division on the second reading of the Registration Bill, which to-day left the Government in a majority of fourteen. How that came about has been abundantly and satisfactorily explained. It was all right. There was no defection from the support of the Government. Every individual case was explicable. Only, as a net result, one of the principal measures with which the fate of the Ministry is bound up passed its second reading by a narrow majority of fourteen.

As Sir William Harcourt discovered before yesterday, to attempt to carry on the work of the country with a Liberal majority of forty is a miserable business. With the Conservatives in power, and whomsoever Heaven please as Leader, a majority of forty would be abundant strength. In ancient Rome, as Macaulay hymns it, none were for a party, all were for the State. The Liberals of to-day vary this condition to the extent that none is for the party, but each is for himself.

Mr. Saunders, it should be said to his
credit, does not often claim his privilege
of being heard from his place in the
House of Commons. He is an influence
that is felt rather than heard. Whenever the Government get in a tight place the question is asked, "What is Saunders going to do ?" It is pretty safe to assume that he will go against the Ministry the electors of Walworth returned him to support. He adroitly varies the procedure in a manner that invests his action with the charm of the unexpected. On the day preceding the particular crisis now pending representatives of news agencies pursued doubtful members through the lobby with inquiry as to how they were going to vote. Some made answer which indicated that they had at least made up their mind. Mr. Saunders to the last cherished a provoking air of mystery lingering over his action. He might; and again he might not. These considerations were not to be lightly approached, nor was decision to be recklessly determined upon.

"Wait, wait," he murmured in hollow voice, with folded arms and far-away look. "Let us wait and see."

To the news agency man, who wanted a paragraph, this was disappointing. But he was evidently much impressed with the interview, of which the evening papers were able to furnish the anxious public with detailed account.

Mr. Saunders, to do him justice, looks his
part, and on the rare occasions when he
rises to speak reaches his full height.
When he stands before the House, clad in virtue and velveteen, folds his arms, drops his chin on his chest as Napoleon was wont to do when meditating either before or after a battle (according as the artist chanced to come across him), the House feels it is dealing with a Man. Lord Rosebery, lamenting at the

M *

Academy banquet last week the sad sartorial circumstances under which modern Englishmen sit for their portraits, spoke with measured approval of " the black velvet coat with which we are accustomed to associate deep thought and artistic instincts." Mr. Saunders's ordinary dress is not velvet but velveteen, not a coat but a jacket, not black but of a hue mellowed by, if not actually lost in, antiquity. But, though it cannot be said to " associate artistic instincts," to " deep thought " it undoubtedly belongs. It is a sort of garment to be put on only by a man with a purpose.

It is a small thing, characteristic of the member for Walworth, that, as noted in an earlier epoch of his Parliamentary career, no speck of white lights up the grim frontage of his closely-buttoned jacket. As he stood to-night, pausing a moment to survey the scene before he uplifted his voice to denounce a guilty Ministry, he felt he could afford to disregard cheap gibes at his fashion of modestly withholding from public gaze the virgin purity of a possible shirt front. The audience was surprisingly small. It was reasonable to expect that, when opportunity presented itself of learning the momentous decision the member for Walworth had arrived at touching the disposition of his vote, the benches would be crowded to their utmost capacity, the historic chamber throbbing with excitement. It is true the hour was unfortunate. Eight o'clock had chimed from the Clock Tower, and members had weakly gone off to dinner. It was not Mr. Saunders's fault that opportunity was thus limited. He had risen earlier in vain attempt to catch the Speaker's eye at a period of the sitting when the assembly was, in point of numbers, more worthy of the effort about to be put forth. The Speaker, with that perverseness that sometimes affects the Chair even when filled by its most distinguished occupant, had given the preference to Mr. " Tommy " Bowles. Thus Mr. Saunders had bequeathed to him the legacy of empty benches, over which reverberated the hollow tones issuing from remote recesses beneath the tightly-buttoned velveteen jacket.

"This Budget," he said, "is manipulated by the Chancellor of the Exchequer in the interest of the classes. What we want is to catch the capitalist whilst he is living. Instead of which, the capitalist is allowed to go to the edge of the churchyard mould, whilst his property is protected without being taxed."

It was quite by accident that during the delivery of this portentous passage Mr. Saunders fixed a gloomy eye on Mr. John Aird, simplest-mannered of semi-millionaires, who, uneasily conscious of the attention, took an early opportunity of leaving the House.

13th May. A Peer of Parliament. The House of Lords has had a stroke of luck in the death of the fourth Marquis of Ailesbury. It is true he never troubled the place with his presence, nor hung up his well-known overcoat, with the bone buttons as big as saucers, upon the pegs which cluster in the outer lobby before the golden gate. His tastes lay in other directions. Still, there was always apprehension that he might turn up on some critical occasion, and there was no authority here, as at Newmarket, to "warn him off."

The only pathetic touch about this vulgar, rowdy career is that it closed at the age of thirty-one. By that time Lord Ailesbury had managed to make things hum. In his day the late Marquis of Hastings stood pretty high amidst luminaries illustrating the beauty and usefulness of the peerage. Lord Hastings died at twenty-six. His brother-marquis, having five years' further run, filled up the added period with undiminished vigour. Before he came of age he had nearly ruined his family, his grandfather and predecessor in the title being compelled to sell the Yorkshire estates in order to pay the debts of the promising heir. The story of Savernake and the struggles of the helpless family to defend it from this unworthy scion of the race is a story told at dismal length in the courts of law.

The comparative lull in the political world which comes with Whitsun week has been broken by the announcement of Mr. Mundella's resignation of the Presidency of the Board of Trade. Ever since Mr. Justice Vaughan Williams concluded his summing up in the case of the New Zealand Loan Company, the Opposition press have clamoured for this sequence. Neither the judge nor his partisan critics charge the member for Sheffield with fraudulent knowledge, much less intent; but the circumstances are peculiar. If this were an ordinary case, it would be necessary for the Board of Trade, with the judge's charge before them, to consider what, if any, steps should be taken against the directors. One of the directors in the New Zealand Loan Company being head of the Board of Trade, it will be perceived that the situation was awkward. Mr. Mundella has smoothed it by resigning, careful to insist on the specific ground that, looking at his peculiar official position, and desirous that the public service should in no way suffer, he felt it his imperative duty, " alike to the officers of my department and to my colleagues in the Government," to take this step.

This is undoubtedly the end, calamitous as unexpected, of an honourable and useful public career. Mr. Mundella entered the House of Commons in 1868, and has ever since taken an active part in its debates and business. He will be accompanied in his retirement by the consciousness of innocence of active wrongdoing and by the assurance that even in his fall he has done a public service. There is no doubt that the blow is the result of the concentrated

18th May.
Mr. Mundella's
Resignation.

exasperation in the public mind with the *laches*
of the directors of public companies responsible
for the financial cataclysm of the past eight or ten
months and for the widespread misery superinduced.
In the period of inflation that preceded the collapse
there was unquestionably a disposition on the part
of members of Parliament and other prominent public
men to trade upon their positions by accepting paid
places on the directorate of various companies. Some
multiplied these appointments to an extent which
no man lacking encyclopædic knowledge and un-
trammelled leisure could honestly cope with.

Mr. Mundella entered the House whilst
24th May. questions were still going forward. As
he passed to the corner seat behind the
Treasury Bench, where so many ex-Ministers have
sat, he was received with a loud cheer from the
Ministerial side. The seat has of late been in the
occupation of Mr. Stansfeld, another ex-Cabinet
Minister of a Liberal Administration. For his old
colleague, Mr. Stansfeld promptly made way, moving
lower down. It was close upon six o'clock when the
Speaker called on the late President of the Board of
Trade. The sympathetic cheers with which he had
early been greeted were renewed as he stood before
the House, not without personal sign of suffering
undergone. He observed the precaution of writing
out his brief statement, and for the most part he read
it. The Opposition took no part in the friendly
reception which the right hon. gentleman met with
from the crowded benches to the right of the Speaker.
They were surprised into a cheer when Mr. Mundella
stated that when his name was first mentioned in
connection with the proceedings in the Court of Law,
he had placed his office at the disposal of Lord
Rosebery. Apart from the kindly reluctance of the
Premier, Mr. Mundella, in a voice broken with
emotion, admitted he was loth to leave unfinished

work to which he had devoted the best years of his life, and for the furtherance of which he found opportunity in his official position. The speech, which from the outset struck a high tone, was delivered with much dignity and occasional pathos. Mr. Mundella resumed his seat amid cheers that now came from all parts of the crowded House.

CHAPTER XXVIII.

SELF-EFFACEMENT OF THE IRISH MEMBERS.

As soon as the House got into Committee of Supply on the Civil Service Estimates, Mr. Alpheus Cleophas Morton moved to diminish the vote of £4,897,350 by the sum of £2,000, being the subvention granted by the State to the Commissariat Department of the House of Commons. Dr. Clark in his genial way put the matter in another form, declaring that the House was " sponging on the nation to the amount of £2,000 a year, in order that members' dinners might come a little cheaper." Colonel Nolan took what, at the outset, appeared higher ground. From a personal point of view, he had only to lament a tendency, Batavian in its impulse, to clap on 40 per cent. to the price of wines —a process, it should be said, in some cases necessary to give the article even an appearance of value. That was unprincipled conduct on the part of the Committee from which members personally suffered. Colonel Nolan's generous soul bled for the waiter. He drew a graphic picture of " Robert " with a large family (possibly a bedridden mother) looking on, whilst a member luxuriated in the rich spring soup that bubbles up from the House of Commons kitchen, or made-believe to crunch between his teeth the limp and lukewarm whitebait, the waiter meanwhile steeped in gloomy reflection upon his inadequate wage and the strong improbability of its being supplemented by a tip from Lucullus.

" How can a man dine in comfort in such circumstances ? " Colonel Nolan asked, personally

25th May.
The Dinner
Question.

addressing the Chairman of Committees, whose acquaintance with the House of Commons cuisine is extensive and peculiar.

Perhaps this parenthetical remark was a mistake. The House listened with sympathy whilst the Colonel, speaking two hundred words a minute, piled up the agony of the waiter. It was kindly meant, unselfishly done. But when, even in an aside, he turned the light on the pampered diner, and with swift touch pictured his disappointment with the asparagus because the woes of the waiter vulgarly obtruded themselves at the feast, the selfish Sybarite stood confessed.

Mr. Alpheus Cleophas Morton was not influenced in his action either by consideration of the hard lot of the waiter, who, it seems, for five days' work gets from 29s. to 35s. in wages and meals worth 12s. 6d., or by the distress which overwhelms a man accustomed to a decent meal when he sits down to the scramble of a House of Commons dinner. The member for Peterborough is always wanting to know, and of late his curiosity has been excited by the mystery that broods over the receipts and expenditure of the Kitchen Committee. All the members who constitute that body are well-dressed, most of them wear watches, chains, and rings. Some have of late taken to coming down to the House in private carriages. Mr. Morton makes no accusation, refrains even from the echo of a note of imputation. Only, why do not the Committee set forth in parallel columns details of their income and expenditure, and frankly state what becomes of the enormous profits they must make from a monopoly of commissariat supply for 670 gentlemen, with glass and crockery, coals and gas free, and a subvention of £2,000 a year taken out of the pocket of the working man ? The Kitchen Committee declining to produce a return setting forth these particulars, Mr. Morton now proposed to fine them for their contumacy by withdrawal of the annual grant.

The opportunity was seized by Mr. Sydney Herbert, who graces the chair of the Kitchen Committee, to make a statement that casts a final pall of gloom over the whole business. It appears that not only are the House of Commons dinners disappointing, badly cooked, and rampageously served, but, even with extraneous advantages possessed by no other club in London, the financial result is as often a deficit as it shows an immaterial surplus. The experiment of placing the commissariat arrangements under the direction of a Committee of Members on the basis of a club arrangement has been tried now for some years. For the Committee, who give up much time and thought to the work, it has proved a thankless task. For members the result is a matter of perpetual and occasionally petulant complaint. The House of Commons has been likened to a Nasmyth hammer, that can, with nicely-adjusted stroke, disestablish a church or sanction by its vote the annual payment to the rat-catcher at Buckingham Palace. To-day's debate brought into strong light the fact, patent to some members on four nights in every week, that it has not yet been able to devise a scheme whereby it can provide itself with a simple dinner at a reasonable price.

30th May.
Heroic Silence. One of the most remarkable features of the House of Commons' life in the present Parliament continues to be the self-effacement of the Irish members. What it must cost them to sit day after day and hour after hour listening to others talking, they dumb, may possibly be hereafter told in the anguished pages of a private diary. At present it can only be guessed at. Looking at Mr. William O'Brien seated in his old place below the gangway, or Mr. Sexton still watchful at his post near the gangway, it seems impossible to connect them

with the eager, passionate personalities that a few
years ago used to dominate the House.   It is hard to
recall any incident of patriotic effort which, for sublime
self-sacrifice, equals the persistent silence in the House
of Commons of these two men.

When opportunity comes, and they may speak,
not only without damaging the cause they have at
heart, but even with wholesome effect upon the
enemy, it is seized with glad delight.   Such an
opening presented itself to-day.   Of the first three
Orders of the Day, placed in that favourable position
by the rule that governs post-Whitsuntide survivals,
the third was a Bill repealing the Coercion Act.   The
two earlier Bills were non-contentious measures which
had reached the report stage, and were regarded with
such general favour that there was every expectation
of the House consenting to read them a third time
and so ensure their passing this Session.   In such
case the Irish Bill would be reached at a period of
the afternoon when it might certainly be carried.
Some Conservative tacticians saw a great opportunity
of out-generalling the Irish.   If they only talked
round Sir Richard Webster's Prevention of Cruelty
to Children Bill for a sufficiently long period they
would shunt Colonel Nolan and the Coercion Repeal
Bill.   No harm would be done, since their friend
would get his Bill, and the enemy would be dis-
comfited.

But the Irish members are a dangerous lot to play
Parliamentary games with.   When the Tories had
been at it for a couple of hours Colonel Nolan entered
indignant protest by moving the adjournment of the
debate.   That was a proposition the Speaker, of
course, could not accept.   On its being set aside open
war was declared.   Mr. Tim Healy, who had joyously
scented the battle from afar, rushed to the front, took
command of the proceedings, and utterly routed the
enemy.   An admirable Bill was lost.   That was a

matter of sincere regret. But melancholy on the
part of the lookers-on was mitigated by the exquisite
comedy in which Mr. Tim Healy and the Conservative
ex-Attorney-General played the principal parts. Sir
Richard Webster put on his most subdued appearance,
whilst Tim, exulting in his rare opportunity, flouted
and gibed, keeping the House in a roar of laughter.

It is now recognised that, whatever may
8th June. In Committee on the Budget. befall the rest of the colossal programme
of the Government, the Budget Bill will be
enacted very much in the form in which
it was introduced. With an active, well-led Opposition the mills of the House of Commons grind
slowly ; but this particular piece of work will have to
be put through. The conviction of such inevitableness
is worth more than a score of votes to Ministers. It
alone could keep men alive through such experience
as has befallen · the House of Commons during the
past week. It was dry enough at the outset when
debate arose on the second reading of the Bill. But
there were broad principles to be discussed, and there
was the excitement of uncertainty as to how the
Government majority might be affected by details of
the scheme. All the giants of debate severally
descended into the arena, and did their best with
broadsword and pike. But the exhilaration, such as
it was, cannot be maintained night after night in
Committee, with Mr. Grant Lawson, Mr. Butcher, and
Mr. Byrne twittering round crumbs of controversy
dropped from the table of Succession Duty.

For a moment to-day the saddened Com-
Merciless. mittee lifted up its head to gaze in amazement upon Colonel Kenyon-Slaney. That
gallant warrior, returning apparently from a distant
campaign, beyond the reach of Parliamentary reports,
presented himself as the mover of an amendment
providing that all property passing at death should
be separated, one section ranking as personal, the

other as real property, being taxed accordingly. Considering that the main principle of the Bill is the assimilation of real and personal property for the purposes of taxation, that the principle had been affirmed on the second reading, assent being reiterated in a dozen divisions on the first clause, it might reasonably be thought that the Chairman would interpose, courteously inform Colonel Kenyon-Slaney of what had taken place in his assumed absence, and pass on to the next amendment. But the beneficence of Parliamentary procedure in favour of doing the same thing over and over again is past belief, and Mr. Mellor might not interfere.

Colonel Kenyon-Slaney's amendment was in order. Still the Committee instinctively felt that was no reason why he should be so unmercifully brisk in manner when recommending it to their favourable notice. In his retirement, whether on sea or land, the Colonel had evidently laid himself out for a supreme endeavour. The Chancellor of the Exchequer might have had his occasional opportunity. Mr. Goschen might from time to time have commanded the attention of the Senate on a subject on which he is past master. Even Mr. "Tommy" Bowles may since the House got into Committee have said a word or two. Now the debate was really going to begin, and the member for North Shropshire should lead it.

Debate in Committee is presumably conducted on quite different lines from those followed when the Speaker is in the chair. In the latter case a man may deliver an oration. In the former he is supposed to converse, much as he would if seated at a table, conducting ordinary commercial or professional business. This is a rule that might serve for ordinary people. For Colonel Kenyon-Slaney, coming quite fresh to the task, with mind unprejudiced by reiterated argument and face bronzed by sun and wind, nothing less would do than the fine old-fashioned oration, of the kind that has often made the rafters ring in the consecrated roof of the college debating society.

He chanced to have got home just in time to seize a most excellent opportunity. It fell to his lot to resume the debate as early as four o'clock in the afternoon, the House being still crowded with members gathered for the varied interest of the question hour, their withers yet unwrung. It was a great opportunity, and the returned traveller had, happily, spared no pains to make himself equal to it. His few remarks were neatly written out on a prodigious sheaf of notes, wherein, as was presently shown, he had the advantage of Mr. Butcher. That learned gentleman, also having an amendment to propose, felt it would never do for an equity barrister in fairly good practice to present himself to the view of a critical House of Commons dependent upon written notes for the current of his speech. In an ordinary debate he would probably have acquitted himself admirably without extraneous aid of that kind. For the purpose of his argument it was necessary to quote a series of supposititious cases in which members of respectable families were shown to be unjustly treated by the operation of this iniquitous Bill.

Mr. Courtney's Puzzle. Mr. Courtney had set himself a similar task and, scorning written notes, had come to a disastrous end. As he went on, piling sons upon brothers, bringing in the deceased father, and throwing a sort of limelight reflection on some mysterious predeceased elder brother, the Committee, after groping hopelessly for some time, came to the conclusion that he had lapsed into one of his familiar lectures on proportional representation as applicable to a large family.

"Do I make myself understood?" he asked at the end of a breathless sentence that somewhat resembled a citation from the Book of Kings tracing back a genealogy to Father Abraham. The Committee, wrought into almost hysterical condition by the tension of trying to follow the right hon. gentleman and make quite sure whether it was the elder brother or the second son whose hard-earned legacy would disappear under the operation of the Budget Bill, burst into a fit of uncontrollable laughter, leaving Mr. Courtney abashed at the discovery that, after all, he is a humorist.

A Three-Card Trick. Mr. Butcher by taking thought believed he had avoided a similar pitfall. He wrote down his genealogies on three small cards, capable of being held in the palm of the hand without attracting the attention of the audience. On each was drawn a genealogical tree, neatly setting forth in varied form a state of things that demonstrated the impracticability and the tyranny of Sir William Harcourt's cherished scheme. But the three-card trick, apparently so simple of accomplishment, is proverbially delusive. Mr. Butcher got his cards mixed. The three family trees had their branches hopelessly interlaced, and the Committee went off into another roar of laughter at sight of Mr. Butcher's face staring aghast into the palm of his hand, his speech brought to a temporary pause by discovery that he had killed the wrong member of the family, and that legacy duty was, according to his account, being paid by the dead man.

Colonel Kenyon-Slaney's fully-written-out notes prevented accident of this kind. He stopped not nor faltered even when interrupted by cry of "Question! Question!" when he read a page or two that unblushingly recalled the friendly Lemprière. For half an hour he spoke at the top of his voice, for the most part with a p a smile on his face that gave the last touch of provocation to prematurely aged men who had heard it full a hundred times, whilst

Colonel Kenyon-Slaney, to whom it was delightfully fresh and new, had been enjoying himself—possibly in that "jungle" he bodily dragged in amid his wealth of picturesque, if not pertinent, illustration.

14th June. The Angel in the House.

Mr. Byles inquired whether there is any rule which prevents women from seating themselves in the Strangers' Gallery over the clock. The First Commissioner explained that for more than a century, between 1675 and 1778, the presence of women in the gallery below the bar was permitted. On the 2nd of February, 1778, a crisis came. A member "spied strangers," and the male section meekly withdrew. The ladies were at first permitted to remain, but, an order being made for their retirement, they positively declined to go. As Mr. Herbert Gladstone euphemistically put it, "their exclusion was effected, but not until they had exhibited such persevering reluctance to obey the order that they interrupted the business of the House for nearly two hours." Since that day, he added, ladies have never been allowed to sit within the House itself. Mr. W. M'Laren, who seemed well up in the subject, added that similar unruly conduct had on one occasion prevailed in the House of Lords. Their lordships, more forgiving than the Commons, had, after an interval, given orders that the ladies might be again admitted, and to this day they are privileged to sit or stand in the pens under the Strangers' Gallery.

15th June. Mr. Gladstone's Young Men.

If Mr. Gladstone had never done anything but select Mr. Arthur Peel for the Speakership, he would have established an unassailable position as a judge of character. But he also picked out Mr. Asquith for the Home Secretaryship, on the face of it a not less unexpected or audacious choice. Mr. Asquith, it is true, had made a more marked impression upon the House than had Mr. Peel when he was placed on the pinnacle.

Through the Session of 1892 Mr. Gladstone in private conversation spoke of the member for Fife in terms which predestined him to office should the wheel of fortune at the general election place the Liberals in power. But the fondest fancy did not go beyond expectation of the Solicitor-Generalship. Mr. Gladstone knew his man better, and endowed the country with the best Home Secretary of modern times. Also he gave impetus to a career which, should it run the ordinary term of life, will certainly be crowned with the Premiership.

When, at a bound, Mr. Asquith took his seat on the Treasury Bench and in the Cabinet there were candid friends who feared the dizzy height would be too much for him. His Parliamentary speeches were, they conceded, admirably effective ; but they were the result of prolonged effort, their well-turned phrases being committed to memory under the glimpses of the midnight lamp.

"Stop," they said, "till Asquith is faced by the difficulties that environ a Minister on the Treasury Bench—the necessity for rising at any hour to wind up a debate, or the more constant ordeal of interrogation. Then, you'll see, he'll halt and stumble."

As everyone knows, the Home Secretary has been weighed in these balances, and, so far from being found wanting, has bumped the beam. Some great Parliamentarians are born, like Mr. Gladstone; some are made, like Mr. Arthur Balfour. Mr. Asquith comes under the former head, and, with fuller opportunity, he has at a stride passed into possession of his birthright in the front rank of Parliamentary debaters.

Mr. Herbert Gladstone. The Home Secretary's success, brilliant as it is, does not obscure that of other of the young men whom Mr. Gladstone picked out from back benches in the House of Commons and for the first time called to office. Mr. Herbert

Gladstone does not strictly come within this category, since he had been in office before 1892. He is new in the sense that he had a fresh lease of life when he became the only one on the Treasury Bench bearing his name. Overshadowed by the colossal figure of his father, he never had a chance, or, to be more exact, he habitually shrank from effort to create one. It was more than a graceful thing on the part of Lord Rosebery to promote the Under-Secretary of the Home Office to the head of an administrative Department. He has proved himself an admirable First Commissioner of Works, and displays great dexterity in replying to the sometimes embarrassing questions put to him by his former Radical associates.

Mr. Acland, as Minister for Education, has been so great a success that at one time he was threatened with having concentrated upon him the public utterances of the Marquis of Salisbury. Mr. Herbert Gardner at the Board of Agriculture has succeeded in inspiring Mr. Cobb with confidence, whilst he has not forfeited the esteem of Mr. Chaplin. Mr. Robertson, an admirable debater, has proved a capable as well as a Civil Lord of the Admiralty; whilst Mr. Seale-Hayne has maintained with dignity the secret of what the Paymaster-General does.

This, with the exception of the Junior Lords of the Treasury, completes the list of the men who, at the invitation of Mr. Gladstone, in 1892 took office for the first time. All the Whips save Mr. Marjoribanks were then new to office, and a better team were never got together. For the first time in recent memory the Liberal Whips met on equal terms with their Conservative *confrères*, with the result that through troublesome times the Ministerial majority was uniformly kept up at its maximum figure.

Mr. Thomas Ellis. When the sins of the fathers were visited on the children, and Mr. Marjoribanks, withdrawn from a scene of hard labour endeared to him by superlative success, went to the House of Lords, another bold step was taken in the direction of selecting for the Chief Whip a young and comparatively untried man. This experiment has been amply justified in the case of Mr. Thomas Ellis. There is a disposition occasionally to compare his majorities with those Mr. Marjoribanks was accustomed to secure through the Session of 1893. The comparison is obviously unfair. At that time the Liberal Party in the House of Commons, united under the magnetic influence of Mr. Gladstone, voted as one man, and, above all, were sustained by the unanimous and constant support of the Irish members. The pressure of the Home Rule Bill being withdrawn, the Irish Party has broken to pieces, and even the larger section, still faithful to Ministers, are not constrained by national considerations to be in their places from day to day. Beyond this is the loosened bond of discipline in the Ministerial ranks following on the retirement of Mr. Gladstone. In such circumstances Lord Tweedmouth would be the first to admit that the majorities secured by Mr. Ellis and his staff compare favourably with those Mr. Marjoribanks used to muster in the Home Rule Session.

"Bob" Reid and "Frank" Lockwood.
The latest appointment to Ministerial office is a fresh triumph of the principle of the infusion of new blood. Mr. Reid has been Solicitor-General for only a few weeks. The House of Commons, the surest and quickest judge of character in the world, regards as a matter of course his promotion to the Attorney-Generalship as part of the readjustment of offices consequent on the death of Lord Coleridge. The new Solicitor-General took to the Treasury Bench as if he had been cradled there, and has proved of invaluable service to Sir William Harcourt in charge of a measure the intricacies of which are quite unintelligible to the great majority of members of the House of Commons.

Lord Rosebery will forthwith have to appoint a new Solicitor-General, a task in which he was assisted by the newspapers in announcements contemporaneously made with that of the death of the Lord Chief Justice.

It is an odd but not inexplicable thing that in these earliest lists the name of Mr. Frank Lockwood did not appear. That is entirely due to a habit of self-effacement which the member for York may, in the public interest, carry too far. There were some, including the present Solicitor-General, who thought and said that the position of Mr. Lockwood in the country and at the Bar gave him a prior claim when a short time back one of the law offices of the Crown was vacant. The vehemence with which Mr. Lockwood denied this assertion, and the ardour with which he espoused the cause of Mr. Reid, led to the conclusion that he did not care for office, content to enjoy the brilliant position he has, unaided, won for himself at the Bar. It is evident that his constituents, who have a nearer acquaintance with his feelings, take another view of the matter. The offer generously made by the spokesmen of the Conservative Party in York to refrain from opposition should Mr. Lockwood present himself for re-election on accepting the Solicitor-Generalship is a rare testimony of his hold upon public opinion and on the esteem of those who are brought into contact with him. Even if it were otherwise, and there was prospect of his having to fight for his seat, it would be suicidal to establish the rule that conspicuous merit should have a justly-earned prize withheld from it on the ground that it has succeeded in holding for the Liberals a seat won only by hard fighting. It has somehow come to pass that Mr. Lockwood has never had that chance of making his mark in the House of Commons which, considering his achievements at the bar and on the public platform, seemed a certainty. It will come to him with the Solicitor-Generalship.

CHAPTER XXIX.

PEGGING AWAY AT THE BUDGET.

23rd June.
Sir Julian
Goldsmid in
the Chair.

SIR WILLIAM HARCOURT still resists the demand impatiently made upon him to shorten proceedings in Committee on the Budget Bill by systematic use of the closure. Hesitation arises out of disinclination to check the right of free speech in discussion of Ways and Means, even when opposition is undisguisedly obstructive. This moderation is grudgingly acquiesced in by the Ministerial party in the House of Commons. But there is much to be said for it. Apart from the constitutional question, it is certain that a good deal of time would be occupied in taking divisions on the closure and in straining to the utmost opportunities for talking. Angry passions would rise, and there might even be a repetition of the scene that made memorable a summer month of last year.

As it is, the Committee plods along night after night, thinking it has done well if before progress is reported a Clause is added to the Bill. If the public, looking on from outside, regard the dilatory proceedings with impatience, what must be the sufferings of those who night after night sit it through ? Perhaps, with the exception of the hapless Chairman, there are none who are literally present from first to last. Even Mr. Mellor from time to time takes an hour's rest, Sir Julian Goldsmid succeeding him in the chair.

Then is witnessed a scene that must delight the soul of Sir William Harcourt. Out of the chair, Sir Julian Goldsmid is an uncompromising " Unionist," not too often speaking, but in all divisions taking his part in thwarting the Government and blocking the progress of their principal measures. Once in the chair, Sir Julian is as absolutely transformed as was Bottom. He becomes a stern, uncompromising champion of Parliamentary order, and is ruthless in the suppression of obstructive tactics. To-night it was worth sitting hour after hour in the dull atmosphere to be present just before midnight, when Sir Richard Webster, flinging himself into the fray that suddenly raged between the two Front Benches, began to rate the Chancellor of the Exchequer. The Deputy-Chairman was upon him in a moment, pinning him to the ground with sharp reproof for indulgence in personalities, and sternly directing the flood of discussion back into the channels of the Clause. Sir Richard Webster's face at this unexpected rebuff from a political friend was a charming study.

24th June. Lord Randolph Churchill. Lord Randolph Churchill is busy preparing for a long journey. He sails on Wednesday for New York, and will thence journey westward till he comes to the uttermost east. The voyage can scarcely be accomplished under a year, which shows either that Lord Randolph does not anticipate a General Election before midsummer next; that he is so confident of winning Mr. Shaw-Lefevre's seat that he can afford to be absent through the contest; or that he has relinquished for the present further pursuit of political life. The latter would be a melancholy conclusion of a career at one time meteoric in its brilliancy. Everyone hopes that Lord Randolph may return with renewed health and vigour. He was quite a new man when he came back from his African excursion, but the impetus then received did not last. It is characteristic of him that, although shattered in health, he has through the Session insisted on taking a prominent part in debate. His once fine voice has failed him, and the House, after some moments of strained attention, gives up the effort to follow his speech.

That this loss of his hold on an assembly he once swayed is due to physical rather than intellectual failure appears from testimony of the highest value. Lord Randolph's last speech in the House of Commons was delivered on the Uganda Question. Members, as usual, complained that they could not hear him. Mr. Bryce, who sat immediately opposite on the Treasury Bench, tells me he heard every word, and affirms that the speech was a masterly dealing with the subject, equal to anything Lord Randolph had done in earlier days.

25th June.
The Eldest
Son Problem.

The gloom of a week's talk round the Budget Bill was to-night relieved by a flash from the Treasury Bench. Discussing one of the innumerable amendments, Sir William Harcourt said a suggestion had been brought under his notice dealing with the question of eldest sons. It was proposed that at a certain age—what limit was fixed he would not mention— the father should withdraw from active control and enjoyment of his estates and should live upon the allowance he had been accustomed to make to his eldest son. One effect of general adoption of this system would be that the allowance of eldest sons would increase, the fathers being careful thereby to make suitable provision for their own advancing years. Sir William Harcourt was so encouraged by the success of this little joke that he elaborated that other happy illustration of the earlier Sovereigns of the House of Brunswick who, whenever things went wrong at Windsor or Westminster, threatened to go back to Hanover. So, he put it, the English land-owners, resenting an equitable readjustment of taxation, threaten to leave the country, a prospect the Chancellor of the Exchequer was able to view with equanimity born of incredulity.

The House of Commons cherishes these little things. Trifling as they may seem, they are rare oases in a melancholy Sahara. Human nature is ever prone to exaggerate current conditions and to talk about the best of times and the worst of times. It seems safe to say that just now the House of Commons is more unrelievedly dull than it has been in recent memory. At the end of the fifth week—or is it the fifteenth?—in Committee on the Budget Bill even Mr. Tommy Bowles begins to pall on the tired palate. There is a feeling that Mr. Byrne is too abundant and Mr. Bartley a bore. The prevailing influence has overcome the customary high spirits of the Chancellor of the Exchequer, who sits -by the hour an image of woe.

27th June. Lord R. Churchill's Last Voyage. Lord Randolph Churchill started to-day on his long voyage. He will be away probably for at least a year. He is going round the world, but does not propose to include Australia in his route.. He will cross the American continent by devious lines, take ship at San Francisco and steam to Yokohama. After a while spent in the dominion of the Mikado he goes on to India, where he hopes to have some sport that will pay him for the long journey. Next he goes to Burmah, and so home, it is hoped in renewed health and strength.

"I want to see the frontiers of India which I extended, and Burmah which I annexed."

As he said this to me at the farewell dinner given by him on Saturday to a few personal friends, his face was lit up by some of its old brightness. But the man who was once the Leader of the House of Commons, the terror as well as the strength of the Conservative party, is a sad wreck. It is characteristic of him that, being ordered abroad by medical advice, he should choose this highway of travel. Most men, overwrought as he is, would have

found seclusion and rest in Norway, or some remote
part of Scotland. Lord Randolph goes straight oft
to breathe, physically and intellectually, the electric
atmosphere of the United States, and proceeds along
the route where he will be fêted at every stopping-
place, and will find no green pastures where he
might lie down to rest.

When he went to Africa, two years, ago there
was keen competition amongst newspaper proprietors
for contributions from his pen. Sir Edward Lawson,
of the *Daily Telegraph*, offered him £100 for a
letter a column and a half long. The proprietors of
the *Daily Graphic*, then newly-born, capped this by
a proposal to give him 2,000 guineas for twenty letters,
a temptation Lord Randolph found irresistible. On
this longer journey he will confine his journalistic
enterprise to writing four letters for a Paris journal.
According to his present intention, they will be
confined to a diary of his experiences in big-game
hunting in India.

It was a notable gathering, arranged with much
care, that met at dinner at Grosvenor Square on Saturday, to say good-bye to him whom they all affectionately
spoke of as "Randolph." Its composition indicated the
many-sidedness of the character of the host. On his
right hand sat Mr. Arthur Balfour, once his subaltern,
now the successor of his brilliant career. Next to
the Cromwellian ex-Chief Secretary of Ireland sat
Mr. John Morley, the present ruler. In due order,
travelling to the right, were Sir Francis Knollys,
Secretary to the Prince of Wales; Mr. Henry Arthur
Jones, author of *The Masqueraders* and a long list
of other plays that have filled London theatres; Sir
Algernon Borthwick, proprietor of the *Morning
Post;* Sir Michael Hicks-Beach, the only man Lord
Randolph did not quarrel with when he left Lord
Salisbury's Ministry; Sir Edward Lawson, of the *Daily
Telegraph;* Sir Henry Calcraft, a high civil functionary

for more than a generation a prominent person in the
inner circles of London Society; Sir George Lewis, of
Ely Place, Holborn; Mr. Dicey, late editor of the
Observer; Mr. Henry Labouchere; Mr. Rochefort
Maguire, Mr. Rhodes' earliest emissary to Lo Bengula;
Mr. David Plunket, most charming of men, most
graceful of speakers in the House of Commons; and
Mr. Henry Chaplin, first President of the Board of
Agriculture. Sir William Harcourt, Mr. Asquith, and
Mr. Henry Irving were prevented by other engage-
ments from being present.

Lord Randolph was in high spirits, full of delight
at the prospect of his journey. But the unspoken
feeling among the company was that the shadow of
an unbidden Guest darkened the festive board, and
that on saying "Good-night" to our host as we parted
we were truly saying "Good-bye."

28th June.
Mr. Keir-
Hardie on
Royalty.
Mr. Keir-Hardie has not been altogether a
success in the House of Commons. It is
one of the best-known peculiarities of that
inscrutable assembly that men who enter
it amid a blare of trumpets find exceptional difficulty
in establishing a position. A well-known illustration
of this axiom is found in the case of Mr. John Stuart
Mill. There are some others of later date whom it
would be invidious to mention. There is no resemblance immediately apparent between the author
of a System of Logic and the member for West Ham.
But whilst Mr. John Stuart Mill and some other
Parliamentary failures took their seats heralded by
the acclaim won by literary and other non-political
work, Mr. Keir-Hardie was accompanied almost to the
door of the House of Commons by the blare of literally
brazen trumpets. When the new Parliament opened,
his friends were so elate at the addition made to the
debating power and personal character of the House
that they brought the member for West Ham down
to Palace Yard in an open chaise, with trumpets

N

also and shawms. On the threshold of his political career Mr. Keir-Hardie discovered how inconveniently autocratic is police authority. No one said him nay when he drove through the public thoroughfares in his triumphal car. But when he wanted to continue his progress across Palace Yard and dismount almost at the doors of the House of Commons, with a send-off from the trumpets probably playing "Dysie" or "Ta-ra-ra-Boom-de-ay," the police uplifted white-gloved hands. The member for West Ham would, of course, have passage made for him. But there was no pathway across Palace Yard for the two-horse shay, the big drum, the trumpet, or the shawms.

Whilst the fulfilment of this pictorial approach was lacking, enough was done to fix attention on a new member who in this fashion approached the scene of his labour. Mr. Keir-Hardie was careful to keep the thing going. He was not the only so-called Labour member. To mention only three, there are Mr. Burt, so modest that the House is apt to forget that he is Secretary to the Board of Trade; Mr. Fenwick, who speaks rarely, but is listened to with a respect that modest merit ever commands in the House of Commons; and Mr. John Burns, perhaps the most influential private member the House contains. These gentlemen, though proud of their record as working men, are in the matter of dress content to conform to ordinary regulations. Short of wearing a kammerband, they are not distinguishable even in the hottest weather from the gentlemen of England who sit below the gangway on the right of the Speaker.

During the Great Dock Strike, that brought Mr. John Burns into prominent notice, a good deal was heard about a straw hat he was then accustomed to wear. It had much to do with floating him into Parliamentary life, and the temptation to wear it at Westminster must have•been almost overpowering.

Mr. Burns resisted and surmounted the temptation. According to the local tradition in Battersea, he sold the straw hat to an enthusiastic admirer and gave the money towards the foundation of a chapel. When Mr. Burt was first returned for Morpeth he brought with him to Westminster the low-crowned hat that had been his pride on high days and holidays in Northumberland. But when he became a Minister he put it away, and habitually wears a tall hat, a circumstance that may, perhaps, partly account for a certain subdued expression that ever clouds his face.

Mr. Keir-Hardie is not as other representatives of Labour, and felt bound to assert the difference so that he might read who ran. At the time he entered Parliament it came to pass that the wearing of low-crowned hats of various colours had become so common in the House that it was hardly noticed. Mr. John Martin, the first to infringe constitutional usage in this respect, was early in his Parliamentary career invited by Mr. Brand, then Speaker, to a private interview. Mr. Brand admitted that he had no authority over headgear worn in the immediate precincts of the House. But within the bar, with the Mace on the table and the Speaker in the chair, a low-crowned hat could not be permitted to appear on the head of a member. The fact that Mr. Martin never after wore his billycock in the House shows how far we have travelled since that day, dead not quite twenty years. Now anything in the shape of a hat may be worn in the House of Commons—from the elaborate edifice under which a casual glimpse of Mr. Cremer is caught, down to Mr. Keir-Hardie's Cap of Liberty.

It was this cap that at once fixed Mr. Keir-Hardie's position in the House of Commons. The low-crowned hat, in whatever shape, material, or colour, is a compromise between gentility and individuality. Taken in conjunction with a short jacket, a pair of trousers frayed at the heel, a flannel shirt of dubious colour, a tweed cap stuck at the back of a shock of uncombed hair, it unmistakably means business. On the whole, in view of this remorseless get-up, Mr. Keir-Hardie has been disappointing. More was justly expected of a man so aggressively labelled " Independent."

Happily Providence, which has endowed the member for West Ham with a taste for dress, has withheld from him the gift of fluency. By far the most coherent speech he has made since he entered the House was that which to-day commanded a crowded audience. It is a curious comment on the waywardness of the House of Commons that whilst Sir William Harcourt, moving the Address of Congratulation on the birth of the Royal Prince, had but scant audience, Mr. Keir-Hardie, stumbling through his awkward sentences, addressed an audience that crowded every bench. Not the least interested, or interesting, section of the audience was found in the Peers' Gallery, where Lord Rowton sat, supported on one side by Earl Spencer, and on the other by the Duke of Devonshire. Lord Rowton, who is certainly younger than the late Mr. Monty Corry, was well enough. He has found the secret of perpetual youth in the faculty of being interested in the widest scope of events, big or little. But for Lord Spencer, with the British Navy on his hands, and the Duke of Devonshire, with the growing encumbrance of Chatsworth looming in the shadow beyond the passing of the Budget Bill, it seemed odd that they should think it worth while to pay a rare visit to the House of Commons to hear Mr. Keir-Hardie talk cheap fustian.

It was, nevertheless, a striking scene, on which the House of Commons may well pride itself. It has its opinion of Mr. Keir-Hardie's sincerity, which may or may not be well founded. Apart from matters of conviction or instincts of good taste, there was nothing attractive in the speech partly read by the unkempt figure, by strange unconscious irony standing by the very seat where through more than a generation Mr. Newdegate uplifted his voice against the advance of Democracy. But Mr. Keir-Hardie is a member of Parliament duly returned. Theoretically he stands on equal footing with the best-born or the most brilliant intellect amongst them. Above all, the House of Commons is the Palladium of freedom of speech, and, within certain well-understood if not easily defined limits, a member has the right to say what he pleases, however distasteful it may be to his hearers. Once there was a swift murmur of indignant protest when, speaking of the infant Prince, Mr. Keir-Hardie descended to a coarse jibe which even he upon reflection must regret. Again, when he opened an attack on the Prince of Wales, Colonel Saunderson was stung to move that he be no longer heard. It was a tempting opening for reprisal. Old members recalled the precedent when, Mr. O'Donnell retailing spiteful gossip about M. Challemel-Lacour, then newly appointed as Minister of France at the Court of St. James's, no less a person than Mr. Gladstone submitted and carried a similar motion. Happily the impulse was only momentary. The better, finer instinct prevailed, and Mr. Keir-Hardie suffered the worse punishment of being permitted to recite the whole of his screed.

Through the greater part of the week the House of Commons has had the opportunity of judging how it might jog along under the Leadership of Mr. Campbell-Bannerman. From the point of view of the Minister for War the experiment lacks something of completeness of condition. He was not through this period Leader of the House, was not even Deputy-Leader, merely the Minister in charge of the Estimates under discussion. He therefore lacked the authority which presumably pertains to the post, though Sir

*6th July.
In Committee
of Supply.*

William Harcourt, after six months' experiment, may be inclined to protest that it is sadly overrated. Still, the War Secretary has since Tuesday night been practically manager of the proceedings in the House of Commons. As soon as questions were over, his colleagues have left the Treasury Bench, all save the faithful Financial Secretary to the War Office. Their example has been followed by the large majority of members, and the Secretary of State has settled down for eight hours' pleasant conversation with the colonels, captains, and Private Hanbury.

Mr. Campbell - Bannerman is, happily, gifted by Nature with a temper of almost imperturbable serenity. That there are possibilities of explosions have been hinted more than twice in his Parliamentary career. But, on the whole, he may be counted invulnerable. It was this gift of Nature, combined with a sense of humour that disproves the stale libel about Scotchmen, that made his term of office as Chief Secretary for Ireland a memorable success. When, in 1884, Sir George Trevelyan, prematurely grey-haired, was hounded out of the Irish Office, Mr. Campbell-Bannerman's appearance as his successor took away the breath of the Irish members, then in fullest, most successful practice in the art or science of obstruction. They attempted with the new Secretary the tactics that had almost worried to death the highly-strung nature of his predecessor. Mr. Campbell-Bannerman only smiled at them, or blandly jested at their simulated wrath. As was said at the time, the English Channel in its stormiest moods raged round Beachy Head with equal effect to that wrought upon the new Chief Secretary by the then united Irishmen.

There are some things besides stupidity against which the gods fight in vain. One is found in the persistent drip, drip of speech-making in an exceedingly thin audience, with nothing breaking the silence

The Secretary of State for War.

save the voice of the hon. member and the occasional desperate attempts of Mr. Mellor to rush through the long-delayed vote. If there were any real fight, spirits might rise in the heat of combat, and so the hours pass pleasantly. But through the past melancholy week no one has had anything particular to say or to do beyond seeing that too many votes are not taken at a current sitting. Members are primed by sufferers in some alleged private grievance, on which they descant for a period which they would blush to find was less than half an hour. One day it was Dr. Briggs. To-night it was a happily anonymous probationer at Netley who was dismissed on the alleged ground of drunkenness and misconduct at a dance. Mr. Clancy knew better than that. The probationer in question was an Irishman and a Catholic, and therefore he had been got rid of—drummed out of a force which if it were denuded of Irishmen and Catholics would be perilously attenuated.

"He was drunk," said Mr. Campbell-Bannerman, with temporary sign of irritation at this line of argument.

"Yes," said Mr. Clancy, "'tis true, and pity 'tis 'tis true. But he was drunk in a military, not in a civil sense."

Inevitable Ireland. After this the Committee was quite grateful to be led, also under direction of Mr. Clancy, to consider the main drainage of the City of Dublin. Should the main drains go under Pigeon House Fort, or should they forbear? Mention of Pigeon House Fort reminded Private Hanbury that the Government had offered this place of arms and its site to the Dublin Corporation for £65,000, it having cost the Imperial Exchequer at least £110,000. Was there not something more in this than met the eye? There was, and Mr. Clancy sprang up to drag it to light. Every penny of the original cost had come out of the Irish pocket.

Argal it was quite right to dispose of it to the Dublin Corporation at a reduction on cost price.

" Therefore," cried Mr. Clancy, with a wave of indignant arm towards Private Hanbury, " the ignorant speech just made by the hon. member falls entirely flat."

Mr. Gibson Bowles now appeared on the scene, clearly visible on his lofty brow marks of the wet towel wound round his head whilst considering the Solicitor-General's amendments on the report stage of the Budget Bill. With the Budget still weighing on his mind, he had not much time for consideration of mere Army affairs. But, passing through the House, hearing Captain Bagot and Sir Henry Fletcher saying something about rifle ranges, it occurred to him that it would be useful if he stated what he knew on the subject.

The Goosestep. He rose simultaneously with Colonel Kenyon-Slaney. The Chairman of Committees hastily called on the military gentleman, who at least would know nothing of Death Duties. Colonel Slaney once on his feet, the coast is clear for a considerable time. The gallant member has brought to the highest perfection the adaptation of the military goosestep to the progress of debate in the House of Commons. His phrases are full of what seem well-fitting words; his utterance is unfaltering; his apologetic asides, expressing hope that he does not intrude, are a little tiresome; and his smile of satisfaction at the sound of his own voice becomes in time irritating. But he can, with every appearance of making a speech, say less in half an hour than any man of much longer experience of Parliamentary forms.

Mr. Bowles utilised the interval to retire to his corner in the library, put on a fresh towel, and draft three more amendments to the Solicitor-General's amendments to the Budget Bill. Returning, he was in good time to hear Colonel Kenyon-Slaney talk himself out of breath, and then brought forward his illustration of a rifle-range. The earliest success of this particular rifle-range was, he said, to bombard a gentleman's country house. Hastily turned in another direction, it kept up a continuous fire across a high-road connecting two busy towns. This leading to protest, the range was again altered, and demolished a railway-station. Having cited these remarkable and apposite instances, Mr. Gibson Bowles returned to his study of the amendments to the Budget.

This made an opening for General Fitzwygram, who, the conversation threatening to flag, gave some interesting reminiscences of studies at Eton. Nothing he had learned there, not even cricket, had, he protested, been of the least use to him in after-life. This brought up Mr. Pierpoint, M.A., who adventured the assertion that many hon. members opposite who had learned Latin could not now construe the inscription on a tombstone. That the accomplishment of such a task should be the principal aim of application to study of the Latin tongue struck the Committee as being a little odd.

Whilst members were trying to master this erudite joke, Sir Richard Temple considerately led them aside to consider the delay in the progress of the works at the St. Lucia coaling-station. Next Mr. Alpheus Cleophas Morton appeared on the scene, addressing the Secretary of State for War at considerable length, in a querulous, chiding voice suitable to the conversation of an elderly nurse with a hopelessly refractory boy. Thus the hours sped on, as they had brightly flitted through Tuesday's, Wednesday's, and Thursday's sittings. Mr. Campbell-Bannerman sat patiently listening, and occasionally making deprecatory reply. Mr. Woodall sat by his side, smiling alike on the just and the unjust.

And the votes? Well, three minor ones of a non-contentious character passed through Committee, and may be discussed over again on the Report stage.

N *

CHAPTER XXX.

SOME DEBATERS.

10th July.
Police
Protection.

IT is one of the signs of the brighter times that have dawned for Ireland that the Chief Secretary to the Lord-Lieutenant is able to take his walks abroad without his footsteps being dogged by a couple of friendly detectives. When Mr. Arthur Balfour occupied the position now filled by Mr. John Morley he was night and day under police surveillance. His residence on Carlton House Terrace is so near that it was his regular custom to walk home after the House was up. As he crossed Palace Yard with his long swinging stride two figures issued from under one of the archways and followed him at a distance of twenty paces. He did not seem to notice them, and they went their way with studied appearance of casually walking in the same direction as the tall spare figure that preceded them. But they were seeing the Chief Secretary safely home, and all the way were on the alert. Not only in London or in Dublin was this watch and ward kept over the Chief Secretary. One autumn time during his term of office he spent a month golfing at North Berwick, a quiet village on the Firth of Forth. Hither came also the posse of policemen in plain clothes, guarding his lodgings by night, by day walking up and down the links, probably wondering what delight the eminent statesman under their charge could find in wandering over sandy wastes, striking with clumsy-looking instrument an insignificant white ball.

That this precaution was not unnecessary has since been shown by disclosures made in respect of another Chief Secretary. It has been told how Mr. Forster on one of his visits to Dublin was deliberately doomed to death, and how he escaped the sentence only by the accident of leaving the city by another route than that intended and announced. As far as is yet publicly known no design against the life of Mr. Balfour was plotted. Certainly no overt attack was made, even at a time when his iron hand held crime in Ireland with most relentless grip. This possibly may have been due to the fact that he was so carefully guarded. When Mr. John Morley succeeded him in the government of Ireland the precautions long in force were automatically continued. But Mr. Morley early insisted upon their withdrawal, and now goes about his business, whether in London or Dublin, as if he were an ordinary under-secretary.

12th July.
An
Undelivered
Speech.

The publication of Mr. Gladstone's farewell letter to the electors of Midlothian has been followed by the announcement that he had not intended his speech of 1st March, delivered on the Lords' amendments to the Parish Councils Bill, to be his final word to the House of Commons. This statement has created some surprise, more especially amongst members of Mr. Gladstone's Cabinet. One tells me that at the Council held on the very morning of this speech Mr. Gladstone bade farewell to his colleagues, intimating that never more would he preside over their deliberations. That obviously does not affect the question of his intention with respect to further speech in the House of Commons. The fact that he did not communicate it to even his most intimate friends in the Cabinet does not necessarily imply its non-existence. With all his apparently uncontrollable volubility Mr. Gladstone was by habit exceedingly reticent on personal matters in communication with his Cabinet colleagues. The authority for the statement about the undelivered speech is a gentleman outside the Ministerial circle, whose personal relations with the ex-Premier have for the last three years been particularly close.

The House of Commons thinks with regret of the opportunity it is said to have missed. It is easy to imagine the dramatic scene of the House crowded to its outer doors with members, old and young, waiting to hear the last of an incomparable series of orations. It is a noteworthy but not inexplicable circumstance that none of the men who have filled a large space in the eye of Parliament have taken or made occasion to deliver a valedictory address. The most common reason for this is that, as in the case of Sir Robert Peel and Mr. Bright, to mention two modern instances, the hand of Death, suddenly descending, cut off opportunity. When they walked out of the House on their last visit they did not know they should never enter it again.

By a coincidence rare in their varied lives the chance came both to Mr. Disraeli and Mr. Gladstone, and neither availed himself of it. When, one August night in 1876, Mr. Disraeli resumed his seat after winding up a debate on Turkish iniquities in Bulgaria, not six men in the House knew it was his last speech in the Commons. It contained not the slightest reference which even with later knowledge can be recognised as indicating his intention of presently walking out never more to return. Mr. Gladstone's last speech in the House of Commons was equally free from allusion to the coming event, though in his case it was known that his retirement was a matter of but days or weeks, and many who listened instinctively felt that they would never again see him standing by the Mace.

If anyone, having intimate acquaintance 13th July. both of Mr. George Wyndham and the Mr. George Wyndham. House of Commons, had been asked when the young member for Dover stood on the threshold of Parliamentary life whether he was likely to succeed, the answer would have been emphatically in the affirmative. He has every recommendation that commands success. Of good presence, perfect manner, a pleasing voice, sharp wit, full knowledge, and a pretty turn of phrasing, it seemed that he would walk right into the affection of the House of Commons and gradually work his way into the front rank of debaters. It is too soon to say he has failed. A man in good health at thirty-one may do anything. But he certainly has not yet succeeded.

One reason would probably be found in the fact that a natural modesty invariably leads him to pre-cipitate himself upon the House at the dinner-hour, a period at which a member, though he speak with the tongue of men and angels, has no chance of making a mark. Another, even greater, drawback is indicated in the circumstance that when he finds opportunity he rarely speaks for less than an hour. There are few men in the present House of Commons who can do that safely, and of these the majority, save on rarest occasions, judiciously refrain. It is one of the heaviest responsibilities of Mr. Glad-stone's Parliamentary life that he set, and for years maintained, the fashion of making long speeches. He never repeated his famous feat of speaking for five hours in exposition of a Budget scheme. But up to recent years three hours were thought quite a moderate time for him to talk on big occasions.

For the ordinary member of the House of Commons, and even for others, twenty minutes is the model maximum duration of a speech. Save in the exposition of an intricate legislative scheme, few men have more to say usefully on a particular question than can be put into twenty minutes' talk. No one exemplified this great fact more strikingly than Mr. Disraeli. When, allured by Mr. Gladstone's example, he set himself out for a prodigious harangue he

wasted his forces and wearied his audience. It was his
twenty minutes' speeches that, in his prime, charmed,
if they did not convince, the House of Commons.

It is not Lord Salisbury's manner to
affect mystery, which makes all the
more remarkable his silence to-night.
It was entirely his show.   Lord Rosebery
had proposed to take the second reading of the
Budget Bill on the previous Monday, which would
have been the ordinary course.   Lord Salisbury
insisted on a full week in which to ponder over its
provisions and, presumably, prepare an attack. When
the House met on Thursday there was every sign of
pitched battle.   The benches on both sides were full ;
a double row of peeresses garlanded the side galleries.
The Commons left their chamber to watch the anticipated fight in the Lords.   They filled the pens allotted
to them over the bar, whilst a crowd of Privy
Councillors sat or stood by the steps of the Throne.
Lord Salisbury was early in his place, seating himself
between Lineage and Learning, represented on one
side by the Duke of Rutland, on the other by Lord
Halsbury.

Hour after hour went by.   Speaker succeeded
speaker, and still Lord Salisbury sat unresponsive.
That he was closely following the course of the
debate, and that his mind was actively at work, was
indicated by a curious but not unfamiliar token.
Whilst he sat with folded arms staring straight before
him, his countenance an empty page, his legs moved
with spasmodic activity.   The action was something
like that of a swimmer treading water, and as it was
not intermitted for five minutes through the three
hours' debate, the exercise was equivalent to something not much short of a ten miles' spin.

It was his only contribution to the debate. Whenever a noble lord concluded his remarks, there was
an appreciable pause, and all eyes were turned

*26th July.
The Silence
of Lord
Salisbury.*

towards the Leader of the Opposition. The Duke of
Rutland rose from one side of him and Lord Halsbury
from the other. The Duke of Argyll, the form of
whose speech suggested that he had not intended
to take part in the debate, found the opportunity
irresistible. Still Lord Salisbury sat dumb, pegging
along an imaginary road at something more than
three miles an hour. It is said he was waiting for
Lord Rosebery, and that Lord Rosebery was waiting
for him, reserving to himself the privilege that
pertains to the Leader of the House of having the
last word. Thus on an historic occasion the Earl of
Chatham and Sir Richard Strachan faced each other
on a bloodless field.

However it came about, whether premeditated or
accidental, Lord Salisbury held his peace, presently,
when the Bill had been read a second time, pressing
out through the throng hastening to dress for dinner.
As he towered above the crowd he recalled lines
written just half a century ago by one of the founders
of the school of picturesque Parliamentary sketches:—

> "But who, scarce less by every gazer eyed,
> Walks yonder, swinging with a stalwart stride?
> With that vast bulk of chest and limb assign'd
> So oft to men who subjugate their kind;
> So sturdy Cromwell push'd broad-shoulder'd on;
> So burly Luther breasted Babylon;
> So brawny Cleon bawl'd his Agora down,
> And large-limb'd Mahmoud clutch'd a Prophet's crown!"

These lines from the "New Timon" convey Sir
Edward Bulwer Lytton's impressions of O'Connell's
personal appearance in the House of Commons. So
pliable is the work of genius that to-day they equally
suit quite a different man.

The House of Commons, ever ready to
take a generous view of circumstances, is
quite sure when Mr. Webster is addressing it he thinks he has something to say.

3rd Aug.
An Earnest
Debater.

There is about him an air of earnest conviction which, in early days when, the Metropolitan Board of Works falling to pieces, he came to Westminster, secured him a hearing. By this time the House knows there is nothing to expect. Still, so intensely earnest is the member for St. Pancras, so unhesitating is his flow of words, that members, especially the young and hopeful, sit on listening, certain that by-and-by something will come of it. To-night the Equalisation of Rates Bill was in Committee. The member for St. Pancras has a certain subtle, indescribable personal appearance which suggests that he at least knows all about parish rates. Usually he springs with catapultic force from a bench above the gangway. To-night he strategically compelled attention at the outset of his speech by presenting himself from the front bench below the gangway, standing in the place where in old Fourth-Party days a gentleman whom Mr. T. Healy the other night referred to as "one Mr. Gorst" used to sit in company with the other two-thirds of the party.

Mr. Webster had secured a favourable opportunity of stating his views. His amendment, attached to the first line of the first clause, took precedence of everything else. He, in fact, opened the debate with all the advantage of an audience whose withers were unwrung. There may have been a few galled jades wincing on the Treasury Bench. For the majority of those present there was something more than the ease and restfulness of the opening of a new sitting. For two days many of them had been on strike. They had refrained from either speaking or voting, and had grown weary of the enforced and unaccustomed idleness. Now they were back, eager to make up for lost time by exceptional assiduity.

All would have been more than well with Mr. Webster had he only possessed a clear idea as to where he was going. Unfortunately at the start he got his feet entangled in the meshes of his own amendment. It proposed to omit certain words in Clause I. as a preliminary to substituting others. The Rules of Debate peremptorily limit discussion to the amendment immediately before the House in Committee. Mr. Webster was tied and bound by the necessity of first inducing the Committee to omit from the clause the words "for aiding the equalisation of the rates" before he substituted "in order to further a uniform system of expenditure for sanitary purposes." In his mind his second amendment was always coming up when the vacuum was swept and garnished for the reception and consideration of the first amendment.

Worse still, over the leaf he had a page and a half of other amendments, dealing with the measure in a masterly but merciless fashion. These vaporously hovered over him. He was constantly starting to make excursions down the broad and illimitable · thoroughfare along which they were planted like melancholy poplars. Sometimes he brought himself back and began again. Oftener it was the Chairman's hand, gently but firmly placed upon his collar, that arrested him. Then there were members in various parts of the House popping up to know if this or that were in order. He was ready to receive them, but the frequency of the movement and the growing intricacy of the situation made things more and more hopeless.

Mr. Webster unconsciously added to the uproar by neglecting to observe the custom of resuming his seat when either the Chairman or another member rose to order. The House of Commons, a miracle of patience, will suffer many things; but it will not, whilst debate is going forward, have two members on their feet at the same moment. Deafening cries of "Order! Order!" resounded as Mr. Webster stood waving his manuscript defiantly towards the Chair whenever Mr. Mellor rose to order. Then there was

an Irish member behind, naturally shocked at anything approaching breach of order, who audibly
remonstrated with the member for St. Pancras.   Mr.
Webster grew quite accustomed to this sort of Greek
Chorus.   From time to time, interrupting his exposition of the system of compounding for rates, he
turned his back upon the Chairman and Committee
and responded in colloquial terms.   Once above the
angry shouts this new breach of order evoked he was
heard, rather in sorrow than in anger, remonstrating
with the Chorus, putting before it in some detail a
narrative of opportunities enjoyed through the Session
by Irish members of airing their grievances and inviting it to consider whether, really now, when a
metropolitan member dealing with a question that
affected his constituents, and knowing something
about rates, ventured to address the House he had
not a right to be heard.

Mr. Webster evidently had much more to say
on this point, but just when the appeal and the argument were beginning to have visible effect upon the
Chorus, persistent yells of "Order! Order!" reminded
him that the House looks askance upon the inter-
polation in ordered speech of a personal address to
another member on a back bench.   So he returned to
his amendment, and was endeavouring to show the
hollowness of the pretension that population should be
the basis of a scheme of equalisation of rates, when
the Chairman once more, for the fourth time, as he
ominously remarked, recalled him within the lines of
his amendment.

There is some reason to fear that Dr.
16th Aug. Macgregor regards with unfavourable eye
Two Scots. Mr. Weir's recent proceedings in the
House of Commons.   To the hasty looker-on there
may seem something in common in the Parliamentary
action of the two Scotch members.   Both are irrepressible; both inconsequential; both supernaturally

solemn; and both concerned for the Crofters Bill. It
may be added that each suspects the other of being a
bore, and regrets that a Scottish member should bring
into disrepute the character of his countrymen for
sobriety of sense. But it is certain that Dr. Macgregor
thinks less of Mr. Weir (if that be possible) than Mr.
Weir thinks of Dr. Macgregor. One advantage the
Doctor secures is accidental and due to locality.
Whilst Mr. Weir grazes off thistles on the lowlands by
the Cross Benches, the native impetuosity of The
Macgregor plants his foot on the loftiest heights
behind the Treasury Bench. Here he is seen of all
men, with one arm thrown over the back of the seat,
one hand haughtily disposed in his bosom, whilst he
intellectually, morally, and physically looks down on
Mr. Weir struggling with his *pince-nez* and his prepositions on the floor of the House. After the member
for Ross and Cromarty has floundered through an
incoherent question, delivered in hollow chest-notes,
the House is occasionally delighted by the interposition
of Dr. Macgregor striking an attitude behind the back
of the Chancellor of the Exchequer, whom he highly
disapproves. Oftener, especially since Mr. Weir seems
bent on using these last days of the Session to strike
an average with the compulsory silence of the recess,
he sits silent, looking unutterable things àt his unconscious countryman garrulous in the lowlands.

If these two eminent Scotchmen could only sink
personal ambition, avoid petty jealousy, and work
together for the common good, they might form a
Scotch party, and so complete the international
fissures of the House of Commons recently widened
by the creation of a Welsh party. That is evidently
a concatenation of circumstances that will never be
realised. A Party in the House of Commons implies
a Leader. Whatever Mr. Weir may think of Dr. Macgregor, or Dr. Macgregor of Mr. Weir, the proud spirit
of the one would never brook the tutelage of the other.

In these circumstances Mr. Weir has been A New Party. at liberty to form what he regards as an alliance with Dr. Clark, leaving Dr. Macgregor in gloomy solitude on the heights under the shadow of the gallery. Dr. Clark has long been in search of a Party, who would be disposed to follow him in the endeavour to make everybody, more especially his nominal Leaders, uncomfortable. Several experiments have been made, but incompatibility of temper has in successive cases led to early disruption. Dr. Clark's discovery of a party in the person of Mr. Weir was accidental, not to say providential. It happened in the earliest moments of this morning, when, after an exhilarating night spent in consideration of the Indian Budget, the Orders of the Day were being run through. The speed with which this was accomplished, reflecting much satisfaction on the faces of the Ministers, convinced Dr. Clark that it was his duty to put a spoke in the wheel. Whatever the particular Bill under consideration was does not particularly matter. Any would serve upon which to put the House to the trouble of a division. He accordingly challenged the Chairman's decision that the Ayes had it when the question was put that Clause I. be added to the Bill. Called upon for a co-teller, Dr. Clark, glancing hurriedly round the House, caught sight of Mr. Conybeare. Here was a kindred spirit with whom in days gone by he had heard the chimes at midnight, whilst he raucously obstructed the Government of the day, to whichever camp it belonged, human weakness being shown in a slight preference for making things disagreeable for his own side. He unhesitatingly named the member for Camborne to tell with him.

But Mr. Conybeare is no longer the man A Reformed Malay. he was. In a Parliamentary sense he has abjured sack, and lives cleanly. Dim,

pained memories haunt him of other times, when one
bearing his name had earned the reputation of a
Parliamentary Malay who ran amuck at everything
and everybody, including the Speaker, whom he once
proposed to censure for his conduct in the Chair.
These things are but a disordered dream. The member for Camborne of to-day is almost deaconal in his
bearing, and has come to be regarded as one of the
most esteemed members, admiration being, perhaps,
slightly checked by the weariness born of his monotonous tameness. A flush mounted his pale and
pensive brow when thus called upon by a familiar
voice. Possibly some impulse of the olden time
stirred within his placid bosom. At a period distant
not more than two years he would gladly have obeyed
the summons, if, indeed, as is more likely, he were not
himself leading the attack and calling Dr. Clark to
his assistance. The moment of temptation may have
been anguished. It was brief, and the victory complete. Mr. Conybeare sharply renounced Dr. Clark
and all his works.

"The Noes : None." It was at this time the Party which
essayed to control to-night's business in
Committee of Supply was formed.

"I will tell," said Mr. Weir, in a voice that seemed
to come from the depths of his boots.

Thus backed up, Dr. Clark was master of the
situation—save for one contingency. When the
course of procedure was reformed, cases like this were
taken into account. The Chair, whether occupied by
the Speaker or the Chairman of Committees, was
invested with authority in view of such a proceeding.
Instead of putting the House to the trouble and
inconvenience of passing through the division lobby
and wasting so much time, the Speaker or Chairman,
declaring the motion to be trivial or vexatious, might
call upon members supporting it to stand up in
their places. The Committee clerks would be called

in and would take down their names. If ever there
was a case that demanded this rebuke, surely it was
here presented. All eyes were turned upon Mr. Mellor
in expectation of his invoking this Rule. He refrained, and, though a quarter of an hour was wasted,
the discomfiture of the new Party was, by the apparent clemency, made more conspicuously ignominious.
Not a single member, not even Dr. Macgregor, went
into the Opposition lobby, and the new Party, standing
at the table amid the jeers of the House, made confession that they started on their career unsustained
by a single supporter.

23rd Aug.
A Candidate
for Ministerial
Honours.

The news that Jabez Balfour is about
to revisit his native country has been
received with mixed feeling. For the
most part there is huge satisfaction at
the prospect of the sanctimonious rogue getting some
portion of his deserts. But it is said there is a
narrow circle, well known in the City, who would
much prefer that their old colleague should remain in
retirement in Argentina. For many years he has
been mixed up with most of the big things going in
the City. At one time no prospectus bringing new
and seductive business under the notice of the public
was thought complete without his attractive name on
the directorate. It is whispered that when he finds
himself in the dock, on the eve of inevitable prolonged
seclusion from the world, he will make a clean breast
of everything. There are people in the City who
insist that his flight was arranged by anxious
friends, who have since contributed to his material
comforts, stipulating only that he shall not quit
Argentina. Circumstances have now proved too
strong for him and them, and the judicial proceedings that will follow upon his arrival in England are
looked forward to with peculiar interest.

One circumstance in connection with the busy
life of the ex-member for Croydon is not likely to

come out in the police-court. Regarded from the
present view, it is, indeed, so incredible that I
mention it only upon personal information of the
highest character. When, a little more than two
years ago, Mr. Gladstone was forming his Ministry,
after the General Election, he received directly, or
through the Whips, some remarkable requests for
preferment. Even with his long experience he was
astonished at one or two cases where obscure members of the House of Commons, overcoming their
natural modesty, put forth in detail claims to
office. Among them was Mr. Jabez Balfour, who
confidently asserted his right to be appointed to at
least an Under-Secretaryship. His application was
not addressed personally to the Premier, but reached
him through the usual channel in Parliament Street.
Mr. Balfour recalled how he had always been a liberal
subscriber to the funds of the party: how he had
fought two gallant battles under the Liberal flag at
Croydon and Newington; how he had held Burnley
for the true faith; how almost national in extent
were his services outside politics in inculcating habits
of thrift among the people through such institutions
as, for example, the Liberator Society.

At this time he must have been aware that
the mighty but baseless fabric he had built up was
tottering to a fall. Within twelve months the crash
came, and he was a fugitive from justice. Yet with
that knowledge he did not hesitate to put himself
forward as a candidate for the position of a Minister
of the Crown. Probably it was the last desperate
card he had to play. A Ministerial position might,
peradventure, have helped him to carry on for another
year, or even more, the financial system which,
bursting up, has wrought more woe and misery in
English households than anything that has happened
since the South Sea Bubble. Members of the present
Ministry, aware of this application, will have taken

peculiar interest in the subsequent record of the man
who might have been their colleague.

The truth of the axiom that threatened
25th Aug. men live long is illustrated by the position
Position of
the Ministry. of the Government at the close of their
second Session.   When last year they
began their task, it was lightly but confidently assumed they would break up before Easter.   That
date was fixed since by the time it was reached the
Home Rule Bill would have been introduced, and
might be expected to have worked its disintegrat-
ing effect.   Easter came, Whitsuntide followed, and
Christmas Eve found the House still in Session under
the Leadership of Mr. Gladstone.   Another Parliamentary year has closed, and the most adverse critics
admit that Ministers are in a stronger position
than they have occupied at any time since the General
Election called them into what seemed a frail existence.

The main reason for this—and it is the weakness
as well as the strength of the position—is the fidelity
and the rare reasonableness of the Irish members.
Early forecasts of doom were based upon the conviction, the fruit of long experience, that upon some point
of the Home Rule Bill the Irish wing of the Ministerial party would dislocate itself.   The existence of
the split in the Irish camp made this conclusion of
the matter increasingly probable.   With the best and
most loyal intentions, the larger section of the party,
under the leadership of Mr. Justin McCarthy, would
surely be driven into a compromising attitude by the
extreme policy of the Redmondites.   The Irish voter's
esteem for his Parliamentary representative has ever
been measured by the length to which the hon.
member in his place in the House of Commons was
prepa   to "go agin the Government."   Mr. John
Redmond, having nothing to lose and indefinite
things to get, might be expected to go any distance
in that direction.   Would Mr. McCarthy and his

party be able to hold their own with popular feeling in Ireland if they observed decorous tone and
disciplined habits whilst Mr. Redmond and his merry
men roamed at large, shillelagh in hand ?

The problem has been fully tested, and the Irish
Nationalist members have come forth triumphant.
Some diversion they must needs have, for the Celtic
nature is peculiarly susceptible to the force of habit
and the impulse of instinct. They have quarrelled,
have even enjoyed the luxury of fierce fight; but
the battle has been kept within the bounds of their
own camp. In spite of all temptation, they have
remained faithful to the Ministers who brought in
the Home Rule Bill. At the beginning of this Session
the prophets foresaw disaster for the Government in
the some day accidental absence of the men who
make their majority. It was all very well for the
Irish members to be in daily, hourly attendance
whilst the Home Rule Bill was the first order of the
day. When that was shelved, and Ministers were engaged upon mere English work, or Scotch or Welsh,
it would be idle to expect the Irish always to be found
on the wall of the citadel when the alarm sounded.

Here again the prophets imagined a vain thing.
During the Session which closed to-day the business
has been almost exclusively British. There were
crises in the big fight round the Budget Bill when
the Government majority was expressed by a single
figure; but the diminution was due not to remiss-
ness on the part of the Irish contingent, but to default
amongst English Liberals. On the two occasions
when the Budget Bill was in sore jeopardy every
one of Mr. McCarthy's men was either polled or
paired. This was the more remarkable since the
question at issue, the spirit duties, affected Irish
constituencies in the directly personal manner which,
acting upon some Liberal British brewers and dis-
tillers, proved too strong for their political fealty.

CHAPTER XXXI.

THE SPEAKER AND SIR W. HARCOURT.

THE Parliamentary Session has closed without the customary report of the retirement of the Speaker. Early in the year this rumour was so persistent and circumstantial that Mr. Peel thought it necessary to take note of it. He was good enough to address a letter to me, in which he intimated that he had formed no such definite decision, and would certainly remain at his post as long as health and strength enabled him to perform its duties. Everyone who has business with the House of Commons is delighted to know that Mr. Peel has got through the Session with far more ease and comfort than last Session, for example. It is not probable that in a new Parliament he would accept re-election, though his severance from the high position he has adorned, and whose work he loves, would be a wrench to his keen sensibilities. That, unless his health breaks down, he will stick at his post through the life of the present Parliament is a certainty upon which members on both sides, and above all Ministers, reflect with gratitude. What would become of the present House of Commons if Mr. Peel's stately presence, his firm yet friendly hand, were withdrawn is a contingency from contemplation of which the mind shrinks.

That Mr. Peel is a heaven-born Speaker, perhaps the best that ever sat in the Chair, is a truism of Parliamentary criticism. This makes the more curious and interesting

26th Aug. Mr. Speaker Peel.

How he came to the Chair.

the story of how he got there. A member holding
high position in Mr. Gladstone's Ministry of 1880–85
tells me the secret history of the Premier's choice
of a Speaker to succeed Mr. Brand—a selection which
at the time most surprised those who knew best the
House of Commons.

The position was, in the first place, offered
to Mr. Goschen. Had it been accepted, a good deal
that has since happened would have taken a varied
course. Mr. Goschen, as is well known, is exceedingly
short-sighted. He can with difficulty recognise faces
across the table of the House. It would be hopeless
for members below the g   a to attempt to catch his
eye even when it seemed anxiously to regard them from the
Speaker's Chair. Mr. Goschen was therefore obliged,
much to his regret, to decline a position he is in
many respects admirably qualified to fill. Failing
him, it was decided that Mr. Campbell-Bannerman should be invited to take the Chair—a choice
that would have been applauded on both sides of
the House. Mr. Gladstone was unreservedly at one
with his colleagues in approval of this nomination,
but for personal reasons he desired to pay to the
son of his old and revered chief the compliment of
offering him the Speakership. This was done with
the fuller freedom as everybody, including Mr. Gladstone, was certain the offer would be declined.

Little more than three years earlier Mr. Peel had
resigned the Under-Secretaryship of the Home Office
on the specific ground that its duties overtaxed his
strength. It appeared self-evident that a man whose
state of health did not permit him to hold an Under-
Secretaryship would promptly decline the office
of Speaker, a position scarcely less responsible or
laborious than that of Prime Minister. Mr. Peel
took time to consider the proposal, and, to the amazement of the Cabinet, ended by accepting it. How
little he was known to the House in general, how

412 THE HOME RULE PARLIAMENT.

profoundly hidden under modest mien were his rare qualities, was testified to by the surprise that filled the House when, standing by the steps of the Chair, he electrified the crowded audience by delivery of a magnificent speech.

Sir William Harcourt. Another eminent public man to whom the public insist in attributing a retiring disposition is Sir William Harcourt. This report has at least the foundation in fact that the Chancellor of the Exchequer is in the habit of "giving notice." In the last week of the Session, when disposition was shown by some inconsiderable persons on the Liberal side to criticise his action as Leader of the House, he plainly told them that, if they did not approve his conduct, they had better get someone else to do their work. He is, or was, even more petulant in private communication with his colleagues. Those who know him best believe that this is "only his way," that the impatience with criticism is born of physical and mental fatigue following on the hard work of the Session, and that after a brief holiday he will be a new man.

He has gone off now to seek quiet and rest on the shores of the Lake of Geneva. He carries with him on his holiday trip the consciousness of having done an uncommonly good year's work, considerably adding to his reputation as a statesman. His Budget Bill has already by acclamation been placed on a level with the greatest financial feats of Mr. Gladstone or Sir Robert Peel. It is so big an achievement as to overshadow the rest. But, as Mr. Chamberlain in a moment of unaccountable and unjustly suspected frankness testified, the general record of the Session in the matter of work accomplished will stand comparison with any of recent times. This is the more noteworthy since it has been the shortest Session for fifteen years, its 113 sittings comparing with exactly double the number of its predecessor.

The success of a Session depends in a great measure upon the aptitude and capacity of the Leader, and therefore the credit accruing largely belongs to Sir William Harcourt. In peculiarly trying circumstances he has displayed infinite resource and almost invulnerable patience. He has mastered the great secret, which always eluded Mr. Gladstone, of the desirability of occasionally saying nothing. When compelled to take part in debate or conversation, he has been commendably brief, thus setting an example the result of which has been felt through a sitting, and seen in the amount of work done. There is no place in the world where more strikingly than in the House of Commons is illustrated the truth of the saying that speech is silvern, and silence is golden.

16th Nov.
Lord Randolph
Churchill.
Private accounts of the health of Lord Randolph Churchill are most depressing. So far from having derived benefit from his journey, there are fresh signs of breaking down. There is even talk of impending paralysis. Lord Randolph is not more easy to lead to-day than he was in the prime of health. When he set out from England he had planned a journey round the world on certain lines, and he is determined to fulfil the programme. He looked forward with especial pleasure to shooting big game in India, and it will be a terrible disappointment for him if failing strength precludes his using his gun. It is hoped he will be able to carry out this cherished desire, returning to England in renewed health and strength; but the prospect at the date of the last advices was not promising. To Lady Randolph, the faithful companion of his voyage, the time is one of intense anxiety.

18th Dec.
Chronic
Resignation.
Sir William Harcourt has discovered how much sharper than a serpent's tooth is the pen of the political paragraphist. Ever since the rearrangement of the Ministry

left him the second place, with Lord Rosebery Premier, the Conservative papers have, at brief intervals, put about circumstantial stories affirming differences in the Cabinet which might at any moment lead to disruption. Last week the *Pall Mall Gazette,* jealous for its success in announcing Mr. Gladstone's proximate retirement, came out with a paragraph in large type positively proclaiming the resignation of the Chancellor of the Exchequer. The statement was so definite that even people who had some occasion to know better were staggered. Perhaps the blow fell with most stunning effect upon Sir William Harcourt. He was quietly meditating in his residence in the New Forest when he received a telegram from the editor of the evening paper mentioned.

" We have positive assurance," so it ran, " that you have resigned. Will you please confirm or contradict the report ? Reply paid."

The Chancellor of the Exchequer is an old newspaper hand, and was not to be caught by this attempt to get from him valuable " copy " without the consideration even of benefiting a political friend. He took no notice of the communication, which was followed an hour later by another from one of the news agencies urgently asking for a sign.

The whole business was the effort of an active imagination. Sir William Harcourt is much annoyed at this culminating abuse of newspaper circulation. Talking the matter over with a friend, he recalls an incident in the closing career of Louis XVI. When he was a prisoner at the Tuileries, after arrest on his flight to Varennes, the populace were always suspicious of another escape. They accordingly formed the cheerful habit of turning up at the Tuileries at odd hours of the night and day, calling out for the King, who, wearing the red Cap of Liberty, was obliged to show himself at the window in proof that he had not escaped.

"I cannot, you know," says Sir William, throwing out his hands with gesture of mock despair, "be going to my front-door every day, or even getting up in the dead of the night, to shout out, 'My good newspaper people, I have not resigned.' And yet, if I don't, we have these stupid stories."

CHAPTER XXXII.

LORD RANDOLPH CHURCHILL: HIS LIFE AND DEATH.

Christmas Eve. LORD RANDOLPH CHURCHILL, brought
Lord Randolph home by easy stages from Egypt, arrived
Churchill's at Grosvenor Square to-night, and was
Home-coming. carried into his mother's house to die.
Those coming in personal contact with him have
been prepared for the inevitable event. All
through the year, now nearly worn to its close, it
has been evident he was fatally stricken. It is
characteristic of his dauntless spirit and imperious
nature that almost up to the time when he was
carried ashore from the steamer that brought him to
Marseilles he talked and acted as if he were suffering
from a passing indisposition, and would be quite ready,
when the Session opened, to take his old place and
play his ancient part. Before he started on a journey
planned on an imperial scale it was still more difficult
to convince him that things were strangely altered
since he was wont to command the attention of the
listening Senate and delight enthusiastic meetings
gathered in great halls in the provinces. An affection
of the tongue, precursor of the paralysis that finally
fell upon him, prevented his clearly articulating.
Even in private conversation it was difficult to follow
his meaning, the situation being rendered addition-
ally embarrassing by the fact that within the past
twelve months his sense of hearing, never very acute,
grievously failed.

Long ago, when he was still in fighting trim, it was
curious to note how he and an adversary almost
double his age had precisely the same gesture when

following debate. Mr. Gladstone on one side of the House and Lord Randolph Churchill on the other were often found at the same moment sitting in the same attitude—leaning forward with right hand behind the ear, endeavouring to catch the drift of some ill-spoken sentence.

To those who recalled Lord Randolph's Parliamentary triumphs it was acutely p nfu to see him addressing the present House of Commons. It is happily doubtful whether he ever fully realised how hopelessly deep and wide was the gulf fixed between the Lord Randolph Churchill of 1880–86 and the Parliamentary Prodigal who, two years ago, in the opening Session of the new Parliament, came back to the old familiar scene. When, early in the spring, he returned to London from a political campaign, taking Bradford on the way to Scotland, he assured me he had never addressed such large and enthusiastic audiences. He was elate with the conviction that, having tried his capacity by the severest test, he had shown that he was as good as in his primest days.

A friend who accompanied him on the tour told me later, in a voice broken with emotion, that the expedition had been a pitiful failure. There had, indeed, been crowded halls, filled by the magic of Lord Randolph's name. People who had never seen him in the flesh or heard his voice eagerly availed themselves of the opportunity of looking upon a famous man. Before he had spoken a quarter of an hour the buzz of conversation arose in the hall, the shuffling of feet was heard, and the audience rapidly began to melt away. They could not follow what he was saying, and soon grew tired of the effort to solve the mystery of his strange articulation. Yet Lord Randolph went on to the end, beating his hands together, thumping the desk, uplifting his voice in denunciation or argument, just as he used to do when he held the House of Commons with light, firm touch,

o

and played upon its passions and its humour with master hand.

When last Session opened he had evidently made up his mind to resume his old position in the front rank of the Conservative party. He spoke frequently, always with results that made his friends miserable for the rest of the sitting. Those who were present will never forget the scene one Friday night early in the Session,* when Lord Randolph stood at the table for half an hour, vigorously declaiming inarticulate ramblings, whilst by his side sat his old subaltern, Mr. Arthur Balfour, with head buried in his hands, shutting out the painful sight. There was a time, not severed from that night by many years, when Mr. Balfour, an unconsidered stripling, was ready to fetch and carry tumblers of brandy and soda for Lord Randolph's refreshment, while the Leader of the Fourth Party fulminated against Mr. Gladstone and all his works. Now Arthur Balfour was Leader of the Conservative party, with the Premiership in certain view, whilst Lord Randolph talked to a House whose emptiness was here and there relieved by a few faces that looked on, saddened at evidence of so great and hopeless a fall.

Jan. 25th.
The End.

Exactly a month ago yesterday, on Christmas Eve, Lord Randolph Churchill was carried into his mother's house in Grosvenor Square and laid upon his bed. Just before daybreak yesterday morning he, as the last bulletin of the attendant doctors puts it with simple pathos, "passed away peacefully without pain." It is almost the only passage of Lord Randolph's stormily picturesque life with which a sense of peace is connected. For fifteen years, with modified force since the disease that has carried him off fastened upon him, he was the stormy petrel of English politics. There was —to be exact—one brief period when he assumed

* See page 349.

and maintained a staidness of manner that surprised people more than did his wildest escapade. This was during the few months he led the House of Commons in succession to Sir Michael Hicks-Beach. Nothing could have been better than his manner or more effective than his tactics. It was concluded from study of his earlier habits that he would stamp upon people's toes, scoff at authority, and play the big bad boy with the high office to which he had been so surprisingly called. On the contrary, he displayed a courtesy that was irresistible, a forceful dignity that was commanding. It is true, and it is characteristic of him, that this state of things was the immediate precursor of the most amazing incident in his meteoric career. Just when the House of Commons had grown out of the marvel of discovering the new Lord Randolph in the Leader's seat, it learned that he had resigned office, was no longer Chancellor of the Exchequer or Leader of the House of Commons, and had wilfully and wantonly gone back to his old state of free-lance.

Lord Randolph's intimate friends know the secret history of that fatal turning-point in his career. They know that it was far removed from the influence of childlike impatience and pettiness of wrath to which it was generally attributed. It was rather the result of a shrewdly-planned but over-audacious scheme for obtaining autocratic power. Lord Randolph had resolved to distinguish his term of office as Chancellor of the Exchequer by production of a popular Budget. The Estimates prepared by his colleagues, the Secretary of State for War and the First Lord of the Admiralty, would, if approved by the Cabinet, make such a Budget impossible. After prolonged and occasionally angry controversy the majority of the Cabinet supported the heads of the spending departments against the Chancellor of the Exchequer. Lord Randolph perceived that if he gave way at this crisis

his position in the Cabinet would be permanently
fixed at second-rate rank. Ever ready for battle, he
accepted it at this the earliest moment it was offered,
flinging in the face of his astonished colleagues the
gauntlet of his resignation.

In telling the story to a friend some years later he
did not disguise the fact that his proceeding was based
upon the certainty of success. He was, he felt, indispensable to the Ministry. So he would have been
but for the peculiar, unprecedented condition of affairs
that made it possible for Lord Salisbury at such a
juncture to turn for help outside his own camp.

" I forgot Goschen," said Lord Randolph, looking
back to the height on which he stood on that earlier
Christmas Eve.

That one flaw in an otherwise well-considered
calculation upset everything. Mr. Goschen, still
posing as a Liberal, sound on all points save Home
Rule, was approached with the glittering bait of the
Chancellorship of the Exchequer. He swallowed it, and
Lord Randolph Churchill's game was up. At his age,
with his transcendent abilities, his firm hold on the
democracy, his supremacy in the House of Commons,
there was no reason why he should not retrieve his
position. Once or twice it seemed as if he were bent
on doing so; but he petulantly turned aside, took to
horse-racing, gold-prospecting, special correspondence
for the newspapers, and finally to his bed, where his
closing days were watched by the civilised world with a
solicitude that showed how keen was its sense of the
irreparable loss it was about to sustain.

Lord Randolph Churchill entered the House of
Commons at the general election of 1874. He filled
so large a place in the succeeding Parliament that
there is a disposition to believe he failed to make his
mark in the Parliament which for the first time
placed Mr. Disraeli in power as well as in office.
That is certainly an error. It is true he did not

often speak in the Disraelian Parliament. Whenever he did, he managed to say something that attracted attention. His maiden speech was delivered on the 22nd of May, 1874. He was then in his twenty-fifth year, a slimly-built aristocrat, who conveyed to a not deeply-interested House the impression that after intimate acquaintance with the world he was already aweary of it. The occasion for his speech was the selection of Oxford as a military centre. I forget whether he opposed or commended the project. I remember Sir William Harcourt pointedly complimented him on a speech which, he said, "gave promise of the noble lord's attaining a place of great distinction in the House." Something a little short of this is not an unusual thing to say of a member making his first speech, more especially if he be the son of a Duke. Sir William Harcourt's precise phrase was unusually strong. How literally the prophecy was fulfilled is a matter of history.

Lord Randolph did not speak again during his first Session. In the following year Sir Charles Dilke brought forward what, for a while, became an annual resolution designed to prune the musty privileges of antique boroughs.

Doubtless Lord Randolph was drawn into the controversy by the circumstance that he represented Woodstock, at the time the appanage of ducal Blenheim. He replied to Sir Charles Dilke in a speech sparkling with audacious humour. I fancy he returned to the defence of ancient boroughs when in succeeding Sessions the attack was renewed. A speech that made a more lasting impression upon the House was his still famous attack on Mr. Sclater-Booth. That estimable person was at the time President of the Local Government Board, a circumstance Lord Randolph apparently forgot when, five years later, he found it convenient to belittle the personages occupying the Front Opposition Bench, comparing them disadvantageously with the company under Mr. Disraeli's leadership. Mr. Sclater-Booth had in charge a Bill dealing with local government in counties. Lord Randolph fell upon it tooth and nail, incidentally dealing blows on the placid person of Mr. Sclater-Booth which seriously disturbed that right hon. gentleman's accustomed equanimity.

"It is very remarkable," he said, looking across the gangway at the President of the Local Government Board, who sat with hands folded over his portly paunch, his gaze fixed on the ceiling—" I do not know whether hon. members have noticed it—how often we find mediocrity enriched with a double-barrelled name."

As for the Bill itself, he, in a sentence the acute criticism of which was a foretaste of much to come, described it as " one of those attempts to conciliate the masses by concession of principles dear to them, concession immediately minimised by the details of legislation."

Lord Randolph's earlier speeches were spoken from the third bench above the gangway, a position ordinarily indicative of faithful attachment to the Ministry of the day. It was not without significance that this attack on a Minister and a Ministerial measure—his first deliberate kick over the traces— was delivered from below the gangway. In that part of the House he sat for the rest of the days of the Disraelian Parliament. When he came back in 1880, again returned for Woodstock, he once more placed the gangway between himself and the Conservative leaders. Shortly after the creation of the Fourth Party, Mr. Beresford Hope, who had secured the corner seat of this front bench, was induced to cross the gangway and, as a Privy Councillor, take a place on the Front Opposition Bench. Thereafter Lord Randolph sat in, or stood by, this corner seat, next to Mr. Gladstone, equal with Mr. Parnell, the most prominent figure in a memorable Parliament.

It was in connection with "the Bradlaugh question " he first assumed a position that speedily led him to almost supreme power in the councils of his party. It was not he, but Sir Henry Wolff, who seriously invented "the Bradlaugh question." Lord Randolph did not chance to be in the House when the difficulty first presented itself. It was the 3rd of May, 1880, when Mr. Bradlaugh appeared on the scene. It was just three weeks later that Lord Randolph interposed, some lively debate having taken place in the interval. From Sir Stafford Northcote and other leaders of the Conservative party was hidden the great opportunity fortuitously spread before the Opposition on the threshold of a new Parliament in which Mr. Gladstone was Leader of an overwhelming majority. Lord Randolph saw it, and promptly devoted himself and all his energies to enlarging the view. Aided by Sir Henry Wolff and Mr. (not then Sir John) Gorst, he managed this business with consummate skill and tireless energy. It was the Bradlaugh business that wrought the earliest process of the disintegration of Mr. Gladstone's second Administration, and it was Lord Randolph Churchill's hand that kept things going.

Having once tasted the delight of battle, and discovered that it was possible thus early in the campaign to make an impression on the Ministerial host, the member for Woodstock gave himself up to Parliamentary life. He was always in his place, quick to see opportunities, ruthless in their use. He had succeeded in dragging Sir Stafford Northcote and the " Marshalls and Snelgroves " of the Front Opposition Bench into line on the Bradlaugh business. But they were, in his opinion, "*bourgeois* placemen, honourable Tadpoles, hungry Tapers, Irish lawyers, third-rate statesmen, such as were good enough to fill subordinate offices whilst Lord Beaconsfield was alive." Now, at a time when " the position of the Conservative

party is hopeful and critical," the world looked on at
" a series of neglected opportunities, pusillanimity,
combativeness at wrong moments, vacillation, dread
of responsibility, repression and discouragement of
hard-working followers, collusions with the Government, hankerings after coalitions, jealousies, commonplaces, and want of perception on the part of former
lieutenants of Lord Beaconsfield."

This attack on his esteemed leaders was delivered
in the form of a letter published in April, 1883.   It
shocked faithful Conservatives, who to the number of
two hundred signed an address to Sir Stafford Northcote assuring him of their unshaken loyalty.   Lord
Randolph laughed and went his way, growing daily in
power not only in the House, but in the country.   In
the following year the official chiefs of the party tried
a fall with their embarrassingly lively subaltern, and
were not encouraged by the results to repeat the effort.
Burke at a critical epoch in his career abandoned the
pocket borough of Wendover and stood for populous
Bristol.   Lord Randolph, on the disfranchisement of
Woodstock, came out as a candidate for Birmingham,
delivering a series of speeches which for breadth of
view and incisiveness of touch showed that he was
much more than a political free-lance.   What the
party in the country thought of him was shown by
the fact that he was elected Chairman of the National
Union of Conservative Associations.   His candidature
had been opposed by all the forces at the command
of the official Leaders.   Having won the fight, Lord
Randolph, presaging a more momentous action in the
future, resigned the Chairmanship, and announced his
intention of withdrawing from political life.   It was seen
that he could be more dangerous in that position than
in one more strictly regulated.   Peace was accordingly
patched up—peace made on Lord Randolph's own
terms—and the Conservative party, recognising the
inevitable, began to regard him as their future Leader.

How that expectation was realised, with what amazing subsequent episodes, is well known. For a while after his resignation of the Chancellorship of the Exchequer Lord Randolph hovered in the rear of the Treasury Bench in the House of Commons, a terror to his former colleagues. But he held his hand, once, it should be remembered to the credit of his clear insight, stretching it forth to save his party from a grievous blunder. When in the summer of 1888 the belated Government were contemplating the appointment of the Parnell Commission, Lord Randolph wrote a long and weighty letter to Mr. W. H. Smith warning him against the step. His forecast of the consequences to the Government was realised in every detail. After a while, again sickening of politics, he gave up to Newmarket what was meant for Westminster. At this time he really believed he had for ever done with politics, assuring one of his friends that he took no interest in them, and " would much sooner watch a horse run for the Derby than Arthur Balfour race for the Premiership."

At an age whose youthfulness will proudly bear comparison with all great Parliamentarians (Pitt excepted) Lord Randolph won for himself a position which, for personal fascination and intellectual dominance over the most critical assembly in the world, was exceeded, whilst its meteoric flight lasted, only by that of Mr. Gladstone. He was a man prone rather to multiply enemies than to attach friends. Constitutionally short-tempered, he had a scathing impatience for anything like stupidity, and in discussing persons did not discard an appropriate and effective phrase because its utterance might give pain. His imperfections were chiefly of temper, and were magnified by ill-health. Those who knew him most intimately remained, through strange vicissitudes of fortune, his most faithful and affectionate friends.

o *

CHAPTER XXXIII.

SESSION OF 1895.

MR. CHAMBERLAIN.

AT this present time of writing the Leaders of the Opposition have not definitely settled whether they shall meet the Address with official amendment or whether they shall be content with harassing the Government by less formal attacks. The young bloods of the party are eager for pitched battle. Mr. Balfour, who carries an exceedingly shrewd head on young shoulders, perceives that one result of such tactics would be to unite the Ministerialists on the eve of the Session, and so give the Government a good send-off with their programme. If the Government are placed in a minority in the coming Session, it will not be upon a large issue deliberately chosen for attack, but on some question in Committee, suddenly sprung and with division rushed. Even with the Redmondites going into the lobby with their old allies the Tories, the Government can command a safe majority on any issue directly affecting its existence. Such occasion would arise in the event of an amendment to the Address being moved from the Front Opposition Bench. Mr. Balfour is, therefore, indisposed to give the Government an advantage.

The first night of the new Session, which common report prophesied would be full of alarums and excursions, proved positively dull. Sir George Osborne Morgan, who had proposed to himself a preliminary crusade against the Lords, in the form of indictment of the

2nd Feb. On the Eve of the Session.

5th Feb. A Quiet Opening.

Duke of Westminster in his illegal capacity as almoner
to Church candidates at Parliamentary elections in
Wales, was gently but firmly put on one side by Sir
William Harcourt. Nothing would have pleased the
Opposition more than the opportunity of spending
an hour or two in such a discussion. Sir William
Harcourt is chiefly concerned to forward business. So
the House lost Sir Osborne Morgan's speech. Lord
Wolmer, who was to have indicted Lord Tweedmouth
for attempting to bribe the Irish members, says he
first heard of the project when he took up his
morning newspaper. Sir Henry James succeeded in
raising the question of the validity of the election of
Mr. Broadhurst and Mr. Hazell, seated for Leicester.
Here again Sir William Harcourt's adroit management prevailed. Sir Henry James asked for a Committee to inquire into the matter. Sir William blessed
him, gave him his Committee, and let him go. Thus
it came to pass that earlier rather than later than
usual the Address was moved.

9th Feb.
A Critical
Division.

As in the earliest hour of this morning,
the debate on the first amendment to the
Address concluded, the tellers for the
Ministerial host entered a few seconds
after the tellers on the other side had handed
in their figures, there was in the crowded House
no acute anticipation of the worst or of the best.
It was known the Government were safe on this
particular issue, and the only anxiety was as to
how far the majority might have fallen away from
its pristine strength of forty. Sir William Harcourt's·
speech did not smack of coming defeat. Nor was
Mr. Balfour's tone anticipatory of immediate triumph.
A faint cheer went up from an excited Liberal when
the paper was handed to Mr. Ellis in token that
the majority was with the Government. When
the figures were read out, showing that in a House
of 534 members the Ministerial majority was only

twelve, the Opposition burst into a cheer of triumph, pluckily responded to from the other side. Judging from the general jubilation, the stranger in the gallery would be puzzled to know whether a majority of twelve meant a great victory or a crushing defeat. It is certainly a serious reduction of a majority perilously small at its best, and the credit of bringing it about was reflected in several quarters.

Mr. Chaplin, radiant with smiles, was convinced that a growing belief in Bimetallism had much to do with it. He had seized the opportunity to demonstrate that the only hope for a nation staggering under the weight of poverty lay in what his friend Major Rasch frivolously described as the device of taking a shilling out of your pocket and calling it eighteenpence. Mr. James Lowther, lustily cheering, beheld the rosy dawn of the day of Protection. Twenty-four hours later than Mr. Chaplin's speech, and therefore with more immediate influence on the result, he had preached its gospel. It seemed at the moment as the voice of one crying in the wilderness. Anyhow, here was the Ministerial majority down to twelve. Mr. John Redmond felt that Bimetallism and Protection were all very well in their way. But nine votes dealt out to the right or left meant eighteen on a division. If only seven more righteous men had been found in Ireland he could have turned out a Government that had brought in a Home Rule Bill and had in hand a measure designed to meet the popular demand for amendment of the Land Act. Only an Irishman can appreciate the pure ecstatic pleasure of such reflection shining in such a quarter. Lacking an additional seven, he had not fully succeeded. But he had given harassed Ministers a lesson which would teach them that it was not worth their while exclusively to collogue with the other King of the many-chasméd Irish Brentford.

As for Mr. Keir-Hardie, his triumph was more real and substantial than any other. It had long been a taunt levelled against him by patricians like John Burns, George Howell, and Mr. Cremer that he had no following. His following had now run up to 260, including in its ranks the flower of the Constitutional Party. Not only had they ranged themselves under his leadership, but had "conveyed" his amendment. It was moved and seconded from above the gangway by two of the most respected members of the Carlton Club. But though the voice was the voice of Mr. Jeffreys, there was no mistaking the 'orniness of the hands. It was the property of Mr. Keir-Hardie.

A Brilliant Speech. Whilst satisfaction was, for these various reasons, diffused on the Front Opposition Bench, it seemed to find its fullest expression in the form of the Chancellor of the Exchequer as he stood at the table and summed up a debate that had concerned itself least of all with the condition of the unemployed. For a fighting speech, sparkling with wit, glittering with barbed points skilfully aimed, Sir William Harcourt has, through a long Parliamentary career, never done better. When he began, the House, which, to do it justice, had been frankly tired of the business since its commencement, was nearly empty. Dinner pairs had been made up to half-past ten, and it was ten minutes earlier when the Chancellor of the Exchequer interposed. Gradually the benches filled up. Boisterous laughter, stormy cheers and counter-cheers, thrilled the atmosphere with that electricity which gives the last touch of inspiration to the Parliamentary gladiator. It is some time since Sir William Harcourt had the opportunity of saying a few pleasant things about his former colleague and ancient friend Mr. Goschen. Now it had come, and he used it with added effect, since there had not been dangerous dalliance in preparing his points. The House of Commons, which, like a nursery of children, delights in pictures, gloated over that roughly drawn on a blackboard— Sir William Harcourt, as the moribund King Henry the Fourth, prone on his death-bed, awaking to brief consciousness to find the hand of his expectant heir stretched forth to take the crown which Plantagenet kings apparently wore in bed.

The Royal William.

Recalling Sir William's family descent, there was a peculiar happiness in this appropriation to himself of the *rôle* of the Royal Henry. One could almost see him reclining on a couch in Downing Street, with the royal ermine lending unnecessarily graceful folds to his figure, a belt round his waist, a ruff of lace at his throat, a crown on his head, and the sceptre of his England in his hand. With Mr. Goschen, if the illustration be taken too literally, it begins to halt. He is a little old to be cast for the part. Moreover, none could say of him that—

> " His addiction was to courses vain;
> His companies unlettered, rude and shallow;
> His hours filled up with riots, banquets, sports.
> And never no██ in him any study,
> Any retirement, any sequestration,
> From open haunts and popularity."

But only a carpenter and joiner would pursue this line of criticism. The House of Commons took the reference in its broad application, and roared with delight.

Not less happy was the Chancellor's description of the genesis of the composite amendment upon which the House was about to divide. The agricultural amendment placed on the paper in the name of Mr. Jeffreys had been " transformed at the moment of its projection into an unemployed amendment, and then, by way of make-weight, the textile industries were woven into it" Now, the net was large enough to include all the fishes—"the loose fishes," Sir William added, with a glance across the House at Mr. Keir-Hardie and back across the floor at the bench where Mr. Labouchere and Sir Charles Dilke sat in company —that might be found in the troubled sea.

Whilst Sir William Harcourt's success Mr. Arthur Balfour. was the more brilliant, Mr. Arthur Balfour's was the more substantial. The speech the House had listened to with uproarious applause was an exceedingly hard nut to crack. Mr. Balfour described it as "a coruscation of wit." No one knew better than he of what dangerous materials to the adversary it had been composed. The sketch of the birth of the amendment; the poser as to whether the Opposition took their stand upon Bi-metallism or Protection; the inquiry whether it was proposed to make the Government of the day directly and personally responsible when there was distress amongst the unemployed; the inconvenient recollec-tion of some of Mr. Goschen's former utterances; the citation of Mr. Balfour's reply at Manchester on the question of the unemployed, contrasted with the embarrassing speech of Mr. Chamberlain on the same subject—these points, and some others, presented to the Leader of the Opposition a formidable-looking bunch of nettles. Most men in Mr. Balfour's position would have forthwith attempted to reply point by point. Mr. Balfour, with the instinct and courage of genius, at once grasped the nettle. Instead of showing an apologetic, or even a defiant, front on the points of attack, he forthwith in the first sentence carried the war into the enemy's country.

"Admirable comedy!" he cried. "But what will the ruined farmers and manufacturers think of it? Will they find as much amusement as the House has gained from the coruscation of wit?"

Here was the Chancellor of the Exchequer laugh-ing and making jokes whilst the people were starving!

Of course this is not a quite accurate description of
the fact. But Mr. Balfour was thinking of a hungry
and angry people outside. He did not forget that of
all Nero's career the one thing which has marked
him out most distinctly for the opprobrium of the
modern Man in the Street is the allegation that he
fiddled whilst Rome was burning.

12th Feb.
The Lord
Mayor of
Dublin.

The Lord Mayor and the Sheriffs of
Dublin lent a welcome touch of colour to
the dreary scene at the opening of to-
day's sitting. In accordance with an
ancient privilege, they are permitted to present in
person at the bar of the House any petition with
which they may be charged. The Corporation of
Dublin have prepared a petition praying for the
release of what it describes as "persons convicted
many years ago upon charges connected with insur-
rectionary movements in Ireland." The Lord Mayor
and the Sheriffs jaunting over to London with the
petition presented themselves shortly after three
o'clock at the door of the House. Word being
brought to the Sergeant-at-Arms, he, with a pretty
air of surprise, went to see what was the matter.
Ascertaining who it was, he approached the table
and announced his Lordship. Then, shouldering
the mace, he returned to the door and escorted the
strangers up to the bar, jealously drawn, as it used
to be in the days when Mr. Bradlaugh addressed the
House.

"The Lord Mayor and Sheriffs of the City of
Dublin," the doorkeeper announced in stentorian
voice.

"My Lord Mayor of Dublin," said the Speaker, in
gravest tones, "what have you there?"

The Lord Mayor not only explained that he had a
petition, but insisted on reading every line of it—a
pleasing duty which occupied some moments. The
Speaker ordered it to be brought to the table, the

Clerk acting as emissary; whereupon the Lord Mayor and Sheriffs, bowing low, withdrew.

15th Feb.
A Champion
of the
House of Lords.

Mr. Chamberlain is justly credited with being a statesman whose vision carries him as far into futurity as most men. It is, however, pretty certain that when, ten years ago, he stood up in the town of Denbigh and offered a few remarks on the position of the House of Lords, he had in his mind no forecast of the scene of which he was, for a while, to-night the centre figure. It was not so much that the benches of the House of Commons were crowded when he rose to fulfil a long-pending engagement to speak. That is a condition of affairs to which already in 1885 he had grown accustomed. The peculiar and most striking feature of to-night's gathering was the thronged state of the Peers' Gallery. Noble lords bustled in elate with grateful anticipation of the pleasure of hearing themselves and their cause championed against those who would revile them inasmuch as they toil not, neither do they spin. Amongst them was the Duke of Devonshire, who has private and personal recollections of the biting speech of his trusted friend and colleague. "Late the Leader of the Liberal Party," Lord Hartington now, through no fault of his own, descended to the political level of a duke, took unusual pains to be in early attendance, so that he might not miss a sentence of the speech in which the framer of the unauthorised programme, the promulgator of the "ransom" proposal, the advocate of Irish national aspiration in the Cabinet from which Mr. Forster was driven forth, should trounce the Radicals who threatened to touch with impious hands the ark of the House of Lords.

That nothing should be lacking to the interest of this part of the scene, the Duke of York filled the seat over the clock, from which the pleasant presence

of the Prince of Wales has looked down on many a
historic episode, including the one in which Mr.
Biggar, spying strangers, chuckled when he saw the
Heir to the Throne retire with the other occupants of
the galleries. It was pretty to see how the young
Duke, fresh to the place, fell into exactly the same
attitude of attention his Royal father ever observed,
with elbows resting on the front ledge of the seat,
and honest brown hands crossed, displaying the
abundant white shirt cuff. The Prince of Wales
always seemed to have put on a new pair of gloves
when he came down on field nights to the House of
Commons. To the young Sailor Prince gloves are
evidently a superfluity of awkwardness.

Mr. Chamberlain, having found himself from time
to time in a position of sharp hostility to each political
party, and to almost every section of it, cannot com-
plain if he is not exactly the most popular man in
the House of Commons. Himself a hard-hitter, he
should be the last to resent reprisals. But whatever
feeling, personal or political, may be nursed in
particular parts of the House, where at one time or
other he has sat as a valued ally, a brilliant captain,
was to-night momentarily merged in admiration for
his indomitable courage. Whenever he takes part in
debate on a burning question of the day, whether it
be Home Rule for Ireland, the disestablishment of the
Welsh Church, or the position of the House of Lords,
there hangs over him the shadow of speeches made
on the same subject when, inspired by equally honest
conviction and unfaltering sense of public duty, he took
and expressed views diametrically opposed to those
that commend themselves to his maturer judgment.

In the peculiar circumstances of the day
it is Mr. Chamberlain's misfortune that he
Ghosts.
should be a master of clean-cut phrase, a
forger of unerring bolts of declamation and denunciation. When he has anything to say, whether the

averment be that a particular thing is white or black, he says it in a manner that goes straight home to the understanding and lingers long in the memory. If a wet sponge could be passed over the record of his public speeches up to the end of 1885, and no echo of them linger in the memory of man, his position in the politics of to-day would be immeasurably strengthened. That is impossible. Mr. Chamberlain, when now he rises to address the House of Commons, is ever faced by the ghost of his dead self, wrestling with whom is a much more exhausting and damaging exercise than any mere battling with Sir William Harcourt, Mr. Asquith, or even the ruthless Mr. Tim Healy.

Nothing can exceed the coolness and courage with which he faces these terrible odds. Whilst he is on his legs, and in command of the House, he shows no sign of consciousness of the presence of the supernatural adversary. He knows even better than close students on the Treasury Bench of his former speeches what he once said. If he were disposed to forget particular turns of argument, he has no opportunity, since their echoes rumble daily through every political speech, whether made in Parliament or on the platform. A debater of rare skill, he might, if he chose, shirk nasty turnings that would inevitably lead back to the well-thumbed volume of his speeches published ten years ago. But he takes every fence, dodges no ditch, and on resuming his seat bears with unflinching calmness the inevitable punishment.

Mr. Brunner is, above all things, a busi-
22nd Feb.
A Mysterious
Disappearance. ness man. When he takes a thing in hand he gives himself up entirely to its accomplishment, disregarding minor matters. It was evident when he entered the House this afternoon that he had something on his mind. He had certainly something in his arms—a portly volume portending deep research. He was so profoundly

engrossed in his mission that he constantly popped
up at the wrong moment, with premature effort to
open it. It happened that controversy arose on the
proposal of the London County Council to "convey"
the London Water Works. This was prolonged over
four hours, during the whole of which time Mr.
Brunner sat at attention, his hand on his book, his
eye fixed on the Speaker, prepared to interpose at
the earliest opening.

Members not in the secret observed and greatly
marvelled at this persistence on the part of a person
of naturally retiring disposition. At first there was a
half-wistful suspicion that a new issue at par of shares
in Brunner, Mond and Co. was contemplated, and
that the senior partner, desirous of testifying to his
esteem of co-workers at Westminster, was about to
distribute them. A moment's reflection showed that
this was not the place nor these the circumstances in
which so commendable an intention could be carried
out. As Mr. Brunner continued to pop up whenever
a member taking part in the debate resumed his seat,
it was finally assumed that he had something to say
on the transfer of the waterworks, and it was thought
curious the Speaker should so persistently ignore him.

When, shortly after seven o'clock, the tap of the
water debate was turned off, Mr. Brunner got his
innings, and the mystery was explained only for
mystery to deepen. The volume shook in his hand,
and the *pince-nez*, set awry in the excitement of the
moment, waggled with what, to the imaginative mind,
might be regarded as blood-curdled trepidation, when
in hollow tones Mr. Brunner asked, Where was the
right hon. gentleman the member for West Birmingham when, at midnight, the division was taken on Sir
Henry James's motion censuring the impost of 5 per
cent. duty on yarns and hanks passing the sunlit portals
of Bombay and other cities of our Eastern Empire?

Since Sir Massingberd was Lost, and since Mystery

closed round the vanishing figure of Edwin Drood, no
such clammy story has been told or written as that
which the member for Northwich now hinted at. His
plain, prompt, business manner added something
indescribably effective to the story. According to
this narrative, the last thing seen of Mr. Chamberlain
pending the division in question was when he stood
by the closed lobby door in hurried conversation with
the Sergeant-at-Arms. Under the Standing Orders,
when the House has been cleared for a division the
doors communicating with the outer world are locked.
None can enter and no one can leave. Mr. Brunner,
with perhaps unconscious art, having brought the
story up to this dramatic point, suddenly dropped the
threads, and announced their absolute, as far as his
diligent inquiry had gone, their unaccountable loss.

From his position by the door—assuming the
truth of the evidence that it was not unlocked in
response to his entreaty — Mr. Chamberlain could
withdraw only into the division lobby. Being there,
he must needs join the stream and pass out through
the wicket at the other end, recording his vote. But,
as the division list showed, he had not voted. What
had become of him after his hurried conversation with
the arméd man by the barred door ?

With one accord members turned swift glance
towards the corner seat below the gangway, where,
throughout the debate that seemed to have culminated
in tragedy, Mr. Chamberlain sat applausive of Sir
Henry James's speech. With a feeling of relief they
noted that, whatever mysteries Mr. Brunner's story
concealed, there had been no fatal result. For there
sat Mr. Chamberlain, orchid-decked and smiling. Mr.
Brunner was also conscious of his presence. But it
had the effect rather of whetting than of satisfying
his curiosity. Like the belated king contemplating
the apple in the dumpling, he wanted to know how
he got there.

The Speaker, addressing himself to the subject, did little to solve the mystery. At the outset he shrank from even touching upon it, pleading that it was too late to invoke his judgment or authority. The time to have mentioned the matter was promptly on the mysterious disappearance of the member for West Birmingham, when eye-witnesses might have testified, and bit by bit the story might have been unravelled. Apparently fascinated by the topic, the Speaker contributed not the least interesting chapter. His observations had the advantage, inestimable in the circumstances, of being made in those thrillingly solemn tones which upon occasion sway the angriest passion of the Commons.

"To my knowledge," he said, "members have gone into the lobby" (a brief but perceptible pause, and in deeper tone there fell on the ears of the hushed House the words) "and they did not always come out of the lobby."

That is exactly the case as Mr. Brunner had put it. But for blood-curdling effect the member for Northwich's detailed narrative was nothing compared to that wrought by this single sentence, uttered by the Speaker as, wigged and robed, he stood with majestic mien under the canopy of the Chair.

Only one man in the assembly could have unravelled the secret, and he sat provokingly silent. The incident had followed on a night which, for unforeseen result, exceeded most of the dramatic surprises provided at Westminster. When last night the House met, it was under the shadow— for some in the sunlight—of approaching catastrophe to the Government. The Liberal Unionist leaders, taking their turn in the management of Opposition affairs, had conceived and skilfully worked up an attack upon the Government (based on the Indian cotton duties as affecting the trade of Lancashire) which by common consent was regarded as

far more dangerous than any that had preceded it
during the fortnight's rally round the Address.
Heads had been counted, and the irrefragable logic
of figures demonstrated that, if not placed absolutely
in a minority, the Government would be brought so
low that it would be hopeless for them to attempt
again to lift up their heads. Five-lined whips sent
out from headquarters of the allied forces brought
together a full muster. The Ministerial whips strained
every nerve, but since the Lancashire members were
going against them in a body, hope flickered faintly.
Sir Henry James, leading the attack, showed by
voice and manner how profoundly he was impressed
with his responsibility. When he sat down Mr.
Chamberlain's face was radiant with certainty that
the hours of the Government's life were numbered.
It was pleasing for loyal hearts to reflect that the
temporary absence of Mr. Balfour had wrought no
disadvantage to the common cause.

Then Mr. Henry Fowler spoke, and the carefully-
ordered, skilfully-marshalled host beleaguering the
Treasury Bench began to melt away. Never was
beheld such transformation scene. The apprehended
minority of a dozen gave place to a triumphant
majority of 195, and Mr. Brunner's curiosity as to the
circumstances under which Mr. Chamberlain's name
does not appear in the division list remains unsatisfied.

CHAPTER XXXIV.

WELSH DISESTABLISHMENT.

THE House was only partially filled when 25th Feb. the Home Secretary, finding his long-delayed chance, moved for leave to bring in the Welsh Disestablishment Bill. The benches filled up as it was made known that Mr. Asquith was speaking. The Bishop of St. Asaph's and the Bishop of Bangor shared between them the Peers' Gallery. Briefly summarising the main provisions of the Bill, the Home Secretary gave the first place to the proposal that after the 1st of January, 1897, the Church of England in Wales and Monmouthshire shall cease to be established. The ecclesiastical revenues drawn from within the borders of the Principality—those outside it did not come within the scope of the Bill —are of the gross annual value of £279,000.

As in the Bill of last year, it was proposed to appoint a Commission to superintend the operation of the Act. To the care of Parish Councils, District Councils, and Town Councils would be referred the burial-grounds and glebe lands to be found within their jurisdiction. The tithe rent charge would be vested in the Council of the district in which it arises. Other property, including the Cathedrals, would be handed over to the Commissioners. Vested interests would be cared for by providing that every minister of the Church now in office shall, as long as he performs the duties of his post, receive the emoluments he at present enjoys. If he desire to withdraw from the scene of his labours, the Bill provides an alternative scheme of annuity. The money appropriated from Church revenues is to be devoted, as was proposed last year, to the establishment of cottage hospitals and dispensaries, the engagement of trained nurses for the sick, the building of labourers' dwellings let at reasonable rents, the establishment of village libraries and museums, and the promotion of secondary and higher education.

The exposition of the scheme, delivered in a studiously matter-of-fact tone, was listened to without manifest emotion by gentlemen opposite.

1st March. The sitting was chiefly occupied by The Factories discussion of the Factories and Workand Work- shops Bill, introduced by Mr. Asquith in shops Bill. one of those speeches which are masterpieces of comprehensive lucidity. The main object of the Bill is to extend in various directions the existing law designed for the safety of working people, and to make supplementary provision in cases with which the Act in its present shape does not attempt to deal. The Home Secretary went at considerable length into the details of the measure. Amongst its novelties is an attempt to define overcrowding as applicable to factories and workshops throughout the country. The Bill proposes that the minimum space for every person employed shall be 250 cubic feet, those working overtime having the quantity extended to 400 feet. The law prohibiting children from cleaning machines in motion is to be extended so as to include young persons. The Act of 1891 left to the sanitary authorities the duty of seeing that adequate provisions are made for escape in case of fire. That duty has been neglected, and the Bill proposes to authorise the institution of courts of summary jurisdiction with the power of ordering the setting up of movable fire-escapes wherever need is shown.

Other clauses of the Bill deal with regulation of work done by persons outside the factory; with the hours of labour; with overtime (to be abolished in cases of persons under eighteen, and to be reduced in the case of women). Dock wharves, quays, bakeries, and laundries are to be brought within the Act. Steam laundries are to be treated as factories, other laundries as workshops. Finally, it is proposed that all workshops shall be registered.

The Bill was received with almost alarming unanimity of approval. Such high authorities as Sir John Gorst, Sir Henry James, Mr. Matthews, Mr. Mundella, regarding the proposals from different points of view, agreed in generally commending them.

2nd March. Hats and Seats. Hats played a memorable part in the scene when in the dusk of a February morning seats were scrambled for in anticipation of Mr. Gladstone's exposition of the Clauses of the Home Rule Bill of 1893. That was the occasion when Mr. Austen Chamberlain arrived in Palace Yard in a four-wheeled cab, said to have approached Westminster by the New Cut, certainly loaded with hats of second-hand aspect. Liberal Unionists having seats in the House of Commons not being unwieldy in number, it was possible for an active, able-bodied Whip to secure places for every man. What became of the hats afterwards has never been told. Colonel Saunderson disposed of one early hat by sitting upon it. But he found it obtrusively placed upon the seat he had long been accustomed to fill, and that is on the benches opposite the Liberal Unionist camp.

It was on this occasion that Dr. Tanner, having exhausted the stock of hats available for the service of the Irish Party, took off his coat and attempted to secure a seat by placing his garment upon it. The House of Commons, even in its most unrestrained mood, is subservient to precedent. Hats were all right, even though there might be suspicion as to the circumstances under which they had been obtained for Parliamentary purposes. If a coat were admitted, why not a waistcoat, or even, in case of emergency, a third garment? Dr. Tanner's coat was peremptorily restored to its proper uses, and a spare hat secured the coveted seat for someone else.

That historic scene, not lacking in picturesqueness, will never more be witnessed in the House of Commons. With Monday's sitting a new custom will be grafted on our ancient Constitution. Hitherto members desirous to secure a particular seat, coming down before prayer time, have pegged out their claim by placing their hat on the seat. That is a preliminary and informal arrangement necessary to be followed by ordered steps. What the planting out of the hat does is to secure a place for prayers. When prayers are over, and only then, members present within the locked doors may obtain from the Clerk at the table tickets on which they write their name. These, set in duly provided framework at the back of the benches, establish for the sitting inalienable right to a particular seat. But the tickets are not available until the penalty of being present at prayers has been paid. Obviously there is a considerable interval of time through which the early bird who has caught a seat must walk about without covering for its head. The ingenuity of members has been equal to the occasion. Many are strongly suspected of having two hats. One they place on the seat when they come down to the House. The other is withdrawn from the locker and worn whilst less resourceful colleagues are catching cold.

By the Speaker's instructions a new card has been prepared available for distribution as soon as members begin to congregate. A name written on one of these, and the card placed on a particular seat, secures a position from which a member may give himself up to devotional exercise undisturbed by doubt as to whether he will find a seat for the remainder of the night. There will still remain the necessity of being present at prayers, for, as heretofore, cards to be placed in the framework at the back of the benches will be distributed only to the sound of the last "Amen."

It will be idle for members to imagine that, having obtained one of the new cards and written their name on it, they may forthwith stick it in the back of the bench and go their way, secure in the possession of a seat. The Speaker has not four times in succession served terms of his high office without learning a thing or two. He has had the new cards made of a size that will not fit the receptacle at the back of the bench.

CHAPTER XXXV.

THE NEW SPEAKER.

7th March.
The Speaker's
Levée. THE levée at Speaker's Court last night was one of the most crowded seen in recent times. It was the last time but one Mr. Peel will act as the Parliamentary host, and members of the House of Commons were careful to avail themselves of the opportunity. It would be impossible to exaggerate the painful sensation created by the announcement of his imminent retirement. Every man in the House feels as if he were losing a personal friend. That the withdrawal from the scene of his stately presence must soon come was accepted as inevitable. But it was believed that the event would be postponed till the Dissolution. Let the next Parliament look after itself. The present one, it seemed, would be strengthened and comforted by Mr. Peel's presence to the end.

Mr. Peel intended that his tenancy of the Chair should be prolonged to the termination of the life of the present Parliament. But he did not expect that termination would be so long delayed. When the Session opened there were many who had convinced themselves it would not survive the Easter Recess, if, indeed, it got over the infantile complaint of the Address. Now it has settled down to work, and, save for some unforeseen accident on a side-issue sprung upon a quiet sitting, it will run its ordinary course.

14th March.
Candidates for
the Speaker's
Chair. Who is to succeed Mr. Peel is the question of the hour. At first it looked as if Mr. Courtney was inevitable. But that is a newspaper nomination as distinguished from a House of Commons conclusion. Those

acquainted with the feeling in various parts of the
House know Mr. Courtney never had a chance.
There are three reasons for this conclusion, any one
sufficient in itself. The Conservatives will not have
him; a powerful clique below the gangway on the
Ministerial side have banded themselves against his
claim; the Irish members have never forgiven him
his action on the Home Rule question. It is one of
the elementary conditions of the full success of a
Speaker that his election should be unanimous. To
that end Sir William Harcourt is now working, and
though I believe he is personally inclined to favour
Mr. Courtney's claims, he finds them absolutely
barred.

The Conservatives want to put forward Sir
Matthew White Ridley, but have no intention of
making a fight round his portly body. They will
be content to accept Mr. Campbell-Bannerman,
should he be willing to offer himself for the post.
He has not yet put in an appearance at the House
after his illness, and I cannot say what are his
views on the question. The first impression is that
he will not undertake the office. He is hopelessly
rich and constitutionally fond of leisure. But the
prize is alluring, and there are many who say it will
prove irresistible. Another name mentioned with
increasing favour is that of the Solicitor-General.
Sir Frank Lockwood, like Mr. Campbell-Bannerman,
is popular on both sides, and if the Cabinet were
finally to select him he would be unanimously
elected.

29th March.
Mr.
Gladstone's
Nominee.

Whilst Mr. Gladstone has scrupulously
refrained from public interference on the
question of the Speakership, or any other
matter agitating the political world, it is
too much to suppose that he has not his own views, or
that he restricts their expression in private conversation. There is a charming story current, which is

probably apocryphal, and has at least the recommendation of being harmless. It tells how the topic of the candidature for the Speakership coming up in Mr. Gladstone's presence, as it does just now wherever two or three are gathered together, he said:

"The most remarkable thing in the controversy is that, as far as I know, no one has mentioned the name of the man best suited for the position."

"Who is that?" was eagerly asked.

"Harcourt," said Mr. Gladstone, in that deep voice he employs when moved by strong conviction.

His assumption that the name had not been mentioned in this connection is not quite accurate. A fortnight ago an evening paper boldly adventured the statement that Sir William Harcourt would leave the Treasury for the Speaker's Chair. The report was plainly put forth *pour rire*, and it was laughed at accordingly. Looked at with Mr. Gladstone's graver vision, the suggestion appears most happy, perhaps not the less so because it is impracticable. Sir William Harcourt would not make a great Speaker precisely on the model Mr. Arthur Peel has established for all time. But a great Speaker he certainly would be. He possesses all the elementary qualities that go to make success in this position. To begin with, he belongs to one of the best families in England, and even in these democratic days that is a matter of some importance when the position of the First Commoner of England is in question. Of commanding presence, he would well become the dignity of the Chair. A consummate Parliamentarian, he knows all the ways of the House of Commons, and is in sympathy with all its instincts. The thing is, of course, impossible; but the fancy is not the less alluring. With Sir William Harcourt in the Speaker's Chair life would once more be worth living in the House of Commons.

The crushed worm will turn at last, and
the patience of The MacGregor is not
inexhaustible. From his eyrie behind the
Treasury Bench he has, since the Session
opened, seen and suffered much. There is Mr. Weir,
for example, who constantly assumes to speak for the
Highlands, and has from time to time had the audacity
actually to mention the Crofters. That is an im-
pertinence which has been promptly reproved, as The
MacGregor has the satisfaction of knowing. It is one
of the many quaintnesses of Mr. Weir that no one can
tell beforehand at what particular point he is likely to
present himself in his favourite attitude as a note of
interrogation. He began his Parliamentary career on
the front bench below the gangway, but found the
situation not unattended by inconvenience. He likes
to watch the effect upon Ministers of his terrible gift
of inquiry. If he rises from below the gangway, he
must needs step out a good pace in order to bring the
Treasury Bench into focus. Should he overstep the
matting that skirts the bench, idle members opposite
would only too gladly interrupt him with cries of
"Order! Order!" Of late he has migrated to the
benches opposite, where, facing the Treasury Bench,
he can, as he puts his question, observe at leisure the
writhings of the hapless Minister.

The MacGregor condescends to none of these
small manœuvres. When he entered the House of
Commons, returned by an intelligent constituency as
an avowed supporter of Mr. Gladstone, he fell in
line behind Ministers, prepared to give them a general
support. They have fallen away; he remains steadfast. Seated midway on the fourth bench, with one
hand thrust in his waistcoat and the other negligently
thrown over the back of the bench, his head slightly
bowed with the weight of thought, The MacGregor
diffuses over this quarter of the House an air of
profound wisdom and cultured statesmanship that

is worth twelve votes on a division to a tottering Ministry.

For some time it has been painfully apparent that the relations between The MacGregor and Her Majesty's Ministers were growing strained. He has mourned to them and they have not wept. He has piped to them and they have not danced. In season and out of season (by preference the latter) he has p on them the necessity of setting aside all ressed business and dealing with the woes of the Crofters. When, a week ago, the House was discussing a proposal to establish Home Rule all round, The MacGregor presented himself just as members were about to proceed to the division. It was a few minutes off midnight, when or never the division must be taken. The jealous Southrons greeted his interposition with a howl of despair. If he went on they might closure him. But that meant two divisions instead of one, and in these degenerate days anything that keeps members in attendance five minutes after midnight is hotly resented. The Highlander, when he is not stealing his neighbour's cattle, is always a gentleman, and on this occasion The MacGregor read the House a lesson in manners which, taken to heart, might prove of permanent benefit.

" Sir," he said, with gracious inclination of his head towards the Speaker, " I had prepared an important speech to deliver on this occasion, but in view of the lateness of the hour I will take the liberty of begging the House to accept it as spoken."

One advantage The MacGregor has over the average statesman is the wide diversity of his occupation before he turned his attention to Imperial politics. A Licentiate of the Royal Colleges of Physicians and Surgeons, Edinburgh (1864), he practised at Penrith and passed on to London. " Was public vaccinator at Penrith," so runs the public record; " Resident Physician at the Peebles Hydropathic Institute, Medical

P

Superintendent Barnhill Hospital and Asylum, Glasgow." In this honourable and varied career he acquired his many graces. Presumably from Penrith came his persuasiveness, from Peebles his polish, from Glasgow his grandly grave demeanour.

There are drawbacks from this happy combination of opportunity as there are drops of bitterness in every cup. Although The MacGregor has for some years retired from practice, there yet linger about him a certain professional air and manner that lead to occasional embarrassment. When, for example, he encounters the Secretary of State for Scotland in the lobby or corridor and, pleased with the opportunity, stretches out his right hand to button-hole him for a brief talk about the Crofters, there is a subtle, indescribable something in the gesture that suggests preliminaries to public vaccination. Sir George Trevelyan makes off in another direction with a rapidity that baffles the ordinarily dignified pace of The MacGregor. It is, of course, the purest fancy. But the wisest among us are not wholly free from the thraldom of fancy.

Irritated by this and similar personal discomfiture, weighed down by growing hopelessness of making anything of Sir William Harcourt, The MacGregor to-day strode down to Westminster, inflamed by high resolve. At the Hydropathic Institute, Peebles, when, in days gone by, cases proved refractory, extreme courses were taken with the assistance of the packing sheet. Regarding the Ministry, more especially the Chancellor of the Exchequer, as a refractory patient, it was clear the time had come when resort must bo had to extreme courses. Nothing would have given the late Resident Physician at the Peebles Hydropathic Institute greater pleasure or satisfaction than to lay out Sir William Harcourt or Sir George Trevelyan in packing sheets, and, taking advantage of their recumbent position, bring in a

Bill giving the Crofters all they want on earth or
Skye. That would be unparliamentary, not to say
impracticable. At least The MacGregor could give
them a fright.

Members observing him as he walked to his place
at the morning sitting, with slow swinging stride, indicative of rhythmic thought, could not fail to suspect
that he was moved with purpose higher and deeper
than usual. He sat in his accustomed attitude whilst
members trifled with such questions as Old Age Pen-
sions, the Local Veto Bill, and even the desirability of
Mr. Herbert Gardner's appointing Welsh - speaking
inspectors to visit the agricultural district of Wales.
Where was Wales, and what was Wales that it should
occupy the time of an assembly whose first and
highest duty was claimed by the Highlands of
Scotland? When these matters were disposed of
and the House was about to resume debate on the
second reading of the Irish Land Bill, the figure
of The MacGregor, erect, terrible, was observed on
the skyline of the heights behind the Treasury
Bench.

"Mr. Speaker, sir," he said, in blood-curdling tones,
"with the indulgence of the House I wish to make a
short personal statement."

The hour and the occasion were not favourable for
full development of tragic incident. It was a morning sitting, and the cold grey light of an April day
fell chill on empty benches. The spirits of members,
sapped by the prodigious bout of speechmaking round
the Welsh Disestablishment Bill, had hopelessly sunk
under the infliction of two days' talk on the Irish
Land Bill, the prospect not enlivened even by promise
of a division at the end. It was the third day of
deliberate purposeless waste of time. Less than two
score members were at this moment scattered about
the dreary chamber. But at sound of the phrase
"personal statement" ears were pricked up, and

figures assumed an attitude of attention. What prospect of destruction of the Welsh Church cannot do, what fresh disturbance of the arrangements between landlord and tenant in Ireland cannot accomplish, a personal statement by the most inconsiderable member straightway effects.

Having thus, so to speak, administered a restorative to the jaded audience, The MacGregor, keeping his fingers on its pulse and narrowly watching the effect of its administration, proceeded. Its quickest and most potent effect was, unfortunately, wrought upon the Speaker.

"The Government," The MacGregor continued, "having hitherto failed to legislate for the Highlands, and having now declared through the Leader of the House that they have no time for that purpose, I decline any longer to play merely the part of a voting machine in order to keep a Government in office who have failed to keep their pledges to my constituents. I therefore—" he proceeded, in sterner tones, regarding with withering glance the backs of the heads of Ministers trembling below him.

It was at this point the Speaker interposed. In what may perchance be his last ruling on a point of order, Mr. Peel adjudged the subject-matter of The MacGregor's speech to be outside the domain of personal explanation. There was no help for this. In the freer air of the Highlands, with his foot on his native heath, The MacGregor might have had ready a rejoinder that would have closed the conversation in another way. As it was, he could only say in the jargon of the Southern tongue—

"Of course, Mr. Speaker, I bow to your ruling."

So he sat down, carrying with him the secret of his "therefore." But it is an open secret. Everyone knows that The MacGregor intended to inform recreant Ministers that never more would he be follower of theirs.

Mr. Gully has long shared with Mr.
Arthur Cohen the position of a man for whom "something must be done." In both cases the something has usually taken the form of a judgeship. Whenever there has been a vacancy on the judicial bench the names of these two faithful Liberals have been spoken. For various reasons promotion has been delayed, and now it is coming to Mr. Gully in unexpected manner. It is safe to say that when, in 1886, Mr. Gully defeated Mr. Cavendish Bentinck at Carlisle, he little thought that within ten years he would be Speaker of the House he then modestly entered. He won the seat again at the last General Election by a reduced majority of 143. That, in the present position of parties, was sufficient to shut him out from a judgeship. The Speakership, not being a place of profit under the Crown, does not necessitate re-election on acceptance. Mr. Gully will, therefore, step into the Speaker's Chair without halt or hindrance. There is, of course, the preliminary of election. But the result of that is a foregone conclusion. If the Conservatives run Sir Matthew White Ridley, and bring up all their men to support him, the majority for the new Speaker will not be overwhelming. But it will serve. Even if, what is by no means certain, the Parnellites vote against him, the Ministerial vote will carry him into the Chair.

It is alleged as an objection to Mr. Gully that he is not known to the House generally, is unfamiliar even by sight to scores of members. That is true, but the objection, such as it is, applies with equal force to Sir Matthew White Ridley. A fortnight ago Mr. Chamberlain and Mr. Arthur Balfour were dining at a table where the question of the hour was unreservedly discussed. Sir Matthew White Ridley's name coming up, Mr. Balfour observed it was a curious thing he never heard the member for the

Blackpool Division of Lancashire speak in the House of Commons.

" Neither have I," said Mr. Chamberlain.

The case of Mr. Arthur Peel on the eve of his election did not greatly differ in this respect. Having held subordinate Ministerial office, which gave him a place on the Front Bench, he could not be regarded as dwelling in obscurity. But so retiring was his disposition that, whether on the Treasury Bench or the Front Opposition Bench, he always sat at the extreme end, in the shadow of the Chair he was destined in later years to invest with new dignity and authority. He very rarely spoke, and his nomination for the Chair was quite as much a surprise to men familiar with the House of Commons as Mr. Gully's has proved. It was Mr. Gladstone who picked out Mr. Peel from the crowd. It is Mr. Labouchere whom the House of Commons will have to thank for whatever is in store for it from the Speakership of Mr. Gully.

CHAPTER XXXVI.

THE OLD SPEAKER.

THE prospect of the announcement by the Speaker of his pending retirement succeeded in breaking the spell of the strange apathy that has for the last fortnight hung over the House of Commons. What the peril of the Established Church in Wales could not effect, nor the proposal for fresh development of tenant right in Ireland bring about, was wrought by promise of the spectacle of this afternoon. As the hand of the clock touched half-past three, the hour at which public business commences, the House presented a densely-crowded appearance.

When the Speaker rose, there was a swift simultaneous action as members uncovered, loudly cheering the while.

Mr. Peel paused for a moment, evidently moved by this demonstration. Beginning in low voice, slightly shaken in tone, but deliberate in utterance, he asked leave to intervene for a few moments before the regular business, in order that he might make an announcement. He should have liked to have made it earlier. In deferring it he thought he was, to the best of his power, consulting the convenience of the House. Considerations of health obliged him to come to the decision to retire from the Chair—" a decision," he added in emphatic tones, which marked occasional passages of the speech, "at which I have not arrived, I hope I need not assure the House, without deep deliberation and the utmost reluctance." Elected more than eleven years ago,

thrice re-elected, he had passed through many
Sessions, and desired unreservedly to say that he had
received from all sides of the House a consideration
and a forbearance that had greatly mitigated the
sense of responsibility and alleviated the mere
physical labour of sitting in the Chair. Some of the
Sessions he had passed through were marked by
storm and stress. Some were of comparative repose.
In respect of all, he acknowledged from the bottom of
his heart the way in which members on both sides, in
all parts of the House, had treated him.

"If," he added, in a voice controlled only by
strong effort against gathering emotion, "I have given
offence to any one member, I hope an act of oblivion
may be passed," an appeal responded to by a burst
of hearty cheering. "If," he continued, possibly with
recollection of some generous outbursts which the
House remembers rather with admiration than resentment, "I have deviated from that calm which should
characterise the utterances of the occupant of this
Chair, I hope every member of the House will believe
me when I say that I have never been consciously
actuated by any personal or political feeling"—here
again the stately flow of eloquence was broken in
upon by a cheer—"and that in all I have said I have,
at least to the best of my judgment, tried to consult the advantage and the permanent interests of
this Assembly."

After graceful acknowledgment of the services of
the officers of the House, more especially the Clerks
at the Table, the Speaker, in a fine passage, affirmed
that neither rules nor orders nor Standing Orders
supply permanent and lasting obligation. They
change with circumstance. One thing remains
absolutely essential if the continuity of sentiment
peculiar to the House of Commons is to be maintained. It is that members should pay regard to
those - honourable traditions, to that great code of

unwritten law which is of imperative and stringent obligation. The Speaker would fain hope that by the co-operation of all its members the House of Commons may continue to be a pattern and a model for foreign nations, and to those great peoples who have left our shores, and have carried our blood, our race, our language, our institutions, and our habits of thought to the uttermost parts of the earth.

"With that hope and belief," said the Speaker in parting words, "I couple the earnest but humble prayer that this House may have centuries of honour and dignity and usefulness before it; that it may continue to hold not a prominent only, but a first and foremost position among the legislative assemblies of the world."

As the Speaker resumed his seat, uplifting his voice in the delivery of this passage, another prolonged cheer arose from the throng of members, who felt they were not only losing a supreme Speaker, but were parting from a great orator. Sir William Harcourt, amid approving cheers, declared the House had heard with deep and painful emotion the announcement just made. On whatever benches members might sit the feeling was one of profound regret at the immeasurable loss the House was destined to sustain, and of heartfelt gratitude for the memorable services the Speaker had rendered. He gave notice that he will to-morrow move the thanks of the House to Mr. Peel for his distinguished services in the Chair, and, by a second resolution, a humble address praying her Majesty to confer some signal mark of her Royal favour upon the retiring Speaker.

9th March. Thanks and a Peerage for Mr. Peel.

Sir William Harcourt, on rising to move a resolution conveying the thanks of the House to the Speaker for his distinguished services in the Chair for more than eleven years, was received with general cheering. He commenced by quotation of the passage in Mr. Peel's

P *

speech when, eleven years ago, he took the Chair,
wherein he defined the qualities and conduct necessary in a man who aspired to fill the gr   office of
Speaker. It was needed that he should lay aside all
that is personal, all that is party, all that savours of
political predilection.

"We are here to-day," said the Chancellor of the
Exchequer, amid renewed cheering, "to bear witness
that these honourable pledges have been most honourably fulfilled."

The qualities that go to make up a good Speaker
are not common in their single excellence, most rare
in their happy combination. Sir William drew a
masterly picture of the ideal Speaker, in whom was
found dignity and authority, tempered by urbanity
and kindness, firmness to control, persuasiveness to
counsel, promptitude of decision with ju   of judgment, tact, patience, and firmness. A natural superiority combined with inbred courtesy, an impartial
mind, a tolerant temper, and a reconciling disposition,
accessible to all in public and private, a kind and
prudent counsellor. These are high and exacting
demands, "and in you, Sir," said Sir William, turning
towards the Speaker, "we have found them all fulfilled," an assertion approved by loud cheering. The
real authority of a Speaker depends absolutely on the
confidence of the House of Commons. That confidence Mr. Peel had earned, and with it the esteem, the
reverence, and the affection of members in all parts of
the House.

Sir William Harcourt had, for greater accuracy,
written out his speech on foolscap, and in the delivery
pretty closely followed the text. He does this as
well as it may be done; but the practice inevitably
detracts from the effect of delivery. He is never at
his best on these ceremonial occasions. He falls into
a lugubriousness of tone and manner conducive rather
to smiles than tears. To see him as he stood at the

table, with a foolscap sheet of notes in his hand,
pointing the application of his remarks by steadfastly
regarding the Speaker over his spectacles, the tone
and attitude were much more suggestive of a schoolmaster, impelled by a stern sense of duty, regretfully
expelling a favourite pupil gone hopelessly to the
bad, than the spokesman of the House of Commons
extolling the virtues and accomplishments of the
greatest Speaker of modern times. He seemed to
have come to bury Arthur Peel, not to praise him.

Mr. Arthur Balfour made rapid notes of his speech
as the Chancellor of the Exchequer proceeded with
the delivery of his. By a curious oversight Sir
William, charged with moving the resolution, entirely overlooked it. Mr. Balfour, whether or not
he noticed this omission, assumed that the motion
had been made, and proceeded to second it. Eight
minutes sufficed for the Chancellor's speech. Mr.
Balfour was briefer by a minute.

The resolution of thanks being put from the Chair,
there was a loud cry of "Aye!" in reply to the
challenge of the Speaker, placed in the embarrassing
position of havin to ask the House if it really meant
what had been eloquently said. No voice was raised
in the negative, and on the motion of the Chancellor
of the Exchequer it was agreed that entry should be
made in the journals of the House recording that the
motion had been carried *nemine contradicente.* The
second resolution, asking Her Majesty to confer upon
the retiring Speaker some signal mark of favour, was
approved with equal heartiness, and at the bidding
of the Chair " the Clerk proceeded to read the orders
of the day."

Proceedings in the House of Commons
10th April. to-day, attendant on the election of the
Election of
New Speaker. new Speaker, triumphantly relieved the
Assembly from the charge, persistently
made, of being steeped in hopeless dulness. Consider-

ing that it is the eve of the Easter Recess, the attendance, numbering with tellers and candidates over 560 members, was unexpected. Every bench was crowded, the side galleries thronged, a group of members standing at the Bar completing the inspiration of the scene. There was in the proceedings that touch of the unexpected sorely lacking of late. It was known there would be a division. It was certain that Ministers would carry their nominee. But the precise number of the majority was a matter of anxious speculation, and the particular turn given to the debate by Mr. Arthur Balfour was absolutely unforeseen.

There were some anxious moments as members trooped in from either lobby. At one time it was plain to read on the faces of the Ministers apprehension of the worst. Mr. Campbell-Bannerman was at this critical moment the only occupant of the Treasury Bench who had courage enough to smile. The Opposition, reinforced by the Parnellites, had come in, and it was known their poll had run up to 274 in favour of Sir Matthew White Ridley. That was dangerously near a full half of the number expected to vote. A couple of minutes later Mr. Causton, always to the fore on these occasions, elbowed his way through the crowd at the Bar, and whispered to Mr. Ellis that the Ministerial muster had run up to 285. The word passed along the Treasury Bench, countenances lighting up as if flooded by sunlight. It was not a large majority, but it will serve, and, with the Parnellites marching out shoulder to shoulder with Mr. Chamberlain, in support of the Tory nominee, was certainly as much as could be expected.

The pleasant incident in the proceedings was Mr. Balfour's graceful welcome of the new Speaker when the battle was lost. There had been a stout fight for the empty Chair. There were moments when angry passion rose, and in the temporary absence of a president it seemed as if chaos must come. When the die was cast and the Ministerial party had won, Mr. Arthur Balfour, most doughty of captains, most chivalrous of knights, rose to join in the congratulations offered to the new Speaker by the Chancellor of the Exchequer.

"You have been elected by a majority," said Mr. Balfour, with courtly obeisance to the new Speaker. "You are now, Sir, the representative of the whole House. I desire to tender you, on· behalf of the minority, the expression of our perfect confidence in your impartiality, and to say that you will receive from us every assistance it is in our power to give you in relieving the labour and lightening the responsibility of the heavy task you have undertaken."

These are not formal words. They are instinct with the traditions of the House of Commons. The fight for the Chair was bitter whilst it lasted. Being over, there remains behind no trace of rancour. As Mr. Balfour put it in a phrase, Mr. Gully is now the representative of the whole House.

CHAPTER XXXVII.

LORD ROSEBERY.

THE level course of debate in the House
8th June. of Commons this afternoon was inter-
A Bold
Advertisement. rupted by an unusual scene. Members
were engaged in discussion of a p o
submitted by Mr. Knox for the repeal of the Criminal
Law Procedure (Ireland) Act, 1887, commonly known
as the Coercion Act. The appeal was based upon the
assertion that Ireland is at present in a condition of
peace and order unparalleled in modern history.

. It was while Mr. Morley was speaking that the
scene burst upon the House. Mr. Dunbar Barton
rising to correct the reading of a passage from his
remarks quoted by the Chief Secretary, a stranger
who had been accommodated with one of the favoured
seats on the floor of the House under the gallery
rose and shouted—

"An assassin's blow has been dealt at me. A
stain has been put upon my name, and I hope this
House——"

The House was pretty full at the moment, and
all heads were turned in the direction whence the
interruption came. Cries of "A stranger!" rose from
the benches below the gangway. The Deputy
Sergeant-at-Arms, Mr. Gosset, was in the Chair at
the time. Hastily leaving it, he crossed the gangway, three messengers running to his assistance.
The stranger, who turned out to be O'Donovan
Rossa, was straightway led from the House, the
debate proceeding as if this new development of
self-advertising had not taken place.

Debate in Committee on the Welsh Disestablishment Bill, not otherwise a stirring
proceeding, is notable for bringing to the
front members who are rarely found
running in couples or in a pack. There are, for
example, the cousins Kenyon—the Hon. George
Thomas Kenyon and Colonel Kenyon-Slaney. The
Colonel, who is endowed with that double-barrelled type
of name of which Lord Randolph Spencer-Churchill
once spoke disrespectfully, cannot be accused of limiting
his appearance in the Parliamentary arena to the
Welsh Church question. At this morning's sitting, for
example, he was on his feet for a considerable time
demonstrating, on behalf of "we agriculturists," how
the proposed reimposition of an added sixpence on
beer would, so to speak, knock the spigot out of
the barrel of the State.

Amongst Parliamentary orators Colonel Kenyon-
Slaney enjoys the distinction of saying less
with fuller appearance of saying something than
is within the gift of any of his contemporaries.
An absolutely deaf man of observant habits would
find a rare intellectual treat in watching the Colonel
address the House of Commons, whether the subject
be the specific gravity of worts or the transfer of the
temporalities of the Church in Wales. He has a way
of fixing a guilty Minister with flaming eye, of beating
the air with his hand as if he were pounding the
right hon. gentleman in a mortar, that is exceedingly
impressive. As for words, his wealth is inexhaustible.
This embarrassment of riches leads somewhat to
undue length of sentence, with corresponding obscurity of meaning. But the Colonel goes on, unfaltering, to the end; and whilst the kindly listener
is endeavouring to make out where the last sentence
led to, the Colonel is well through another, punctuated with rapid movement of the right hand,
accentuated by knowing nods of the head, illumined

10th June.
The Cousins
Kenyon.

by the angry flash of the eyes bent on the cowering
Minister.

For simple glibness, for the capacity to turn on
a tap with the certainty that words will flow in level
stream for an hour or, with equal ease, for an hour
and a half, Mr. Griffith-Boscawen may be bracketed
with Colonel Kenyon-Slaney. But, to do the member
for Tunbridge justice, he does not look as if he were
saying anything, whereas Colonel Kenyon-Slaney
invariably does.

The Hon.
George
Thomas.

Neither of these champions of the Church
pleases the House as does the other
Kenyon, member for Denbigh, whom
some day an envious House of Lords
will gather into its fold. When Mr. Kenyon rises
from the bench almost under the shade of the gallery,
where his presence has been long familiar, there is
something almost awesome in the impressiveness
of his manner and the incoherence of his speech.
He looks as if he had a message to deliver which,
told in its entirety, would make his hearers' flesh
creep. In delivering it he sometimes leaves a
sentence unfinished, at others drops his voice to a
blood-curdling whisper, and in the end succeeds in
leaving his audience in doubt as to what it was he
rose to say. But whilst the House, as was the sad
case to-day, cries "Divide!" Divide!" when Colonel
Kenyon-Slaney's tap has been running for half an
hour, it always welcomes the Hon. George Thomas with
hilarious cheer, and follows him with delighted attention as he attempts to thread the maze of his speech.

"The Man
from Shrop-
shire."

Lord Cranborne is another member who,
habitually silent through the ordinary
course of the Session, leaps into attitude
of activity whenever rude hands are
stretched forth to touch the ark of the Church.
Ordinarily a mild-mannered man, he can upon occasion lash himself into a state of righteous fury, his

clenched hands, his face pale to the lips, testifying to the intensity of his emotion. Mr. Stanley Leighton, on the other hand, is able in Committee on the Bill to preserve an outward semblance of equanimity. Of ·a philosophic mind, he recognises that things generally are so bad it is no use loudly lamenting them. It is an odd coincidence, that cannot fairly be laid to the charge of the county, that, like Mr. Kenyon, a Shropshire man, Mr. Stanley Leighton's speech has about it a fine flavour of unintelligibility. Also like Mr. Kenyon, his manner is so impressive that that hardly matters. To see him dallying with his eyeglass, gently impressing invisible points with authoritative forefinger, to hear his pleasant voice, to look upon his figure—the embodiment of the English country gentleman born to the bench of Quarter Sessions—is quite sufficient in satisfaction of reason for his interposition in debate, without too curiously inquiring which side of the argument he is supporting.

The Speaker, impressed by the responsibility of his position, takes a different view of his duty, and is constantly recalling Mr. Stanley Leighton to the course of what at one time seemed to be his argument. But no harm is done. Mr. Leighton bows to the Chair with graceful dignity, swings his pince-nez with fresh conviction, reproachfully but gently wags his forefinger at the impervious Home Secretary, and starts on quite a fresh track.

13th June. A Peer in the House. When the long procession of over a hundred questions drew to a close, the Earl of Selborne, long popular in the Commons as Lord Wolmer, entered accompanied by Mr. Curzon and Mr. St. John Brodrick. Passing down the floor of the House, he took his seat in a place left vacant by the side of Mr. Chamberlain. Mr. Courtney, coming in a few minutes afterwards, found him there, and mastered earlier instinct which impelled him to cry "Order! Order!" No notice was formally taken of this incursion of a more or less belted earl within the sanctuary of the Commons. But a buzz of whispering rising from bench to bench indicated curiosity as to what might follow.

The whole business was arranged with great skill and sedulous attention to order. Mr. Labouchere, whom Lord Selborne had passed on his way to his seat, rose and addressed the Speaker, calling his attention to "the presence in this House of a nobleman elected at the last General Election," but who since then, Mr. Labouchere was informed, had become a peer of the realm. Description of Lord Selborne as a nobleman was corrected by cries of "A stranger!" Mr. Labouchere inquired of the Speaker whether the noble lord had the right to be within the Bar of the House. If not, he added in significant inflection of voice, what steps will be taken in consequence of his being here?

The Speaker forthwith submitted a shorter catechism for the consideration of Lord Selborne. Was it a fact that he had succeeded to the peerage of his father, the late Earl of Selborne?

"Sir," said Lord Selborne, with unfaltering voice, "I am not a Lord of Parliament, but I am a Peer of the Realm."

Continuing the catechism, the Speaker asked whether he had applied for a writ of summons to the House of Peers, or whether it was his immediate intention to do so? Lord Selborne promptly answered that he had not applied, and that it was not his intention so to apply until the House has considered whether he is not still the duly elected representative of West Edinburgh. The Speaker remarked that there is no instance on record, so far as he was able to discover, of such a claim being made as that now submitted. In these circumstances he invited Lord Selborne to retire below the Bar until the question of his right to sit in the House had been decided.

Lord Selborne quickly responded, halting to make low obeisance to the Chair, and then withdrew to the bench under the gallery corresponding to the one occupied by newly-elected members waiting to take the oath.

20th June.
A Scare.

This afternoon Lord Rosebery returned from a Channel cruise in the Admiralty yacht *Enchantress.* It was undertaken by direction of his doctor, and followed close upon the somewhat alarming collapse which marked his speech ten days ago at the National Liberal Club. Those who have suffered from an attack of influenza know something of the pitifully comatose state in which the patient remains, even when he has been pronounced convalescent. Surcease from work and worry is yearned for—is, indeed, indispensable to full recovery. The Prime Minister was forbidden the luxury accorded in similar circumstances to less distinguished people. Before he left his sick-room he was at work with his secretaries, breasting again the boundless sea of work that environs the first Minister of the Crown. When first invited to attend a festival of Radicalism in the marble halls of the National Liberal Club, he judiciously begged to be excused. Forthwith were printed and circulated circumstantial reports of "fresh dissensions in the Cabinet." Lord Rosebery, it was said, would not even be seen on the same platform as Sir William Harcourt. Something too sensitive to the influence of this kind of political warfare, the Premier, convincing himself that he was better, went down to the National Liberal Club, made his way with difficulty through the teeming multitude that thronged its approaches and filled its halls, began a speech, and, midway in its delivery, lost its thread, a painful pause alarming the audience.

After this he went to sea, coming back to-day to hear of fresh and final developments of his fabled

passion for resignation. He arrived in London shortly
after noon. At three o'clock the House of Commons
met. Two hours later it was in a state nearly approaching panic. Lord Rosebery, it was said, had
returned from his trip hopeless as to his health,
broken in spirit, insistent upon resignation. The fact
that the Queen's journey to Balmoral had been postponed was cited as conclusive proof of the urgency of
the Ministerial crisis. Lord Rosebery had undoubtedly
resigned. Inevitably a dissolution must crash down
on the country and on the House.

There is not for this story what Lord Randolph
Churchill, in his energetic fashion, once described as
a shadow of the shade of a leg to stand upon. Lord
Rosebery greatly benefited by his trip, and has
buckled down to work with renewed energy and in the
brightest of spirits. The recollection of the hoax will
not prevent next week or the week after a repetition
of the scare. For political purposes it is effective
even when the artificiality of the process is demonstrated. Though you know it is only "in fun," it is
not comfortable to have someone at irregular intervals
lustily calling out "Fire! fire!" on the top of your
staircase. At best it disturbs the household, and
creates an abiding feeling of uneasiness. That is
what is possibly designed. It is what undoubtedly
happens in the case of these recurrent scares of
resignation of Ministers and imminent dissolution of
Parliament. There is nothing in them to start with;
but if persevered with, something may grow up around
them.

The simple truth is, the Cabinet are still united in
the resolve to peg along at their appointed work. It
is a thankless task, Ministers being faced by a pitiless
Opposition and not backed up by an enthusiastic
army. Nevertheless to-day, as last month, last year,
and the year before, when resignation was spoken of
as finally resolved upon, they will go on bringing in

Bills and trying to pass them. When the end comes, it will be precipitated by accident or wayward defection on the part of a section of their own followers. It will be from the outside of the Cabinet, not from within, that the knell of the present Parliament is sounded.

21st June. "Much Cry and Little Wolmer." At the conclusion of questions the Chancellor of the Exchequer brought in the Report of the Committee appointed to inquire into the question of the succession to the Earldom of Selborne. Contrary to the usual custom, the Report was read by the Clerk at the table. It briefly declared that William Waldegrave Palmer, commonly called Viscount Wolmer, had, since his election to the House of Commons, succeeded to the Earldom of Selborne in the Peerage of the United Kingdom. Mr. Anstruther thereupon moved the issue of a new writ for the election of a member to serve for West Edinburgh.

There was a marked disinclination on the part of the Opposition leaders to take part in the discussion. Mr. Balfour and Sir Henry James, who were present, said nothing. Mr. Chamberlain and Mr. Courtney absented themselves. This evident disposition to get rid of a subject which in the cartoon of *Punch's* new number is summed up under the formula " Great Cry and Little Wolmer " was generally shared, and the writ was forthwith ordered to issue.

"Where is the Old Furniture?" If the shade of Peter Rylands still haunts the House of Commons, moving about with long stride, hailing with ghostly thump on the shoulder a passing friend, shouting " Good Day ! " in echoless whisper, it must shiver to see how low things are sometimes. played in the House. Peter and friends who sat near him below the gangway were wont to look after the pence in the Civil Service Estimates, and were often laughed at for their pains. At least it was better done than the exhibition on which to-day and yesterday old members looked sad-eyed.

By the withdrawal of Dr. Macgregor, left without a rival in his particular walk, Mr. Weir pored over the Civil Service Estimates, wanting to know all manner of things. He was particularly anxious to ascertain what became of the old furniture. There was an item of £3,000 for new furniture. Very well. But where were the articles it had displaced?

"Mr. Mellor," he said, having succeeded with some effort in getting his glasses to sit on his nose whilst he fixed the hapless Chairman with gleaming eye, "where is the old furniture?"

Mr. Mellor moved uneasily in his chair, but if he had any guilty knowledge in the matter he finally decided not to make a clean breast of it. Being in the furniture department, Mr. Weir told the truth about chair and sofa castors. In the public departments, as elsewhere, these are apt to come off. The natural sequence appears to be to have them screwed on.

"Not at all," said Mr. Weir, in tragic tones. "By a regulation in the Works Office castors are replaced only when legs are broken. So, Mr. Mellor, what happens? When a castor comes off a chair or sofa the leg is next morning found broken."

Alpheus Cleophas next came on the scene. He told a thrilling story of how he spent his spare moments, probably with a lighted candle in his hand, perambulating the premises in fruitless search of oil lamps that cost the nation £1,000 a year. And all the while Sir E. Ashmead-Bartlett tossed about on the Front Opposition Bench, seeking for opportunity to show how pitiful great England had become, whilst Willie Redmond waited to pop in with inquiry after an anonymous friend in Ireland who, owing to Ministerial machinations, had "gone out of his mind."

CHAPTER XXXVIII.

D.EFEAT AND DISSOLUTION.

TO-DAY Ministers were defeated upon a
21st June.
Defeat of the
Ministry.
vote taken in Committee on the Army Estimates. The event happened in a House considerably under half its full strength. So absolute was the state of certainty in the quietude of the time that at the general exodus for dinner many members had not observed the ordinary precaution of pairing. To come back to the House, find the Government had been defeated, and one of its principal members threatening to. resign, was a breathless experience for the truants.

It is strongly indicative of the current of events that several members who took part in the division did not think it necessary to wait to hear the figures announced. They took it for granted the Government would have something about their average majority, and there would be an end of it. It was in the smoking-room, the reading-room, or the library many learned the momentous fact that the Government had been defeated on what a Cabinet Minister formally declared was a Vote of Censure.

Mr. Labouchere testifies that, just before the division was called, he was sitting on the terrace with Sir William Harcourt, who observed how pleasant it was to pass an evening without alarms. Another conversation further illustrates the situation as viewed from within. Passing out to the division, Mr. Balfour observed to Mr. Chamberlain, "Well, I suppose they'll have their usual majority."

"Don't you be too sure about that," Mr. Chamberlain oracularly replied.

Within an hour of the fateful division it seemed that, willy-nilly, Lord Rosebery's Ministry were chained to the oar for at least another seven or eight months. On both sides parties had settled down to the prospect of sitting through the drudgery of committee on the Welsh Church Bill, next taking up the Irish Land Bill, meeting again for an autumn session in order to prepare the way for a general election to take place on the new register that comes into force on the 1st of January. Over and over again, on a multiplicity of issues, the Opposition had tried a fall with Ministers. Sometimes, favoured by accidental circumstances, the majority had been reduced once as low as seven. That was invariably the signal for a rally in the Ministerial ranks, and the next night the majority went up considerably above its normal level. The Opposition grew weary of constant sallies against a garrison which, numerically weak, always mustered just enough to beat back the foe.

Killed by a Stray Shot.

The worst of it—or from ex-Ministers' personal point of view the best of it—was that, the activity of the besiegers falling off, the watchfulness of the besieged grew dull. The final and successful blow was delivered on what, regarded in advance, seemed a hopeless line of attack. Among the ablest, certainly the most popular, member of the Government is Mr. Campbell-Bannerman. He has the distinction, rare with a Secretary of State for War, of pleasing both civilians and soldiers. Lord Wolseley, talking to a friend on the subject, emphatically said, " In my experience, pretty long now, Campbell-Bannerman is the most capable War Minister I have known or had dealings with."

The specific charge submitted by an ex-Under-Secretary to the War Office was that Mr. Campbell-

Bannerman had neglected his duty, inasmuch as he had not in store a sufficient stock of cordite for small arms. Mr. Campbell-Bannerman pledged his word as a man, his reputation as a Minister, that the allegation was baseless. He further cited the testimony of Sir Redvers Buller, a soldier who, in peculiar degree, possesses the confidence of the House of Commons. In ordinary cases that would have been more than enough to dispose of the business. The motion, which took the form of a reduction of the Secretary of State's salary, would have been withdrawn ; or, more probably, the committee would have insisted on formally negativing it, in order that there might be placed on record in the journals of the House testimony of their views on the subject.

How little interest was taken in the matter, with what measure of indifference it was regarded, is shown by the fact that many Liberals, including several Ministers, were away unpaired. When the division was taken it appeared that less than one half of a full muster of the House had taken part in it. But the motion had been carried by a majority of seven. Mr. Campbell-Bannerman very properly regarded it as a vote of censure, and will resign. Even were they so disposed, his colleagues can hardly remain in office. As it happens, their inclination jumps with opportunity. So they gratefully go, killed as it were by a stray shot, after having through three troublesome sessions resolutely faced, and successfully resisted, carefully-laid plans of attack carried out by a powerful and well-led army.

For the first time since Mr. Gladstone **24th June.** withdrew from the scene there returned **Ministers** **Resign.** the once-familiar crowd facing, across the roadway, the gates of Palace Yard, a sure token of deeply-moved political feeling. Inside, the House of Commons teemed with excitement. The Speaker took the chair as usual at three o'clock, and a private Bill was solemnly advanced a stage. Thereafter there was nothing to do till the half-hour struck and public business might be entered upon. But no man would risk losing a precious seat by temporarily withdrawing. So they all sat, talking in loud whisper that filled the air as with the murmur of innumerable bees.

The Peers' Gallery was taken by storm immediately after the doors were opened. Lord Spencer, being in the first flight, gained a favoured seat by the clock. Lord Norton, Lord Limerick, and Lord Dunraven were among those who found seats. Lord Ashbourne, less fortunate, stood among the mob of peers shouldering each other at the top of the stairs. He at least could see and hear, efforts wherein a considerable number of peers failed.

At this time the Treasury Bench was so crowded that some Ministers were fain to sit on the gangway steps. Amongst those on the bench were Mr. John Morley, already in holiday dress; Mr. Henry Fowler, Mr. Bryce, Sir George Trevelyan, and Mr. Arnold Morley. Sir R. Reid and Sir F. Lockwood, beautiful in the companionship of their Law Offices of the Crown, were not at this critical moment divided. They sat together at the end of the bench, gaily talking as if lately there had befallen them a stroke of good fortune. Mr. Campbell-Bannerman, entering at ten minutes past three, was greeted with hilarious shout from the Ministerial side, some members rising to their feet to welcome him.

Sir William Harcourt coming in at twenty-five minutes past three, the whole of the occupants of the Ministerial Benches rose, welcoming him with enthusiastic cheer. Three minutes earlier, Mr. Arthur Balfour entering, Conservatives had likewise leaped to their feet, strenuously cheering. The effect of this well-deserved tribute to a popular leader was marred by the accident that almost contemporaneously Mr. Jesse Collings entered from the other side. The opportunity was taken by the Irish members, mustered in large force, to pay him the mock tribute of applause. Last of all came Mr. Chamberlain also. Scarcely had the cheer which greeted the Chancellor of the Exchequer died away than the member for West Birmingham was descried walking with swinging step to his place below the gangway, at the moment occupied by Mr. Courtney. The Dissentient Liberals, not to be outdone by more numerous if not more important sections of party, uprose to cheer. Mr. Courtney, accustomed to control wild emotion, kept his seat. This demonstration was useful as showing how very few the following of Mr. Chamberlain in the House of Commons muster. There was some cheering when Mr. Asquith came in, completing the list of Cabinet Ministers present.

A full minute before the canonical hour Sir William Harcourt stood at the table, again cheered from the Liberal ranks. He spoke only a few minutes, the earlier portion of his speech being delivered in the studiously unemotional manner in which he has been accustomed to indicate the ordinary course of business. The action of the House of Commons on Friday last was, he said, a direct vote of censure on the Secretary for War, " than whom a more able, respected, or popular Minister "—the loud cheers that here broke in upon the sentence prevented its conclusion being heard. The Government associate themselves with Mr. Campbell-Bannerman. The vote had disabled him from proceeding with the Army Estimates in order to obtain those votes in Supply necessary to the public service. In these circumstances, the Government had felt it their duty to tender to the Queen their resignation, and Her Majesty had accepted it. It only remained for them to hold office until their successors were appointed. Sir William Harcourt, in a voice and manner betraying unwonted emotion, offered his grateful thanks to the House for the unfailing assistance it had rendered him in performing the duties of Leader, a post he held to be higher than any other dignity. He acknowledged the courtesy he had received from his political opponents, and, quoting the words of one of his most illustrious predecessors, confessed that his highest ambition was to stand well with the House of Commons.

This portion of the speech drew forth a notable demonstration of personal esteem from the Conservatives. To this feeling Mr. Balfour gave graceful expression, declaring that whatever gentlemen on his side might think of the policy of the Government they recognised in Sir W. Harcourt one of the greatest ornaments of the House, who had always kept in view the preservation of its dignity.

It is noted that in making this response to Sir William Harcourt's appeal for judgment Mr. Balfour was punctilious in declining to assume that the Government had actually been supplanted or was on the verge of quitting office. Taking the view of Friday's vote expressed by the Chancellor of the Exchequer, he urged that the proper course would have been to advise a dissolution. In August, 1892, following upon the motion of Mr. Asquith, the leaders of the present Opposition were made the subject of a Vote of Censure. How after that, in the same Parliament, a party so treated were to be invited to wind up the business of the Session, Mr. Balfour could not see.

"There are," said Lord Rosebery, in an
28th June. unrecorded speech delivered this week
The Happy
Deliverance. at a gathering of private friends, "two supreme pleasures in life. One is ideal, the other real. The ideal is when a man receives the seals of office from the hands of his

Sovereign. The real pleasure comes when he hands them back."

This is true in degree of all Ministries. Undoubtedly it accurately describes the position of the Government over which Lord Rosebery of late presided. Probably there was not on any railway in the kingdom a happier, lighter-hearted group of men than that which to-day went to Windsor to perform the closing scene in their Ministerial life. For them hereafter, whatever befall, a softened gleam of tender recollection will brighten their eyes when they chance to rest on the manly figure of Mr. St. John Brodrick. He has been to them friend and deliverer, and though possibly, if carefully examined, the motives of his action in raising the question of the stock of cordite in store would not prove to be unreservedly benevolent, that is a matter of secondary consideration. What he did was to cut the bonds that had grown intolerably galling. Manumitted Ministers rise up and call him blessed.

There has been idle and malicious talk in some quarters about Friday night's surprise being a deliberate plot on the part of the Unionist Leaders. The surprise, painful in its nature, has been chiefly with Mr. Arthur Balfour and his companions. Undoubtedly the attack on Mr. Campbell-Bannerman was made with intent of harassing the Government. It is the duty of an Opposition to oppose; and when Mr. St. John Brodrick moved to reduce the salary of the Secretary of State for War by the sum of £100 by way of marking the House's distrust of his administration in the matter of cordite stores, he was only doing his duty. It seemed, in the circumstances of the hour, reasonable to expect that the Government would be damaged by having their majority brought down to something below the normal level. To put them in a minority was a task which the irrefragable logic of figures seemed to show impossible. A return

of members present and within sound of the division
bell placed in the hands of Mr. Akers-Douglas at
seven o'clock gave the Government a majority of
fourteen. A similar numbering of the people, made
about the same time by Mr. Ellis, gave a majority of
seventeen.

The bye-play between the Whips when,
A Significant Incident. the division over, they stood at the table
accurately indicates their impressions.
The Clerk handed the paper to Sir William Walrond,
the junior Opposition Whip. He hesitating to receive
it, Mr. Ellis stepped forward and took it as a matter
of course. As with amazed and puzzled look he
studied the position of the figures, Mr. Akers-Douglas
came up and hesitatingly claimed the paper. Mr.
Ellis yielded. Once more confident that the Government could not have been beaten, he took the paper
from Mr. Akers-Douglas's unresisting hand and only
after a long scrutiny, still evidently half doubtful
whether the Clerk had not inadvertently transposed
the figures, he gave it back to the not less perturbed
Opposition Whip.

Thus by unpremeditated, unforeseen accident was
the patiently-played game of the leaders of parties
broken in upon, their cards and counters ruthlessly
swept off the board. Liberal Ministers bound by
their repeated pledges, constrained by political necessities, were bound to go on making-believe to legislate.
No one understood the position more thoroughly than
Mr. Arthur Balfour. Obviously his policy, as Leader
of the Opposition, was to hang on the flanks of the
enemy, harass them at every point, weaken their
morale by reducing their majority to a single figure,
and so wear out their patience that they might some
day be tempted to fling expediency to the winds and
perform an act of political suicide. "Instead of
which," as the judge once said, Mr. St. John Brodrick
takes charge of affairs, and provides the Government

with means of escape from dilemma such as had not
opened up to Fancy in its moments of rarest exaltation.

It is quite possible that but for the acci-
If not Scylla, dent of Friday last the Government ship
Charybdis. might on the Monday following have been
driven on the rocks and made hopeless wreck of. On
that day a point in Committee on the Welsh Disestablishment Bill was to have been reached, at which
those eminent statesmen and unpurchasable patriots,
Mr. Lloyd George and Mr. David Thomas, were to
take matters in hand. The Welsh Church Bill, for
which Nonconformity had long toiled, upon which the
Ministry had staked their existence, not suiting these
gentlemen on a particular point, they were resolved
to wreck it, with it the Ministry, and the other large
measures with which their argosy was freighted.
They had threatened before, and retreated at the
point of impact. They could not, for very shame, play
that part over again. If they had anything like
the following they boasted, the Government would
find themselves in a tight place. They might, indeed
—and some authorities regarded the event as exceedingly probable—have been placed in a minority.

In such case, differing entirely from that established by the success of Mr. Brodrick's action, Ministers
would have been obliged to go to the country with all
their imperfected plans, and with conviction of in-
competency to keep their own party together branded
on their brow. Amongst other disadvantages they
would have been beset by the serious one of having
to commit themselves to a programme, to stand on
the defensive, instead of marshalling their forces for
the more exhilarating and less compromising attitude
of attack.

Matters stand to-day on quite another footing.
The vote of censure on Mr. Campbell-Bannerman
having been carried, there remained nothing for him
but to retire. Ministers could not take the Army

Vote without having a Secretary of State for War. A dissolution might not take place until the Army Vote was passed. Of course the Cabinet might have thrown over Mr. Campbell-Bannerman and placed another Minister at his post. That is a proceeding that does not call for discussion. Failing that, the only course open to Ministers was to resign, casting upon the Opposition the responsibility of dissolving Parliament and canvassing the country upon a programme of constructive legislation, whilst the late Ministry, victims of untoward accident, cut off in the midst of a career of usefulness by a wanton hand, appeal to the sympathies of a generous nation.

As through their troubled existence the foes of the Liberal Ministry have been those of their own household, so in the hour of death their best friend has been the enemy.

8th July.   Parliament dissolved.

INDEX.

Printed by Cassell & Company, Limited. La Belle Sauvage, London, E.C.

A SELECTED LIST

OF

CASSELL & COMPANY'S

PUBLICATIONS.

6 G—a.96

Illustrated, Fine Art, and other Volumes.

Abbeys and Churches of England and Wales, The: Descriptive, Historical, Pictorial. Series II. 21s.

Adventure, The World of. Fully Illustrated. Complete in Three Vols. 9s. each.

Adventures in Criticism. By A. T. QUILLER-COUCH. 6s.

Africa and its Explorers, The Story of. By Dr. ROBERT BROWN, F.R.G.S., &c. With about 800 Original Illustrations. Complete in 4 Vols. 7s. 6d. each.

Agrarian Tenures. By the Rt. Hon. G. SHAW LEFEVRE. 5s.

Allon, Henry, D.D.: Pastor and Teacher. The Story of his Ministry, with Selected Sermons and Addresses. By the Rev. W. HARDY HARWOOD. 6s.

American Life. By PAUL DE ROUSIERS. 12s. 6d.

Animal Painting in Water Colours. With Coloured Plates. 5s.

Animals, Popular History of. By HENRY SCHERREN, F.Z.S. With 13 Coloured Plates and other Illustrations. 7s. 6d.

Arabian Nights Entertainments (Cassell's). With about 400 Illustrations. 10s. 6d.

Architectural Drawing. By R. PHENÉ SPIERS. Illustrated. 10s. 6d.

Art, The Magazine of. Yearly Volume. With about 400 Illustrations, 14 Etchings or Photogravures, and a Series of Full-page Plates. 21s.

Artistic Anatomy. By Prof. M. DUVAL. *Cheap Edition,* 3s. 6d.

Astronomy, The Dawn of. A Study of the Temple Worship and Mythology the Ancient Egyptians. By Professor J. NORMAN LOCKYER, C.B., F.R.S., &c. Illustrated. 21s.

Atlas, The Universal. A New and Complete General Atlas of the World, with 117 Pages of Maps, handsomely produced in Colours, and a Complete Index to about 125,000 Names. List of Maps, Prices, and all particulars on application.

Bashkirtseff, Marie, The Journal of. Translated by MATHILDE BLIND. 7s. 6d.

Battles of the Nineteenth Century. An entirely New and Original Work, with Several Hundred Illustrations. Vol. I. 9s.

"Belle Sauvage" Library, The. Cloth, 2s. (*A complete list of the volumes free on application.*)

Beetles, Butterflies, Moths, and other Insects. By A. W. KAPPEL, F.L.S., F.E.S., and W. EGMONT KIRBY. With 12 Coloured Plates. 3s. 6d.

Biographical Dictionary, Cassell's New. Containing Memoirs of the Mo Eminent Men and Women of all Ages and Countries. *Cheap Edition.* 3s 6d.

Birds' Nests, British: How, Where, and When to Find and Identify By R. KEARTON. With nearly 130 Illustrations of Nests, Eggs, Young, etc., fr Photographs by C. KEARTON. 21s.

Birds' Nests, Eggs, and Egg-Collecting. By R. KEARTON. Illustrated wi 16 Coloured Plates of Eggs. *Revised and Enlarged Edition. Fourth T ousand.* !

Britain's Roll of Glory; or, the Victoria Cross, its Heroes, and the Valour. By D. H PARRY. Illustrated. 7s. 6d.

British Ballads. 275 Original Illustrations. Two Vols. Cloth, 15s.

British Battles on Land and Sea. By JAMES GRANT. With about Illustrations. Four Vols. 4to, £1 16s.; *Library Edition,* Four Vols. £2.

Butterflies and Moths, European. By W. F. KIRBY. With 61 Coloured Plates. 35s

Canaries and Cage-Birds, The Illustrated Book of. By W. A. BLAKSTON W. SWAYSLAND, and A. F. WIENER. With 56 Fac-simile Coloured Plates. 35s.

Captain Horn, The Adventures of. By FRANK STOCKTON. 6s

Capture of the "Estrella," The. By COMMANDER CLAUD HARDING, R.N.

Carnation Manual, The. Edited and Issued by the National Carnation a Picotee Society (Southern Section). 3s. 6d.

Cassell's Family Magazine. Yearly Volume. Illustrated. 7s. 6d.

Cathedrals, Abbeys, and Churches of England and Wales. Descripti Historical, Pictorial. *Popular Edition.* Two Vols. 25s.

Cats and Kittens. By HENRIETTE RONNER. With Portrait and 13 magnific Full-page Photogravure Plates and numerous Illustrations. 4to, £2 10s.

Cavour, Count, and Madame de Circourt. Translated by A. J. BUTLER. 10s.

China Painting. By FLORENCE LEWIS. With Sixteen Coloured Plates, &c.

Choice Dishes at Small Cost. By A. G. PAYNE. *Cheap Edition,* 1s.

Chums. The Illustrated Paper for Boys. Yearly Volume, 8s.

Cities of the World. Four Vols. Illustrated. 7s. 6d. each.

Civil Service, Guide to Employment in the. *Entirely New Edition.* 1s.; cloth, 1s. 6d.

Clinical Manuals for Practitioners and Students of Medicine. (*A List Volumes forwarded post free on application to the Publishers.*)

Cobden Club, Works published for the. (*A Complete List on application.*)

Colonist's Medical Handbook, The. By E. ALFRED BARTON, M.R.C.S.   1

Colour. By Prof. A. H. CHURCH. *New and Enlarged Edition*, 3s. 6d.

Columbus, The Career of. By CHARLES ELTON, F.S.A.   10s. 6d.

Combe, George, The Select Works of. Issued by Authority of the Com Trustees. *Popular Edition*, 1s. each, net.

> **The Constitution of Man. Moral Philosophy. Science and Religion. Discus-ions on Education. American Notes.**

Commons and Forests, English. By the Rt. Hon. G. SHAW LEFEVRE, M.P.   5s

Conquests of the Cross. Edited by EDWIN HODDER. With numerous Origina Illustrations. Complete in Three Vols.   9s. each.

Cookery, A Year's. By PHYLLIS BROWNE. *New and Enlarged Edition*, 3s. 6d

Cookery Book, Cassell's New Universal. By LIZZIE HERITAGE. With 1 Coloured Plates and other Illustrations. 1,344 pages, strongly bound in leather gilt, 6s.

Cookery, Cassell's Popular. With Four Coloured Plates. Cloth gilt, 2s.

Cookery, Cassell's Shilling. 125th Thousand.   1s.

Cookery, Vegetarian. By A. G. PAYNE.   1s. 6d.

Cooking by Gas, The Art of. By MARIE J. SUGG. Illustrated. Cloth, 2s.

Cottage Gardening. Edited by W. ROBINSON, F.L.S. Illustrated. Half yearly Vols., II., III., V., and VI., 2s. 6d. each. Vol. IV., 3s.

Countries of the World, The. By DR. ROBERT BROWN, F.L.S. In Six Vols. with about 750 Illustrations. 7s. 6d. each. Cheap Edition. Vol. I., 6s.

Cyclopædia, Cassell's Concise. Brought down to the latest date. With abou 600 Illustrations. *New and Cheap Edition*, 7s. 6d.

Cyclopædia, Cassell's Miniature. Containing 30,000 Subjects. Cloth, 2s. 6d. half-roxburgh, 4s.

David Balfour, The Adventures of. By R. L. STEVENSON. Illustrate Two Vols.   6s. each.

Part 1.—Kidnapped.   Part 2.—Catriona.

Defoe, Daniel, The Life of. By THOMAS WRIGHT. Illustrated. 21s.

Dictionaries. (For description see alphabetical letter.) Religion, Biographical Encyclopædic, Mechanical, English, English Literature, Domestic. (French, German and Latin, see with *Educational Works*.)

Diet and Cookery for Common Ailments. By a Fellow of the Royal Colleg of Physicians, and PHYLLIS BROWNE.   5s.

Dog, Illustrated Book of the. By VERO SHAW, B.A. With 28 Coloure Plates. Cloth bevelled, 35s. ; half-morocco, 45s.

Domestic Dictionary, The. An Encyclopædia for the Household. Cloth, 7s. 6d

Doré Don Quixote, The. With about 400 Illustrations by GUSTAVE DOR Cheap Edition, bevelled boards, gilt edges, 10s. 6d.

Doré Gallery, The. With 250 Illustrations by GUSTAVE DORÉ. 4to, 42s.

Doré's Dante's Inferno. Illustrated by GUSTAVE DORÉ. *Popular Editio* With Preface by A. J. BUTLER. Cloth gilt or buckram, 7s 6d.

Doré's Dante's Purgatory and Paradise. Illustrated by GUSTAVE DOR Cheap Edition. 7s 6d.

Doré's Milton's Paradise Lost. Illustrated by GUSTAVE DORÉ. 4to, 21 *Popular Edition*. Cloth gilt, or buckram gilt, 7s. 6d.

Dressmaking, Modern. The Elements of. By J. E. DAVIS. Illustrated.

Earth, Our, and its Story. Edited by Dr. ROBERT BROWN, F.L.S. Wit 36 Coloured Plates and 740 Wood Engravings. Complete in Three Vols. 9s. each.

Edinburgh, Old and New, Cassell's. With 600 Illustrations. Three Vol 9s. each ; library binding, £1 10s. the set.

Egypt: Descriptive, Historical, and Picturesque. By Prof. G. EBER Translated by CLARA BELL, with Notes by SAMUEL BIRCH, LL.D., &c. Two Vols. 42

Electric Current, The. How Produced and How Used. By R. MULLINEU WALMSLEY, D.Sc., &c. Illustrated. 10s. 6d.

Electricity, Practical. By Prof. W. E. AYRTON. Illustrated. Cloth, 7s. 6d.

Electricity in the Service of Man. A Popular and Practical Treatise. Wit upwards of 950 Illustrations. *New and Revised Edition*, 10s. 6d.

Employment for Boys on Leaving School, Guide to. By W. S. BEAR F.R.G.S.   1s 6d.

Encyclopædic Dictionary, The. Complete in Fourteen Divisional Vols., 10s. each ; or Seven Vols., half-morocco, 21s. each ; half-russia, 25s. each.

England, Cassell's Illustrated History of. With upwards of 2,000 Illus tions. *New and Revised Edition.* Complete in Eight Vols., 9s. each; cloth and embossed gilt top and headbanded, £4 net the set.

English Dictionary, Cassell's. Containing Definitions of upwards of 100, Words and Phrases. *Cheap Edition*, 3s. 6d. ; *Superior Edition*, 5s.

English Literature, Library of. By Prof. H. MORLEY. In 5 Vols. 7s. 6d. eac

English Literature, Morley's First Sketch of. *Revised Edition*, 7s. 6d.

English Literature, The Story of. By ANNA BUCKLAND. 3s. 6d.

English Writers from the Earliest Period to Shakespeare. By HENR MORLEY. Eleven Vols. 5s. each.

Æsop's Fables. Illustrated by ERNEST GRISET. *Cheap Edition.* Cloth, 3s. 6d. bevelled boards, gilt edges, 5s.

Etiquette of Good Society. *New Edition.* Edited and Revised by LAD COLIN CAMPBELL. 1s. ; cloth, 1s. 6d.

Europe, Cassell's Pocket Guide to. Leather, 6s.

Fairy Tales Far and Near. Retold by Q. Illustrated. 3s. 6d.

Fairway Island. By HORACE HUTCHINSON. 3s. 6d.

Faith Doctor, The. A Novel. By Dr. EDWARD EGGLESTON. 6s.

Family Physician. By Eminent PHYSICIANS and SURGEONS. Cloth, 21s. roxburgh, 25s.

Fiction, Cassell's Popular Library of. 3s. 6d. each.

The Snare of the Fowler. By Mrs. ALEX-ANDER.	"La Bella," and others. By EGER CASTLE.
Out of the Jaws of Death. By FRANK BARRETT.	A Blot of Ink. Translated by Q. and P. M. FRANCKE. 5s.
Fourteen to One, &c. By ELIZABETH STUART PHELPS.	The Avenger of Blood. By J. MA COBBAN.
The Medicine Lady. By L. T. MEADE.	A Modern Dick Whittington. By Ji PAYN.
Leona. By Mrs. MOLESWORTH.	The Man in Black. By STANLEY WEY
Father Stafford. A Novel. By ANTHONY HOPE.	The Doings of Raffles Haw. By A. CON
Dr. Dumány's Wife. By MAURUS JÓKAI.	DOYLE.

Field Naturalist's Handbook, The. By Revs. J. G. WOOD and THEODOR WOOD. *Cheap Edition*, 2s. 6d.

Figuier's Popular Scientific Works. With Several Hundred Illustrations i each. 3s. 6d. each.

The Insect World.	Reptiles and Birds.	The Vegetable Wor
The Human Race.	Mammalia.	Ocean World.
	The World before the Deluge.	

Figure Painting in Water Colours. With 16 Coloured Plates. 7s. 6d.

Flora's Feast. A Masque of Flowers. Penned and Pictured by WALTE CRANE. With 40 pages in Colours. 5s.

Flower Painting, Elementary. With Eight Coloured Plates. 3s.

Flowers, and How to Paint Them. By MAUD NAFTEL. With Coloured Plates.

Football: the Rugby Union Game. Edited by Rev. F. MARSHALL. Illustrat *New and Enlarged Edition.* 7s. 6d.

For Glory and Renown. By D. H. PARRY. Illustrated. 5s.

Fossil Reptiles, A History of British. By Sir RICHARD OWEN, F.R.S., & With 268 Plates. In Four Vols. £12 12s.

France, From the Memoirs of a Minister of. By STANLEY WEYMAN. 6s.

Franco-German War, Cassell's History of the. Complete in Two Vols containing about 500 Illustrations. 9s. each.

Fraser, John Drummond. By PHILALETHES. A Story of Jesuit Intrigue the Church of England. *Cheap Edition.* 1s. 6d.

Free Lance in a Far Land, A. By HERBERT COMPTON. 6s.

Garden Flowers, Familiar. By SHIRLEY HIBBERD. With Coloured Plates F. E. HULME, F.L.S. Complete in Five Series. Cloth gilt, 12s. 6d. each.

Gardening, Cassell's Popular. Illustrated. Complete in Four Vols. 5s. each

Gazetteer of Great Britain and Ireland, Cassell's. With numerous Illustratio and Maps in Colours. Vols. I. and II. 7s. 6d. each.

George Saxon, The Reputation of. By MORLEY ROBERTS. 5s.

Gleanings from Popular Authors. Two Vols. With Original Illustration 9s. each. Two Vols. in One, 15s.

Gulliver's Travels. With 88 Engravings. Cloth, 3s. 6d. ; cloth gilt, 5s.

Gun and its Development, The. By W. W. GREENER. Illustrated. 10s. 6d.

Guns, Modern Shot. By W. W. GREENER. Illustrated. 5s.

Health, The Book of. By Eminent Physicians and Surgeons. Cloth, 21s.

Heavens, The Story of the. By Sir ROBERT STAWELL BALL, LL.D., F.R.S With Coloured Plates and Wood Engravings. *Popular Edition*, 12s. 6d.

Heroes of Britain in Peace and War. With 300 Original Illustrations. *Chea Edition.* Two Vols. 3s. 6d. each ; or Two Vols. in One, cloth gilt, 7s. 6d.

Hiram Golf's Religion; or, the Shoemaker by the Grace of God. 2s.

Hispaniola Plate (1683-1893). By JOHN BLOUNDELLE-BURTON. 6s.

Historic Houses of the United Kingdom. With Contributions by the Rev. Pr fessor BONNEY, F.R.S., and others. Profusely Illustrated. 10s. 6d.

History, A Footnote to. Eight Years of Trouble in Samoa. By R. L. STEVENSON. 6s

Home Life of the Ancient Greeks, The. Translated by ALICE ZIMMERN Illustrated. *Cheap Edition.* 5s.

H..rse, The Book of the. By SAMUEL SIDNEY. With 17 Full-page Collot Plates of Celebrated Horses of the Day, and numerous other Illustrations. Cloth,

Horses and Dogs. By O. EERELMAN. With Descriptive Text. Transla from the Dutch by CLARA BELL. With Author's portrait and Fifteen Full-page other Illustrations. 25s. net.

Houghton, Lord : The Life, Letters, and Friendships of Richard Mon Milnes, First Lord Houghton. By Sir WEMYSS REID. Two Vols. 32s.

Household, Cassell's Book of the. Illustrated. Complete in Four Vols. 5s. each or Four Vols. in Two, half-morocco, 25s.

Hygiene and Public Health. By B. ARTHUR WHITELEGGE, M.D. Illustrated *New and Revised Edition.* 7s. 6d.

Impregnable City, The. By MAX PEMBERTON. 6s.

India, Cassell's History of. By JAMES GRANT. With 400 Illustrations. Tw Vols., 9s. each, or One Vol., 15s.

In-door Amusements, Card Games, and Fireside Fun, Cassell's Book o With numerous Illustrations. *Cheap Edition.* Cloth, 2s.

Iron Pirate, The. By MAX PEMBERTON. Illustrated. 5s.

Island Nights' Entertainments. By R. L. STEVENSON. Illustrated, 6s.

Italy from the Fall of Napoleon in 1815 to 1890. By J. W. PROBYN. 3s.

Kennel Guide, Practical. By Dr. GORDON STABLES. Illustrated. *Cheap Edition*, 1

Khiva, A Ride to. Travels and Adventures in Central Asia. By Col. FRE BURNABY. *New Edition.* With Portrait and Seven Illustrations. 3s. 6d.

King George, In the Days of. By COL. PERCY GROVES. Illustrated. 1s. 6d

King's Hussar, A. Memoirs of a Troop Sergeant-Major of the 14th (King's Hussars. Edited by HERBERT COMPTON. 6s.

Ladies' Physician, The. By a London Physician. *Cheap Edition, Revised an Enlarged.* 3s. 6d.

Lady's Dressing Room, The. Translated from the French by LADY COLI CAMPBELL. 3s. 6d.

Lady Biddy Fane, The Admirable. By FRANK BARRETT. *New Edition* With 12 Full-page Illustrations. 6s.

Lake Dwellings of Europe. By ROBERT MUNRO, M.D., M.A. Cloth, 31s. 6d.

Letters, The Highway of; and its Echoes of Famous Footsteps. By THOMA ARCHER. Illustrated, 10s. 6d.

Letts's Diaries and other Time-saving Publications are now published exclu sively by CASSELL & COMPANY. (*A List sent post free on application.*)

Lisbeth. A Novel. By LESLIE KEITH. *Cheap Edition.* One Vol. 6s.

List, ye Landsmen ! A Romance of Incident. By W. CLARK RUSSELL. 6s.

Little Minister, The. By J. M. BARRIE. *Illustrated Edition*, 6s.

Little Squire, The. A Story of Three. By Mrs. HENRY DE LA PASTURE. 3s. 6d

Lobengula, Three Years with, and Experiences in South Africa. By J COOPER-CHADWICK. *Cheap Edition.* 2s. 6d.

Locomotive Engine, The Biography of a. By HENRY FRITH. 3s. 6d.

Loftus, Lord Augustus, P.C., G.C.B., The Diplomatic Reminiscences of. Firs Series. With Portrait. Two Vols. 32s. Second Series. Two Vols 32s.

London, Greater. By EDWARD WALFORD. Two Vols. With about 4 Illustrations. 9s. each. *Library Edition.* Two Vols. £1 the set.

London, Old and New. By WALTER THORNBURY and EDWARD WALFOR Six Vols., with about 1,200 Illustrations. Cloth, 9s. each. *Library Edition*, £3.

London, The Queen's. With nearly 400 Superb Views. 9s.

Medical Handbook of Life Assurance. By JAMES EDWARD POLLOCK, M.D., and JAMES CHISHOLM. *New and Revised Edition.* 7s. 6d.

Medicine, Manuals for Students of. (*A List forwarded post free on application.*)

Modern Europe, A History of. By C. A. FYFFE, M.A. *Cheap Edition in One Volume,* 10s. 6d.; *Library Edition, Illustrated,* 3 vols , 7s. 6d. each.

Music, Illustrated History of. By EMIL NAUMANN. Edited by the Rev. Sir F. A. GORE OUSELEY, Bart. Illustrated. Two Vols. 31s. 6d.

National Library, Cassell's. Consisting of 214 Volumes. Paper covers, 3d. ; cloth, 6d. (*A Complete List of the Volumes post free on application.*)

Natural History, Cassell's Concise. By E. PERCEVAL WRIGHT, M.A., M.D., F.L.S. With several Hundred Illustrations. 7s. 6d. ; also kept half bound.

Natural History, Cassell's New. Edited by P. MARTIN DUNCAN, M.B., F.R.S., F.G.S. Complete in Six Vols. With about 2,000 Illustrations. Cloth, 9s. each.

Nature's Wonder Workers. By KATE R. LOVELL. Illustrated. 3s. 6d.

Nelson, The Life of. By ROBERT SOUTHEY. Illustrated with Eight Plates. 3s. 6d.

New Zealand, Pictorial. With Preface by Sir W. B. PERCEVAL, K.C.M.G. Illust. 6s.

Nursing for the Home and for the Hospital, A Handbook of. By CATHERIN J. WOOD. *Cheap Edition,* 1s. 6d. ; cloth, 2s.

Nursing of Sick Children, A Handbook for the. By CATHERINE J. WOOD. 2s. 6d.

Old Dorset. Chapters in the History of the County. By H. J. MOULE, M.A. 10s. 6d.

Old Maids and Young. By ELSA D'ESTERRE-KEELING. 6s.

Old Boy's Yarns, An. By HAROLD AVERY. With 8 Plates. 3s. 6d.

Our Own Country. Six Vols. With 1,200 Illustrations. Cloth, 7s. 6d. each.

Painting, The English School of. By ERNEST CHESNEAU. *Cheap Edition,* 3s. 6d.

Paris, Old and New. Profusely Illustrated. Complete in Two Volumes. 9s. each, or gilt edges, 10s. 6d. each.

Peoples of the World, The. By Dr. ROBERT BROWN, F.L.S. Complete in S' Vols. With Illustrations. 7s. 6d. each.

Photography for Amateurs. By T. C. HEPWORTH. Illustrated. 1s. ; cloth, 1s. 6d.

Phrase and Fable, Dr. Brewer's Dictionary of. Giving the Derivation, Source or Origin of Common Phrases, Allusions, and Words that have a Tale to Tell *Entirely New and largely increased Edition.* 10s. 6d. Also in half-morocco.

Physiology for Students, Elementary. By ALFRED T. SCHOFIELD, M.D., M R.C.S. With Two Coloured Plates and numerous Illustrations. *New Edition.* 5s

Picturesque America. Complete in Four Vols., with 48 Exquisite Steel Plates and about 800 Original Wood Engravings. £2 2s. each. *Popular Edition,* Vol I. and II., price 18s each.

Picturesque Canada. With about 600 Original Illustrations. Two Vols. £6 6s. these

Picturesque Europe. Complete in Five Vols. Each containing 13 Exquisite Ste Plates, from Original Drawings, and nearly 200 Original Illustrations. £21 ; ha morocco, £31 10s. ; morocco gilt, £52 10s. *Popular Edition.* In Five Vols. 18s. eac

Picturesque Mediterranean, The. With a Series of Magnificent Illustratio from Original Designs by leading Artists of the day. Two Vols. Cloth, £2 2s. eac

Pigeon Keeper, The Practical. By LEWIS WRIGHT. Illustrated. 3s. 6d.

Pigeons, Fulton's Book of. Edited by LEWIS WRIGHT. Revised, Enlarge and Supplemented by the Rev. W. F. LUMLEY. With 50 Full-page Illustration *Popular Edition.* In One Vol., 10s. 6d.

Planet, The Story of Our. By the Rev. Prof. BONNEY, F.R.S., &c. Wit Coloured Plates and Maps and about 100 Illustrations. 31s. 6d.

Pocket Library, Cassell's. Cloth, 1s. 4d. each.

A King's Diary. By PERCY WHITE.	**The Little Huguenot.** By MAX PEMBERTO
A White Baby. By JAMES WELSH.	A Whirl Asunder. By GERTRUDE ATHE
Lady Bonnie's Experiment. By TIGHE HOPKINS.	TON.
	The Paying Guest. By GEO. GISSING.

Polytechnic Series, The. Practical Illustrated Manuals. (*A List will sent on application.*)

Pomona's Travels. By FRANK R. STOCKTON. Illustrated. 5s.

Portrait Gallery, Cassell's Universal. Containing 240 Portraits of Celebrate Men and Women of the Day. With brief Memoirs and *facsimile* Autograph Cloth. 6s.

Portrait Gallery, The Cabinet. Complete in Five Series, each containing Cabinet Photographs o Eminent Men and Women of the day 15s. each.

Poultry, The Book of. By LEWIS WRIGHT. *Popular Edition.* Illustrated. 10s. 6d.

Poultry, The Illustrated Book of. By LEWIS WRIGHT. With Fifty Exquisit Coloured Plates, and numerous Wood Engravings. *Revised Edition.* Cloth, gil edges, *price on application*; half-morocco, £2 2s

"Punch," The History of. By M. H. SPIELMANN. With nearly 170 Illustra tions, Portraits and Facsimiles. Cloth, 16s. ; *Large Paper Edition*, £2 2s. net.

Prison Princess, A. By MAJOR ARTHUR GRIFFITHS. 6s.

Q's Works, Uniform Edition of. 5s. each.

Dead Man's Rock.	The Astonishing History of Troy Town.
The Splendid Spur.	"I Saw Three Ships," and other Winter's Tale
The Blue Pavilions.	Noughts and Crosses.
The Delectable Duchy.	Stories, Studies, and Sketches.

Queen Summer; or, The Tourney of the Lily and the Rose. Penned an Portrayed by WALTER CRANE. With 40 pages in Colours. 6s.

Queen, The People's Life of their. By Rev. E. J. HARDY, M.A. 1s.

Queen Victoria, The Life and Times of. By ROBERT WILSON. Complete i 2 Vols. With numerous Illustrations. 9s. each.

Queen's Scarlet, The. By G. MANVILLE FENN. Illustrated. 5s.

Rabbit-Keeper, The Practical. By CUNICULUS. Illustrated. 3s. 6d.

Railway Guides, Official Illustrated. With Illustrations on nearly every page Maps, &c. Paper covers, 1s.; cloth, 2s.

London and North Western Railway.	Great Eastern Railway.
Great Western Railway.	London and South Western Railway.
Midland R ilway.	London, Brighton and South Coast Railway.
Great Northern Railway.	South Eastern Railway.

Railway Guides, Official Illustrated. Abridged and Popular Editions. Pape covers, 3d. each.

Great Eastern Railway.	London and South Wes'ern Railway.
London and North Western Railway.	London, Brighton and South O a t Railway

Railways, Our. Their Origin, Development, Incident, and Romance. B JOHN PENDLETON. Illustrated. 2 Vols., demy 8vo, 24s.

Red Terror, The. A Story of the Paris Commune. By EDWARD KING. Illus trated. 3s. 6d.

Rivers of Great Britain: Descriptive, Historical, Pictorial.
The Royal River: The Thames from Source to Sea. *Popular Edition,* 16s.
Rivers of the East Coast. With highly-finished Engravings. *Popular Edition,* 16s.

Robinson Crusoe. *Cassell's New Fine-Art Edition.* With upwards of 1 Original Illustrations. 7s. 6d. *Cheap Edition,* 3s. 6d. or 5s.

Romance, The World of. Illustrated. One Vol., cloth, 9s.

Ronner, Henriette, The Painter of Cat-Life and Cat-Character. By M. H SPIELMANN. Containing a Series of beautiful Phototype Illustrations. 12s.

Royal Academy Pictures, 1895. With upwards of 200 magnificent reproduction of Pictures in the Royal Academy of 1895. 7s. 6d.

Russo-Turkish War, Cassell's History of. With about 500 Illustrations Tw Vols., 9s. each ; library binding, One Vol., 15s.

Sala, George Augustus, The Life and Adventures of. By Himself. *Libra Edition* in Two Vols. 32s. *Cheap Edition,* One Vol., 7s. 6d.

Saturday Journal, Cassell's. Illustrated throughout. Yearly Vol., 7s. 6d.

Scarabæus. The Story of an African Beetle. By THE MARQUISE CLAR LANZA and JAMES CLARENCE HARVEY. *Cheap Edition,* 3s. 6d.

Schoolmaster Sketches. By J. T. MACNAMARA. 2s. 6d.

Science for All. Edited by Dr. ROBERT BROWN, M.A., F.L.S., &c. *Revis Edition.* With 1,500 Illustrations. Five Vols. 9s. each.

Science Series, The Century. Consisting of Biographies of Eminent Scientifi Men of the present Century. Edited by Sir HENRY ROSCOE, D.C L., F.R.S ; M.P Crown 8vo, 3s. 6d. each.
John Dalton and the Rise of Modern Chemistry. By Sir HENRY E. ROSCOE, F.R.S.
Major Rennell, F.R.S., and the Rise of English Geography. By CLEMENTS R. MARK HAM, C.B., F.R.S., President of the Royal Geographical Society.
Justus Von Liebig: His Life and Work. By W. A SH. NSTONE.
The Herschels and Modern Astronomy. By Miss AGNES M. CLERKE.
Charles Lyell and Modern Geology. By Professor T. G. BONNEY, F.R.S.
J. Clerk Maxwell and Modern Physics. By R. T. GLAZEBROOK, F.R.S.

Scotland, Picturesque and Traditional. A Pilgrimage with Staff an Knapsack. By G. E. EYRE-TODD. 6s.

Sea, The Story of the. An Entirely New and Original Work. Edited by Illustrated. Vol. I. 9s.

Sea-Wolves, The. By MAX PEMBERTON. Illustrated. 6s.

Shadow of a Song, The. A Novel. By CECIL HARLEY. 5s.

Shaftesbury, The Seventh Earl of, K.G., The Life and Work of. By EDWI
HODDER. Illustrated. *Cheap Edition,* 3s. 6d.

Shakespeare, Cassell's Quarto Edition. Edited by CHARLES and MARY COWDE
CLARKE, and containing about 600 Illustrations by H. C. SELOUS. Complete
Three Vols., cloth gilt, £3 3s.—Also published in Three separate Vols., in cloth
viz. :—The COMEDIES, 21s.; The HISTORICAL PLAYS, 18s. 6d.; The TRAGEDIES, 25s

Shakespeare, The England of. *New Edition.* By E. GOADBY. With Ful
page Illustrations. Crown 8vo, 224 pages, 2s. 6d.

Shakespeare, The Plays of. Edited by Prof. HENRY MORLEY. Complete i
Thirteen Vols. Complete in 13 Vols., cloth, in box, 21s.; also 39 Vols., cloth, in box,
21s.; half-morocco, cloth sides, 42s.

Shakspere, The International *Edition de luxe.*
King Henry VIII. By Sir JAMES LINTON, P.R.I. *(Price on application.)*
Othello. Illustrated by FRANK DICKSEE, R.A. £3 10s.
King Henry IV. Illustrated by Herr EDUARD GRÜTZNER. £3 10s.
As You Like It. Illustrated by the late Mons. ÉMILE BAYARD. £3 10s.

Shakspere, The Leopold. With 400 Illustrations, and an Introduction by F. J.
FURNIVALL. *Cheap Edition,* 3s. 6d. Cloth gilt, gilt edges, 5s.; roxburgh, 7s. 6d.

Shakspere, The Royal. With Exquisite Steel Plates and Wood Engravings.
Three Vols. 15s. each.

Sketches, The Art of Making and Using. From the French of G. FRAIPONT.
By CLARA BELL. With Fifty Illustrations. 2s. 6d.

Smuggling Days and Smuggling Ways; or, The Story of a Lost Art. B
Commander the Hon HENRY N. SHORE, R.N. Illustrated. Cloth, 7s. 6d.

Social England. A Record of the Progress of the People. By various writers
Edited by H. D. TRAILL, D.C.L. Vols. I., II., and III., 15s. each. Vol. IV., 17s.

Social Welfare, Subjects of. By LORD PLAYFAIR, K.C.B., &c. 7s. 6d.

Sorrow, The Highway of. By HESBA STRETTON and a well-known Russia
exile. 6s.

Sports and Pastimes, Cassell's Complete Book of. *Cheap Edition,* 3s. 6d.

Squire, The. By MRS. PARR. *Cheap Edition in one Vol.,* 3s. 6d.

Standishs of High Acre, The. A Novel. By GILBERT SHELDON. Two Vols. 21s.

Star-Land. By Sir ROBERT STAWELL BALL, LL.D., &c. Illustrated. 6s.

Statesmen, Past and Future. 6s.

Story of Francis Cludde, The. A Novel. By STANLEY J. WEYMAN. 6s.

Sun, The Story of the. By Sir ROBERT STAWELL BALL, LL.D., F.R.S., F.R.A.S.
With Eight Coloured Plates and other Illustrations. 21s.

Sunshine Series, Cassell's. In Vols. 1s. each. *A List post free on application.*

Sybil Knox; or, Home Again. A Story of To-day. By E. E. HALE. 6s.

Taxation, Municipal, at Home and Abroad. By J. J. O'MEARA. 7s. 6d.

Thackeray in America, With. By EYRE CROWE, A.R.A. Illustrated. 10s. 6d

Thames, The Tidal. By GRANT ALLEN. With India Proof Impressions of 2
Magnificent Full-page Photogravure Plates, and many other Illustrations, afte
original drawings by W L. WYLLIE, A.R.A. Half-morocco, gilt, gilt edges, £5 15s. 6d

The "Belle Sauvage" Library. Cloth, 2s. each. A Complete List of th
Volumes post free on application.

The Short Story Library. 5s. each. List of Vols. on application.

Things I have Seen and People I have Known. By G. A. SALA. With Portrai
and Autograph. 2 Vols. 21s.

Thorough Good Cook, The. By GEORGE AUGUSTUS SALA. With 900 Recipes. 21s

To Punish the Czar: A Story of the Crimea. By HORACE HUTCHINSON
Illustrated. 3s. 6d.

"Treasure Island" Series, The. *Cheap Illustrated Edition.* Cloth, 3s. 6d. each
Treasure Island. By ROBERT LOUIS STEVENSON.
The Master of Ballantrae. By ROBERT LOUIS STEVENSON.
The Black Arrow: A Tale of the Two Roses. By ROBERT LOUIS STEVENSON.
King Solomon's Mines. By H. RIDER HAGGARD.

Treatment, The Year-Book of, for 1896. A Critical Review for Practitioners o
Medicine and Surgery. Twelfth Year of Issue. 7s. 6d.

Trees, Familiar. By Prof. G. S. BOULGER, F.L.S., F.G.S. Two Series. W'
Forty Coloured Plates in each. *(Price on application.)*

Tuxter's Little Maid. By G. B. BURGIN. 6s.

Bibles and Religious Works.

Bible Biographies. Illustrated. 2s. 6d. each.

The Story of Joseph. Its Lessons for To-Day. By the Rev. GEORGE BAINTON.
The Sto y of Moses and Joshua. By the Rev. J. TELFORD.
The Story of Judges. By the Rev. J. WYCLIFFE GEDGE.
The Story of Samuel and Saul. By the Rev. D. C. TOVEY.
The Story of David. By the Rev. J. WILD.

The Story of Jesus. In Verse. By J. R. MACDUFF, D.D.

Bible, Cassell's Illustrated Family. With 900 Illustrations. Leather, gilt edges, £2 10s. ; full morocco, £3 10s.

Bible, The, and the Holy Land, New Light on. By B. T. A. EVETTS, M.A. Illu trated. Cloth, 21s.

Bible Educator, The. Edited by E. H. PLUMPTRE, D.D. With Illustrations, Maps, &c. Four Vols., cloth, 6s. each.

Bible Manual, Cassell's Illustrated. By the Rev. ROBERT HUNTER, LL.D. Illustrated. 7s. 6d.

Bible Student in the British Museum, The. By the Rev. J. G. KITCHIN, M.A. *Entirely New and Revised Edition,* 1s. 4d.

Biblewomen and Nurses. Yearly Vol., 3s.

Bunyan, Cassell's Illustrated. With 200 Original Illustrations. *Cheap Edition,* 7s 6d.

Bunyan's Pilgrim's Progress (Cassell's Illustrated). 4to. *Cheap Edition,* 3s. 6d.

Child's Bible, The. With 200 Illustrations. Demy 4to, 830 pp. 150*th Thousand.* *Cheap Edition,* 7s. 6d. *Superior Edition,* with 6 Coloured Plates, gilt edges, 10s. 6d.

Child's Life of Christ, The. Complete in One Handsome Volume, with about 200 Original Illustrations. *Cheap Edition,* cloth, 7s. 6d. ; or with 6 Coloured Plates, cloth, gilt edges, 10s. 6d. Demy 4to, gilt edges, 21s.

Commentary, The New Testament, for English Readers. Edited by the Rt. Rev. C. J. ELLICOTT, D.D., Lord Bishop of Gloucester and Bristol. In Three Vols. 21s. each.

Vol. I.—The Four Gospels.
Vol. II.—The Acts. Romans. Corinthians, Galatians.
Vol. III.—The remaining Books of the New Testament.

Commentary, The Old Testament, for English Readers. Edited by the Rt. Rev. C. J. ELLICOTT, D.D., Lord Bishop of Gloucester and Bristol. Complete in 5 Vols. 21s. each.

Vol. I.—Genesis to Numbers.
Vol. II.—Deuteronomy to Samuel II.
Vol. III.—Kings I. to Esther.
Vol. IV.—Job to Isaiah.
Vol. V.—Jeremiah to Malachi.

Commentary, The New Testament. Edited by Bishop ELLICOTT. Handy Volume Edition. Suitable for School and General Use.

St. Matthew. 3s. 6d.	Romans. 2s. 6d.	Titus, Philemon, Hebrews, and James. 3s.
St. Mark. 3s.	Corinthians I. and II. 3s.	
St. Luke. 3s 6d.	Galatians, Ephesians, and Philippians. 3s.	Peter, Jude, and John. 3s.
St. John. 3s. 6d		The Revelation. 3s.
The Acts of the Apostles. 3s. 6d.	Colossians, Thessalonians, and Timothy. 3s.	An Introduction to the New Testament. 2s. 6d.

Commentary, The Old Testament. Edited by Bishop ELLICOTT. Handy Volume Edition. Suitable for School and General Use.

Genesis. 3s. 6d.	Leviticus. 3s.	Deuteronomy. 2s. 6d.
Exodus. 3s.	Numbers. 2s. 6d.	

Dictionary of Religion, The. An Encyclopædia of Christian and other Religious Doctrines, Denominations, Sects, Heresies, Ecclesiastical Terms, History, Biography, &c. &c. By the Rev. WILLIAM BENHAM, B D. *Cheap Edition,* 10s. 6d.

Doré Bible. With 230 Illustrations by GUSTAVE DORE. *Original Edition.* Two Vols., best morocco, gilt edges, £15. *Popular Edition.* With Full-page Illustrations. In One Vol. 15s. Also in leather binding. (*Price on application.*)

Early Days of Christianity, The. By the Very Rev. Dean FARRAR, D.D., F.R.S. LIBRARY EDITION. Two Vols., 24s. ; morocco £2 2s. POPULAR EDITION. Complete in One Vol., cloth, 6s. ; cloth, gilt edges, 7s. 6d. ; Persian morocco, 10s. 6d. ; tree-calf, 15s.

Family Prayer-Book, The. Edited by the Rev. Canon GARBETT, M.A., and the Rev S. MARTIN. With Full-page Illustrations *New Edition.* Cloth, 7s. 6d.

Gleanirgs after Harvest. Studies and Sketches By the Rev. JOHN R. VERNON, M.A

"Graven in the Rock;" or, the Historical Accuracy of the Bible confirmed by reference to the Assyrian and Egyptian Sculptures in the British Museum and else where. By the Rev. Dr. SAMUEL KINNS, F.R.A.S.. &c. &c. Illustrated. *Library Edition*, in Two Volumes, cloth, with top edges gilded, 15s.

"Heart Chords." A Series of Works by Eminent Divines. Bound in cloth, red edges, 1s. each.

My Father. By the Right Rev. Ashton Oxenden, late Bishop of Montreal.
My Bible. By the Rt. Rev. W. Boyd Carpenter, Bishop of Ripon.
My Work for God. By the Right Rev. Bishop Cotterill.
My Object in Life. By the Very Rev. Dean Farrar, D.D.
My Aspirations. By the Rev. G. Matheson, D.D.
My Emotional Life. By Preb. Chadwick, D.D.
My Body. By the Rev. Prof W. G. Blaikie, D.D.
My Soul. By the Rev. P. B. Power, M.A.

My Growth in Divine Life. By the Rev. Prebendary Reynolds, M.A.
My Hereafter. By the Very Rev. Dean Bickersteth.
My Walk with God. By the Very Rev. Dean Montgomery.
My Aids to the Divine Life. By the Very Rev. Dean Boyle.
My Sources of Strength. By the Rev. E. E. Jenkins. M.A.
My Comfort in Sorrow. By Hugh Macmillan, D.D.

Helps to Belief. A Series of Helpful Manuals on the Religious Difficulties of the Day. Edited by the Rev. TEIGNMOUTH SHORE, M.A., Canon of Worcester, and Chaplain-in-Ordinary to the Queen. Cloth, 1s. each.

CREATION. By **Harvey Goodwin, D.D.**, late Lord Bishop of Carlisle.
MIRACLES. By the **Rev. Brownlow Maitland, M.A.**
PRAYER. By the **Rev. Canon Shore, M.A.**

THE DIVINITY OF OUR LORD. By the Lord Bishop of Derry.
THE ATONEMENT. By **William Connor Magee, D.D.**, Late Archbishop of York.

Holy Land and the Bible, The. A Book of Scripture Illustrations gathered in Palestine By the Rev. CUNNINGHAM GEIKIE, D.D., LL.D. (Edin.). *Illustrated Edition.* One Vol. 21s.

Life of Christ, The. By the Very Rev. Dean FARRAR, D.D., F.R.S., Chaplain-in-Ordinary to the Queen.
POPULAR EDITION, Revised and Enlarged, extra crown 8vo cloth gilt, 7s. 6d.
CHEAP ILLUSTRATED EDITION. Cloth, 7s. 6d. Cloth, full gilt, gilt edges, 10s. 6d.
LIBRARY EDITION. Two Vols. Cloth, 24s.; morocco, 42s.

Marriage Ring, The. By WILLIAM LANDELS, D.D. Bound in white leatherette. *New and Cheaper Edition.* 3s. 6d.

Moses and Geology; or, the Harmony of the Bible with Science. By the Rev. SAMUEL KINNS, Ph.D., F.R.A.S. Illustrated. *Library Edition*, revised to date, 10s. 6d.

My Last Will and Testament. By HYACINTHE LOYSON (PÈRE HYACINTHE). Translated by FABIAN WARE. 1s.; cloth, 1s. 6d.

New Light on the Bible and the Holy Land. By BASIL T. A. EVETTS, M.A. Illustrated. Cloth, 7s. 6d.

Old and New Testaments, Plain Introductions to the Books of the. Containing Contributions by many Eminent Divines. In Two Vols., 3s. 6d. each.

Plain Introductions to the Books of the Old Testament. 336 pages. Edited by the Right Rev. C. J. ELLICOTT, D.D., Lord Bishop of Gloucester and Bristol. 3s. 6d.

Plain Introductions to the Books of the New Testament. 304 pages. Edited by the Right Rev. C. J. ELLICOTT, D.D., Lord Bishop of Gloucester and Bristol. 3s. 6d.

Protestantism, The History of. By the Rev. J. A. WYLIE, LL.D. Containing upwards of 600 Original Illustrations. Three Vols., 27s.

"Quiver" Yearly Volume, The. With about 600 Original Illustrations and Coloured Frontispiece. 7s. 6d. Also Monthly, 6d.

St. George for England; and other Sermons preached to Children. *Fifth Edition.* By the Rev. T. TEIGNMOUTH SHORE, M.A., Canon of Worcester. 5s.

St. Paul, The Life and Work of. By the Very Rev. Dean FARRAR, D.D., F.R.S.
LIBRARY EDITION. Two Vols., cloth, 24s.; calf, 42s.
ILLUSTRATED EDITION, One Vol., £1 1s.; morocco, £2 2s.
POPULAR EDITION. One Vol., 8vo, cloth, 6s.; cloth, gilt edges, 7s. 6d.; Persian morocco, 10s. 6d.; tree-calf, 15s.

Searchings in the Silence. By Rev. GEORGE MATHESON, D.D. 3s. 6d.

Shall We Know One Another in Heaven? By the Rt. Rev. J. C. RYLE, D.D., Bishop of Liverpool. *New and Enlarged Edition.* Paper covers, 6d.

Shortened Church Services and Hymns, suitable for use at Children's Services. Compiled by the Rev. T. TEIGNMOUTH SHORE, M.A., Canon of Worcester. *Enlarged Edition.* 1s.

Signa Christi: Evidences of Christianity set forth in the Person and Work of Christ. By the Rev. JAMES AITCHISON. 2s. 6d.

Educational Works and Students' Manuals.

Agricultural Text-Books, Cassell's. (The "Downton" Series.) Fully Illustrat
Edited by JOHN WRIGHTSON, Professor of Agriculture. **Soils and Manures.**
J. M. H. Munro, D.Sc. (London), F.I.C., F.C.S. 2s. 6d. **Farm Crops.** By P
fessor Wrighton. 2s. 6d. **Live Stock.** By Professor Wrighton. 2s. 6d.

Alphabet, Cassell's Pictorial. Mounted on Linen, with rollers. 3s. 6d.

Arithmetic :—Howard's Art of Reckoning. By C. F. HOWARD. Paper, 1s.
cloth, 2s. *Enlarged Edition,* 5s.

Arithmetics, The "Belle Sauvage." By GEORGE RICKS, B.Sc. Lond. Wi
Test Cards. (*List on application.*)

Atlas, Cassell's Popular. Containing 24 Coloured Maps. 2s. 6d.

Book-Keeping. By THEODORE JONES. FOR SCHOOLS, 2s. ; or cloth, 3s. Fo
THE MILLION, 2s. ; or cloth, 3s. Books for Jones's System, Ruled Sets of, 2s.

British Empire Map of the World. New Map for Schools and Institutes. B
G. R. PARKIN and J. G. BARTHOLOMEW, F.R.G.S. Mounted on cloth, varnish
and with Rollers or Folded. 25s.

Chemistry, The Public School. By J. H. ANDERSON, M.A. 2s. 6d.

Cookery for Schools. By LIZZIE HERITAGE. 6d.

Dulce Domum. Rhymes and Songs for Children. Edited by JOHN FARMER,
Editor of "Gaudeamus," &c. Old Notation and Words, 5s. N.3.—The Words
the Songs in "Dulce Domum" (with the Airs both in Tonic Sol-Fa and Old Notatio
can be had in Two Parts, 6d. each.

English Literature, A First Sketch of, from the Earliest Period to the Pre
Time. By Prof. HENRY MORLEY. 7s. 6d.

Euclid, Cassell's. Edited by Prof. WALLACE, M.A. 1s.

Euclid, The First Four Books of. *New Edition.* In paper, 6d. ; cloth, 9d.

French, Cassell's Lessons in. *New and Revised Edition.* Parts I. and II., each,
2s. 6d. ; complete, 4s. 6d. Key, 1s. 6d.

French-English and English-French Dictionary. *Entirely New and Enla
Edition.* 1,150 pages, 8vo, cloth, 3s. 6d. ; superior binding, 5s.

French Reader, Cassell's Public School. By GUILLAUME S. CONRAD. 2s.

Galbraith and Haughton's Scientific Manuals.
Plane Trigonometry. 2s. 6d. Euclid. Books I., II., III. 2s. 6d. Books IV., V., VI. 2s.
Mathematical Tables. 3s. 6d. Mechanics. 3s. 6d. Natural Philosophy. 3s. 6d. Opt
2s. 6d. Hydrostatics. 3s. 6d. Steam Engine. 3s. 6d. Algebra. Part I, cloth, 2s. 6d.
plete, 7s. 6d. Tides and Tidal Currents. with Tidal Cards, 3s.

Gaudeamus. Songs for Colleges and Schools. Edited by JOHN FARMER.
Words only, paper, 6d. ; cloth, 9d.

Geometrical Drawing for Army Candidates. By H. T. LILLEY, M.A. 2s.

Geometry, First Elements of Experimental. By PAUL BERT. Illustrated. 1s.

Geometry, Practical Solid. By Major ROSS, R.E. 2s.

German Dictionary, Cassell's New. German-English, English-German. *Che
Edition,* cloth, 3s. 6d. ; superior binding, 5s.

German Reading, First Lessons in. By A. JÄGST. Illustrated. 1s.

Hand and Eye Training. By GEORGE RICKS, B.Sc., and JOSEPH VAUGHAN
Illustrated. Vol. I. Designing with Coloured Papers. Vol. II. Cardboard Work
2s. each. Vol. III. Colour Work and Design, 3s.

Hand and Eye Training. By G. RICKS, B.Sc. Two Vols., with 16 Colour
Plates in each Vol. Crown 4to, 6s. each.

"Hand and Eye Training" Cards for Class Work. Five sets in case. 1s. eac

Historical Cartoons, Cassell's Coloured. Size 45 in. × 35 in. 2s. each. Mount
on canvas and varnished, with rollers, 5s. each. (Descriptive pamphlet, 16 pp., 1d.)

Italian Lessons, with Exercises, Cassell's. In One Vol. 3s. 6d.

Latin Dictionary, Cassell's New. (Latin-English and English-Latin.) Revi
by J. R. V. MARCHANT, M.A., and J. F. CHARLES, B.A. 3s. 6d. ; superi
binding, 5s.

Latin Primer, The New. By Prof. J. P. POSTGATE. 2s. 6d.

Latin Primer, The First. By Prof. POSTGATE. 1s.

Lessons in Our Laws ; or, Talks at Broadacre Farm. By H. F. LESTER, B. Part I. : THE MAKERS AND CARRIERS-OUT OF THE LAW. Part II. : LAW COUR AND LOCAL RULE, &c. 1s. 6d. each.

Little Folks' History of England. By ISA CRAIG-KNOX. Illustrated. 1s. 6d.

Making of the Home, The. By Mrs. SAMUEL A. BARNETT. 1s. 6d.

Marlborough Books :—Arithmetic Examples. 3s. French Exercises. 3s. 6d. Fren Grammar. 2s. 6d. German Grammar. 3s. 6d.

Mechanics for Young Beginners, A First Book of. By the Rev. J. G. EASTO M.A. 4s. 6d.

Mechanics and Machine Design, Numerical Examples in Practical. R. G. BLAINE, M.E. *New Edition, Revised and Enlarged.* With 79 Illustratio Cloth, 2s. 6d.

Natural History Coloured Wall Sheets, Cassell's New. Consisting of subjects. Size, 39 by 31 in. Mounted on rollers and varnished. 3s. each.

Object Lessons from Nature. By Prof. L. C. MIALL, F.L.S., F.G.S. F Illustrated. *New and Enlarged Edition.* Two Vols. 1s. 6d. each.

Physiology for Schools. By ALFRED T. SCHOFIELD, M.D., M.R.C.S., & Illustrated. 1s. 9d. Three Parts, paper covers, 5d. each; or cloth limp, 6d. each.

Poetry Readers, Cassell's New. Illustrated. 12 Books. 1d. each. Cloth, 1s. 6

Popular Educator, Cassell's New. With Revised Text, New Maps, New Colour Plates, New Type, &c. Complete in Eight Vols., 5s. each ; or Eight Vols. Four, half-morocco, 50s.

Readers, Cassell's "Belle Sauvage." An Entirely New Series. Fully Ill trated. Strongly bound in cloth. (*List on application.*)

Reader, The Citizen. By H. O. ARNOLD-FORSTER, M.P. Cloth, 1s. 6d. ; also Scottish Edition, cloth, 1s. 6d.

Reader, The Temperance. By Rev. J. DENNIS HIRD. 1s. 6d.

Readers, Cassell's "Higher Class." (*List on application.*)

Readers, Cassell's Readable. Illustrated. (*List on application.*)

Readers for Infant Schools, Coloured. Three Books. 4d. each.

Readers, Geographical, Cassell's New. With Numerous Illustrations in ea Book. (*List on application.*)

Readers, The Modern Geographical. Illustrated throughout. (*List on application.*)

Readers, The Modern School. Illustrated. (*List on application.*)

Reading and Spelling Book, Cassell's Illustrated. 1s.

Round the Empire. By G. R. PARKIN. With a Preface by the Rt. Hon. Earl of Rosebery, K.G. Fully Illustrated. 1s. 6d.

Science Applied to Work. By J. A. BOWER. Illustrated. 1s.

Science of Every-Day Life. By J. A. BOWER. Illustrated. 1s.

Sculpture, A Primer of. By E. ROSCOE MULLINS. Illustrated. 2s. 6d.

Shade from Models, Common Objects, and Casts of Ornament, How to. B W. E. SPARKES. With 25 Plates by the Author. 3s.

Shakspere's Plays for School Use. Illustrated. 9 Books. 6d. each.

Spelling, A Complete Manual of. By J. D. MORELL, LL.D. 1s.

Technical Educator, Cassell's New. An entirely New Cyclopædia of Techni Education, with Coloured Plates and Engravings. Complete in Six Vols., 5s. each.

Technical Manuals, Cassell's. Illustrated throughout. 16 Vols., from 2s. to 4s. 6d. (*List free on application.*)

Technology, Manuals of. Edited by Prof. AYRTON, F.R.S., and RICHARD WORMELL, D.Sc., M.A. Illustrated throughout. (*List on application.*)

Things New and Old ; or, Stories from English History. By H. O. ARNOLD-FORSTER, M.P. Fully Illustrated. Strongly bound in Cloth. Standards I and II., 9d. each ; Standard III., 1s. ; Standard IV., 1s. 3d. ; Standards V. and VI., 1s. 6d. each ; Standard VII., 1s. 8d.

World of Ours, This. By H. O. ARNOLD-FORSTER, M.P. Fully Illustrated. 3s. 6d.

𝔅ooks for 𝔜oung 𝔓eople.

"Little Folks" Half-Yearly Volume. Containing 432 pages of Letterpress, with Pictures on nearly every page, together with Six Full-page Plates printed in Colours. Coloured boards, 3s. 6d. ; or cloth gilt, gilt edges, 5s.

Bo-Peep. A Book for the Little Ones. With Original Stories and Verses. Illustrated with beautiful Pictures on nearly every page, and Four Full-page Plates in Colours. Yearly Vol. Elegant picture boards, 2s. 6d ; cloth, 3s. 6d.

Beneath the Banner. Being Narratives of Noble Lives and Brave Deeds. By F. J. CROSS. Illustrated. Limp cloth, 1s. ; cloth boards, gilt edges, 2s.

Good Morning ! Good Night ! Morning and Evening Readings for Children, by the Author of ' Beneath the Banner." Fully Illustrated. Limp cloth, 1s., or cloth boards, gilt edges, 2s.

Five Stars in a Little Pool. By EDITH CARRINGTON. Illustrated. 6s.

Beyond the Blue Mountains. By L. T. MEADE. Illustrated. 5s.

The Cost of a Mistake. By SARAH PITT. Illustrated. *New Edition.* 2s. 6d.

The Peep of Day. Cassell's Illustrated Edition. 2s. 6d.

Maggie Steele's Diary. By E. A. DILLWYN. 2s. 6d.

A Book of Merry Tales. By MAGGIE BROWNE, SHEILA, ISABEL WILSON, and C. L. MATÉAUX. Illustrated. 3s. 6d.

A Sunday Story-Book. By MAGGIE BROWNE, SAM BROWNE, and AUNT ETHEL. Illustrated. 3s. 6d.

A Bundle of Tales. By MAGGIE BROWNE, SAM BROWNE, & AUNT ETHEL. 3s. 6d.

Story Poems for Young and Old. By E. DAVENPORT. 3s. 6d.

Pleasant Work for Busy Fingers. By MAGGIE BROWNE. Illustrated. 5s.

Magic at Home. By Prof. HOFFMAN. Fully Illustrated. A Series of easy and startling Conjuring Tricks for Beginners. Cloth gilt, 3s 6d.

Schoolroom and Home Theatricals. By ARTHUR WAUGH. With Illustrations by H. A. J. MILES. *New Edition.* Cloth, 1s. 6d.

Little Mother Bunch. By Mrs. MOLESWORTH. Illustrated. *New Edition.* 2s. 6d.

Heroes of Every-Day Life. By LAURA LANE. With about 20 Full-page Illustrations. 256 pages, crown 8vo, cloth, 2s. 6d.

Ships, Sailors, and the Sea. By R. J. CORNEWALL-JONES. Illustrated throughout, and containing a Coloured Plate of Naval Flags. *Cheap Edition*, 2s 6d.

Gift Books for Young People. By Popular Authors. With Four Original Illustrations in each. Cloth gilt, 1s. 6d. each.

The Boy Hunters of Kentucky. By Edward S. Ellis.	Jack Marston's Anchor.
Red Feather: a Tale of the American Frontier. By Edward S Ellis.	Frank's Life-Battle.
Fritters; or, "It's a Long Lane that has no Turning."	Major Monk's Motto; or, "Look Before you Leap."
Trixy; or, "Those who Live in Glass Houses shouldn't throw Stones."	Tim Thomson's Trial; or, "All is not Gold that Glitters."
The Two Hardcastles.	Ursula's Stumbling-Block.
Seeking a City.	Ruth's Life-Work; or, "No Pains, no Gains."
Rhoda's Reward.	Rags and Rainbows.
	Uncle William's Charge.
	Pretty Pink's Purpose.

"Golden Mottoes" Series, The. Each Book containing 208 pages, with Four full-page Original Illustrations. Crown 8vo, cloth gilt, 2s. each.

"Nil Desperandum." By the Rev. F. Langbridge, M.A.	"Honour is my Guide." By Jeanie Hering (Mrs. Adams-Acton).
"Bear and Forbear." By Sarah Pitt.	"Aim at a Sure End." By Emily Searchfield.
"Foremost if I Can." By Helen Atteridge.	"He Conquers who Endures." By the Author of "May Cunningham's Trial," &c.

"Cross and Crown" Series, The. With Four Illustrations in each Book. Crown 8vo, 256 pages, 2s. 6d. each.

Heroes of the Indian Empire ; or, Stories of Valour and Victory. By Ernest Foster.	By Fire and Sword: A Story of the Huguenots. By Thomas Archer.
Through Trial to Triumph; or, "The Royal Way.' By Madeline Bonavia Hunt.	Adam Hepburn's Vow : A Tale of Kirk and Covenant. By Annie S. Swan.
In Letters of Flame : a Story of the Waldenses. By C. L. Matéaux.	No. XIII. ; or, The Story of the Lost Vestal. A Tale of Early Christian Days. By Emma Marshall.
Strong to Suffer: a Story of the Jews. By E. Wynne.	Freedom's Sword: A Story of the Days of Wallace and Bruce. By Annie S. Swan.